An Assessment of Climate Change and the Vulnerability of Wildlife in the Sky Islands of the Southwest

Sharon J. Coe, Deborah M. Finch, Megan M. Friggens

United States Department of Agriculture / Forest Service
Rocky Mountain Research Station

General Technical Report RMRS-GTR-273

April 2012

ABSTRACT

We evaluated the historical and projected trends in climate and vegetation relevant to the Coronado National Forest in southeast Arizona, USA. We then applied this information in an assessment of the vulnerability of 30 species of terrestrial vertebrates on the Coronado National Forest to the potential effects of future climate change. We used a pilot version of a decision-support tool developed by the U.S. Department of Agriculture, Forest Service, Rocky Mountain Research Station that produces scores that represent relative measures of vulnerability to climate change as related to habitat, physiology, phenology, and biotic interactions. Over the next ~100 years, increased temperature and aridity are projected for the region, as well as a reduction in forested areas. All 30 species were considered vulnerable with respect to at least some criteria comprising the decision-support tool. The elegant trogon (*Trogon elegans*) and Tarahumara frog (*Rana tarahumarae*) were tied for the largest vulnerability score. The Slevin's bunchgrass lizard (*Sceloporus slevini*) had the smallest vulnerability score. While species varied in their expected responses to climate change, most appeared to be vulnerable relative to one or more expected negative impacts to their habitat, such as an overall reduction in suitable habitat. The assessment results can be used by USFS managers in climate change adaptation planning for these species and their habitats by helping to identify goals for adaptation planning.

Keywords: climate change, vulnerability assessment, wildlife management, Coronado National Forest, decision-support tool

AUTHORS

Sharon J. Coe is a Postdoctoral Researcher with the USFS Rocky Mountain Research Station in Albuquerque, New Mexico, in collaboration with the University of Arizona. She holds both a Ph.D. and an M.Sc. degree in Biology from the University of California, Riverside. She is researching the vulnerability of wildlife to climate change and the effects on wildlife from vegetation treatments to reduce fire risk.

Deborah M. Finch is the Program Manager for the Grassland, Shrubland, and Desert Ecosystems Program at USFS Rocky Mountain Research Station in Albuquerque, New Mexico. She received her B.S. degree in Wildlife Management from Humboldt State University, her M.S. degree in Zoology and Physiology from Arizona State University, and her Ph.D. in Zoology and Range Science from University of Wyoming, Laramie.

Megan M. Friggens is a Research Ecologist with the USFS Rocky Mountain Research Station in Albuquerque, New Mexico, where she has worked on the development and application of tools and assessments regarding the vulnerability of species to climate change. She obtained a B.S. and M.S. degree in Biology from the University of New Mexico and a Ph.D. in Forest Science from Northern Arizona University. She is researching disturbance (fire, drought, land conversion, and climate change), impacts on wildlife species, and wildlife disease ecology.

PREFACE

The success and persistence of plants and animals in their natural environments is inextricably linked to climate. While species in North America have experienced historical variation in climate, a relatively rapid increase in global temperature has the potential to create unique environmental conditions for plant and animal species relative to their recent evolutionary past. Mean global surface temperature has increased over the last 157 years (i.e., over the instrumental record; Trenberth and others 2007). The global average temperature increased 0.35 °C from the 1910s to the 1940s and then 0.55 °C from the 1970s to the end of 2006. Temperatures are projected to increase in the United States, overall, and in the Southwest specifically, according to a variety of climate change models. There is substantial support for a projected increase in surface-air temperatures in the United States of 2 °C during the next century on an annual-mean basis; some models predict temperature increases exceeding 4 °C (Christensen and others 2007).

How to manage for the effects of climate change on plant and animal species has become an increasing concern for resource managers and others whose goal it is to maintain species viability into the future. The U.S. Forest Service (USFS) has identified climate change as an important force that puts ecosystems at risk. USFS (2011a) identifies the need for "science-based assessments of the relative vulnerability of key ecosystem components" to address risks and vulnerabilities of national resources. It also states the need to identify knowledge gaps and management outcomes under climate change. Each National Forest and National Grassland is required to meet standards in 11 areas related to climate change planning, and each is evaluated annually for achievement using a "scorecard" system (USFS 2011b). One criterion is education of all employees on the causes and impacts of climate change. Another criterion measures the extent to which information about the vulnerability of key resources and ecosystem elements to climate change is used in decision-making.

The Coronado National Forest (CNF) is located in southeastern Arizona and includes the Peloncillo Mountains that extend into southwestern New Mexico (Fig.1.1). The National Forest encompasses large areas of a group of high-elevation mountains called the Sky Islands. In this report, we provide information about climate change and a vulnerability assessment of 30 species on the CNF based on the possible effects of climate change over the next ~100 years. Vulnerability assessments are discussed in more detail in Chapter 2, but overall, they can be used to help set management priorities and to develop strategies for responding to climate change ("adaptation strategies;" Glick and others 2011). Assessing vulnerability to climate change requires knowledge of possible changes in temperature, precipitation, and vegetation. We review these potential changes in Chapter 1, which is used as a basis for the species vulnerability assessment presented in Chapter 2. Readers who are interested primarily in a review of climate and potential climate-related changes in the Southwest (here, mainly Arizona and New Mexico) will find that information within Chapter 1. Readers who are interested primarily in the evaluation of species vulnerability, and not specifically the evaluation of climate, can proceed directly to Chapter 2.

REFERENCES

Bagne, K.E., M.M. Friggens, and D.M. Finch. 2011. A system for assessing vulnerability of species (SAVS) to climate change. Gen. Tech. Rep. RMRS-GTR-257. Fort Collins, CO: U.S. Department of Agriculture, Forest Service, Rocky Mountain Research Station. 28 p.

Christensen, J.H., B. Hewitson, A. Busuioc, [and others]. 2007. Regional climate projections. In: Solomon, S., D. Qin, M. Manning, Z. Chen, M. Marquis, K.B. Averyt, M. Tignor, and H.L. Miller, eds. Climate Change 2007. The Physical Science Basis. Contribution of Working Group I to the Fourth Assessment Report of the Intergovernmental Panel on Climate Change. Cambridge, United Kingdom: Cambridge University Press.

Glick, P., B.A. Stein, and N.A. Edelson, eds. 2011. Scanning the Conservation Horizon: A Guide to Climate Change Vulnerability Assessment. Washington, DC: National Wildlife Federation. Available: www.nwf.org/vulnerabilityguide.

Trenberth, K.E., P.D. Jones, P. Ambenje, [and others]. 2007. Observations: Surface and atmospheric climate change. In: Solomon, S., D. Qin, M. Manning, Z. Chen, M. Marquis, K.B. Averyt, M. Tignor and H.L. Miller, eds. Climate Change 2007: The Physical

Science Basis. Contribution of Working Group I to the Fourth Assessment Report of the Intergovernmental Panel on Climate Change. Cambridge, United Kingdom: Cambridge University Press.

U.S. Forest Service [USFS]. 2011a. National roadmap for responding to climate change. FS-957b. Washington, DC: U.S. Department of Agriculture, Forest Service. Available: http://www.fs.fed.us/climatechange/pdf/Roadmapfinal.pdf.

U.S. Forest Service [USFS]. 2011b. Navigating the climate change performance scorecard. Washington, DC: U.S. Department of Agriculture, Forest Service. Available: http://fsweb.wo.fs.fed.us/chief/climatechange/scorecard%20guidance%20document%201-21-2011.pdf.

ACKNOWLEDGMENTS

Funding was provided by the USFS Washington Office Research and Development. This work was also supported by a Joint Venture Agreement (08-JV 11221632-279) between the University of Arizona School of Natural Resources and the Environment and the Rocky Mountain Research Station. We thank Larry Jones and Rick Gerhardt on the Coronado National Forest for providing information on the local ecology of some of the species we assessed, and for helping to locate unpublished reports within USFS and at other resource agencies. We also thank the following individuals for providing unpublished documents and/or other species information: Jim Heffelfinger (Arizona Game and Fish Department), Jim Rorabaugh (United States Fish and Wildlife Service; Tucson, Arizona), and Michelle Christman (United States Fish and Wildlife Service; Albuquerque, New Mexico). The staff of the National Forest Service Library located numerous documents. Dr. Karen Bagne, Dr. Megan Friggens, and Dr. Deborah Finch developed the decision-support tool. Dr. Terry Rich (United States Fish and Wildlife Service) and Dr. Carolyn Enquist (The Wildlife Conservation Society, USA National Phenology Network) provided many helpful suggestions on an earlier draft of this document. David Hawksworth, David Trujillo, and the staff of the publishing unit of USFS Rocky Mountain Research Station provided helpful editing and graphics assistance.

CONTENTS

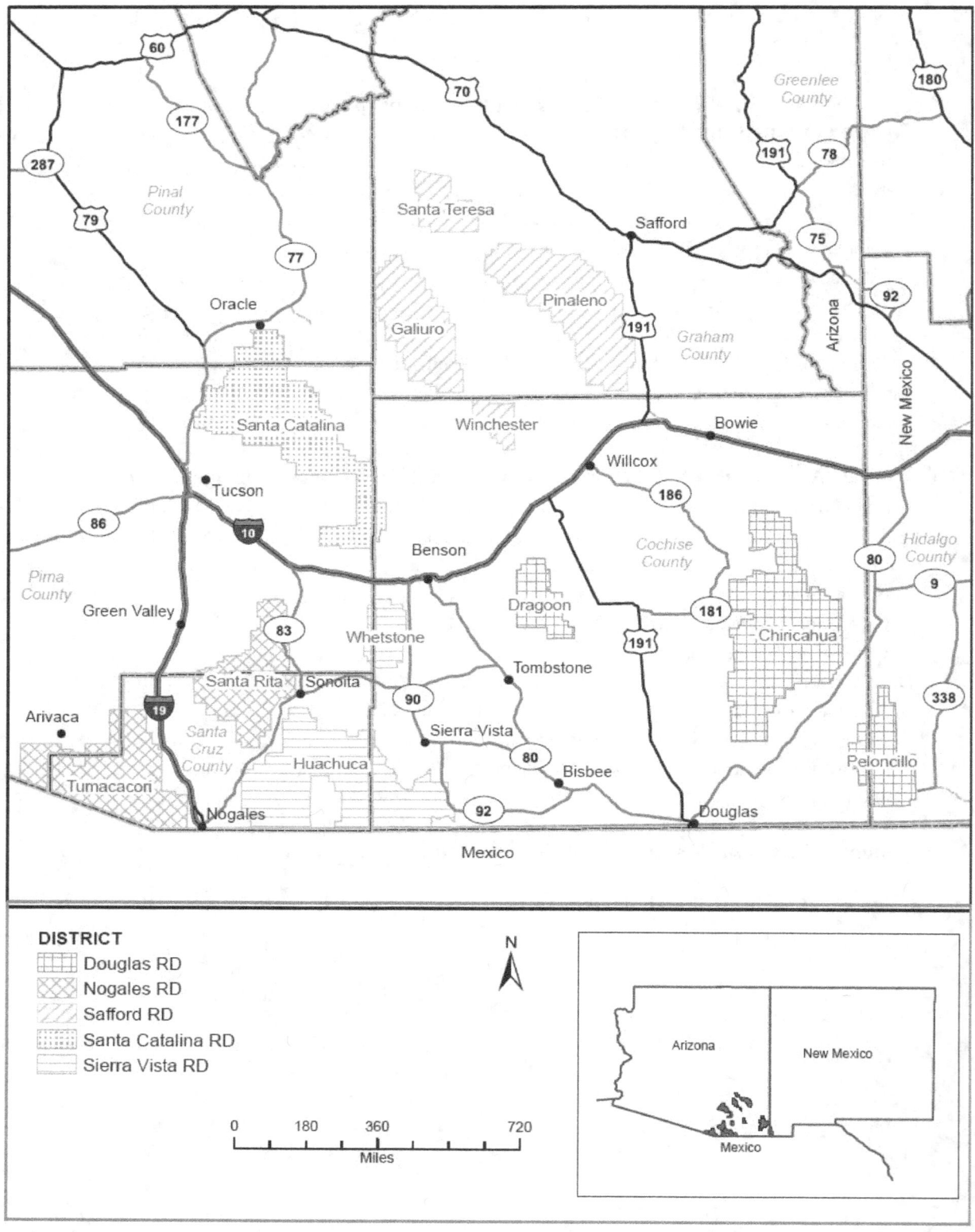

Figure 1.1. The CNF is located in southeastern Arizona and southwestern New Mexico. Twelve EMAs are located across five ranger districts (RD) on the CNF.

Chapter 1: A Review of Historical Trends and Projections for Future Change of Climate and Vegetation

Introduction

The Coronado National Forest (CNF) encompasses portions of multiple mountain ranges that are part of a sky island archipelago located where the Rocky Mountains converge with the Sierra Madre Occidental of Mexico. Sky islands are mountain ranges separated by low-lying valleys that can act as barriers to movement by some species. There are roughly 26 sky island complexes worldwide (Warshall 1995). The Madrean sky island region is located in the southwestern United States (southeastern Arizona and southwestern New Mexico) and northwestern Mexico. The north-south orientation produces climatic variation that is absent in archipelagos that are oriented east-west (e.g., Great Basin; Warshall 1995). The Madrean archipelago provides a "stepping stone" between the Rocky Mountains and plateaus to the north and the Sierra Madre plateau and its mountains to the south (Warshall 1995). Within the United States, the Madrean sky islands are noted for their high floral diversity (McLaughlin 1995). It is here that the Holoarctic and Neatropic floral provinces meet, as do the Neotropic and Nearctic faunal realms (Warshall 1995).

Within the United States it is likely that the southwest will experience some of the greatest extremes in temperatures and aridity as a result of climate change. Northern regions of North America are expected to experience the greatest warming during winter, but in southwestern areas, warming is expected to be greatest in summer (Christensen and others 2007). Annual mean precipitation is also likely to decrease, whereas in Canada and the northeastern United States, rainfall is expected to increase. Increased aridity in the Madrean sky islands is expected to have negative consequences for its flora and fauna. To address possible impacts to vertebrate species (see Chapter 2), we identified expected or possible changes in climate and vegetation for the CNF through a combination of literature review, online tools, and vegetation projections.

Methods

The CNF consists of 720,340 ha divided into twelve Environmental Management Areas (EMAs; Fig.1.1) between ~33°3' and 31°20' latitude. Elevation on CNF ranges from 914 m to 3267 m (3000 ft. to 10,720 ft.). The twelve EMAs coincide primarily with the mountain ranges that they encompass. The exceptions are the Tumacacori EMA, which includes both the Tumacacori Mountains and the Pajarito Mountains, and the Huachuca EMA, which includes the Huachuca Mountains, the Canelo Hills, and the Patagonia Mountains. Major vegetation community types on CNF, from lowest elevation to highest, are Sonoran and Chihuahuan desert, semi-desert grassland, interior chaparral, Madrean encinal woodland, Madrean pine/oak woodland, ponderosa pine, mixed conifer forest, and spruce-fir forest (USFS 2009). The two plant communities that comprise the greatest area are semi-desert grassland (~26% of total area) and Madrean encinal woodland (~42%). Three major riparian plant communities are recognized: cottonwood willow, mixed broadleaf deciduous, and montane willow.

We reviewed scientific literature regarding historical trends in climate and vegetation that were applicable to Arizona and the southwestern United States, and we modeled projections for the Twenty-first Century. We used an online tool called "Climate Wizard" for both historical climate data, and for projections of temperature and precipitation (http://www.climatewizard.org/; data downloaded August 2009). Historical data in Climate Wizard were developed using the PRISM (Parameter-elevation Regressions on Independent Slopes Model) climate mapping system. Projections in Climate Wizard used the ensemble of three General Circulation Models: MIROC3.2 (medres), CSIRO-MK3.0, and UKMO-HadCM3.

We used projections of vegetation change in the western United States that were generated by Rehfeldt and others (2006) as predictors of possible change within CNF. This approach predicts where *suitable climate* for various plant communities will exist in the future based on current climate associations of plant communities. Rehfeldt and others (2006) used multivariate regression tree models to predict changes in total area with suitable climate for Brown vegetation communities (Brown 1998) using: (1) plant presence-absence data, (2) an algorithm called "Random Forests," and (3) input from a climate model at 1-km resolution. They used climate variables that were related to summer and winter temperatures, measures of available moisture, length of frost-free season, and the interaction between temperature and precipitation. The IPCC IS92a scenario (1% increase in greenhouse gases per year after 1990) was used as well as the average of two General Circulation Models (HadCM3GGA1 and CGCM2_ghga). We created maps of current vegetation (Year 2005) and projected change (Year 2090) in suitable climate for vegetation for each EMA on the CNF in ArcMap 9.3 using raster images produced by Rehfeldt and others (2006) (available from http://forest.moscowfsl.wsu.edu/climate/customData/) and shapefiles for each of the ranger districts using boundary data obtained from the USFS ("Administrative_ Boundaries" available from http://www fs fed.us/r3/gis/cor_gis.shtml). For each of the eight vegetation communities identified, we calculated the percent area of suitable climate for year 2005 and year 2090.

For information on possible future conditions in Mexico, Central America, and South America, where migratory species spend part of the year, we relied on published literature sources. Obtaining climate change information for areas utilized outside of the CNF was complicated by the fact that specific over-wintering areas and migratory routes of most species are generally not well known. We focused on general projections for large geographic areas.

Results

Temperature, Precipitation, and Hydrology

Historical trends

Considering large-scale trends in temperature, global mean surface temperatures have risen by almost 1 °C in the last 100 years (0.74 ± 0.18 °C over the period 1906-2005 when estimated by a linear trend; Trenberth and others 2007). In the last 50 years, the rate of warming has been roughly twice that. The greatest warming over land has occurred in winter (December-February) and in spring (March-May) in the Northern Hemisphere. In mid-latitude regions, there has been a reduction in the number of frost days and daily cold extremes and an increase in the number of warm extremes (Trenberth and others 2007).

Temperature in Arizona fluctuates seasonally with the coldest temperatures occurring in mid-winter and the hottest occurring in mid-summer (Sheppard and others 2002). Along the southern portion of the state, mean annual temperatures increase from west to east, as well as from high to low elevation. A combination of paleo-climate records and modern records (i.e., from weather stations that began recording temperature in the mid- to late-1800s) indicate that the recent warming trend in the southwestern United States is unprecedented in the last 400 years (Sheppard and others 2002), with the warmest year in the Twentieth Century being 1934 (Sheppard and others 1999). In the Sonoran Desert, between 1960 and 2000, winter and spring temperatures increased, the frequency of freezing temperatures decreased, and minimum winter temperatures increased (Weiss and Overpeck 2005). Local land use and multi-decadal modes (e.g., Pacific Decadal Oscillation, or PDO) did not appear to have driven these warming trends. According to Climate Wizard, over the latter half of the Twentieth Century, most of the CNF experienced an increase in winter temperature (December-February; Fig. 1.2).

Precipitation in Arizona and New Mexico falls primarily in the summer and winter; spring and fall are often comparatively dry. The North American monsoon is an important precipitation phenomenon, bringing as much as 50% of the annual rainfall to Arizona and New Mexico from July through September (Sheppard and others 2002). Moisture from oceanic sources leads to convective storms when conditions in the Southwest cause air masses to rise. The timing of precipitation from monsoons varies seasonally, annually, and decadally. Inter-annual variation results, in part, from the relative location of the Bermuda subtropical ridge; a northward shift in the ridge is associated with wet summers in Arizona (Sheppard and others 1999). The effect of the El Niño-Southern Oscillation (ENSO) on monsoonal patterns is unclear (Sheppard and others 2002). The penetration of tropical hurricanes in late summer and fall from farther south and west can also bring large amounts of rainfall over large areas of the Southwest in a relatively short period. In winter, a second peak of precipitation occurs, generally between November and March, falling as snow at high elevations. Winter climate variability is influenced by a number of phenomena, including the Pacific/North American pattern, Southwestern troughing, ENSO, and PDO. See Sheppard and others (2002) for a review.

Historical trends in precipitation in the Southwest differ depending on which months of the year, which years, and what regions are considered. From 1900 to 2005, in the southwestern United States, northwestern Mexico, and Baja Peninsula, there was a trend of decreasing annual precipitation (1-2% per decade) based on Global Historical Climatology Network data from the National Climatic Data Center (Trenbreth and others 2007). This contrasts with a general increase in precipitation over much of North America over the same period and based on the same data source (Trenbreth and others 2007). Using a different data set (based on a global network called "CRU TS2.1") and looking at only the latter half of the century (1950-2000), Wang and others (2009) reported that in much of Arizona, mean precipitation increased in all seasons except for the June to August period. Regonda and others (2005) found that many recording stations in Arizona showed increases in the amount of winter precipitation. Anderson and others (2010) reported no trend for changes in summer monsoonal precipitation from July to September in Arizona from 1931 to 2000; increases were observed in areas to the north in Utah and Colorado, which are considered outside of the core monsoonal region.

Large among-year variation in precipitation has been observed in the Southwest. For example, a "seasonal precipitation reversal" occurred in the mid-2000s in Arizona (Goodrich and Ellis 2008). The second wettest winter on record in Arizona occurred in 2004/2005 and ameliorated a drought that had been ongoing in some parts of the state since 1996. This very wet year was followed in 2005/2006 by the driest winter in the instrumental record for most regions in Arizona since 1895. The authors noted a trend for increasing variability in inter-annual winter precipitation in Arizona, particularly since the 1960s.

Recurrent droughts are common in the mid-latitudes, including North America. Globally, droughts have become more common since the 1970s, as measured by the Palmer Drought Severity Index (Trenbreth and others 2007), which uses precipitation, temperature, and local water content data to assess soil moisture. Decreased precipitation on land and increased temperatures have contributed to more areas experiencing drought. Diminished snowpack in the western United States also appears to have contributed to a reduction in moisture availability. According to McCabe and others (2004), over the coterminous United States, 52% of the spatial and temporal variance in multidecadal drought frequency is explained by the PDO and the Atlantic

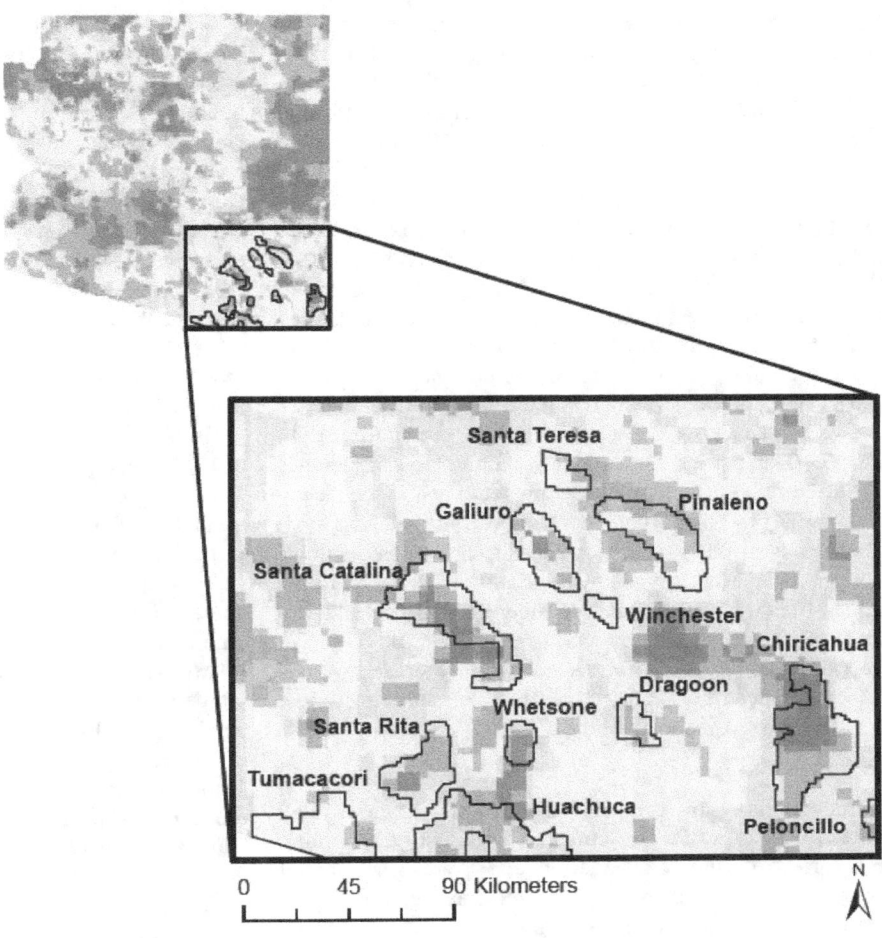

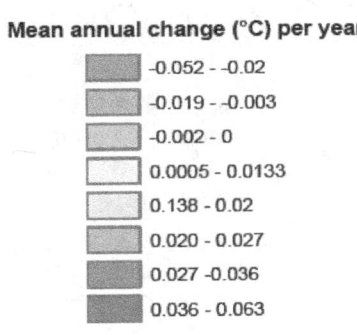

Mean annual change (°C) per year

- -0.052 - -0.02
- -0.019 - -0.003
- -0.002 - 0
- 0.0005 - 0.0133
- 0.138 - 0.02
- 0.020 - 0.027
- 0.027 -0.036
- 0.036 - 0.063

Figure 1.2. Winter temperatures (December-February) in southeastern Arizona increased over 1951-2006. Many areas within the CNF showed warming trends. Source: Climate Wizard (www.climatewizard.org).

Multidecadal Oscillation (AMO), with 22% being attributable to a "complex spatial pattern of positive and negative trends in drought occurrence possibly related to increasing Northern Hemisphere temperatures or some other unidirectional climate trend." The authors found that droughts in the 1990s were associated with a North Atlantic warming (positive AMO) and a northeastern and tropical cooling (negative PDO).

Drought is considered a normal phenomenon in the Southwest (Weiss and others 2009). The effects of ENSO modulate drought conditions on inter-annual and decadal timeframes (Cook and others 2009). When sea surface temperatures in the eastern tropical Pacific are lower than normal (also known as "La Niña"), conditions in the southwestern United States are drier than normal. Over the last approximately 100 years, the most notable droughts in the Southwest occurred in (1) the late 1890s and early 1900s, (2) the 1950s, and (3) the early 2000s (Seager and others 2005; Trenberth and others 2007; Weiss and others 2009). La Niña conditions were present in the Southwest drought of the 1950s and at the beginning of the Twenty-First Century; additional conditions at that time included the cold phase of the PDO, the warm phase of the AMO, and the positive phase of the Eastern Pacific Oscillation (EPO; Quiring and

Goodrich 2008). Tree ring data in the Upper Colorado River Basin (including portions of Wyoming, Utah, Colorado, Arizona, and New Mexico) indicated that the more recent drought from 1999 to 2004 was the seventh worst for that area in approximately 500 years (Piechota 2004).

Changes in flow in rivers and streams also have been documented in the western United States, including reduced snowpack in winter (Knowles and others 2006) and earlier peak streamflow in spring (Cayan and others 2001). Regonda and others (2005) found that many streams in snowmelt-dominated river basins in the western United States from 1950 to 1999 showed advances in peak spring flows, including a site located in central-eastern Arizona. The trend for earlier streamflow in the western United States (Stewart and others 2005) has been most apparent from 1947 to 2003 (Hamlet and others 2007). An analysis of changes in 14 free-flowing, snowmelt-dominated rivers in the Rocky Mountains of Canada and the United States during various periods in the 1900s showed that winter season flows (December to March) were often slightly increased, but the larger effect was a decrease in summer flows (Rood and others 2008). Spring peak flow was often earlier and larger. In the Sierra Nevada of California, April to July streamflow has decreased since the 1950s; in contrast, autumn streamflow has increased (Aguado and others 1992).

Projected changes

Temperatures are projected to increase in the United States overall, and in the Southwest specifically, according to a variety of climate change models. There is substantial support for a projected increase in U.S. surface-air temperatures of 2 °C during the next century on an annual-mean basis; however, some models predict temperature increases exceeding 4 °C (Christensen and others 2007). Increases in summer temperatures are expected to be the largest in the Southwest. Fewer frost days across the United States are also predicted, and the lowest winter temperatures are likely to increase more than average winter temperatures. Dominguez and others (2010) indicated that there is growing consensus that the Southwest will become drier and hotter in the coming century, and that there will be an amplification of aridity during La Niña conditions. Storms may become more intense but less frequent, resulting in an overall increase in aridity (Trenberth and others 2005). According to Climate Wizard, under the A2 and A1B emission scenarios (IPCC 4th Assessment) and the "ensemble average" of models MIROC3.2 (medres), CSIRO-MK3.0, and UKMO-HadCM3, temperatures in the region encompassing the CNF are projected to rise by a few degrees Celsius relative to 1961 to 1990 in each of four seasons from 2049 to 2069 (Fig. 1.3). This is generally consistent with IPCC projections for the Southwest (Christensen and others 2007). Temperature projections under the A1B scenario based on 22 Global Climate Models downscaled to the Southern Colorado Plateau (includes northern Arizona) predicted increased mean annual temperatures through the year 2100 by as much as 4 °C (Garfin and others 2009). The 22-model average projected temperatures increasing above the Twentieth Century average by 2.2 °C by 2030.

Reduced annual rainfall in the Southwest is predicted (Table 1.1) as well as reduced moisture availability and reduced snowpack in areas that typically receive snowfall. Climate Wizard (under the A2 and A1B emission scenarios and the "ensemble average" of MIROC3.2 (medres), CSIRO-MK3.0, and UKMO-HadCM3) generally projected precipitation decreases for the period 2049 to 2069 (relative to 1961 to 1990), with the largest decreases projected for spring (Fig. 1.4). The 22-model ensemble average by Garfin

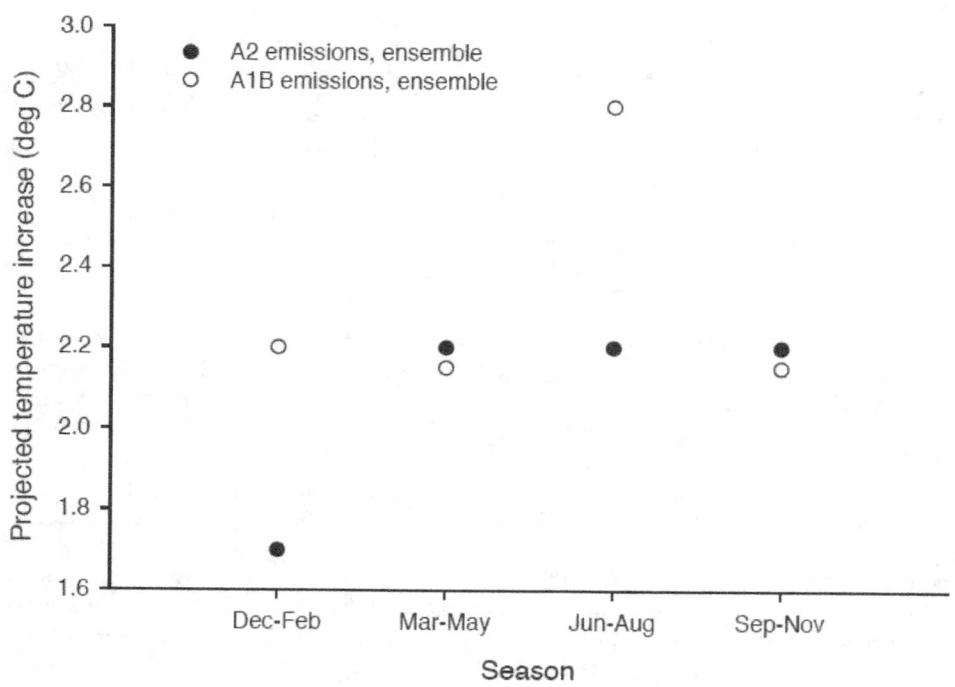

Figure 1.3. Temperature increases projected for southeastern Arizona for the period 2049-2069 as compared to the baseline period 1961-1990, based on analysis by Climate Wizard (www.climatewizard.org) under two IPCC emissions scenarios (A2 and A1B) and using the ensemble average for General Circulation Model (models used in ensemble average: MIROC3.2 [medres], CSIRO-MK3.0, and UKMO-HadCM3).

Table 1.1. Projected changes in moisture-related phenomena in the United States.

Condition predicted for future	Region			Source	Comments
	U.S.	South-western U.S.	Other		
Less precipitation		X		Christensen and others 2007	In the Southwest, less rainfall in winter (December-February) and summer (June-August), which contrasts with projections of increased precipitation in northeastern North America.
		X		Seager and others 2007	Based on a multimodel ensemble mean, climate becomes drier and shows a continued drying trend beginning in the late 1900s and early 2000s.
			X	Garfin and others 2009	Based on a 22-model ensemble average, precipitation expected to decline in the southern Colorado Plateau.
Greater aridity and increased droughts		X		Seager and others 2007	Dryness evaluated in terms of precipitation minus evaporation. Predict that "future droughts…will be worse than any since Medieval period."
	X			Field and others 2007	Increased evaporation due to higher temperatures.
Reduced snowpack	X			Christensen and others 2007	General decrease in snow depth from delayed autumn snowfall and earlier melting in spring. Some models may underestimate warming in high altitudes in western U.S. associated with snow-albedo feedback.
Reduced summer stream flow	X			Field and others 2007	Projected for mountain snowmelt-dominated watersheds.

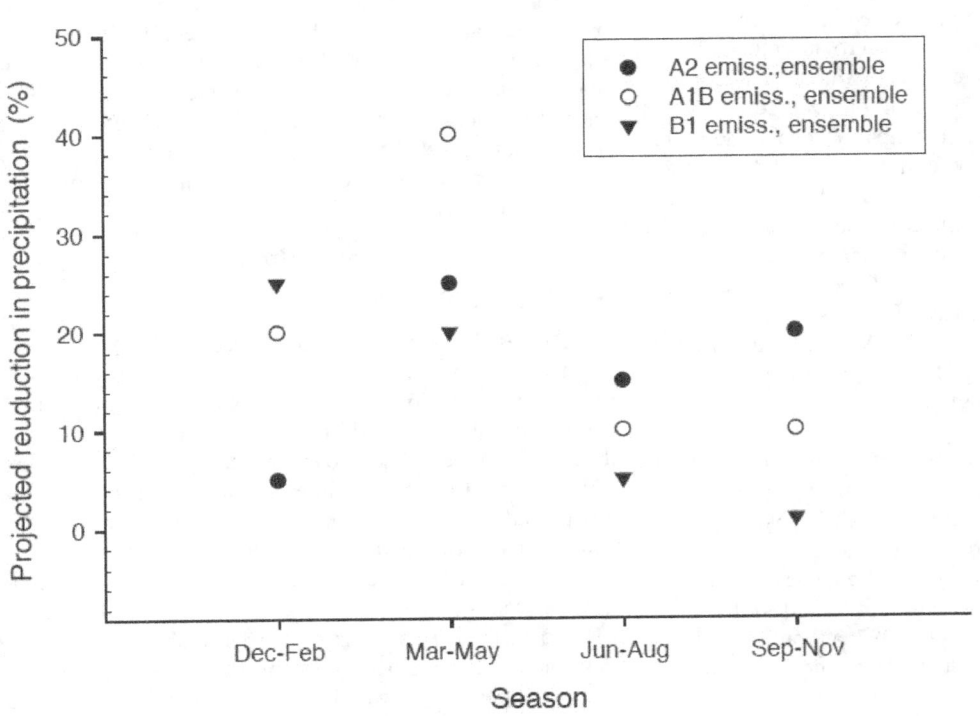

Figure 1.4. Precipitation changes projected for southeastern Arizona for the period 2049-2069 as compared to the baseline period 1961-1990, based on analysis by Climate Wizard (www.climatewizard.org) under three IPCC emissions scenarios (A2, A1B, and B1) and using the ensemble average for General Circulation Model (models used in ensemble average: MIROC3.2 [medres], CSIRO-MK3.0, and UKMO-HadCM3). We used values for the area encompassing the Huachuca EMA, and expect that values for the other EMAs would be similar.

and others (2009) projected a 6% decrease in annual precipitation by the end of the 2000s. The authors found that agreement among a subset of the 22 Global Climate Models was greatest for the May to June period, with rainfall projected to decline by 11 to 45% during the Twenty-First Century. Output from individual models varied more than for temperature, differing in the magnitude and direction of projected precipitation changes. This was possibly due to some of the Global Climate Models modeling historical climate poorly. Dominquez and others (2010) indicated that all of the models used in the IPCC AR4 significantly overestimate winter precipitation and do not simulate well the precipitation associated with the North American Monsoon.

Extreme Weather Events

Historical trends

One analysis of temperature patterns in North America since the 1960s found that in Arizona, there has been a trend for fewer cold days (i.e., the number of days above the 90th percentile of minimum temperature; Peterson and others 2008). The authors also found a trend for heavier rainfall in some parts of Arizona, and a trend for lighter rainfall in other areas.

Tropical cyclones (also known as hurricanes) develop mainly in the tropics over large bodies of warm water and lose strength as they pass over land, although heavy rains can fall inland. In late summer and early fall, rainfall from tropical cyclones can reach the Southwest when tropical cyclones in the eastern Pacific Ocean penetrate northeastward (Sheppard and others 2002). Most tropical storms that bring rainfall to Arizona are from storms in the eastern Pacific Ocean. However, the majority of tropical storms in the eastern Pacific do not track into the Southwest (Corbosiero and others 2009). From 1958 to 2003, one to three tropical cyclones and their remnants affected the Southwest each year, typically in September (Corbosiero and others 2009). It is estimated that "direct impacts" (which include heavy rainfall) from a tropical storm occur, on average, every 4.5 years in Arizona, but "indirect impacts" occur more frequently (Carter 2002). The western portions of Arizona are most likely to be affected. The number of tropical storms that impact Arizona does not appear to be greater in El Niño years (Carter 2002), although other characteristics of tropical cyclones may be (Carter 2002; Corbosiero and others 2009). High rainfall from tropical cyclones has been associated with extreme flooding events in Arizona (e.g., Tropical Storm Norma in September of 1970) and with much-needed rainfall during times of drought (e.g., Tropical Storm Olivia in October 2000).

Globally, there has been a trend of longer cyclone storm lifetime and greater storm intensity since approximately 1970 (Trenberth and others 2007), and the North Pacific Ocean is one of the top three oceanic areas with the largest increases in cyclone severity. The frequency of cyclones in winter (November to March) in mid-latitudes (30-60°N) decreased over the period 1959 to 1997, although the intensity of cyclones increased in both mid- and high latitudes

(McCabe and others 2001). Emanuel (2005) found that since the mid-1970s, there has been a trend of longer storm lifetimes and greater storm intensities. A review of data from 1970 to 2004 for six ocean basins that support tropical cyclones found no clear linear trend in the number of cyclone days but observed a decadal oscillation, particularly in the number of storm days (Webster and others 2005). The exception was the North Atlantic Ocean, which showed a significant increase in frequency and duration commencing in 1995, possibly associated with global warming.

Projected changes

Projections by Diffenbaugh and Ashfaq (2010) based on a large number of climate model experiments under the A1B scenario showed a potential for a significant increase in the number of times the historical hottest-season temperature threshold will be exceeded over the next 30 years throughout the United States. In the western United States, an increase in the frequency and duration of heat waves is expected (Christensen and others 2007). Assuming a doubling of CO_2 over pre-industrial levels, most hydrologic basins in California are predicted to experience an increase in "extremely hot days" (i.e., days in which the daily maximum temperature is above the 95th percentile of daily maximum temperatures in each year, which corresponds to the 18th hottest maximum in a year) and an increase in periods of prolonged extreme temperature or "hot spells" (i.e., the maximum temperature exceeds the long-term 95th percentile for seven or more days; Bell and others 2004).

Tebaldi and others (2006) examined the potential for increases in precipitation intensity on a global scale under the A1B emissions scenario. Globally, the mid-latitudes and high-latitudes of the northern hemisphere showed a statistically significant increase in precipitation intensity. Areas including the Southwest were outside of this range and interpretation was less clear. Emanuel (2005) predicted that hurricane intensity will increase under global climate change, but noted that predictions regarding hurricane frequency are inconsistent. Webster and others (2005) cited six studies that modeled cyclone patterns under doubled CO_2 levels that gave contradictory results, although most predicted increased hurricane intensity.

Vegetation

Historical trends

Changes in temperature and precipitation can affect vegetation communities in a variety of ways, including vegetation mortality, changes in phenology, changes in competitive ability, and shifts in range. Globally, multi-year droughts have been linked to tree mortality (Allen and others 2010). A rapid increase in tree mortality rates in the western United States in unmanaged forests in recent decades could not be attributed solely to aging of large trees, and higher ambient temperature was considered a likely contributor (Van Mantgem and others 2009). In northern New Mexico in the 1950s, there was a large shift (of 2 km or more) in the ecotone between semi-arid ponderosa pine forest and piñon-juniper woodland in less than five years as a result of ponderosa pine mortality associated with severe drought (Allen and Breshears 1998). From 2002 to 2003, a regional-scale die-off in woodlands in the Southwest was associated with drought and beetle infestations (Breshears and others 2005). At one study site, more than 90% of piñon pine (*Pinus edulis*) died following 15 months of depleted soil water content. During the drought years of 1942 to 1957 (considered the most extreme in the Southwest in the past 400 years), there was wide-ranging mortality of plants in shrublands, woodlands, and forests; there also was an increase in the rate at which shrubs encroached into grasslands (Swetnam and Betancourt 1998). In contrast, a 20-ha study site in Chihuahuan Desert in southeastern Arizona where grazing was excluded showed an increase in the density of woody shrubs since the 1970s that was attributed to an increase in winter precipitation (Brown and others 1997).

Changes in temperature and precipitation can lead to changes in the range of plant species along altitudinal gradients. In the Santa Catalina Mountains of southeastern Arizona, Crimmins and others (2009) recorded flowering dates of several hundred plant species over the period 1984 to 2003. Ninety-three species (25.6%) showed a significant shift in flowering range between the first half and the latter half of the study period. A variety of responses was observed: some species' flowering range shifted upslope, some expanded upslope (increase in range), others contracted upslope, and still others expanded downslope. These changes coincided with a general warming in most seasons between the first half and the latter half of the 20-year study period. Plants at higher elevations in the Santa Catalina Mountains responded differently to climate variables than species at lower elevations (Crimmins and others 2007). From 1984 to 2003, the diversity of species in bloom at lower elevations was strongly related to precipitation, whereas at high elevations, it was heavily influenced by temperature.

Generally, there has been a trend in the United States of increased forest fire activity, including on USFS lands (Stephens 2005). The recurrence of regionally synchronized fires over many centuries in the Southwest demonstrates that climate plays an important role in fire patterns, although fuel accumulation as a result of fire suppression beginning in the early 1900s has also contributed to fire activity (Swetnam and Betancourt 1998). There was an increase in the area over which stand-replacing fires occurred between 1984 and 2006 in portions of California and Nevada, and an increase in mean and maximum fire size and the area burned annually (Miller and others 2009). The patterns in California and Nevada appeared to be related to hotter air temperatures and reduced precipitation. The forested area that burned between 1987 and 2003 in the western United States (including Arizona) was 6.7 times more than that burned from 1970 to 1986 (Westerling and others 2006) and the mean length of the fire season increased by 78 days in the latter period compared to the earlier period (1970-1986). The increase in fires was associated with an increase in temperature and earlier snowmelt; of the 34 years studied, years with earlier snowmelt had five times more wildfires than those with later snowmelt. Littell and others (2009) found that in the western

United States, "wildfire area burned" (WFAB, or total hectares burned) over a variety of vegetation types from 1916 to 2003 showed strong associations with climate. WFAB in mountainous ecoprovinces showed strong relationships with low precipitation, low Palmer Drought Severity Index, and high temperature, whereas in grass- and shrub-dominated ecoprovinces, WFAB showed strong relationships to precipitation levels the preceding winter. The authors indicated that although fire suppression and fuel treatments likely had an influence on area burned, climate had a significant affect.

On the CNF, fire exclusion has been associated with a high density of small-diameter trees in ponderosa pine forest, mixed conifer forest, and spruce-fir forest and shrub invasion in semi-desert grasslands (USFS 2009). Furthermore, vegetation communities have been altered for long periods after fire. Following a severe crown fire in Madrean oak-pine woodland in southeast Arizona (i.e., 10-ha Rattlesnake Fire) oaks resprouted more and oak seedlings grew faster than pine, which the authors expected to cause a shift to a more homogenous oak woodland (Barton 2002).

Projected changes

Experiments, including those that increase CO_2 levels, provide some insight into how plants may respond to changing abiotic conditions. The effects of changes in CO_2 have been shown to vary with precipitation. In the Mojave Desert, three species of shrubs significantly increased above-ground production in response to experimentally elevated CO_2 in one year with anomalously high rainfall but not in three years with below-average rainfall (Housman and others 2006). New shoot production by a dominant shrub under elevated CO_2 was not enhanced in a drought year but was enhanced in a high rainfall year, and above-ground production was higher for an exotic annual grass than for native annuals, which the authors suggested might lead to higher dominance of that species (Smith and others 2000).

Increased insect outbreaks that lead to increased tree mortality are projected for forests in North America (Logan and others 2003; Field and others 2007; Bentz and others 2010). Based on the 2002/2003 regional-scale die-off in Southwest woodlands associated with drought and beetle infestations, Breshears and others (2005) projected more severe and extensive die-offs should air temperatures continue to rise. Insect outbreaks leading to vegetation mortality are already considered a threat to multiple vegetation communities on CNF (USFS 2009), and this threat is likely to worsen.

Changes in the timing of stream peak flow have the potential to alter conditions for riparian plant species. Based on observations of an earlier spring peak flow and reduced summer and autumn flows in 14 rivers in the Rocky Mountains, Rood and others (2008) predicted a possible mismatch between seasonal flow and both seedling establishment and seed release. A decline in late summer flows was thought to be one of the greater, if not greatest, impacts to floodplain forests, potentially imposing drought stress along reaches in arid and semi-arid regions, with a likely negative impact on willows (*Salix* spp.) and cottonwoods (*Populus* spp.). The effect of earlier peak flow on flooding regimes and

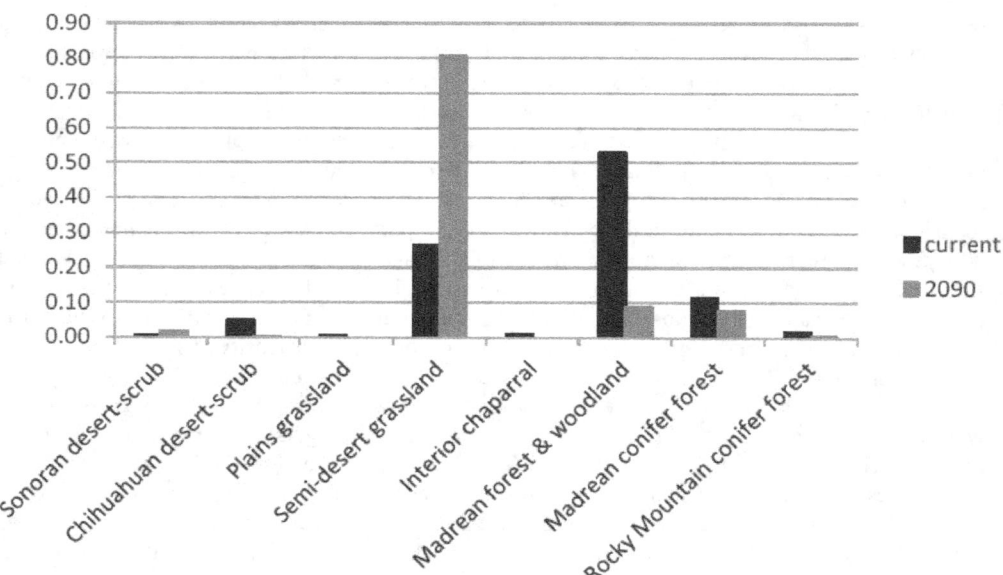

Figure 1.5. Proportion of eight vegetation communities estimated as occurring on the CNF and the proportion of area predicted to have suitable climate for the eight communities by year 2090 using models developed by Rehfeldt and others (2006).

establishment of riparian vegetation is expected to vary by site and be difficult to predict (Poff 2002).

Using the Rehfeldt vegetation models, we projected for year 2090 a decline in the amount of total area on the CNF that would possess suitable climate for Madrean forest and woodland and Madrean conifer forest, and an increase in area with suitable climate for semi-desert grassland (Fig. 1.5). Projected change in area with suitable climate for other communities, which occur in much smaller proportion, are as follows: a slight increase for Sonoran desert scrub, and a slight decrease for Chihuahuan desert scrub, plains grassland, interior chaparral, and Rocky Mountain conifer forest (Fig. 1.5). We considered possible explanations for why the area for Sonoran desert scrub was projected to increase yet Chihuahuan desert scrub was projected to decrease. Similarly, area for plains grassland was expected to decrease yet semi-desert grassland was projected to increase. Possible explanations are measurement error relating to the large scale of the analysis, and the small scale of the units that desert scrub and plains grasslands comprise in this study.

Projected changes in vegetation for a portion of the Saguaro National Park in Tucson, Arizona, were similar qualitatively to those predicted by our analysis with the Rehfeldt models, although the vegetation categories were somewhat different (Kupfer and others 2005). Assuming a temperature rise of 4 °C and either no change in precipitation, a 10% decrease, or a 10% increase, both desert scrub and desert savanna/grassland were projected to increase, and Madrean woodland and forest and montane conifer forest were expected to decrease.

Forest fires are expected to increase under future climate change, and riparian areas are expected to continue to be threatened by high intensity fire. Flannigan and others (2000) modeled an index of forest fire potential for North America under a scenario of doubling of CO_2 levels. For two different GCMs, Arizona showed an increase in the index of fire potential. Vegetation communities on CNF are already considered at risk from fire (USFS 2009). High intensity fire is a threat to woodlands, forests, and riparian areas, and high frequency fires are a concern in chaparral.

Onset of Spring

Changes in the onset of spring in North America are expected (Field and others 2007). In the western United States, first blooming dates for common purple lilac (*Syringa vulgaris f. purpurea* Hort. Ex Schelle) and honeysuckle (*Lonicera tatarica* cv., "Arnold Red," and *L. korolkowii stopf*, var. zebelli) and the spring pulse in snow-fed streamflow have been earlier since the 1970s, coincident with warmer-than-average spring temperatures (Cayan and others 2001). Over the period from 1950 to 1999 there were significant trends for earlier timing of the spring warm spell in the western United States (defined as the seven-day period when daily maximum temperatures were above 12 °C), including at several weather stations in Arizona (Regonda and others 2005). The flowering dates of shrubs in the northern Sonoran Desert advanced from 1894 to 2004 (Bowers 2007).

In the Santa Catalina Mountains of southeastern Arizona, over the period 1984 to 2003, the onset of flowering in plant species at low elevations was driven most frequently by temperature and precipitation during the prior autumn, whereas at high elevations first flowering was more frequently associated with spring temperatures (Crimmins and others 2010). Approximately 10% of species showed a significant shift in date of first flowering over the study period, with most tending toward a later onset. The authors suggested that some species may have shown later onset as a result of decreased autumn precipitation, whereas others may have responded to a slight decrease in spring temperature.

Reports of earlier phenology in North American fauna include earlier dates of calling in several species of frogs in New York from 1990 to 1999 compared to 1900 to 1912

(Gibbs and Breisch 2001); species included gray treefrog (*Hyla versicolor*), spring peeper (*Pseudacris crucifer*), American bullfrog (*Rana catesbeiana*), and wood frog (*Rana sylvatica*). Blaustein and others (2001) found that some species of frogs in North America have shown a trend toward earlier breeding while others have not.

Conditions for Species That Migrate South of the United States

In general, increased temperatures are projected for Central America (Magrin and others 2007: Fig. 13.1 and Table 13.4). Observed trends in rainfall for Central America vary, with increases in some areas and decreases in others (Magrin and others 2007: Fig. 13.1). In South America (Magrin and others 2007), temperature increases are occurring in many areas (and glaciers have retreated in Columbia, Peru, and Ecuador). Northern areas are expected to become drier and tropical forests are expected to be replaced by savannahs with a general increase in risk of fire; southern areas are expected to become more suitable for tropical vegetation. In southern Mexico, between 1960 and 2004, average and maximum temperatures increased and were generally unrelated to ENSO or PDO (Peralta-Hernandez and others 2009). In this same study, a slight non-statistically significant decrease in precipitation was observed.

Summary

Overall, we provided support for the likelihood of the following key environmental changes on the CNF: increased average annual temperature and temperature extremes; reduced average annual precipitation, including a reduction in snowfall and snowpack, changes to the timing of peak stream flow, particularly those fed directly by snowmelt; increased wildfire activity; and a reduction in riparian forest and woodlands.

References

Aguado, E., D. Cayan, L. Riddle, and M. Roos. 1992. Climatic fluctuations and the timing of west-coast streamflow. Journal of Climate 5:1468-1483.

Allen, C.D., and D.D. Breshears. 1998. Drought-induced shift of a forest-woodland ecotone: rapid landscape response to climate variation. Proceedings of the National Academy of Sciences 14839-14842.

Allen, C.D., A.K. Macalady, H. Chenchouni, [and others]. 2010. A global overview of drought and heat-induced tree mortality reveals emerging climate change risks for forests. Forest Ecology and Management 259:660-684.

Anderson, B.T., J. Wang, G. Salvucci, S. Gopal, and S. Islam. 2010. Observed trends in summertime precipitation over the southwestern United States. Journal of Climate 23:1937-1944.

Barton, A.M. 2002. Intense wildfire in southeastern Arizona: transformation of a Madrean oak-pine forest to oak woodland. Forest Ecology and Management 165:205-212.

Bell, J.L., L.C. Sloan, and M.A. Snyder. 2004. Regional changes in extreme climatic events: a future climate scenario. Journal of Climate 17:81-87.

Bentz, B.J., J. Régnière, C.J. Fettig, E.M. Hansen, J.L. Hayes, J.A. Hicke, R.G. Kelsey, J.F. Negrón, and S.J. Seybold. 2010. Climate change and bark beetles of the western United States and Canada: direct and indirect impacts. BioScience 60:602-613.

Blaustein, A.R., L.K. Belden, D.H. Olson, D.M. Green, T.L. Root, and J.M. Kiesecker. 2001. Amphibian breeding and climate change. Conservation Biology 15:1804-1809.

Bowers, J.E. 2007. Has climatic warming altered spring flowering date of Sonoran Desert shrubs? Southwestern Naturalist 52:347-355.

Breshears, D.D., N.S. Cobb, P.M. Rich, K.P. Price, C.D. Allen, R.G. Balice, W.H. Romme, J.H. Kastens, M. Lisa Floyd, J. Belnap, J.J. Anderson, O.B. Myers, and C.W. Meyer. 2005. Regional vegetation die-off in response to global-change-type drought. Proceedings of the National Academy of Sciences 102:15144-15148.

Brown, D.E., F. Reichenbacher, S.E. Franson. 1998. A classification of North American biotic communities. Salt Lake City, UT: University of Utah Press. 141 p.

Brown, J.H., T.J. Valone, and C.G. Curtin. 1997. Reorganization of an arid ecosystem in response to recent climate change. Proceedings of the National Academy of Sciences 94:9729-9733.

Carter, R. 2002. Tropical storm impacts on Arizona and New Mexico. El Niño-Drought Initiative (END InSight), August 2002, Climate Assessment for the Southwest Project, University of Arizona. Available: http://www.climas.arizona.edu/feature-articles/august-2002-Carter.

Cayan, D.R., S.A. Karrerdiener, M.D. Dettinger, J.M. Caprio, and D.H. Peterson. 2001. Changes in the onset of spring in the western United States. Bulletin of the American Meteorological Society 82:399-415.

Christensen, J.H., B. Hewitson, A. Busuioc, [and others]. 2007. Regional climate projections. In: Solomon, S., D. Qin, M. Manning, Z. Chen, M. Marquis, K.B. Averyt, M. Tignor, and H.L. Miller, eds. Climate Change 2007: The Physical Science Basis. Contribution of Working Group I to the Fourth Assessment Report of the Intergovernmental Panel on Climate Change. Cambridge, United Kingdom: Cambridge University Press.

Cook, B.I., R.L. Miller, and R. Seager. 2009. Amplification of the North American "Dust Bowl" drought through human-induced land degradation. Proceedings of the National Academy of Sciences 13:4997-5001.

Corbosiero, K.L., M.J. Dickinson, and L.F. Bosart. 2009. The contribution of eastern North Pacific tropical cyclones to the rainfall climatology of the southwest United States. Monthly Weather Review 137:2415-2435.

Crimmins, T.M., M.A Crimmins, and C.D. Bertelsen. 2009. Flowering range changes across an elevation gradient in response to warming summer temperatures. Global Change Biology 15:1141-1152.

Crimmins, T.M., M.A Crimmins, and C.D. Bertelsen. 2010. Complex responses to climate drivers in onset of spring flowering across a semi-arid elevation gradient. Journal of Ecology 98:1042-1051.

Crimmins, T.M., M.A. Crimmins, D. Bertelsen, and J. Balmat. 2007. Relationships between alpha diversity of plant species in bloom and climatic variables across and elevation gradient. International Journal of Biometeorology 52:353-366.

Diffenbaugh, N.S., and M. Ashfaq. 2010. Intensification of hot extremes in the United States. Geophysical Research Letters 37:L15701 (5 p.).

Dominguez, F., J. Cañon, and J. Valdes. 2010. IPCC-AR4 climate simulations for the Southwestern US: the importance of future ENSO projections. Climatic Change 99:499-514.

Emanuel, K. 2005. Increasing destructiveness of tropical cyclones over the past 30 years. Nature 436:686-688.

Field, C.B., L.D. Mortsch, M. Brklacich, D.L. Forbes, P. Kovacs, J.A. Patz, S.W. Running, and M.J. Scott. 2007. In: Parry, M.L., O.F. Canziani, J.P. Palutikof, P.J. van der Linden, and C.E. Hanson, eds. Climate Change 2007: Impacts, Adaptation and Vulnerability. Contribution of Working Group II to the Fourth Assessment Report of the Intergovernmental Panel on Climate Change. Cambridge, United Kingdom: Cambridge University Press: 617-652.

Flannigan, M.D., B.J. Stocks, and B.M. Wotton. 2000. Climate change and forest fires. Science of the Total Environment 262:221-229.

Garfin, G., J. Eischeid, M. Lenart, K. Cole, K. Ironside, and N. Cobb, 2009. Downscaling climate projections in topographically diverse landscapes of the Colorado Plateau in the arid southwestern United States. In: Van Riper, C. III, T. Sisk, and B. Wakeling, eds. The Colorado Plateau IV: Proceedings of the 9th Biennial Conference on Colorado Plateau Research; October, 2007. Tucson: University of Arizona Press: p. 21-44.

Gibbs, J.P., and A.R. Breisch. 2001. Climate warming and calling phenology of frogs near Ithaca, New York, 1900-1999. Conservation Biology 15:1175-1178.

Goodrich, G.B., and A.W. Ellis. 2008. Climatic controls and hydrologic impacts of a recent extreme season precipitation reversal in Arizona. Journal of Applied Meteorology and Climatology 47:498-508.

Hamlet, A.F., P.W. Mote, M.P. Clark, and D.P. Lettenmeier. 2007. Twentieth-century trends in runoff, evapotranspiration, and soil moisture in the western United States. Journal of Climate 20:1468-1486.

Housman, D.C., E. Naumburg, T.E. Huxman, T.N. Charlet, R.W. Nowak, and S.D. Smith. 2006. Increases in desert shrub productivity under elevated carbon dioxide vary with water availability. Ecosystems 9:374-385.

Knowles, N., M.D. Dettinger, and D.R. Cayan. 2006. Trends in snowfall versus rainfall in the western United States. Journal of Climate 19:4545-4559.

Kupfer, J.A., J. Balmat, and J.L. Smith. 2005. Shifts in the potential distribution of sky island plant communities in response to climate change. In: Gottfried, G.J., B.S. Gebow, L.G. Eskew, and C.B. Edminster, comps. 2005. Connecting mountain islands and desert seas: biodiversity and management of the Madrean Archipelago II. 2004 May 11-15; Tucson, AZ. Proc. RMRS-P-36. Fort Collins, CO: U.S. Department of Agriculture, Forest Service, Rocky Mountain Research Station. 631 p.

Littell, J.S., D. McKenzie, D.L. Peterson, and A.L. Westerling. 2009. Climate and wildfire area burned in western U.S. ecoprovinces, 1916-2003. Ecological Applications 19:1003-2001.

Logan, J.A., J. Régnière, and J.A. Powell. 2003. Assessing the impacts of global warming on forest pest dynamics. Frontiers in Ecology and the Environment 1:130-137.

Magrin, G., C. Gay García, D. Cruz Choque, J.C. Giménez, A.R. Moreno, G.J. Nagy, C. Nobre, and A. Villamizar. 2007. Latin America. In: Parry, M.L., O.F. Canziani, J.P. Palutikof, P.J. van der Linden, and C.E. Hanson, eds. Climate Change 2007: Impacts, Adaptation and Vulnerability. Contribution of Working Group II to the Fourth Assessment Report of the Intergovernmental Panel on Climate Change. Cambridge, United Kingdom: Cambridge University Press: 581-615.

McCabe, G.J., M.P. Clark, and M.C. Serreze. 2001. Trends in Northern Hemisphere surface cyclone frequency and intensity. Journal of Climate 14:2763-2768.

McCabe, G.J., M.A. Palecki, and J.L. Betancourt. 2004. Pacific and Atlantic Ocean influences on multidecadal drought frequency in the United States. Proceedings of the National Academy of Sciences 101:4136-4141.

McLaughlin, S.P. 1995. An overview of the flora of the Sky Islands, southeastern Arizona: diversity, affinities, insularity. In: DeBano, L.H., P.F. Ffolliott, A. Ortega-Rubio, G. Gottfried, R.H. Hamre, and C.B. Edminster, tech. coords. Biodiversity and management of the Madrean Archipelago: the Sky Islands of southwestern United States and northwestern Mexico. 1994 Sept. 19-23; Tucson, AZ. Gen. Tech. Rep. RM-GTR-264. Fort Collins, CO: U.S. Department of Agriculture, Forest Service, Rocky Mountain Forest and Range Experiment Station. 669 p.

Miller, J.D., H.D. Safford, M. Crimmins, and A.E. Thode. 2009. Quantitative evidence for increasing forest fire severity in the Sierra Nevada and southern Cascade Mountains, California and Nevada, USA. Ecosystems 12:16-32.

Peralta-Hernandez, A., R.C. Balling, Jr., and L.R. Barba-Martinez. 2009. Analysis of near-surface diurnal temperature variations and trends in southern Mexico. International Journal of Climatology 29:205-209.

Peterson, T.C., X. Zhang, M. Brunet-India, and J.L. Vázquez-Aguirre. 2008. Changes in North American extremes derived from daily weather data. Journal of Geophysical Research 113. D07113. 9 p.

Piechota, T., J. Timilsena, G. Tootle, and H. Hidalgo. 2004. The western drought: How bad is it? Eos 85:301-304.

Poff, N.L. 2002. Ecological response to and management of increased flooding caused by climate change. Philosophical Transactions of the Royal Society of London A 360:1497-1510.

Quiring, S.M., and G.B Goodrich. 2008. Nature and causes of the 2002 to 2004 drought in the southwestern United States compared with the historic 1953 to 1957 drought. Climate Research 36:41-52.

Regonda, S.K., B. Rajagopalan, M. Clark, and J. Pitlick. 2005. Seasonal cycle shifts in hydroclimatology over the Western United States. Journal of Climate 18:372-384.

Rehfeldt, G.E., N.L. Crookston, M.V. Warwell, and J.S. Evans. 2006. Empirical analyses of plant-climate relationships for the western United States. International Journal of Plant Science 167:1123-1150.

Rood, S.B., J. Pan, K.M. Gill, C.G. Franks, G.M. Samuelson, and A. Shepard. 2008. Declining summer flows of the Rocky Mountain rivers: Changing seasonal hydrology and probable impacts of floodplain forests. Journal of Hydrology 349:397-410.

Seager, R., Y. Kushnir, C. Herweijer, N. Naik, and J. Velez. 2005. Modeling of tropical forcing of persistent droughts and pluvials over western North America: 1865-2000. Journal of Climate 18:4065-4088.

Seager, R., M. Tang, Y. Kushnir, J. Lu, G. Vecchi, H.-P. Huang, N. Harnik, A. Leetmaa, N.-C. Lau, C. Li, J. Velez, and N. Naik. 2007. Model projections of an imminent transition to a more arid climate in southwestern North America. Science 316:1181-1184.

Sheppard, P.R., A.C. Comrie, G.D. Packin, K. Angersbach, and M.K. Hughes. 1999. The climate of the Southwest. CLIMAS Report Series, CL1-99. University of Arizona, Institute for the Study of Planet Earth. Available: http://www.climas.arizona.edu/files/climas/pubs/cl1-99.pdf.

Sheppard, P.R., A.C. Comrie, G.D. Packin, K. Angersbach, and M.K. Hughes. 2002. The climate of the US Southwest. Climate Research 21:219-238.

Smith, S.D., T.E. Huxman, S.F. Zitzer, T.N. Charlet, D.C. Housman, J.S. Coleman, L.K. Fenstermaker, J.R. Seemann, and R.S. Nowak. 2000. Elevated CO_2 increases productivity and invasive species success in an arid ecosystem. Nature 408:79-81.

Stewart, I.T., D.R. Cayan, and M.D. Dettinger. 2005. Changes toward earlier streamflow timing across western North America. Journal of Climate 18:1136-1154.

Stephens, S.L. 2005. Forest fire causes and extent on United States Forest Service lands. International Journal of Wildland Fire 14:213-222.

Swetnam, T.W., and J.L. Betancourt. 1998. Mesoscale disturbance and ecological response to decadal climate variability in the American Southwest. Journal of Climate 11:3128-3147.

Tebaldi, C., K. Hayhoe, J.M. Arblaster, and G.A. Meehl. 2006. Going to the extremes: An intercomparison of model-simulated historical and future changes in extreme events. Climatic Change 79:185-211.

Trenberth, K.E., P.D. Jones, P. Ambenje, R. Bojariu, D. Easterling, A. Klein Tank, D. Parker, F. Rahimzadeh, J.A. Renwick, M. Rusticucci, B. Soden, and P. Zhai. 2007. Observations: Surface and atmospheric climate change. In: Solomon, S., D. Qin, M. Manning, Z. Chen, M. Marquis, K.B. Averyt, M. Tignor, and H.L. Miller, eds. Climate Change 2007: The Physical Science Basis. Contribution of Working Group I to the Fourth Assessment Report of the Intergovernmental Panel on Climate Change. Cambridge, United Kingdom: Cambridge University Press.

Trenberth, K.E., J. Fasullo, and L. Smith. 2005. Trends and variability in column-integrated atmospheric water vapor. Climate Dynamics 24:741-758.

U.S. Forest Service [USFS]. 2009. Draft Coronado National Forest ecological sustainability report. Tucson, AZ: U.S. Department of Agriculture, Forest Service. Available: http://www fs fed.us/r3/coronado/plan-revision/documents/final/cnf-ecological-sustainability-report-final-022009.pdf.

Van Mantgem, P.J., N.L. Stephenson, J.C. Byrne, L.D. Daniels, J.R. Frankline, P.Z. Fule, M.E. Harmon, A.J. Larson, J.M. Smith, A.H. Taylor, and T.T. Veblen. 2009. Widespread increase of tree mortality rates in the western United States. Science 323:521-523.

Wang, H., J.A. Schubert, M. Suarez, J. Chen, M. Hoerling, A. Kumar, and P. Pegion. 2009. Attribution of the seasonality and regionality in climate trends over the United States during 1950-2000. Journal of Climate 22:2571-2590.

Warshall, P. 1995. The Madrean Sky Island Archipelago: A planetary overview. In: DeBano, L.H., P.F. Ffolliott, A. Ortega-Rubio, G. Gottfried, R.H. Hamre, and C.B. Edminster, tech. coords. Biodiversity and management of the Madrean Archipelago: The Sky Islands of southwestern United States and northwestern Mexico. 1994 Sept. 19-23; Tucson, AZ. Gen. Tech. Rep. RM-GTR-264. Fort Collins, CO: U.S. Department of Agriculture, Forest Service, Rocky Mountain Forest and Range Experiment Station. 669 p.

Webster, P.J., G.J. Holland, J.A. Curry, and H.-R. Chang. 2005. Changes in tropical cyclone number, duration, and intensity in a warming environment. Science 309:1844-1846.

Westerling, A.L., H.G. Hidalgo, D.R. Cayan, and T.W. Swetnam. 2006. Warming and earlier spring increase western U.S. forest wildfire activity. Science 313:940-943.

Weiss, J.L., C.L. Castro, and J.T. Overpeck. 2009. Distinguishing pronounced droughts in the southwestern United States: seasonality and effects of warmer temperatures. Journal of Climate 22:5918-5932.

Weiss, J.L., and J.T. Overpeck. 2005. Is the Sonoran Desert losing its cool? Global Change Ecology 11:2065-2077.

Chapter 2: An Assessment of the Vulnerability of Wildlife to Climate Change

Introduction

The process of identifying what types of climate change impacts are likely to be experienced by ecosystems, plant communities, and/or species can help to focus decisions regarding conserving natural resources under a changing climate. Rowland and others (2011) summarized some of the approaches that have been used to evaluate potential impacts on animal species, including: (1) using observations of paleoecological data (past 1000-10,000 years) and/or more recent data (Twentieth Century) to evaluate changes in distributions of species as correlated with climate; (2) species distribution modeling (e.g., bioclimatic envelope modeling, and niche modeling) to predict the future range of a species relative to changes in climate and/or distributions of plant species on which a species depends; and (3) vulnerability indices to identify the relative vulnerability of species. Each approach has benefits and limitations. While niche modeling can produce very useful information for how species' distributions may change (Peterson and others 2002; Preston and others 2008), the method can be relatively data intensive and requires application of analytical methods that may go beyond the time available to resource managers. Field experiments that manipulate water, temperature, and/or CO_2 levels (Smith and others 2000; Housman and others 2006; Mikkelsen and others 2008) provide insight into how vegetation may change but are generally the purview of research scientists, not resource managers. Vulnerability indices (of the type described by Rowland et al. 2011) tend to rely on existing data and can be less quantitatively intensive. They can be applied to geographic units, species' habitats, and species themselves, and are set in a framework that explicitly considers sensitivity and exposure to climate change.

The IPCC defines vulnerability (Schneider and others 2001) as the extent to which a system (or species) is susceptible to sustaining damage from climate change; vulnerability is considered to be a function of sensitivity and exposure to climate change as well as adaptive capacity. Sensitivity refers to the degree to which a system or species will respond to a given change in climate, whereas exposure is the degree to which a species or system is expected to experience projected changes in climate. Adaptive capacity refers to the degree to which a species or system can reduce or moderate the potential impact of climate change. A resilient system or population is one that is not sensitive to climate variability and change and has the capacity to adapt.

Glick and others (2011) described the results of several case studies that used vulnerability indices. Application of NatureServe's Climate Change Vulnerability Index to 216 species in Nevada identified several relatively common species (e.g., American pika [*Ochotona princeps*], bighorn sheep, and sagebrush vole [*Lemmiscus curtatus*]) as

vulnerable to climate change. Another assessment using the U.S. Environmental Protection Agency's Threatened and Endangered Species Vulnerability Framework evaluated six Federally listed vertebrate species and categorized each into one of three different levels of vulnerability to climate change.

Our goal was to assess the relative vulnerability of 30 vertebrate species on CNF to assist wildlife managers in on-going efforts to set conservation priorities under climate change. However, our results also may be of interest to efforts for species conservation on other public and private lands in the region. We used a vulnerability index system that was a pilot of a decision-support tool developed by USFS Rocky Mountain Research Station. It produced scores reflecting relative measures of vulnerability to climate change with respect to habitat, physiology, phenology, and biotic interactions.

Methods

The 30 vertebrate species we assessed (Appendix A) were identified by CNF biologists (R. Gerhardt and L. Jones) as being high priority for assessing vulnerability. These species had one or more of the following designations: (1) USFS Species of Concern, (2) USFS Species of Interest, (3) species that are otherwise of concern to USFS, (4) Federally listed as Endangered or Threatened species under the Endangered Species Act, (5) Federal Species of Concern; (6) federal Candidate for Listing, (7) Federal "under review" species. By taxonomic grouping, the 30 species consisted of 8 birds, 13 mammals, 5 reptiles, and 4 amphibians. Twenty-nine of the 30 species are known to occur on CNF. The mesquite mouse (*Peromyscus merriami*) potentially occurs on CNF based on known nearby locations (Jones, personal communication). We evaluated vulnerability by considering species on all relevant EMAs simultaneously (i.e., we did not assess vulnerability separately for each EMA). Two species—the American bullfrog and the Abert's squirrel (*Sciurus aberti*; Fig. 2.1)—are of concern because they are not native to CNF and potentially, or are known to, compete with native species.

We used a pilot version of a decision-support tool called a System for Assessing Vulnerability of Species (SAVS). SAVS was developed by the USFS Rocky Mountain Research Station to assess the vulnerability of terrestrial vertebrates to climate change (Bagne and others 2011). It consists of 25 questions based on criteria or factors that are expected to predict relative vulnerability to climate change. Questions, and their multiple choice options, are grouped into four categories as they relate to habitat, physiology, phenology, and biotic interactions (Fig. 2.2; Appendix B). Each question addresses one or two of the following aspects of

Figure 2.1. The Abert's squirrel (*Sciurus aberti*) is native to northern Arizona but was introduced to the CNF. The species is considered a potential competitor of the Mount Graham red squirrel (*Tamiasciurus hudsonicus grahamensis*), a Federally listed endangered species. *Photo: Sally King, National Park Service (Wikimedia Commons).*

Figure 2.2. A summary of the factors (and their grouping into four categories) used in the vulnerability assessment.

HABITAT

- Breeding habitat area
- Non-breeding habitat area
- Habitat components required for breeding season
- Habitat components required for non-breeding season
- Habitat quality and reproductive success
- Habitat quality and survival
- Ability to colonize new areas
- Use of migratory or transitional areas

PHYSIOLOGY

- Impacts to physiological tolerances
- Temperature-dependent sex determination
- Exposure to extreme weather
- Limitations to daily active period
- Metabolic energy savings (torpor, hibernation)
- Type of metabolism and ability to store energy
- Alternative life history strategies
- Lifespan

PHENOLOGY

- Use of temperature and moisture cues
- Reproduction and survival relative to resource availability (event timing)
- Separation of cues relative to resource availability (mismatch potential)
- Number of breeding attempts per year

BIOTIC INTERACTIONS

- Impacts on primary food resources if not a diet generalist
- Changes to predation levels if limited diversity of predators
- Changes in symbiotic relationships
- Potential for change in disease incidence causing widespread mortality
- Changes to influence of competitors

vulnerability: exposure, sensitivity, and/or adaptive capacity. For each question, one multiple-choice option is selected by the user, with each option having a different point value. Responses that are considered to reflect vulnerability to climate change have a positive point value; those considered to reflect resilience to climate change have a negative point value. Responses considered to reflect "no affect" (or neither a benefit nor a cost) from climate change have a point value of zero. For our study, a single biologist (S. Coe) assessed all 30 species.

For each species, we calculated a score using responses from all questions (called an "overall score") and a separate sub-score for each of the four categories (called a "categorical score"). Possible overall scores ranged from -20 to +20, and possible categorical scores ranged from -5 to +5. Formulas that we used to calculate these scores adjusted for different numbers of questions within each category. For a given species, a positive overall score (and a positive categorical score) resulted when more multiple-choice responses were chosen that had positive values than negative values. A score of zero was obtained either when all questions were scored a zero or when the positive point totals offset the negative point totals.

An uncertainty score accounted for variation in the amount of data used (i.e., available data) to answer each question. We scored uncertainty for each category in the following way: zero points when information was available for most questions in the respective category; one point when information was available for some questions or when most of the information used was from similar species; and two points if there was little information for the species or similar species beyond broad generalizations. We summed the uncertainty scores in each category to create an overall uncertainty score. The uncertainty values are distinct from the vulnerability scores.

For species-specific biological information, we used published literature sources obtained by searching the Web of Science® database of primary literature using the name of each species and/or sub-species. We also used unpublished agency documents and conference proceedings, as these sources often contained important information specific to populations in Arizona and/or the Southwest.

We assessed vulnerability of species on the CNF assuming that the following changes are likely to occur, based on the results of our climate change review (see Chapter 1):

- An increase in average temperature, including an increase in winter minimum temperatures;

- An increase in the frequency of temperature extremes (although the precise frequency, intensity, and duration of such events remains unclear);

- A reduction in snowpack (greater fraction of winter precipitation falling as snow);

- An increase in aridity and drought as a result of reduced average precipitation, altered precipitation regimes, and/or an increase in evaporation relative to precipitation;

- Alterations to the timing of peak stream flows in spring, particularly in streams that occur in snowmelt drainages, and reduced average stream flow during other times of year;

- An increase in the frequency and intensity of wildfire;

- A reduction in riparian, forest, and woodland communities; a possible increase in semi-desert grassland.

With respect to impacts from wildfire, we considered direct loss of habitat and did not include direct mortality of species from fire or smoke. Given the uncertainty in projections for precipitation intensity by Meehl and others (2005; see Chapter 1), we did not assume increases in precipitation intensity. For each long-distance migratory species, we present in Appendix B the information used to evaluate potential impacts to non-breeding habitats. Our assessment focused on the direct impacts of climate change on species; we did not incorporate potential impacts from anthropogenic responses that may occur in response to planning for climate change (e.g., increases in wind turbines for wind energy to reduce greenhouse gas emissions).

Results

Overall Scores

We calculated overall scores using all 25 questions; possible scores ranged from -20 to +20. Actual overall scores ranged from +9.9 to -0.4 (Fig. 2.3 and Table 2.1). Twenty-nine of the 30 species assessed received overall scores >0. More than half of the species (67%) had a score >+5.0, which is roughly the mid-point in the range of scores received. The two species with the largest scores were the elegant trogon (Fig. 2.4) and Tarahumara frog (Fig. 2.5)—both received an overall score of +9.9. They both received positive scores ("vulnerable") on 13 questions, a score of zero ("neutral") on 10 questions, and negative scores ("resilient") on 2 questions, but they differed on which questions they were scored vulnerable.

The lowest-scoring species were the mesquite mouse and desert bighorn sheep (Ovis canadensis mexicana), which both received +1.3, and Slevin's bunchgrass lizard (-0.4). Slevin's bunchgrass lizard received negative scores ("resilient") on 7 questions, positive scores ("vulnerable") on 7 questions, and a score of zero ("neutral") on 11 questions.

The highest scores were not limited to a single taxonomic category. Species with the highest ~30% of the scores (i.e., ≥+7.0) consisted of one or more species in each of the four taxonomic categories—birds, mammals, reptiles, and amphibians. The taxonomic group with the highest average overall score was birds (+7.4), followed by amphibians (+6.9), mammals (+5.0), and reptiles (+3.9).

The five species with the largest overall scores (Fig. 2.3) are associated with riparian habitat. However, additional species use riparian habitat, such as the Sonoran tiger salamander (Ambystoma tigrinum stebbinsi) and the American bullfrog, and received lower scores (+4.4 and +3.7, respectively).

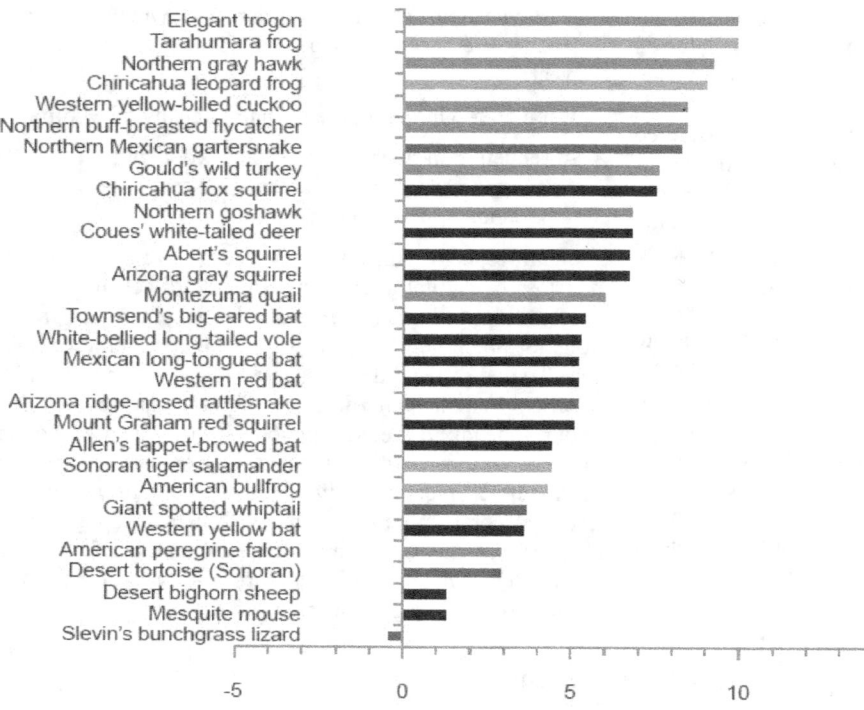

Figure 2.3. Vulnerability scores ("overall scores") for the 30 species assessed on the CNF. Colors indicate taxonomic category (birds = red, mammals = black, reptiles = purple, and amphibians = green).

Figure 2.4. The elegant trogon (*Trogon elegans*) had the largest vulnerability score of the bird species assessed and was tied with Tarahumara frog (*Rana tarahumarae*) for the largest vulnerability score of the 30 species. *Photo: Dominic Sherony (Wikimedia Commons).*

Figure 2.5. The Tarahumara frog (*Rana tarahumarae*) had the largest vulnerability score of the amphibian species assessed and was tied with the elegant trogon for the largest vulnerability score of the 30 species. *Photo: Jim Rorabaugh, U.S. Fish and Wildlife Service (Wikimedia Commons).*

USDA Forest Service RMRS-GTR-273. 2012.

Table 2.1. Vulnerability scores (overall and categorical) for species assessed on CNF (n = 30). Possible overall scores range -20 to 20. Possible scores in four categories (habitat, physiology, phenology, and biotic interactions) range -5 to 5.

Species	Overall Score	Categorical Scores			
		Habitat	Physiology	Phenology	Biotic interactions
Elegant trogon	9.9	2.9	2.1	5.0	0.0
Tarahumara frog	9.9	3.5	2.9	2.1	0.0
Northern gray hawk	9.2	2.4	2.1	3.8	1.0
Chiricahua leopard frog	9.0	4.0	2.9	-0.8	0.0
Western yellow-billed cuckoo	8.4	2.4	2.1	3.8	0.0
Northern buff-breasted flycatcher	8.4	2.4	2.1	3.8	0.0
Northern Mexican gartnersnake	8.3	3.5	1.4	2.1	0.0
Gould's wild turkey	7.6	2.9	2.1	-0.4	1.0
Chiricahua fox squirrel	7.5	3.4	0.7	0.8	1.0
Coues' white-tailed deer	6.8	3.4	0.7	1.3	0.0
Northern goshawk	6.8	2.4	2.1	0.8	0.0
Arizona gray squirrel	6.7	3.4	0.7	0.8	0.0
Abert's squirrel	6.7	3.4	0.7	0.8	0.0
Montezuma quail	6.0	0.9	2.1	2.1	1.0
Townsend's big-eared bat	5.4	2.4	-0.8	2.1	1.0
White-bellied long-tailed vole	5.3	2.5	0.7	-0.4	1.0
Western red bat	5.2	2.9	-0.7	2.5	0.0
Mexican long-tongued bat	5.2	1.9	-0.7	3.8	1.0
Arizona ridge-nosed rattlesnake	5.2	2.5	0.0	2.1	0.0
Mount Graham red squirrel	5.1	3.4	-0.7	0.8	0.0
Sonoran tiger salamander	4.4	1.5	0.7	2.1	0.0
Allen's lappet-browed bat	4.4	2.9	-0.7	0.8	0.0
American bullfrog	4.3	2.4	0.7	-0.8	0.0
Giant spotted whiptail	3.7	2.5	0.0	-0.8	0.0
Western yellow bat	3.6	2.4	-0.7	0.8	0.0
Desert tortoise (Sonoran)	2.9	0.5	0.7	2.1	0.0
American peregrine falcon	2.9	-0.1	2.1	2.5	-1.0
Mesquite mouse	1.3	2.5	-0.7	-3.3	0.0
Desert bighorn sheep	1.3	-0.1	1.4	-0.4	0.0
Slevin's bunchgrass lizard	-0.4	-2.3	1.4	2.1	0.0

Categorical Scores

We calculated categorical scores for each of the four categories; possible scores ranged +5 to -5. The average score and range in the first three categories across all species were as follows:

- habitat = +2.3; +4.0 to -2.3 (Fig. 2.6; Table 2.1);

- physiology = +0.9; +2.9 to -0.8 (Fig. 2.7; Table 2.1);

- phenology = +1.4; +5.0 to -3.0 (Fig. 2.8; Table 2.1).

In the biotic interactions category, only three values were obtained: +1.0, 0.0, and -1.0 with an average of +0.2. Within the habitat, physiology, and phenology categories, the majority of species received scores >0 (27 species, 21 species, and 23 species, respectively).

In the habitat category, which had the highest average score, the Chiricahua leopard frog (*Rana chiricahuensis*) received the highest score (Figs. 2.6 and 2.9). The species with the lowest score was Slevin's bunchgrass lizard (-2.3). The highest average score by taxonomic group was for amphibians (+2.9), followed by mammals (+2.7), birds (+2.1), and reptiles (+1.3). All bird and mammal species had scores >0 except for the American peregrine falcon (*Falco peregrinus anatum*; Fig. 2.10) and desert bighorn sheep (Fig. 2.11). Three of the four reptiles also scored >0 (Fig. 2.12A), as did all amphibians (Fig. 2.12B).

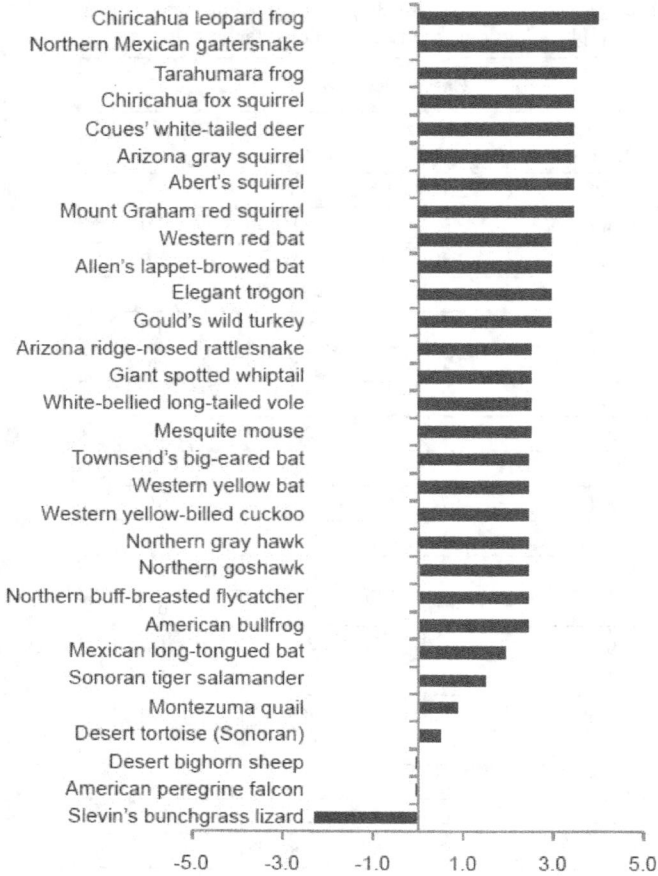

Figure 2.6. Vulnerability scores in the habitat category for the 30 species assessed on the CNF.

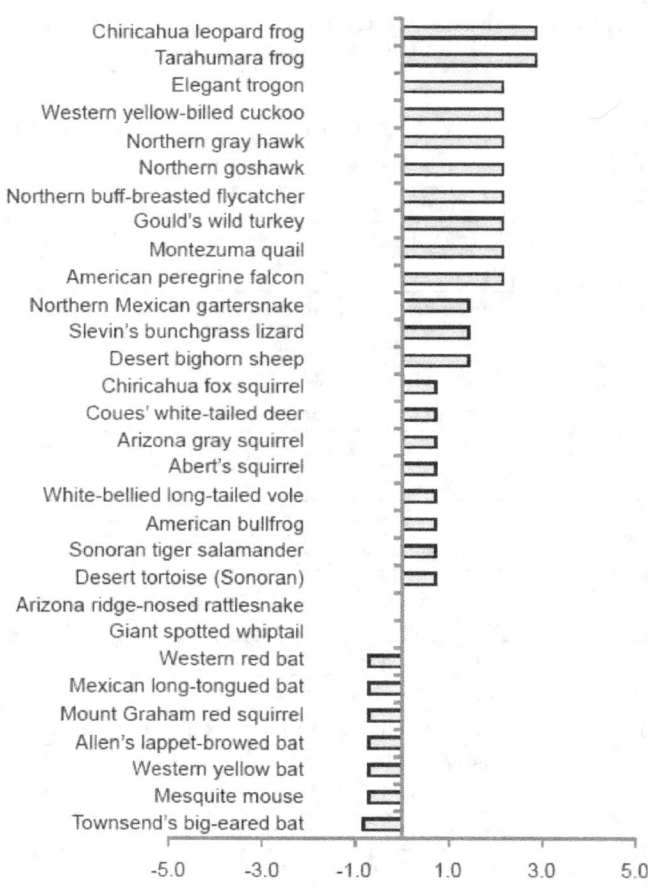

Figure 2.7. Vulnerability scores in the physiology category for the 30 species assessed on the CNF.

In the physiology category, the Tarahumara frog and the Chiricahua leopard frog were tied for the highest score (+2.9; Fig. 2.7). Both of these species were scored as "vulnerable" for five of the eight criteria, "neutral" for two criteria, and "resilient" on one criterion (see respective species accounts, Appendix B). The pattern of scores was notably different from those in the habitat category, with eight of the 21 species having a very small positive score (+0.71; Fig. 2.7 and Table 2.1). The highest average score by taxonomic group was for birds (+2.1), followed by amphibians (+1.8), reptiles (+0.7), and mammals (0.0). All bird and amphibian species had scores >0 (Figs. 2.10 and 2.12B, respectively), whereas roughly half of the mammals had scores <0 (Fig. 2.11), and two of the five reptiles received a score of 0 (Fig. 2.12A).

The phenology category had the second-highest average score after the habitat category. The elegant trogon received the largest score (+5.0; Fig. 2.8), and the mesquite mouse received the smallest score (-3.3). The highest average score by taxonomic group was received by birds (+2.3), followed by reptiles (+1.5), mammals (+0.8), and amphibians (+0.6). All but 1 bird species received a score >0, as did 10 of 13 mammals, 4 of 5 reptiles, and 2 of 4 amphibians.

In the biotic interactions category, most species (n = 22) obtained a score of 0.0, seven species scored 1.0, and one scored -1.0 (American peregrine falcon). Birds and mammals had an average score of 0.3, and amphibians and reptiles had an average score of 0.0.

Uncertainty Scores

Uncertainty scores were not incorporated into vulnerability scores, but rather, helped to identify the relative amount of information used to select responses in each category, which, in turn, identified where further information or research could prove beneficial. Possible scores for uncertainty ranged from 0 to 8, with higher scores indicating greater uncertainty. In our study, scores for uncertainty for each species ranged from 0 to 7 (Table 2.2). Desert bighorn sheep was scored a 0 and Mexican long-tongued bat (*Choeronycteris mexicana*) was scored a 7. The mean uncertainty score was 2.6.

For most species, uncertainty was lowest in the habitat category. Within this category, one criterion for which there was often no information was "habitat quality" (relating variation in habitat quality to variation in reproductive success and survival). Also, there was uncertainty for questions

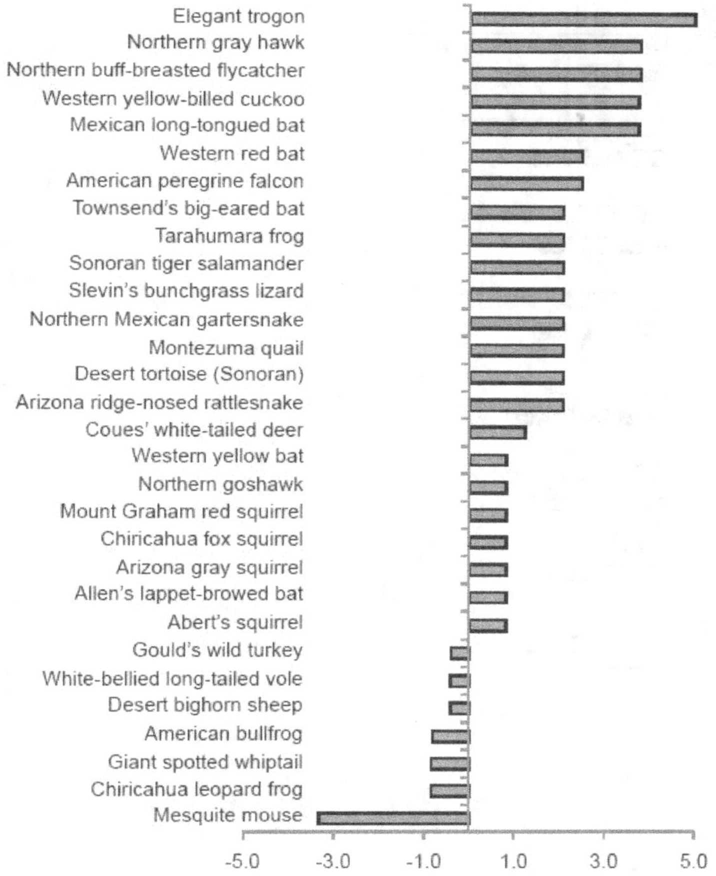

Elegant trogon
Northern gray hawk
Northern buff-breasted flycatcher
Western yellow-billed cuckoo
Mexican long-tongued bat
Western red bat
American peregrine falcon
Townsend's big-eared bat
Tarahumara frog
Sonoran tiger salamander
Slevin's bunchgrass lizard
Northern Mexican gartersnake
Montezuma quail
Desert tortoise (Sonoran)
Arizona ridge-nosed rattlesnake
Coues' white-tailed deer
Western yellow bat
Northern goshawk
Mount Graham red squirrel
Chiricahua fox squirrel
Arizona gray squirrel
Allen's lappet-browed bat
Abert's squirrel
Gould's wild turkey
White-bellied long-tailed vole
Desert bighorn sheep
American bullfrog
Giant spotted whiptail
Chiricahua leopard frog
Mesquite mouse

-5.0   -3.0   -1.0   1.0   3.0   5.0

Figure 2.9. The Chiricahua leopard frog received the highest score for vulnerability in the habitat category. *Photo: Jim Rorabaugh, U.S. Fish and Wildlife Service (Wikimedia Commons).*

Figure 2.8. Vulnerability scores in the phenology category for the 30 species assessed on the CNF.

related to non-breeding habitat for migratory species because the wintering locations of migratory species are typically not well known, and climate projections for Mexico, Central, and South America were broad-scale in scope.

For most species, there was also a lack of information for questions in the physiology category. For example, we found little information in the published literature on the ability of species to deal with heat extremes and drought in natural settings. For the criteria in the category of biotic interactions, there was little information on competitors of individual species. Also, for most species, the literature suggested that a suite of predators existed. Many, if not most, species were identified as susceptible to a variety of diseases, but we found few reports of widespread mortality from the many diseases that species potentially experience, and there was relatively little information projecting how climate change might alter the prevalence of the diseases identified.

Discussion

Our assessment of 30 species showed that most species have vulnerability according to the multiple criteria

comprising the assessment system we used, and all species had vulnerability in some areas. Even the species with a negative overall score (<0)—the Slevin's bunchgrass lizard—was scored as vulnerable for seven criteria. In general, species with the largest overall scores were associated with riparian habitat, which is expected to decline with increasing temperatures. However, not all species associated with riparian habitat had the largest overall scores.

It is difficult to predict what the relative importance of different traits to a species' survival will be under climate change. Criteria in the questionnaire each had equal, or roughly equal, weight. However, in reality, one or more criteria may exert a disproportionate influence on a species' survival relative to other criteria. Furthermore, additional factors that influence species' vulnerability under climate change likely exist. Thus, small differences in scores may or may not reflect large differences in actual vulnerability. The ranking of species by scores (as we presented in graphical and tabular format) can be used to guide further investigations regarding the specific areas of vulnerability of a species or set of species. Ranks should not, however, be assumed to predict the relative probability of population decline. Rather, scores on individual questions should

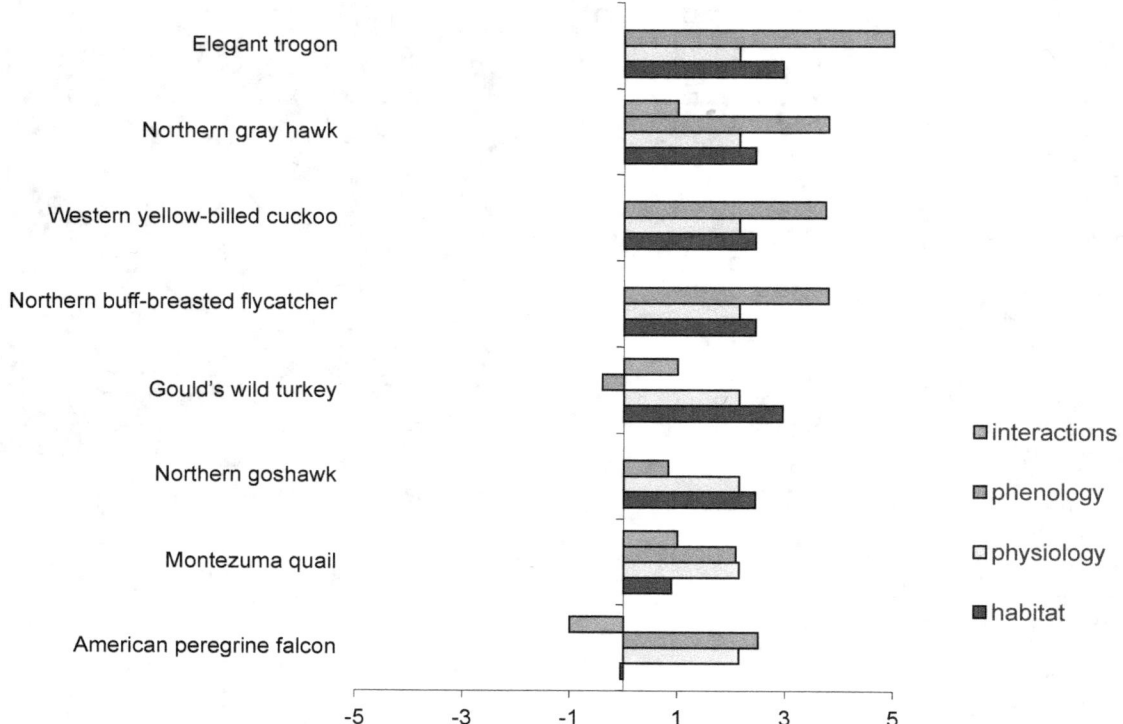

Figure 2.10. Vulnerability scores within each category for species of birds assessed on the CNF.

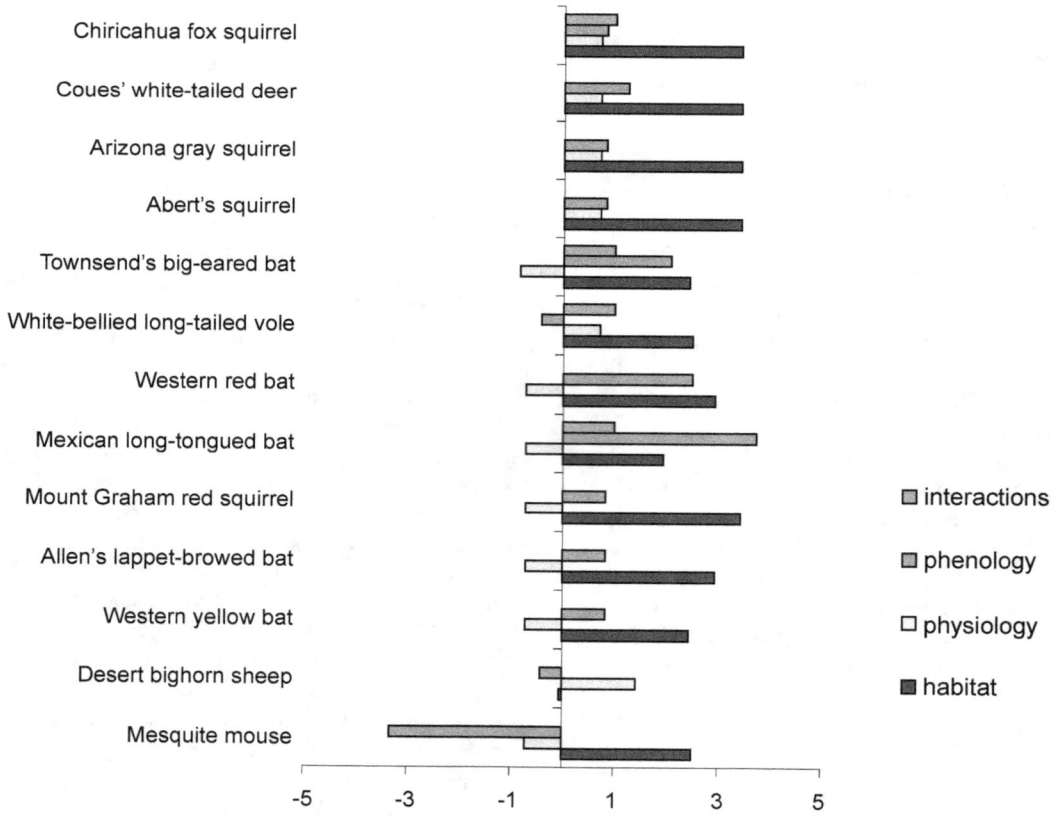

Figure 2.11. Vulnerability scores within each category for species of mammals assessed on the CNF.

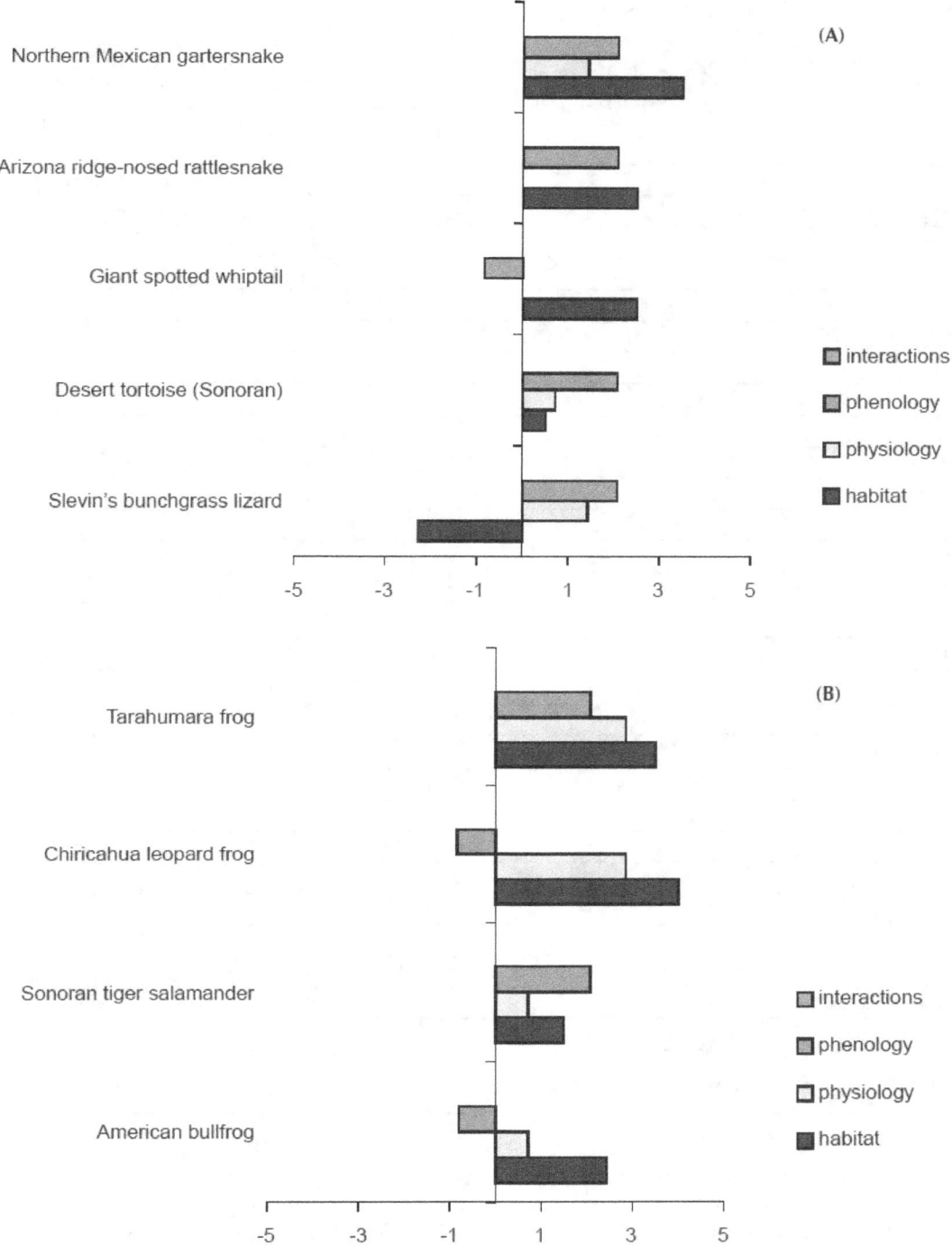

Figure 2.12. Vulnerability scores within each category for species of (A) reptiles and (B) amphibians assessed on the CNF.

Table 2.2. Uncertainty scores for species assessed on CNF (n=30). Possible scores within a category are 0, 1, or 2, for a possible total uncertainty score ranging from 0 to 8

Species	Overall Uncertainty Score	Uncertainty Score Within Category			
		Habitat	Physiology	Phenology	Biotic interactions
Elegant trogon	3	0	2	0	1
Tarahumara frog	2	0	2	0	0
Northern gray hawk	4	0	2	0	2
Chiricahua leopard frog	4	0	2	1	1
Western yellow-billed cuckoo	2	0	1	0	1
Northern buff-breasted flycatcher	5	1	2	1	1
Northern Mexican gartersnake	3	0	1	1	1
Gould's wild turkey	1	0	1	0	0
Chiricahua fox squirrel	4	0	1	2	1
Coues' white-tailed deer	2	0	1	1	0
Northern goshawk	1	0	1	0	0
Arizona gray squirrel	2	0	1	0	1
Abert's squirrel	1	0	1	0	0
Montezuma quail	3	0	2	0	1
Townsend's big-eared bat	3	0	1	1	1
White-bellied long-tailed vole	4	1	1	1	1
Western red bat	4	1	1	1	1
Mexican long-tongued bat	7	2	2	1	2
Arizona ridge-nosed rattlesnake	4	0	1	1	2
Mount Graham red squirrel	3	0	1	1	1
Sonoran tiger salamander	1	0	1	0	0
Allen's lappet-browed bat	4	1	1	1	1
American bullfrog	1	0	1	0	0
Giant spotted whiptail	5	1	1	1	2
Western yellow bat	4	1	1	1	1
Desert tortoise (Sonoran)	1	0	1	0	0
American peregrine falcon	2	0	1	1	0
Mesquite mouse	5	2	1	1	1
Desert bighorn sheep	0	0	0	0	0
Slevin's bunchgrass lizard	4	0	1	1	2

be examined and considered in terms of how each criterion potentially contributes to vulnerability or resilience. For example, the elegant trogon and Tarahumara frog both had the same overall score and the same number of questions for which they were scored as vulnerable, but their categorical scores differed, thus reflecting differences in the criteria for which they were considered vulnerable.

The fact that the largest overall scores were not limited to a single taxonomic category suggests that traits of individual species, not just of major taxonomic groups, were important contributors to vulnerability scores. For example, the two species with the largest overall scores were from different taxonomic groups. Also, the two reptiles with the largest overall scores—northern Mexican gartersnake [*Thamnophis*

eques megalops] and Arizona ridge-nosed rattlesnake [*Crotalus willardi willardi*])—each had overall scores closer to species of mammals and birds than to each other or to other reptiles.

Within the habitat category, the Chiricahua leopard frog received the highest score in part due to its dependence on standing water during the breeding season and its low dispersal tendency. Low dispersal ability was a trait common to all of the amphibians and contributed to that group having the highest average score, as did the expectation that habitat for three of the four species will decline. The fourth amphibian—Sonoran tiger salamander—was projected to experience some habitat loss (a decline in Madrean oak woodland) and some increase in habitat (expansion of grasslands). Similarly, a high average score for mammals was influenced by a predicted decline in habitat for 12 of the 13 species (the exception being the desert bighorn sheep). In contrast to the amphibians, the mammals were considered to be good dispersers and, thus, able to move to new areas in response to changes in habitat, with the exception of mesquite mouse and white-bellied long-tailed vole (*Microtus longicaudus leucophaeus*). Among birds, the only species for which habitat was projected not to decrease was the American peregrine falcon, a species that occupies a variety of habitat types. The only bird species that was considered vulnerable due to low dispersal was the Montezuma quail (*Cyrtonyx montezumae*). All five reptiles were considered poor dispersers, and habitat for three was projected to decrease. Projected increases in grasslands are expected to provide some benefit to the Slevin's bunchgrass lizard. The Sonoran desert tortoise (*Gopherus agassizii*, Sonoran population) was scored as "neutral" with respect to habitat changes given the potential for an increase in desert scrub.

In the physiology category, the Tarahumara frog and the Chiricahua leopard frog had the largest scores and were considered vulnerable on the same criteria. Factors contributing to their vulnerability were the potential for: (1) a drier environment to lead to reduced over-wintering survival and reduced activity periods, (2) mortality from an increase in spring flooding, and (3) multi-year droughts to reduce the success and/or number of breeding events across years. The existence of terrestrial and aquatic adult forms in the Sonoran tiger salamander was considered a life history strategy that might confer an advantage when resources and climate conditions are variable. The bird species also showed many areas of vulnerability in the physiology category, and all were considered vulnerable on the same criteria, including the inability of these species to conserve energetic resources by undergoing torpor, their relatively short lifespan, and their endothermic physiology. The lack of alternative life history strategies had a neutral effect on their scores. Uncertainty regarding potential behavioral responses to increases in temperature reduced our capacity to predict physiological thresholds and effects on activity periods. Also, had there been more certainty with respect to predictions related to an increase in hurricane frequency, we would have considered this potential extreme weather pattern a threat to the bird species that migrate long distances to the south.

As with birds, the uncertainty regarding possible behavioral coping responses to high temperature led us to assign neutral scores for the squirrels, bats, and rodents for questions regarding physiological thresholds and changes in activity periods. Heat stress in summer has been documented as an important issue for desert bighorn sheep. It is possible that Coues' white-tailed deer (*Odocoileus virginianus couesi*), another large ungulate, would have similar physiological issues, although their use of more wooded habitats may help to reduce their exposure. The ability of the bat and squirrel species to reduce metabolic demands through torpor or other means of inhibiting metabolism was considered an advantage. The Mount Graham red squirrel (*Tamiasciurus hudsonicus grahamensis*) is reported as able to store food in the long term, which may reduce its vulnerability to energetic issues associated with climate-related reductions in food resources; it is the only genus of tree squirrel in North America that stores substantial quantities of food. Lastly, scores for the five reptile species varied considerably due, in part, to variation in life history, and we refer the reader to individual species accounts for the sources of that variation (Appendix B).

Birds, on average, had the largest scores in the phenology category. Although only two species were scored as vulnerable to potential changes in temperature and moisture cues (elegant trogon and Montezuma quail), all but two species (Gould's wild turkey [*Meleagris gallopavo mexicana*] and American peregrine falcon) were considered to be vulnerable with respect to "event timing" (association between fecundity and survival relative to potential changes in the timing of environmental factors that influence both). The geographic separation of breeding and wintering grounds for several of the bird species increased the mean score of the birds. Lastly, all species were considered to have a temporally limited breeding period.

Mammals, on average, scored low in the phenology category. Only one species (Towsend's big-eared bat, *Corynorhinus townsendii*) was scored as vulnerable with respect to temperature and moisture cues. All but three species (Coues' white-tailed deer, desert bighorn sheep, and mesquite mouse) were considered vulnerable to "event timing" (Question 2 in Phenology; Appendix B). As with the migratory birds, migratory bats have the potential for mismatched phenology in breeding. Only the mesquite mouse and white-bellied long-tailed vole were documented as having multiple breeding attempts in a single year. The amphibian and reptile species were considered vulnerable to changes in cues used for breeding and event timing, and resilient relative to the separation in time and space between cues that initiate breeding and resources for breeding. Two of the amphibians (Tarahumara frog and Sonoran tiger salamander) and one of the reptiles (giant spotted whiptail, *Aspidoscelis burti stictogrammus*) were scored as vulnerable due to a relatively short breeding period.

The preponderance of scores of zero in the biotic interactions category reflects the fact that many species were considered neither vulnerable nor resilient (i.e., score of 0) for many or all criteria. Most species in this assessment were considered to be diet generalists, to be preyed upon by a variety of predators, and to have a variety of competitive relationships, all of which led to "neutral" scores. The elegant trogon was the only species scored as having a symbiotic relationship because it depends on other species to excavate nesting cavities in trees. However, it is likely that climate change will indeed influence relationships many species have with food, interactions with predators and competitors, and susceptibility to disease. These relationships are complex due to the number of variables involved and how they interact. Predicting what and how changes may occur is difficult. Additional information and more complex analyses are needed to identify the specific impacts of climate change on species interactions.

In considering the results of assessments of potential future impacts from climate change, it is important to recognize that uncertainty exists. Predictions for how temperature, precipitation, and vegetation may change in the future are inherently uncertain. These uncertainties include (but are not limited to) "the natural internal variability of the climate system, the trajectories of future emissions of greenhouse gases and aerosols, and the response of the global climate system to any given set of future emissions/concentrations (Mearns 2010, adapted from Cox and Stephenson 2007)." The method we used to estimate change in plant communities was based upon where suitable climate for vegetation communities might exist in the future. However, additional factors are expected to influence shifts in plant species distributions, such as carbon dioxide levels, nutrients, soil conditions, competitive interactions among species, differential rates of dispersal and survival (McKenney and others 2007), and the interactions of these variables. Also, it is unclear how climate change may alter the relationship between native and invasive species (e.g., buffel grass invasion into desert scrub on CNF).

With respect to application of the questionnaire, one biologist assessed all species, which eliminated between-user variability in applying information from literature sources and subsequently selecting among multiple-choice responses. Having multiple biologists score the same species would have been more labor intensive and was beyond the scope of our project. However, doing so would have allowed us to evaluate whether differential expertise among biologists would have resulted in different scores. Lastly, because we used a pilot version of SAVS, our scores are not directly comparable to SAVS assessments (Bagne and others 2011).

Management Considerations

Identifying Goals for Adaptation Planning

Adaptation planning involves management focused on reducing the negative impacts of climate change (Blate and others 2009). Climate change creates additional considerations for managers who are already addressing a variety of threats such as invasive species, urban and suburban encroachment, disease, and the like. A crucial step for managers is to identify goals under climate change in a broad sense. For example, some concepts that might be addressed are the extent to which management should aim at maintaining threatened and endangered species versus biodiversity in general, or whether efforts should be focused on trying to resist changes to the distribution and species composition of plant communities. Identifying these kinds of goals will help to set the context under which subsequent decisions are made.

One approach in climate change adaptation planning is to consider long-term versus short-term options. Blate and others (2009) recommended managing for change as resilience thresholds are crossed in the long term, and building resistance and resilience to climate change in the short term so that natural resources are better able to withstand change.

Glick and others (2011) identified the following possible approaches "(1) building resistance to climate-related stressors as a way of maintaining high-priority species or systems; (2) enhancing resilience in order to provide species and systems with a better chance for accommodating and weathering changes; and (3) anticipating and facilitating ecological transitions that reflect the changing environmental conditions."

A variety of planning processes are underway to help wildlife managers identify conservation goals and develop management strategies. Governmental organizations such as the USFS, U.S. Fish and Wildlife Service, and the U.S. Geological Survey have assigned staff to climate change issues and have offered webinars and workshops. Video lectures, case studies of adaptation planning on National Forests, and other sources of information such as announcements for workshops can be found on the website of USFS Climate Change Resource Center (http://www.fs.fed.us/ccrc/). The U.S. Department of Interior (DOI) has established Landscape Conservation Cooperatives that consist of partnerships between public and private entities to develop large-scale conservation efforts that address a variety of impacts, including those of climate change. U.S. DOI is also establishing eight regional Climate Science Centers to address issues related to climate change. Non-profit organizations such as the Sky Island Alliance (http://www.skyislandalliance.org/), The Nature Conservancy, and the Wildlife Conservation Society have sponsored climate change planning workshops for lands in the western and southwestern United States. The Nature Conservancy established the Southwest Climate Change Initiative, which brought together state, Federal, and non-Governmental entities in Colorado, New Mexico, Utah, and Arizona to develop strategies to address climate change. Managers can seek more information through this wide array of entities for more guidance in setting goals for climate change adaptation planning.

Using Assessment Results in Adaptation Planning

The results of our vulnerability assessment can assist wildlife managers in making decisions regarding conservation under climate change. Incorporating the results into decision-making by USFS personnel helps to meet the objectives of the USFS Climate Change Performance Scorecard (USFS 2011).

In terms of the types of conservation techniques that might be considered, Heller and Zevaleta (2009) provided an extensive review of strategies identified in the scientific literature for managing for biodiversity under climate change. These include (but are not limited to):

(1) increasing connectivity;

(2) integrating climate change planning into planning exercises;

(3) mitigating non-climate change threats;

(4) studying responses of species to climate change;

(5) translocating species;

(6) increasing the number of reserves;

(7) increasing and maintaining basic monitoring programs.

The range in elevation on the CNF means that some species may be able to move upslope in the face of increasing temperatures. Thus, maintaining corridors that allow connectivity across altitude may assist some species on the CNF to locate more suitable conditions as the environment changes. Reducing non-climate threats might involve reducing bufflegrass invasion, reducing populations of non-native amphibians and fish, etc. Examples of various management techniques are also outlined in Bagne and others (2011, Table 5); these examples may help managers to develop appropriate approaches for reducing the vulnerability of species of interest. We also encourage managers to consider how ongoing management activities may apply.

Managers can use our assessment in a variety of ways to consider management strategies. First, we encourage managers to keep in mind the assumptions and uncertainties inherent to assessments during the decision-making process. Also, the results should be used in conjunction with additional information on species (e.g., known range size and population size).

Managers who want to focus on activities that could reduce the vulnerability of many species can examine categorical scores for all taxonomic groups combined and see that the majority of species on the CNF showed some vulnerability to criteria that fell within the habitat category. However, before actions are undertaken, managers should evaluate to what extent activities that are geared toward highly vulnerable species might act as additional stressors on these species during implementation. For example, forest thinning and prescribed fire to reduce fire risk in areas occupied by highly vulnerable species may have immediate consequences for survival of those species. One alternative might be to thin and prescribe burn in adjacent locations, thus avoiding direct negative effects. Ultimately, activities that reduce the potential for catastrophic wildfire may help to reduce the vulnerability of the species that depend on Madrean forest and woodland.

Efforts to maintain and/or increase dispersal into more suitable areas as environmental conditions change, or translocation of individuals, might be considered for species that were considered vulnerable due to low dispersal. Some management actions can increase resilience for criteria in more than one category. For instance, a number of the criteria that fall under the physiology category are related to impacts from possible alterations to habitat condition and use (e.g., physiological impacts on amphibians from the drying of ponds for breeding, or the potential for spring flooding). Thus, modifications to habitat conditions might be effective management strategies.

Managers may also want to use information on species distribution or population size and stability in applying the assessment results. For example, the elegant trogon was considered vulnerable on more criteria than any of the bird species. Within the United States, this species has a very small distribution (southern Arizona and New Mexico).

Depending on other management goals for this species on CNF, its limited distribution could be sufficient to prioritize its conservation on CNF lands. On the other hand, a highly vulnerable species with a small population size may be more difficult or costly to manage under changing conditions than a species that is more abundant and considered less vulnerable.

Vulnerability scores can be placed in a geographic context to visualize landscape-scale patterns of vulnerability. Davison and others (2012) combined species vulnerability scores with models of species' distributions for 15 species on CNF. A "cross-species vulnerability index" was created by: (1) summing the vulnerability scores for species with potential or known habitat in each 30-m map pixel on the CNF, and (2) dividing it by the associated number of species. Cross-species vulnerability was greater in woodlands and lower in desert scrub areas.

For examples of how results of other assessments have been applied, readers should review the seven case studies in Glick and others (2011). For example, the Nevada Natural Heritage Program plans to use the results to identify what species they will monitor (pp. 85-95). An assessment of vulnerability of Chesapeake Bay to sea-level rise identified the need to protect remaining marsh patches (pp. 114-121).

Uncertainty scores for each category, and summed for each species, helped to identify general areas where information is lacking. Filling data gaps (e.g., through new research) would reduce uncertainty associated with assessing species vulnerability and would improve managers' capacity to predict the outcomes of management activities.

References

Bagne, K.E., M.M. Friggens, and D.M. Finch. 2011. A system for assessing vulnerability of species (SAVS) to climate change. Gen. Tech. Rep. RMRS-GTR-257. Fort Collins, CO: U. S. Department of Agriculture, Forest Service, Rocky Mountain Research Station. 28 p.

Blate, G.M., L.A. Joyce, J.S. Littell, S.G. McNulty, C.I. Millar, S.C. Moser, R.P. Neilson, K. O'Halloran, and D.L. Peterson. 2009. Adapting to climate change in United States National Forests. Unasylva 221/232:57-62.

Davison, J., S. Coe, D. Finch, E. Rowland, M. Friggens, and L.J. Graumlich. 2012. Bringing indices of species vulnerability to climate change into geographic space: An assessment across the Coronado National Forest. Biodiversity and Conservation. 21:189-204.

Glick, P., B.A. Stein, and N.A. Edelson, eds. 2011. Scanning the conservation horizon: A guide to climate change vulnerability assessment. Washington, DC: National Wildlife Federation. Available: www.nwf.org/vulnerabilityguide.

Heller, N.E., and E.S. Zavaleta. 2009. Biodiversity management in the face of climate change: A review of 22 years of recommendations. Biological Conservation 142:14-32.

Housman, D.C., E. Naumburg, T.E. Huxman, T.N. Charlet, R.W. Nowak, and S.D. Smith. 2006. Increases in desert shrub productivity under elevated carbon dioxide vary with water availability. Ecosystems 9:374-385.

Jones, Larry. 2011. [Personal communication]. May 18, 2011. Tucson, AZ: U.S. Department of Agriculture, Forest Service, Coronado National Forest, Assistant Program Manager for Wildlife, Fish, and Rare Plants.

McKenney, D.W., J.H. Pedlar, K. Lawrence, K. Campbell, and M.F. Hutchinson. 2007. Potential impacts of climate change on the distribution of North American trees. Bioscience 57:939-948.

Mearns, L.O. 2010. The drama of uncertainty. Climatic Change 100:77-85.

Mikkelsen, T.N., C. Beier, S. Jonasson, [and others]. 2008. Experimental design of multifactor climate change experiments with elevated CO2, warming and drought: The CLIMAITE project. Functional Ecology 22:185-195.

Peterson, A.T., M.A. Ortega-Huerta, J. Bartley, V. Sanchez-Corderos, Jorge Soberon, R.H. Buddemeier, and D.R.B. Stockwell. 2002. Future projections for Mexican faunas under global climate change scenarios. Nature 416:626-629.

Preston, K.L., J.T. Rotenberry, R.A. Redak, and M.F. Allen. 2008. Habitat shifts of endangered species under altered climate conditions: Importance of biotic interactions. Global Change Biology 14:2501-2515.

Rowland, E.L., J.E. Davison, and L.J. Graumlich. 2011. Approaches to evaluating climate change impacts on species: A guide to initiating the adaptation planning process. Environmental Management 47:322-337.

Schneider, S., J. Sarukhan, J. Adejuwon, C. Azar, W. Baethgen, C. Hope, R. Moss, N. Leary, R. Richels, J.-P. van Ypersele. 2001. Overview of impacts, adaptation, and vulnerability to climate change. In: Houghton, J.T., Y. Ding, D.J. Griggs, M. Noguer, P.J. van der Linden, X. Dai, K. Maskell, and C.A. Johnson, eds. Climate Change 2001: The Scientific Basis. Contribution of Working Group I to the Third Assessment Report of the Intergovernmental Panel on Climate Change. Cambridge, United Kingdom: Cambridge University Press: 889.

U.S. Forest Service [USFS]. 2009. Draft Coronado National Forest ecological sustainability report. Tucson, AZ: U.S. Department of Agriculture, Forest Service. Available at: http://www fs fed.us/r3/coronado/plan-revision/documents/final/cnf-ecological-sustainability-report-final-022009.pdf.

U.S. Forest Service [USFS]. 2011. Navigating the climate change performance scorecard. Available: http://fsweb.wo.fs.fed.us/chief/climatechange/scorecard%20guidance%20document% 201-21-2011.pdf.

Appendix A: Terrestrial Vertebrate Species Assessed

Species on the Coronado National Forest (CNF) that were assessed for their vulnerability to climate change (n=30). An "x" indicates an Environmental Management Area (EMA) with actual or potential habitat according to: (1) the CNF Draft Ecological Sustainability Report (USFS 2009), or (2) personal communications. Personal communications indicated with an asterisk (see respective species account in Appendix B for citations)

Common name	Status[1]	Peloncillo	Chiricahua	Dragoon	Tumacacori	Santa Rita	Huachuca	Whetstone	Pinaleño	Winchester	Galiuro	Santa Teresa	Santa Catalina
BIRDS													
Northern goshawk	USFS-2	X	X	X	X	X	X	X	X	X	X	X	X
Northern gray hawk*	USFS Sensitive, FSOC	X			X	X	X				X		
American peregrine falcon	USFS-1	X	X	X	X	X	X	X	X	X	X	X	X
Gould's wild turkey	USFS-2	X	X		X	X	X		X		X		X
Montezuma quail	USFS-2	X	X		X	X							
Western yellow-billed cuckoo	USFS-1, FCL					X	X						
Elegant trogon	USFS-2	X	X		X	X	X						
Northern buff-breasted flycatcher	USFS-2, FUR	X	X		X	X							X
MAMMALS													
Mexican long-tongued bat	USFS-2, FSOC	X	X	X	X	X	X	X					X
Western yellow bat	USFS-2	X	X	X	X	X	X	X	X	X	X	X	X
Western red bat	USFS-2, FSOC	X	X	X	X	X	X	X	X		X		
Allen's lappet-browed bat	USFS Sensitive		X						X		X		
Townsend's big-eared bat*	USFS Sensitive, FSOC	X	X	X	X	X	X	X	X	X	X	X	X
Abert's squirrel*	USFS-2 (non-native)								X				X
Arizona gray squirrel	USFS-2				X	X	X						X
Chiricahua fox squirrel	USFS-1		X										
Mount Graham red squirrel	Federally Endangered								X				
Mesquite mouse* (aka Merriam's mouse)	USFS Sensitive				X	X	X						X
White-bellied long-tailed vole	USFS-1								X				
Coues' white-tailed deer	USFS-2	X	X	X	X	X	X	X	X	X	X	X	X
Desert bighorn sheep	USFS-2	X									X		X
REPTILES													
Sonoran desert tortoise	USFS-2, FCL				X						X		X

Common name	Status[1]	Environmental Management Area											
		Peloncillo	Chiricahua	Dragoon	Tumacacori	Santa Rita	Huachuca	Whetstone	Pinaleño	Winchester	Galiuro	Santa Teresa	Santa Catalina
Slevin's bunchgrass lizard	USFS-2	X	X	X		X	X	X					
Giant spotted whiptail	USFS-2	X			X	X	X		X	X	X	X	X
Northern Mexican gartersnake	USFS-2, FCL				X	X	X						
Arizona ridge-nosed rattlesnake	USFS-2					X	X	X					
AMPHIBIANS													
Sonoran tiger salamander	Federally Endangered						X						
American bullfrog*	USFS-2 (non-native)	X	X	X	X	X	X	X	X	X	X	X	X
Chiricahua leopard frog	Federally Threatened	X	X	X	X	X	X				X		
Tarahumara frog	USFS-1, FSOC					X							

[1]Status designations are as follows: (1) USFS-1 for USFS Species of Concern; (2) USFS-2 for USFS Species of Interest; (3) USFS Sensitive = additional species of interest; (4) FSOC= Federal Species of Concern (U.S. Fish and Wildlife Service); (5) FCL = Federal Candidate for Listing (USFWS); (6) FUR = Federal "Under Review" (USFWS). Species may have additional designations assigned by Arizona Game and Fish Department or by other entities. Sources: USFS (2009), USFWS website (http://www.fws.gov/endangered/species/).

Appendix B: Species Vulnerability Assessments

Habitat: Northern goshawk (*Accipiter gentilis*)			
Trait/Quality	**Question**	**Background info. & explanation of score**	**Points**
1. Area and distribution: *breeding*	Is the area or location of the associated vegetation type used for breeding activities by this species expected to change?	From Squires and Reynolds (1997): In the western hemisphere, this species breeds across Canada and much of Alaska, the western half of the United States, and portions of western Mexico. Much of its range is year-round, although additional wintering areas are identified in areas outside its year-round range. Southeast Arizona is identified as including year-round areas and wintering portions of this species' range.

Northern goshawks nest in most forest types across their geographic range from as low as sea level to as high as alpine (Squires and Reynolds 1997). On the Kaibab Plateau in northern Arizona, this species nests in ponderosa pine forests and in mixed conifer; some nests were found in spruce-fir (Reynolds and others 1994). Other goshawk populations in the western United States use forests that include Douglas-fir, various pine species, and aspen (see references in Squires and Reynolds 1997). The Arizona Breeding Bird Atlas (Corman and Wise-Gervais 2005) reports that for the state overall, 41% of observations of this species during the breeding season were in pure ponderosa pine forest and 26% were in mixed conifer (Douglas-fir, white fir, ponderosa pine, and aspen). In the mountains of southeastern Arizona, specifically, observers noted this species most often in "Madrean pine-oak woodlands dominated by Chihuahuan, Apache, and ponderosa pine forests with a scattered evergreen oak and juniper understory" and fewer observations in spruce-fir or areas dominated by ponderosa or pinyon pine.

Mature to old-growth forests with mostly large trees are typically used for nesting (references in Squires and Reynolds 1997). High canopy closure (60-90%) is also typical (references in Squires and Reynolds 1997) and was observed to be one of the most uniform characteristics of nesting areas (Hayward and Escaño 1989 as cited in Squires and Reynolds 1997).

Water, ranging from a pond or small stream to a large river or lake, is often present near nests (references in Squires and Reynolds 1997), although it is not considered a habitat requirement (references in Squires and Reynolds 1997).

Across its range, this species hunts in diverse habitats (open-sage steppes and dense forests, including riparian areas). In northern Arizona, this species has been observed to forage in forests with greater canopy closure and greater density of trees relative to contrast plots (Beier and Drennan 1997 as cited in Squires and Reynolds 1997).

This species, or its potential habitat, occurs on all 12 of the EMAs on CNF (USFS 2009). Projections of suitable climate for vegetation communities forest-wide (Chapter 1) predicted declines in suitable climate for all plant community types, with the exception of increased suitable climate for semi-desert grassland and small increases in Sonoran desert scrub (present in small amounts on the CNF).

Projected reductions in forested habitats will reduce breeding habitat for this species. | 2 |
| 2. Area and distribution: *non-breeding* | Is the area or location of the associated vegetation type used for non-breeding activities by this species expected to change? | Use of areas in winter is not well understood, and most data are from Europe (Squires and Reynolds 1997). Wintering goshawks in the Rocky Mountains were observed using cottonwood riparian areas (Squires and Ruggiero 1995 as cited in Squires and Reynolds 1997), aspen, spruce/fir, lodgepole pine, ponderosa pine, and open habitats (Squires and Reynolds 1997).

The northern goshawks that breed in Arizona are considered year-round residents (see Habitat, Question 8), so we assumed that in Arizona non-breeding habitat is similar, or the same as, breeding habitat. | 2 |
| 3. Habitat components: | Are specific habitat components | Populations in the western United States typically nest in conifers (references in Squires and Reynolds 1997). This includes ponderosa pine, Douglas-fir, white fir, California red fir, western larch, western hemlock, | 1 |

Habitat: Northern goshawk (*Accipiter gentilis*)			
Trait/Quality	**Question**	**Background info. & explanation of score**	**Points**
breeding	required for breeding expected to change?	and lodgepole pine. In the Southwest, ponderosa pine is used frequently (references in Squires and Reynolds 1997), and nests are usually in the largest trees of the stand (references in Squires and Reynolds 1997). Increased tree mortality from reduced annual precipitation, increased fires, and increased insect infestations is expected to reduce the abundance of large trees capable of supporting raptor nests and perches.	
4. Habitat components: *non-breeding*	Are specific habitat components required for survival during non-breeding periods expected to change?	Winter habitat use is poorly understood and roosting habitat is not described (Squires and Reynolds 1997). However, this species is presumed to use trees for roosting and perching.	1
5. Habitat quality and reproduction	Are features of the habitat associated with better reproductive success expected to change?	Found no information in Squires and Reynolds (1997) on whether there are known habitat features associated with variation in reproductive success. Variation among sites has been observed; in a 2-year study on 3 National Forests in eastern Oregon, productivity varied between years and among landscapes on the same study areas (DeStefano and others 1994). Although not pertaining to reproductive success, Squires and Reynolds (1997) indicated that the relationship between environmental conditions such as vegetative type and landscape characteristics and how they affect breeding densities is not well understood; the authors also indicated that yearly occupancy rates are highly variable and may be related fluctuations in prey densities and severe (cold) weather conditions.	0
6. Habitat quality and survival	Are features of the habitat associated with better survival expected to change?	Winter habitat use is poorly understood (Squires and Reynolds 1997).	0
7. Ability to colonize new areas	What is this species' capacity and tendency to disperse?	We considered birds to be very mobile due to their capacity for flight and, thus, overall able to colonize new areas.	-1
8. Migratory or transitional habitats	Does this species require additional habitats during migration that are separated from breeding and non-breeding habitats?	This species is considered primarily a year-round resident in Arizona (Corman and Wise-Gervais 2005). Individuals nesting at high elevations have been observed moving to lower elevations in winter (Millsap 1981 as cited in Corman and Wise-Gervais 2005). However, such movements not considered to require significantly different types of habitat.	0

Physiology: Northern goshawk (*Accipiter gentilis*)			
Trait/Quality	**Question**	**Background info. & explanation of score**	**Points**
1. Physiological thresholds	Are physiological thresholds related to temperature or moisture expected to change?	In the western hemisphere, the range of northern goshawk is the United States, Canada and portions of western Mexico. The CNF is in the southern portion of the species' latitudinal range. Use of water for drinking is unknown (Squires and Reynolds 1997). We found no information on tolerance of extreme heat in Web of Science database search on species and "tolerance." With the exception of cases of extreme heat rises, presumably could tolerate increases of several degrees C. Shaded habitat might reduce effects of solar radiation on rise in body temperature, although shade from trees expected to decline with time.	0

Physiology: Northern goshawk (*Accipiter gentilis*)			
Trait/Quality	**Question**	**Background info. & explanation of score**	**Points**
2. Sex ratio	Is sex ratio determined by temperature?	No. Temperature-dependent sex determination is mainly observed in reptiles and fish (Manolakou and others 2006).	0
3. Exposure to extreme weather conditions	Are extreme weather or disturbance events that result in direct mortality or reproductive failure expected to change?	Increase in frequency of heat waves is predicted for southwestern United States. Overall, not clear to what extent timing and intensity of heat waves will affect survival and reproduction. We considered it unlikely that heat waves would cause widespread mortality for this species. Individuals that breed in CNF are believed to winter there as well, so they would not be exposed to potential changes in storms along a migratory route. Exposure to cold and rain has been attributed to egg and chick mortality (see references in Squires and Reynolds 1997). Not expected that cold or rain will increase during breeding season under climate change. See also Physiology, Question 1.	0
4. Limitations to active period	Are projected temperature or precipitation regimes that influence activity period of species expected to change?	This species is a diurnal forager but does not show diurnal rhythms of foraging activity; timing of hunting depends on activity patterns of the prey (Squires and Reynolds 1997). No information found in Squires and Reynolds (1997) indicating limits on activity period relative to high temperatures. With the exception of cases of extreme heat rises, seems unlikely for seasonal or daily active periods to be directly restricted to the point of significantly reducing survival. Unclear to what extent prey activity might be reduced due to temperature increases and how that might indirectly affect this species. See also Physiology, Question 1.	0
5. Metabolic inhibition	Does this species possess an ability to reduce metabolic energy or water requirements?	No reports of torpor in Squires and Reynolds (1997). No citations of torpor found in Web of Science database. Based on this information, we assumed that the species does not use torpor.	1
6. Survival during resource limitation	Does this species have lower energy requirements or possess the capacity to store energy or water in the long term?	This species caches prey, primarily when nestlings are small; most cached items are retrieved the same day (Schnell 1958 as cited in Squires and Reynolds 1997), so not considered a long-term food storage behavior.	1
7. Variable life history	Does this species have alternative life history strategies to cope with variable resources or climate conditions?	No variable life history strategies.	0
8. Reproduction in variable environments	Can this species outlive periods where reproduction is limited?	Longevity record (i.e., longest-lived individual recorded) of a wild bird is at least 11 years (Fowler 1985 as cited in Squires and Reynolds 1997). A 6-year mark-recapture study in northern Arizona estimated annual survival of birds greater than 1 year old to be 69% for males and 87% for females (unpublished data cited in Squires and Reynolds 1997). Periods of extreme reductions in rainfall may last 5 years. If these conditions reduce food resources to the point that birds have insufficient food for breeding, most of the population would not survive longer than the periods of limited reproduction.	1

Phenology: Northern goshawk (*Accipiter gentilis*)

Trait/Quality	Question	Background info. & explanation of score	Points
1. Cues	Does this species use temperature or moisture cues to initiate activities related to fecundity or survival?	This species is a "predictable breeder," meaning its breeding season occurs at the same time each year (i.e., spring). In predictable breeders, photoperiod is the predominant proximate factor leading to gonadal changes required for reproduction (Dawson and others 2001). It should be noted that, in general, birds also use local predictive information, including temperature, availability of food, and rainfall, to make short-term adjustments to reproductive timing, (Wingfield 2008), although this short-term adjustment is not addressed by this question (see Bagne and others 2011).	0
2. Event timing	Are activities related to species' fecundity or survival tied to discrete events that are expected to change?	Food availability is believed to strongly affect population dynamics in the northern goshawk (Squires and Reynolds 1997). Many raptor species that consume rodents show large variation in annual production of young in relation to fluctuations in levels of their prey (see references in Durant and others 2000; Newton 1998; and Steenhof and others 1997). A food supplementation study in New Mexico showed that in one year (but not another), supplemented nests had a substantially higher nestling survival rate relative to control nests; however, the authors indicated that the mechanism was lower predation of treatment birds, probably due to increased time spent guarding nests by the female (Ward and Kennedy 1996). Changes in the timing of precipitation and increases in temperature have the potential to alter the timing of prey availability and abundance and, hence, fecundity.	1
3. Mismatch potential	What is the separation in time or space between cues that initiate activities and discrete events that provide critical resources?	This species is a year-round resident in Arizona. Typically, increases in prey abundance (a critical resource) occur in spring, so there is little temporal separation. There is no spatial separation since the species is a year-round resident.	–1
4. Resilience to timing mismatches during breeding	Does this species employ strategies or have traits that increase the likelihood of reproduction co-occurring with important events?	This species has only one brood per year; laying replacement clutches has been observed but is considered rare (Squires and Reynolds 1997).	1

Biotic interactions: Northern goshawk (*Accipiter gentilis*)

Trait/Quality	Question	Background info. & explanation of score	Points
1. Food resources	Are important food resources for this species expected to change?	This species consumes a variety of relatively large-bodied birds and mammals, with main foods consisting of ground and tree squirrels, rabbits and hares, large passerines, woodpeckers, game birds, and corvids (Squires and Reynolds 1997). In Arizona, this species was observed preying on Abert's squirrels (Westcott 1964 as cited in Squires and Reynolds 1997). Therefore, it has generalist prey habits.	0
2. Predators	Are important predator	Northern goshawks have relatively few natural predators (Squires and Reynolds 1997). Documented nestling predators include mammals and	0

Biotic interactions: Northern goshawk (*Accipiter gentilis*)			
Trait/Quality	Question	Background info. & explanation of score	Points
	populations expected to change?	great horned owls; adult predators include eagles, marten, and great horned owls. Limited information on how predation affects goshawk populations (Squires and Reynolds 1997).	
3. Symbionts	Are populations of symbiotic species expected to change?	None known.	0
4. Disease	Is prevalence of diseases known to cause widespread mortality or reproductive failure in this species expected to change?	A variety of diseases and parasites (both ecto- and internal) are reported for the northern goshawk (Squires and Reynolds 1997). Trichomoniasis, a disease caused by the protozoan parasite *Trichomonas gallinae*, can be acquired by goshawks and other raptors by consuming infected columbids (doves and pigeons). The parasite causes significant mortality in nestlings and fledglings in urban-nesting Cooper's hawks in Arizona (Boal and others 1998 as cited in Rosenfield and others 2002). However, in 48 nests in non-urban areas of Wisconsin, North Dakota, and British Columbia, the parasite prevalence was very low with no attributable nestling mortality. It appears that the disease may be more of a concern to urban populations of raptors where columbids are more abundant. For example, Krone and others (2005) investigated the prevalence of the parasite in northern goshawks that had colonized urban and suburban areas of Berlin, Germany.	0
5. Competitors	Are populations of important competing species expected to change?	No information was found in Squires and Reynolds (1997) documenting inter-specific competitive interactions.	0

Literature Cited

Bagne, K.E., M.M. Friggens, and D.M. Finch. 2011. A system for assessing vulnerability of species (SAVS) to climate change. Gen. Tech. Rep. RMRS-GTR-257. Fort Collins, CO: U.S. Department of Agriculture, Forest Service, Rocky Mountain Research Station. 28 p.

Corman, T.E., and C. Wise-Gervais, eds. 2005. Arizona breeding bird atlas. Albuquerque, NM: University of New Mexico Press.

Dawson, A., V.M. King, G.E. Bentley, and G.F. Ball. 2001. Photoperiodic control of seasonality in birds. Journal of Biological Rhythms 16:365-380.

DeStefano, S., S.K. Daw, S.M. Desimone, and E.C. Meslow. 1994. Density and productivity of northern goshawks: implications for monitoring and management. Studies in Avian Biology 16:88-91.

Durant, J.M., S. Massemin, C. Thouzeau, and Y. Handrich. 2000. Body reserves and nutritional needs during laying preparation in barn owls. Journal of Comparative Physiology B 170:253-260.

Krone, O., R. Altenkamp, and N. Kenntner. 2005. Prevalence of *Trichomonas gallinae* in northern goshawks from the Berlin area of northeastern Germany. Journal of Wildlife Diseases 41:304-309.

Newton, I. 1998. Population limitation in birds. New York: Academic Press. 597 p.

Reynolds, R.T., S.M. Joy, and D.G. Leslie. 1994. Nest productivity, fidelity, and spacing of northern goshawks in northern Arizona. Studies in Avian Biology 16:106-113.

Rosenfield, R.N., J. Bielefeldt, L.J. Rosenfield, S.J. Taft, R.K. Murphy, and A.C. Stewart. 2002. Prevalence of *Trichomonas gallinae* in nestling Cooper's hawks among three North American populations. Wilson Bulletin 114:145-147.

Squires, J.R. and R.T. Reynolds. 1997. Northern Goshawk (*Accipiter gentilis*) In: Poole, A., ed. The birds of North America online. Ithaca, NY: Cornell Lab of Ornithology. Available: http://bna.birds.cornell.edu/bna/species/298doi:10.2173/bna.298.

Steenhof, K., M.N. Kochert, and T.L. McDonald. 1997. Interactive effects of prey and weather on golden eagle reproduction. Journal of Animal Ecology 66:350-362.

U.S. Forest Service [USFS]. 2009. Draft Coronado National Forest ecological sustainability report. Tucson, AZ: U.S. Department of Agriculture, Forest Service. Available: http://www.fs.fed.us/r3/coronado/plan-revision/documents/final/cnf-ecological-sustainability-report-final-022009.pdf.

Ward, J.M., and P.L. Kennedy. 1996. Effects of supplemental food on size and survival of juvenile northern goshawks. Auk 113:200-208.

Wingfield, J.C. 2008. Comparative endocrinology, environment, and global change. General and Comparative Endocrinology 157:207-216.

Habitat: Northern gray hawk (*Buteo nitidus plagiata*)			
Trait/Quality	Question	Background info. & explanation of score	Points
1. Area and distribution: *breeding*	Is the area or location of the associated vegetation type used for breeding activities by this species expected to change?	**Taxonomic note:** The 47th Supplement to the American Ornithologists' Union Checklist of North American Birds recognizes *Asturina nitida* as *Buteo nitida* (Bibles and others 2002). Also, Bibles and others (2002) indicated that the sub-species *plagiata* occurs in Arizona (now, *Buteo nitidus plagiata*; some authors use *maxima*).	2
		In the United States northern gray hawks breed in a very limited range (Arizona and Texas, sporadically in New Mexico) and is considered uncommon in the United States, with likely fewer than 100 nesting pairs (Bibles and others 2002). Most nesting records in Arizona are in the south-central part of the state (in the counties of Cochise, Pima, Pinal, and Santa Cruz), particularly along San Pedro River and its tributaries, Sonoita and Arivaca Creeks, and the southernmost reaches of the Santa Cruz River and its tributaries. Based on observations by Arizona Breeding Bird Atlas (ABBA) observers (Corman 2005), this raptor was considered to be locally common on portions of the San Pedro River with perennial flow and on parts of the Cienega Creek and Sonoita Creek; observations also documented on the Santa Cruz River.	
		In the United States and northern Mexico, gray hawks forage mostly in mesquite woodlands and nests in adjacent forests of cottonwood and willow that occur along streams and rivers (Bibles and others 2002). Approximately 73% of the observations during the ABBA surveys (n=55) were reported from areas with perennial or intermittent streams dominated by tall Fremont cottonwood and Goodding willow, typically with stands of velvet mesquite (Corman 2005). Most of the remaining observations were made in riparian woodlands containing Arizona sycamore, often with cottonwoods and willows; and in some cases, individuals were observed nesting in drier drainages containing Madrean evergreen oaks, Arizona walnut, velvet ash, and netleaf hackberry. Observations of nesting birds by ABBA recorders were at elevations ranging 594-1524 m. (1950-5000 ft).	
		Mesquite is considered important for breeding; nesting is often in lone cottonwood trees surrounded by mesquite woodland (Glinski 1988; Bibles 1999). Historically, gray hawks used mesquite 12-15 m tall, but mesquite this tall has become rare in Arizona. Corman (2005) indicated that some nesting territories had been lost due to wildfires and depletion of groundwater from drought and pumping.	

Trait/Quality	Question	Background info. & explanation of score	Points
Habitat: Northern gray hawk (_Buteo nitidus plagiata_)			
		Northern gray hawks are known, or have the potential, to occur on the following EMAs: Peloncillo, Tumacacori, Santa Rita, Huachuca, and Galiuro (Jones, personal communication). Projections of suitable climate for vegetation communities on these five EMAs (Chapter 1) predicted a decline in the total areas that would have suitable climate for Madrean forest and woodland and Madrean conifer forest and an increase in areas that would have suitable climate for semi-desert grassland. Riparian habitats are predicted to decline due to decreased stream flows (on average), increased aridity, and an increased risk of fires.	
2. Area and distribution: _non-breeding_	Is the area or location of the associated vegetation type used for non-breeding activities by this species expected to change?	Bibles and others (2002) indicated that the _plagiata_ subspecies occurs in Arizona, New Mexico, Texas, and south to northwest Costa Rica, so we assumed that breeders in the United States are not likely to migrate farther south than Costa Rica, where other sub-species occur. According to Bibles and others (2002), little information exists on winter habitat. In Sonora, Mexico, gray hawks occupy Sinaloan deciduous forest and Sinaloan thorn scrub (Monson 1986 as cited in Bibles and others 2002), the latter being similar to mesquite forests used for foraging in Arizona. Glinski (1998) indicated that gray hawks in the tropics prefer xeric second-growth and thorn forests. Overall, expected that drier conditions will occur in wintering range for this species, leading to reduction in trees.	2
3. Habitat components: _breeding_	Are specific habitat components required for breeding expected to change?	No information found in Bibles and others (2002) to indicate presence of habitat components for breeding. Bibles and others (2002) indicated no information on drinking behavior, and we found no other indication that gray hawks require standing water. Glinski (1988) indicated that they tend not to occupy forests without tropical-subtropical thorn scrub and woodland elements, so this was considered under Habitat, Question 1.	0
4. Habitat components: _non-breeding_	Are specific habitat components required for survival during non-breeding periods expected to change?	No information found in Bibles and others (2002) to indicate presence of habitat components for survival on non-breeding periods.	0
5. Habitat quality and reproduction	Are features of the habitat associated with better reproductive success expected to change?	In Arizona, habitat quality determined by the amount of mesquite within the home range (Bibles 1999). We considered mesquite likely to decline under climate change.	1
6. Habitat quality and survival	Are features of the habitat associated with better survival expected to change?	No information was found in Bibles and others (2002); given the gaps in knowledge on gray hawks, it is likely that if there are any such features, they have not been quantified.	0
7. Ability to colonize new areas	What is this species' capacity and tendency to disperse?	We considered birds to be very mobile due to their capacity for flight and, thus, overall able to colonize new areas.	-1
8. Migratory or transitional habitats	Does this species require additional habitats during migration that are separated from breeding and non-	Bibles and others (2002) indicated that populations in the United States and northern Mexico are migratory. In Arizona, individuals have been observed in December (Glinski 1988), and there are unverified reports throughout winter months. Most individuals depart from Arizona by late September or early October (Corman 2005). However, Bibles and others (2002) indicated that it is	1

Habitat: Northern gray hawk (*Buteo nitidus plagiata*)			
Trait/Quality	**Question**	**Background info. & explanation of score**	**Points**
	breeding habitats?	unknown whether individuals observed in areas of year-round residency are migrants or are remaining in the breeding area year-round. Overall, while some may over-winter in Arizona, the majority of those that breed in Arizona are expected to migrate south of the United States for winter.	

Physiology: Northern gray hawk (*Buteo nitidus plagiata*)			
Trait/Quality	**Question**	**Background info. & explanation of score**	**Points**
1. Physiological thresholds	Are limiting physiological conditions expected to change?	Bibles and others (2002) indicated no information on drinking behavior or temperature regulation for this species. Red-shouldered hawk (*Buteo lineatus*) is likely the most closely related North American species based on morphology and ecology, but there is no information on temperature regulation in the Birds of North America species account for that species. We assumed that the northern gray hawk is capable of behavioral thermoregulation. With the exception of rare cases of extreme heat rises, presumably could tolerate increases of several degrees C.	0
2. Sex ratio	Is sex ratio determined by temperature?	No. Temperature-dependent sex determination is mainly observed in reptiles and fish (Manolakou and others 2006).	0
3. Exposure to extreme weather conditions	Are extreme weather or disturbance events that result in direct mortality or reproductive failure expected to change?	Increase in frequency of heat waves is predicted for the southwestern United States. Overall, not clear to what extent timing and intensity of heat waves will affect survival and reproduction. We considered it unlikely that heat waves would cause widespread mortality. Not clear where Arizona breeders over-winter or whether they would be exposed to hurricanes. Hurricane intensity is expected to increase under global climate change, but frequency predictions are inconsistent (Emanuel 2005); frequency increase likely more detrimental overall to migrating populations than intensity since hurricane-level winds already detrimental to migrants.	0
4. Limitations to active period	Are projected temperature or precipitation regimes that influence activity period of species expected to change?	Gray hawks forage diurnally. In Arizona, foraging activity peaks during mid-morning and early evening, with the least amount of foraging at mid-day, presumably related to activity patterns of prey species (Bibles and others 2002). No information was found in Bibles and others (2002) that indicated limits on activity period relative to high temperatures. With the exception of cases of extreme heat rises, we considered it unlikely that seasonal or daily active periods would be directly restricted to the point of significantly reducing survival.	0
5. Metabolic inhibition	Does this species possess an ability to reduce metabolic energy or water requirements?	No information on energetics and metabolism was reported in Bibles and others (2002), but we assumed that gray hawks do not undergo torpor based on the lack of documentation of torpor in numerous other raptor species.	1
6. Survival during resource	Does this species have lower energy	Gray hawks have been observed to cache prey (e.g., gartersnakes, partly eaten birds, and cottontail rabbits) on large horizontal limbs	1

Physiology: Northern gray hawk (*Buteo nitidus plagiata*)			
Trait/Quality	Question	Background info. & explanation of score	Points
limitation	requirements or possess the capacity to store energy or water in the long term?	(Bibles and others 2002). Cached food is available for a few days at most, so we did not consider this long-term food storage.	
7. Variable life history	Does this species have alternative life history strategies to cope with variable resources or climate conditions?	No variable life history strategies.	0
8. Reproduction in variable environments	Can this species outlive periods where reproduction is limited?	First breeding typically in at least the third calendar year, but occasionally in the second calendar year (Bibles and others 2002). There is no information on lifespan (Bibles and others 2002). In the red-shouldered hawk, a similar species, mean survival in one study was ~2 years; another study found 95% mortality of nestlings within 5.2 years (references in Dykstra and others 2008). Periods of extreme reductions in rainfall may last 5 years. If these conditions reduce food resources to the point that birds have insufficient food for breeding, we considered it possible that much of the population would not survive longer than periods of limited reproduction.	1

Phenology: Northern gray hawk (*Buteo nitidus plagiata*)			
Trait/Quality	Question	Background info. & explanation of score	Points
1. Cues	Does this species use temperature or moisture cues to initiate activities related to fecundity or survival?	Individuals arrive in Arizona generally in mid-March, and egg laying typically occurs in early May (Glinski 1998). Nest building or nest repairing has been observed in April and early May by ABBA recorders (Corman 2005). Northern gray hawks are a predictable breeder, meaning the breeding season occurs at the same time each year (i.e., spring). In predictable breeders, photoperiod is the predominant proximate factor leading to gonadal changes required for reproduction (Dawson and others 2001). It should be noted that, in general, birds also use local predictive information such as temperature, food availability, and rainfall to make short-term adjustments to reproductive timing (Wingfield 2008), although this short-term adjustment is not addressed by this question (see Bagne and others 2011).	0
2. Event timing	Are activities related to species' fecundity or survival tied to discrete events that are expected to change?	Changes in the timing of precipitation and increases in temperature have the potential to alter the timing of prey (reptiles, particularly lizards) availability and abundance, which, in turn, could influence fecundity of gray hawks.	1
3. Mismatch potential	What is the separation in time or space between cues that initiate activities and discrete events that provide critical resources?	Given that northern gray hawks are migratory, critical resources for breeding (such as food) occur far from where individuals over-winter; thus, individuals have no direct information about resource abundance on the breeding grounds in a given year when they initiate migration from their wintering grounds.	1

Phenology: Northern gray hawk (*Buteo nitidus plagiata*)			
Trait/Quality	**Question**	**Background info. & explanation of score**	**Points**
4. Resilience to timing mismatches during breeding	Does this species employ strategies or have traits that increase the likelihood of reproduction co-occurring with important events?	Considered to rear only one brood per season, although individuals may re-nest if original clutch fails prior to hatching (Bibles and others 2002).	1

Biotic interactions: Northern gray hawk (*Buteo nitidus plagiata*)			
Trait/Quality	**Question**	**Background info. & explanation of score**	**Points**
1. Food resources	Are important food resources for this species expected to change?	Gray hawks appear to eat mostly reptiles throughout its range, although studies of diet mostly have been on individuals in northern part of the species' range (Bibles and others 2002). Glinski (1988) observed that 74% of prey that were delivered to nestlings were lizards, 5% were gartersnakes, 11% were nestling and adult birds, and 10% were mammals. Gray hawks are able to hunt terrestrial and arboreal lizards due to their ability to maneuver well in flight (Glinski 1998). Bibles and others (2002) indicated that the gray hawk diet (ostensibly in United States) is dominated by whiptail lizards (*Cnemidophorus* spp.) and spiny lizards (*Sceloporus* spp.). Amadon and Phillips (1939) considered it possible that the distribution of the gray hawk might be determined by the occurrence of a few reptile species. Overall, it appears that gray hawks may depend mostly on just a few species of lizards which will probably be negatively impacted by climate change (particularly in the habitat shared by the gray hawk).	1
2. Predators	Are important predator populations expected to change?	Bibles and others (2002) indicated that there is little information on predation in gray hawks. The great horned owl is a documented nestling predator and the red-tailed hawk is a potential predator; the amount of nest predation by mammals is not known. Bibles and others (2002) considered that owl predation may be a significant source of mortality for both gray hawk adults and nestlings. We considered it likely that there is a suite of predators.	0
3. Symbionts	Are populations of symbiotic species expected to change?	No indication of symbiotic relationships in Bibles and others (2002).	0
4. Disease	Is prevalence of diseases known to cause widespread mortality or reproductive failure in this species expected to change?	Bibles and others (2002) indicated that there is little information on diseases and body parasites. Nestling mortality has been attributed to trichomoniasis (caused by *Trichomonas gallinae*; Stensrude 1965 as cited in Bibles and others 2002).	0
5. Competitors	Are populations of important competing species expected to change?	Bibles and others (2002) indicated a lack of information on competition. Glinski (1998) listed eight species of raptors found nesting within ~1 km of nesting gray hawks. Successful nesting documented within 50 m of nests of Cooper's hawk, red-tailed hawk, and zone-tailed hawks (Glinski and Millsap 1987 as cited in Bibles and others 2002).	0

Literature Cited

Amadon, D., and A.R. Phillips. 1939. Notes on the Mexican goshawk. Auk 56:183-184.

Bagne, K.E., M.M. Friggens, and D.M. Finch. 2011. A system for assessing vulnerability of species (SAVS) to climate change. Gen. Tech. Rep. RMRS-GTR-257. Fort Collins, CO: U.S. Department of Agriculture, Forest Service, Rocky Mountain Research Station. 28 p.

Bibles, B.D., R.L. Glinski, and R.R. Johnson. 2002. Gray Hawk (*Asturina nitida*). In: Poole, A., ed. The birds of North America online. Ithaca, NY: Cornell Lab of Ornithology. Available: http://bna.birds.cornell.edu/bna/species/652; doi:10.2173/bna.652.

Bibles, B.D. 1999. The relationship between productivity and habitat quality in gray hawks. Dissertation. University of Arizona, Tucson.

Corman, T.E. 2005. Gray Hawk. In: Corman, T.E., and C. Wise-Gervais, eds. The Arizona Breeding Bird Atlas. Albuquerque, NM: University of New Mexico Press: 136-137.

Dawson, A., V.M. King, G.E. Bentley, and G.F. Ball. 2001. Photoperiodic control of seasonality in birds. Journal of Biological Rhythms 16:365-380.

Dykstra, C.R., J.L. Hays, and S.T. Crocoll. 2008. Red-shouldered Hawk (*Buteo lineatus*). In: Poole, A., ed. The birds of North America online. Ithaca, NY: Cornell Lab of Ornithology. Available: http://bna.birds.cornell.edu/bna/species/107; doi:10.2173/bna.107.

Emanuel, K. 2005. Increasing destructiveness of tropical cyclones over the past 30 years. Nature 436:686-688.

Glinski, R.L. 1988. Gray Hawk. In: Glinski R.L., and others, eds. Proceedings of the Southwest Raptor Management Symposium and Workshop. Washington, DC: National Wildlife Federation: 83-86.

Glinski, R.L. 1998. Gray Hawk (*Buteo nitidus*). In: The Raptors of Arizona. Tucson: University of Arizona Press, and Phoenix: Arizona Game and Fish Department: 82-85.

Jones, Larry. 2010. [Personal communication]. February 17, 2010. Tucson, AZ: U.S. Department of Agriculture, Forest Service, Coronado National Forest, Assistant Program Manager for Wildlife, Fish, and Rare Plants.

Manolakou, P., G. Lavranos, and R. Angelopoulou. 2006. Molecular patterns of sex determination in the animal kingdom: a comparative study of the biology of reproduction. Reproductive Biology and Endocrinology 4:59.

U.S. Forest Service [USFS]. 2009. Draft Coronado National Forest ecological sustainability report. Tucson, AZ: U.S. Department of Agriculture, Forest Service. Available: http://www fs.fed.us/r3/coronado/plan-revision/documents/final/cnf-ecological-sustainability-report-final-022009.pdf.

Wingfield, J.C. 2008. Comparative endocrinology, environment, and global change. General and Comparative Endocrinology 157:207-216.

Habitat: American peregrine falcon (*Falco peregrinus anatum*)			
Trait/Quality	**Question**	**Background info. & explanation of score**	**Points**
1. Area and distribution: *breeding*	Is the area or location of the associated vegetation type used for breeding activities by this species expected to change?	**Taxonomic note:** This is one of three sub-species that occur in the United States (White and others 2002), and it occurs in North America, from south of the tundra in Canada to northern Mexico, except for the Pacific Northwest. Peregrine falcons occupy numerous terrestrial biomes in North America with no clear preference for one type, although there may be higher densities in tundra and on the coasts. Burger (2005) indicated that topographic relief and prey base is more important than vegetation in terms of where this species occurs. ABBA observers recorded peregrine falcons in 22 habitat types, ranging from forest to desert to wetland. Almost 48% of observations were in forested areas (pinyon pine-juniper, evergreen oaks, ponderosa pine, and mixed conifer), and 33% were in desert scrub containing sagebrush and other shrubs, and Sonoran desert scrub near water. Hunts in the open sky above treetops and rarely nests in desert mountain ranges in areas that are not near large bodies of water (Burger 2005). In New Mexico in the breeding season, most likely to be seen in areas with cliffs and canyons with open areas for pursuing prey (Stahlecker 2010). Glinski (1998) estimated that more than 200 pairs nest in Arizona. American peregrine falcons occur, or potential habitat exists, on all 12 of the EMAs on CNF (USFS 2009). Projections of suitable climate for vegetation communities forest-wide (Chapter 1) predicted declines in suitable climate for all plant community types with the exception of increases of suitable climate for semi-desert grassland and small increases in Sonoran desert scrub (present in small amounts on the CNF). Overall, we assumed that loss of forest and woodlands will not significantly reduce breeding habitat on CNF.	0
2. Area and distribution: *non-breeding*	Is the area or location of the associated vegetation type used for non-breeding activities by this species expected to change?	Peregrine falcons occupy a wide range of habitats as a result of their large geographical range (White and others 2002). In New Mexico in the non-breeding season, they are most likely to be seen along bodies of water or other areas where there are large concentrations of prey (Stahlecker 2010). See also Habitat, Question 8. Overall, because peregrine falcons occupy a variety of habitats we considered it likely that individuals would be able to respond to changes reductions in forests and woodlands.	0
3. Habitat components: *breeding*	Are specific habitat components required for breeding expected to change?	Cliffs and other structures for nesting are important for this species. Most commonly occupied habitats contain cliffs, and eggs are laid in a scrape (White and others 2002). Nesting in human-based structures (buildings and bridges) is often aided by an artificial nestbox. Reports of using abandoned osprey or raven nests on towers and eagle nests in trees in Alaska (references in White and others 2002). In Arizona, all peregrine falcon eyries have been on cliff faces, canyon walls, spires, and, in some cases, on rocky ridges and outcrops (Burger 2005). Most commonly individuals search for prey from a perched position, but also while flying (White and others 2002). Often perches on cliffs, especially in breeding season. No change expected in the number of suitable cliff sites under projected climate change.	0
4. Habitat components:	Are specific habitat components required for	In fall and winter, peregrine falcons often hunt from lower perches than in the breeding season (including trees, utility poles, fence posts, banks, mounds, driftwood (Dekker 1980, 1999 as cited in White and	0

Habitat: American peregrine falcon (*Falco peregrinus anatum*)			
Trait/Quality	**Question**	**Background info. & explanation of score**	**Points**
non-breeding	survival during non-breeding periods expected to change?	others 2002). Unclear whether reduction in number of trees, if used in wintering areas, could reduce number of non-cliff perches.	
5. Habitat quality and reproduction	Are features of the habitat associated with better reproductive success expected to change?	No information found in White and others (2002) tying specific habitat features to greater reproductive success. Kauffman and others (2003) found that American peregrine falcons in urban areas in California had higher fecundity rates than those in rural habitats. Differential productivity among years and among regions in the United States is documented and thought to be related to differences in prey availability (see White and others 2003), but no clear ties to specific habitat features have been identified, particularly to features that are likely to be altered under climate change.	0
6. Habitat quality and survival	Are features of the habitat associated with better survival expected to change?	No information found (see Habitat, Question 5).	0
7. Ability to colonize new areas	What is this species' capacity and tendency to disperse?	We considered birds to be very mobile due to their capacity for flight and, thus, overall able to colonize new areas. Some peregrine falcons migrate very long distances.	-1
8. Migratory or transitional habitats	Does this species require additional habitats during migration that are separated from breeding and non-breeding habitats?	Populations across this species' breeding range in the United States vary in whether they over-winter or migrate long distances to wintering grounds; birds breeding in northernmost areas of the continent in tundra typically migrate the farthest south (central Argentina and Chile), and those that breed farther south travel shorter distances (White and others 2002). Burger (2005) indicated that some individuals in Arizona remain near nesting areas year-round, whereas others move to lowlands or migrate south. Stahlecker (2010) indicated that it is likely that most individuals breeding in Arizona over-winter south of New Mexico, although there are consistent winter observations of the species in southern New Mexico. Overall, some individuals appear to leave Arizona in winter.	1

Physiology: American peregrine falcon (*Falco peregrinus anatum*)			
Trait/Quality	**Question**	**Background info. & explanation of score**	**Points**
1. Physiological thresholds	Are limiting physiological conditions expected to change?	Most peregrine falcons can maintain a relatively constant cloacal temperature over a span of air temperature ranging 20-50 °C (White and others 2002). They thermoregulate primarily through behavioral adjustments (such as seeking favorable microclimates, drooping legs or wings, orienting body differently relative to sun, panting, erecting feathers), evaporative cooling, and adjusting body insulation to decrease the amount of heat lost (White and others 2002).	0
		Reported to drink frequently but it is not clear whether water is required. Adults and juveniles also bathe.	
		Female peregrine falcons nesting on south slopes and where there is little vegetation screening (e.g., in the Arctic) often shade eggs/small young from heat and sun rather than incubating, and heat stress of both adults and young can occur (White and others 2002).	
		With the exception of rare cases of extreme heat rises, presumably could tolerate increases of several degrees C.	

Physiology: American peregrine falcon (*Falco peregrinus anatum*)			
Trait/Quality	**Question**	**Background info. & explanation of score**	**Points**
2. Sex ratio	Is sex ratio determined by temperature?	No. Temperature-dependent sex determination is mainly observed in reptiles and fish (Manolakou et al. 2006).	0
3. Exposure to extreme weather conditions	Are extreme weather or disturbance events that result in direct mortality or reproductive failure expected to change?	Increase in frequency of heat waves is predicted for southwestern United States. Overall, it is not clear to what extent timing and intensity of heat waves will have on survival and reproduction. We considered it unlikely that heat waves would cause widespread mortality for this species. See also Physiology, Question 1. Not clear where individuals who breed in Arizona over-winter or whether they would be exposed to hurricanes. Hurricane intensity is expected to increase under global climate change, but frequency predictions are inconsistent (Emanuel 2005); frequency increase would likely be more detrimental overall to migrating populations than intensity since hurricane-level winds already detrimental to migrants.	0
4. Limitations to active period	Are projected temperature or precipitation regimes that influence activity period of species expected to change?	Peregrine falcons are diurnal foragers. No information found in White and others (2002) indicating limits on activity period relative to high temperatures. See also Physiology, Question 1. With the exception of cases of extreme heat rises, it seems unlikely that seasonal or daily active periods would be directly restricted to the point of significantly reduced survival.	0
5. Metabolic inhibition	Does this species possess an ability to reduce metabolic energy or water requirements?	No reports of torpor in White and others (2002).	1
6. Survival during resource limitation	Does this species have lower energy requirements or possess the capacity to store energy or water in the long term?	Peregrine falcons cache surplus prey, particularly during the breeding season, in apparent response to short periods when prey is unavailable (e.g., daily or multiple-day periods, including during stormy conditions) (White and others 2002). Cached food would be available for a few days at most, so we did not consider this long-term food storage.	1
7. Variable life history	Does this species have alternative life history strategies to cope with variable resources or climate conditions?	No variable life history strategies.	0
8. Reproduction in variable environments	Can this species outlive periods where reproduction is limited?	Longevity records for banded birds (i.e., longest-lived birds recorded) range 16-20 years (White and others 2002). White and others (1992) cited studies with values of adult survival rates of ranging from 63-100%. White and others (2002) estimated that for a population where adult survival rate is 70% per year, the median adult life (after second year) is about 2 years (mean 2.8 years), assuming that rate does not change with age. This translates into at 10 years, 3% of cohort would still be alive. Periods of extreme reductions in rainfall may last 5 years. If these conditions reduce food resources to the point that birds have insufficient food for breeding, it is possible that much of the population would not survive longer than the period of limited reproduction, particularly if drought conditions reduced annual survival rates below 70%.	1

USDA Forest Service RMRS-GTR-273. 2012.

Phenology: American peregrine falcon (*Falco peregrinus anatum*)

Trait/Quality	Question	Background info. & explanation of score	Points
1. Cues	Does this species use temperature or moisture cues to initiate activities related to fecundity or survival?	Burger (2005) indicated that ABBA observers documented courtship displays and pair formation beginning in March. In Arizona, eggs are typically laid between mid-March and mid-May (Glinski 1998). This species is a predictable breeder, meaning its breeding season occurs at the same time each year (i.e., spring). In predictable breeders, photoperiod is the predominant proximate factor leading to gonadal changes required for reproduction (Dawson and others 2001). It should be noted that, in general, birds also use local predictive information such as temperature, availability of food, and rainfall to make short-term adjustments to reproductive timing(Wingfield 2008), although this short-term adjustment is not addressed by this question (see Bagne and others 2011).	0
2. Event timing	Are activities related to species' fecundity or survival tied to discrete events that are expected to change?	Given the diversity of prey consumed, it is not clear that changes in the timing of precipitation and increases in temperature would alter the timing of prey availability and abundance, and, hence, fecundity.	0
3. Mismatch potential	What is the separation in time or space between cues that initiate activities and discrete events that provide critical resources?	We assumed that at least some individuals that breed on the CNF migrate south for winter. For those individuals that do, critical resources for breeding (such as food) occur far from where individuals over-winter; thus, individuals have no direct information about resource abundance on the breeding grounds when they initiate migration.	1
4. Resilience to timing mismatches during breeding	Does this species employ strategies or have traits that increase the likelihood of reproduction co-occurring with important events?	Peregrine falcons have not been known to rear more than one brood per year, but they can lay a second clutch if the first one fails relatively early in nesting (White and others 2002).	1

Biotic interactions: American peregrine falcon (*Falco peregrinus anatum*)

Trait/Quality	Question	Background info. & explanation of score	Points
1. Food resources	Are important food resources for this species expected to change?	Peregrine falcons consume mostly birds (estimated at 77-99% based on frequency) ranging in size from songbirds to small geese, occasionally mammals (most frequently bats, microtines, squirrels, and rats), and rarely amphibians, fish, and insects (references in White and others 2002). They search for prey from a perch or while in the air, the majority of which is caught in the air during flight but some prey is taken from the water surface or ground (references in White and others 2002). Overall, individuals consume a variety of prey.	0
2. Predators	Are important predator populations expected to change?	Large birds (e.g., eagles and great horned owls) are generally the only predators of adult peregrine falcons. Mammals (e.g., bears, fox, and cats) and predatory birds (e.g., great horned owls and golden eagles) predate nestlings and juveniles (White and others 2002). In the	-1

Biotic interactions: American peregrine falcon (*Falco peregrinus anatum*)			
Trait/Quality	Question	Background info. & explanation of score	Points
		northeastern United States, owls are responsible for >25% of peregrine falcon mortality. Owls and eagles are expected to be negatively impacted by climate change.	
3. Symbionts	Are populations of symbiotic species expected to change?	No indication of symbiotic relationship was found in White and others (1992).	0
4. Disease	Is prevalence of diseases known to cause widespread mortality or reproductive failure in this species expected to change?	Peregrine falcons are known to be hosts to a variety of parasites, bacteria, viruses, etc., as reviewed in White and others (2002), including avian pox, Newcastle disease, parasitic worms, various mites, lice, and flies. Mortality from *Clostridium botulinum* Type C and *Trichomonas gallinae* acquired from prey (references in White and others 2002). No large-scale die-offs from diseases were indicated by White and others (2002). Mortality from collisions with buildings and vehicles was more substantial than from starvation and disease in one study (see White and others 2002).	0
5. Competitors	Are populations of important competing species expected to change?	"…relations with great horned owl (*Bubo virginianus*) are inconsistent and puzzling: Some pairs nest close to owls with little conflict; others harass owls at every opportunity and occasionally kill them; but many pairs of owls dominate and drive off or kill neighboring peregrines, adults and young" (White and others 2002). No clear pattern of competition with other raptor species, and, as indicated by White and others (2002), not easy to categorize interactions with other raptors as predator defense versus competitive interactions. White and others (2002) reviewed multiple studies for interference of other raptor species on peregrine falcons and concluded that the studies "indicate little effect on territorial spacing per se or direct competition for food; but, depending on structure and availability of nest sites (cliffs), individuals of one species can influence choice of nest site by other, heterospecific individuals."	0

Literature Cited

Bagne, K.E., M.M. Friggens, and D.M. Finch. 2011. A system for assessing vulnerability of species (SAVS) to climate change. Gen. Tech. Rep. RMRS-GTR-257. Fort Collins, CO: U.S. Department of Agriculture, Forest Service, Rocky Mountain Research Station. 28 p.

Burger, B. 2005. Peregrine Falcon. In: Corman, T.E., and C. Wise-Gervais, eds. The Arizona Breeding Bird Atlas. Albuquerque, NM: University of New Mexico Press: 156-157.

Dawson, A., V.M. King, G.E. Bentley, G.F. Ball. 2001. Photoperiodic control of seasonality in birds. Journal of Biological Rhythms 16:365-380.

Emanuel, K. 2005. Increasing destructiveness of tropical cyclones over the past 30 years. Nature 436:686-688.

Glinski, R.L. 1998. Peregrine Falcon (*Falco peregrinus*). In: Glinski, R.L., ed. The Raptors of Arizona. Tucson: University of Arizona Press.

Kauffman, M.J., W.F. Frick, and J. Linthicum. 2003. Estimation of habitat-specific demography and population growth for Peregrine Falcons in California. Ecological Applications 13:1802-1816.

Manolakou, P., G. Lavranos, and R. Angelopoulou. 2006. Molecular patterns of sex determination in the animal kingdom: a comparative study of the biology of reproduction. Reproductive Biology and Endocrinology 4:59.

Stahlecker, D.W. 2010. Peregrine falcon (*Falco peregrinus*). In: Cartron, J-L.E. Raptors of New Mexico. Albuquerque, NM: University of New Mexico Press: 445-459.

U.S. Forest Service [USFS]. 2009. Draft Coronado National Forest Ecological Sustainability Report. Tucson, AZ: U.S. Department of Agriculture, Forest Service. Available: http://www fs fed.us/r3/coronado/plan-revision/documents/final/cnf-ecological-sustainability-report-final-022009.pdf.

White, C.M., N.J. Clum, T.J. Cade, and W.G. Hunt. 2002. Peregrine Falcon (*Falco peregrinus*). In: Poole, A., ed. The Birds of North America Online. Ithaca, NY: Cornell Lab of Ornithology. Available: http://bna.birds.cornell.edu/bna/species/660; doi:10.2173/bna.660.

Wingfield, J.C. 2008. Comparative endocrinology, environment, and global change. General and Comparative Endocrinology 157:207-216.

Habitat: Gould's wild turkey (*Meleagris gallopavo mexicana*)			
Trait/Quality	Question	Background info. & explanation of score	Points
1. Area and distribution: *breeding*	Is the area or location of the associated vegetation type used for breeding activities by this species expected to change?	This sub-species occurs in only a few areas in southwestern United States: — Huachuca Mountains (Arizona); — Peloncillo Mountains (Arizona and New Mexico); — Galiuro Mountains; and — some riparian areas of southeastern Arizona (e.g., Bonita Creek, San Pedro River, and San Bernardino Valley; Heffelfinger and others 2000). See Mock and others (2001) and Heffelfinger and others (2000) for a review of historical information regarding turkey sub-species in Arizona, including introduction and later removal of Merriam's sub-species in the Huachuca Mountains. Gould's wild turkeys were re-established into the Huachuca Mountains in 1983 and 1987 (Mock and others 2001) and into the Galiuro Mountains in 1994 and 1997 (Heffelfinger and others 2000). Mock and others (2001) stated that the population at that time was estimated to be around 70-150 individuals. In the Sierra Madre Occidental in Mexico, Gould's wild turkey was reported to occur in mountainous pine forest and pine-oak woodlands (Aldrich 1967 as cited in York and Schemnitz 2003). In western Chihuahua in Mexico, this sub-species reported in evergreen woodland and forest communities (Lafon-Terrazas 1997 as cited in York and Schemnitz 2003). In southeastern Arizona, ABBA surveyors reported wild turkeys in evergreen oak woodlands, Madrean pine-oak forests, and sycamore-dominated drainages (Moors 2005). In the Peloncillo Mountains in New Mexico (York and Schemnitz 2003), hens used three types of pinyon-juniper woodland in winter: riparian type, savannah type, and open woodland where tree species included Chihuahuan pine, silverleaf oak, Toumey oak, and Emory oak. In spring, individuals used similar areas. Riparian habitats were used heavily in spring and summer and were considered to be critical to continued survival of this population. Madrean oak woodland was the habitat occupied in the Peloncillo Mountains (Potter 1984). Open grasslands are an important foraging habitat across the range of the wild turkey (Gardner 2004). Grassy meadows or forest openings with herbaceous vegetation are important for rearing broods (Heffelfinger and others 2000). Gould's wild turkeys occur, or potential habitat exists, on the following EMAs: Peloncillo, Chiricahua, Tumacacori, Santa Rita, Huachuca, Pinaleño, Galiuro, and Santa Catalina (USFS 2009). Projections of suitable climate for vegetation communities	2

Habitat: Gould's wild turkey (*Meleagris gallopavo mexicana*)			
Trait/Quality	**Question**	**Background info. & explanation of score**	**Points**
		(Chapter 1) on Coronado NF predicted declines in suitable conditions for Madrean forest and woodland, Madrean conifer forest, and Rocky Mountain conifer forest, and increases in suitable conditions for semi-desert grassland and, to a lesser extent, Sonoran desert scrub. Overall, we expected that projected reductions in forest and woodland habitats (from drought, pest infestation, and high intensity fires) will reduce breeding habitat.	
2. Area and distribution: *non-breeding*	Is the area or location of the associated vegetation type used for non-breeding activities by this species expected to change?	See Habitat, Question 1 above and Habitat, Question 8 below.	2
3. Habitat components: *breeding*	Are specific habitat components required for breeding expected to change?	Wild turkeys nest on the ground (hen scratches shallow depression; Eaton 1992). Trees are important for roosting; in the Peloncillo Mountains, Chihuahuan pines were used almost exclusively at 15 known roost sites (Potter 1984). Wild turkeys, regardless of species, select trees with large lateral branches (Schorger 1966 as cited in Eaton 1992). Downed logs are important as loafing sites (Heffelfinger and others 2000). We considered large trees and downed logs to be important to individuals during the breeding season (as well as during the non-breeding season), although they may not be specifically required to breed successfully. Eaton (1992) indicated that wild turkeys will drink water where available, but did not indicate that this is a requirement; therefore, we did not consider standing water a requirement.	1
4. Habitat components: *non-breeding*	Are specific habitat components required for survival during non-breeding periods expected to change?	See Habitat, Question 3 above.	1
5. Habitat quality and reproduction	Are features of the habitat associated with better reproductive success expected to change?	Little information found. Eaton (1992) indicated a need to synthesize the considerable amount of data that exist on wild turkey habitat, home range, and movements into a generalized theory of habitat use.	0
6. Habitat quality and survival	Are features of the habitat associated with better survival expected to change?	Little information for this sub-species. Mast-producing trees are crucial to over-winter survival; a lack of mast results in reduced over-winter survival (Heffelfinger and others 2000). Increased aridity has the potential to reduce the number of mast-producing trees.	1
7. Ability to colonize new areas	What is this species' capacity and tendency to disperse?	Several hens of this sub-species in New Mexico had mean annual home ranges of 4385 ha based on radio-telemetry observations (York and Schemnitz 2003). Movements were greatest in summer; the mean maximum distance moved over the course of the study (n=3) was 10.9 km. This study was conducted during a drought period, and the authors indicated that they expected home ranges would be smaller in non-drought periods when food would be more available and individuals would not need to travel as far to meet their nutritional needs. Juveniles disperse in their first spring, at ~8 months post-hatch; in Pennsylvania, wild turkeys dispersed at a rate of about 8 km per year (references in Eaton 1992).	-1

USDA Forest Service RMRS-GTR-273. 2012.

Habitat: Gould's wild turkey (*Meleagris gallopavo mexicana*)			
Trait/Quality	**Question**	**Background info. & explanation of score**	**Points**
		We considered Gould's wild turkey to be highly mobile and able to colonize new areas.	
8. Migratory or transitional habitats	Does this species require additional habitats during migration that are separated from breeding and non-breeding habitats?	Wild turkeys are non-migratory (Eaton 1992). Potter (1984) did not observe separate summer and winter ranges in the Peloncillo Mountains. However, in one year, three radio-equipped hens in the Peloncillo Mountains moved south approximately 6 km from their winter home range to an area where they bred (York and Schemnitz 2003).	0

Physiology: Gould's wild turkey (*Meleagris gallopavo mexicana*)			
Trait/Quality	**Question**	**Background info. & explanation of score**	**Points**
1. Physiological thresholds	Are limiting physiological conditions expected to change?	Eaton (1992) indicated that wild turkeys will drink water where available, but did not indicate that this is a requirement. Feeds for 2-3 hours after leaving roost at dawn, depending on how abundant food is, and again for 2-3 hours before roosting at the end of the day (Eaton 1992), therefore, not actively foraging during hottest part of day. No information found on tolerance of extreme heat in Eaton (1992) or via a Web of Science database search. With the exception of rare cases of extreme heat rises, presumably could tolerate increases of several degrees C. Shaded habitat might reduce effects of solar radiation on rise in body temperature in the short term, but shade from trees expected to decline with time.	0
2. Sex ratio	Is sex ratio determined by temperature?	No. Temperature-dependent sex determination is mainly observed in reptiles and fish (Manolakou et al. 2006).	0
3. Exposure to extreme weather conditions	Are extreme weather or disturbance events that result in direct mortality or reproductive failure expected to change?	Increase in frequency of heat waves is predicted for southwestern United States. Overall, not clear to what extent timing and intensity of heat waves will effect survival and reproduction. We considered it unlikely that heat waves would cause widespread mortality. See also Physiology, Question 1.	0
4. Limitations to active period	Are projected temperature or precipitation regimes that influence activity period of species expected to change?	Feeds for 2-3 hours after leaving roost at dawn, depending on how abundant food is, and again for 2-3 hours before roosting at the end of the day (Eaton 1992). No information was found in Eaton (1992) indicating limits on activity period relative to high temperatures. With the exception of cases of extreme heat rises, it seems unlikely that seasonal or daily active periods would be directly and significantly restricted.	0
5. Metabolic inhibition	Does this species possess an ability to reduce metabolic energy or water requirements?	No information in Eaton (1992) to suggest that wild turkeys use torpor.	1
6. Survival during resource limitation	Does this species have lower energy requirements or possess the capacity to store energy or water in the long term?	No information in Eaton (1992) to indicate that wild turkeys store food.	1

Physiology: Gould's wild turkey (*Meleagris gallopavo mexicana*)

Trait/Quality	Question	Background info. & explanation of score	Points
7. Variable life history	Does this species have alternative life history strategies to cope with variable resources or climate conditions?	No variable life history strategies.	0
8. Reproduction in variable environments	Can this species outlive periods where reproduction is limited?	While longevity records (i.e., longest-lived birds recorded) for wild turkeys include at least two individuals known to have lived in the wild at least 10 years, band recoveries of juveniles in West Virginia and Florida estimated mean life expectancy as a little more than 1 year of age, with mean mortality rates per year of 76% and 60% (Mosby 1967 as cited in Eaton 1992). Periods of extreme reductions in rainfall may last 5 years. If this condition reduces food resources to the point that birds have insufficient food for breeding, most of the population would not survive longer than the period of limited reproduction.	1

Phenology: Gould's wild turkey (*Meleagris gallopavo mexicana*)

Trait/Quality	Question	Background info. & explanation of score	Points
1. Cues	Does this species use temperature or moisture cues to initiate activities related to fecundity or survival?	Gardner (2004) indicated that wild turkeys are polygamous and that breeding behavior begins in late winter as daylight increases. In southeastern Arizona, wild turkeys begin breeding in late February when males begin displaying to females and it continues into late March and early April, at which time hens begin to lay (Moors 2005). In general, bird species use local predictive information, including temperature, availability of food, and rainfall, to make short-term adjustments to reproductive timing (Wingfield 2008), although this behavior is not addressed by this question (see Bagne and others 2011).	0
2. Event timing	Are activities related to species' fecundity or survival tied to discrete events that are expected to change?	Reductions in precipitation and increases in temperature may alter the abundance of plant food, though it is not clear that timing would be altered. Food abundance is covered in Biotic Interactions, Question 1.	0
3. Mismatch potential	What is the separation in time or space between cues that initiate activities and discrete events that provide critical resources?	Gould's wild turkeys are year-round residents. Typically, increases in food occur in spring, so there is little temporal separation. There is no spatial separation since they are year-round residents.	-1
4. Resilience to timing mismatches during breeding	Does this species employ strategies or have traits that increase the likelihood of reproduction co-occurring with important events?	Wild turkeys generally have just one clutch per season (Eaton 1992). Re-nesting after predation is considered common if predation occurs during laying or at the beginning of incubation. It is rare that a second brood will be initiated after loss of a first brood.	1

Biotic interactions: Gould's wild turkey (*Meleagris gallopavo mexicana*)			
Trait/Quality	**Question**	**Background info. & explanation of score**	**Points**
1. Food resources	Are important food resources for this species expected to change?	Eaton (1992) referred to wild turkeys as "extremely adaptable and catholic in feeding." A literature review indicated that wild turkeys throughout the United States and Mexico eat the same general types of food: hard and soft mast, green forage, seeds, agricultural crops, and animal matter (Hurst 1992 as cited in Gardner 2004). In New Mexico, this sub-species was reported to consume a variety of foods across the year (York and Schemnitz 2003). Juniper and manzanita fruits were common and, overall, were considered important to this sub-species. In spring, this sub-species consumed pinyon nuts and acorns, mustard forbs (early spring), and a variety of grass seeds (e.g., pinyon ricegrass and sideoats grama). After summer rains, consumption of grass seeds (e.g., barnyard grass) and insects increased. Potter (1984) indicated that late monsoonal rains could reduce insects and succulent vegetation for young poults. Although this sub-species eats a variety of foods across the year, the score for this question reflects potential reduction in fruit and seed crops. For example, reduced crops of acorns are expected as a result of reduced precipitation in the short term (Zlotin and Parmenter 2008); and in the long term, less food from these sources is expected as a result of reduced tree cover.	1
2. Predators	Are important predator populations expected to change?	Humans are the most common predator of wild turkeys (Eaton 1992). Potter (1984) considered potential predators in the Peloncillo Mountains to be coyote, bobcat, mountain lion, golden eagle, and great horned owl. However, inspection of coyote scat did not result in any recognizable wild turkey remains. Fox, skunk, crow, coati, and feral hog were considered potential nest predators. Schemnitz and Zeedyk (1992) noted that no Gould's wild turkey remains were observed in 239 coyote droppings and 83 great horned owl pellets. Overall, this species has a variety of predators.	0
3. Symbionts	Are populations of symbiotic species expected to change?	No indication of symbiotic relationships was found in Eaton (1992).	0
4. Disease	Is prevalence of diseases known to cause widespread mortality or reproductive failure in this species expected to change?	Heffelfinger and others (2000) indicated that no diseases had been identified in recent work with Gould's wild turkey populations and translocations from Mexico. A variety of viral and bacterial diseases may infect wild turkeys (Hopkins and others 1990). Seemingly healthy individuals may be carrying pathogenic mycoplasmas (Fritz and others 1992). Schemnitz and Zeedyk (1992) noted that relatively little is known about diseases and parasites in Gould's wild turkey. According to references in Eaton (1992), significant diseases for wild turkeys, in general, are blackhead (histomoniasis, caused by protozoan *Histomonas meleagradis*), coli-granuloma, fowl pox (caused by a strain of avian pox virus), and fowl cholera (caused by bacterium *Pasteurella multocida*). Approximately 25% of the wild turkeys found sick or dead in 8 southeastern states were diagnosed with avian pox, and ~12% were diagnosed with blackhead disease (Davidson and others 1985 as cited in Davidson and Wentworth 1992). It appears that it avian pox may be more prevalent in the southeastern United States (Davidson and Wentworth 1992). There is little information to suggest that large outbreaks of these diseases have occurred in Gould's wild turkey. Unclear whether prevalence of the diseases might be influenced by climate change.	0

Biotic interactions: Gould's wild turkey (*Meleagris gallopavo mexicana*)			
Trait/Quality	**Question**	**Background info. & explanation of score**	**Points**
5. Competitors	Are populations of important competing species expected to change?	Potter (1984) indicated that deer are probably strong competitors for food only when herds are over populated and the understory becomes significantly depleted. Feral hogs are considered potentially strong competitors during times of food shortage. Potter (1984) speculated that, in the Peloncillo Mountains, wild turkeys might compete with raptors such as goshawks and red-tailed hawks for large trees that turkeys need for roosting and goshawks need for nesting.	0
		Hurt (1992) stated that while competition for food among turkeys, deer, hogs, and many other species occurs, the extent to which it limits wild turkey populations is unclear. In one area in Florida, deer and hog populations were large and grazing was intensive, but wild turkey populations were large as well (Williams 1981 as cited in Hurst 1992).	
		Overall, species has a variety of competitors.	

Literature Cited

Bagne, K.E., M.M. Friggens, and D.M. Finch. 2011. A system for assessing vulnerability of species (SAVS) to climate change. Gen. Tech. Rep. RMRS-GTR-257. Fort Collins, CO: U.S. Department of Agriculture, Forest Service, Rocky Mountain Research Station. 28 p.

Davidson, W.R., and E.J. Wentworth. 1992. Population influences: diseases and parasites. In: Dickson, J.G., ed. The Wild Turkey: Biology and Management. Harrisburg, PA: Stackpole Books: 101-118.

Eaton, S.W. 1992. Wild Turkey (*Meleagris gallopavo*). In: Poole, A., ed. The birds of North America online. Ithaca, NY: Cornell Lab of Ornithology. Available: http://bna.birds.cornell.edu/bna/species/022. doi: 10.2173/bna.22.

Fritz, B.A., C.B. Thomas, and T.M. Yull. 1992. Serological and microbial survey of *Mycoplasma gallisepticum* in wild turkeys (*Meleagris gallopavo*) from six western states. Journal of Wildlife Diseases 28:10-20.

Gardner, S. 2004. Strategic plan for Wild Turkey management. Sacramento, CA: California Department of Fish and Game. Available: http://www.dfg.ca.gov/wildlife/hunting/uplandgame/docs/turkplan_04.pdf.

Heffelfinger, J., B. Wakeling, J. Millican, S. Stone, T. Skiner, M. Fredlake, and M. Adkins. 2000. Southeastern Arizona wild turkey management plan. Available: http://www.azgfd.gov/pdfs/h_f/management/SoutheasternArizonaWildTurke%20ManagementPlan.pdf.

Hopkins, B.A., J.K. Skeeles, G.E. Houghten, D. Siagle, and K. Gardner. 1990. A survey of infectious diseases in wild turkeys (*Meleagris gallopavo silvestris*) from Arkansas. Journal of Wildlife Diseases 26:468-472.

Hurst, G.A.1992. Foods and feeding In: Dickson, J.G., ed. The Wild Turkey: Biology and Management. Harrisburg, PA: Stackpole Books: 66-83.

Manolakou, P., G. Lavranos, and R. Angelopoulou. 2006. Molecular patterns of sex determination in the animal kingdom: a comparative study of the biology of reproduction. Reproductive Biology and Endocrinology 4:59.

Mock, K.E., T.C. Theimer, B.F. Wakeling, O.E. Rhodes, D.L. Greenberg, and P. Keim. 2001. Verifying the origins of a reintroduced population of Gould's wild turkey. Journal of Wildlife Management 65:871-879.

Moors, A. 2005. Wild Turkey In: Corman, T.E., and C. Wise-Gervais, ed. The Arizona Breeding Bird Atlas. Albuquerque, NM: University of New Mexico Press: 80-81.

Potter, T.D. 1984. Status and ecology of Gould's turkey. Thesis. New Mexico State University, Las Cruces.

Schemnitz, S.D., and W.D. Zeedyk. 1992. Gould's Turkey In: Dickson, J.G., ed. The Wild Turkey: Biology and Management. Harrisburg, PA: Stackpole Books: 350-360.

U.S. Forest Service [USFS]. 2009. Draft Coronado National Forest ecological sustainability report. Tucson, AZ: U.S. Department of Agriculture, Forest Service. Available: http://www.fs fed.us/r3/coronado/plan-revision/documents/final/cnf-ecological-sustainability-report-final-022009.pdf.

Wingfield, J.C. 2008. Comparative endocrinology, environment, and global change. General and Comparative Endocrinology 157:207-216.

York, D.L., and S.D. Schemnitz. 2003. Home range, habitat use, and diet of Gould's turkeys, Peloncillo Mountains, New Mexico. Southwestern Naturalist 48:231-240.

Zlotin, R.I., and R.R. Parmenter. 2008. Patterns of mast production in pinyon and juniper woodlands along a precipitation gradient in central New Mexico (Sevilleta National Wildlife Refuge). Journal of Arid Environments 72:1562-1572.

Habitat: Montezuma quail (*Cyrtonyx montezumae*)

Trait/Quality	Question	Background info. & explanation of score	Points
1. Area and distribution: *breeding*	Is the area or location of the associated vegetation type used for breeding activities by this species expected to change?	The Montezuma quail occurs year-round in the United States in limited areas in Arizona, New Mexico, and Texas. Its distribution extends into Mexico, where it also occurs year-round. In Arizona, this species is found in south and central mountain ranges and has been reported in: Baboquivari, San Luis, Pajarito, Atascosa, Canelo Hills, Tumacacori, Santa Rita, Patagonia, Huachuca, and Chiricahua Mountains, with smaller populations in Catalina, Rincon, Galiuro, Dragoon, Pinaleño, and Whetstone Mountains and in the forested Mogollon Rim north of Gila River Mountains (references in Stromberg 2000). ABBA observers recently confirmed this species presence in the Peloncillo, Chiricahua, Baboquivari, Rincon, and Pinaleño Mountains; it was not observed in the Santa Catalina, Galiuro, or Pinal Mountains, but this species often goes undetected when present (Corman and Wise-Gervais 2005). Closely associated with oak woodlands. In Arizona, individuals chose areas with higher grass cover and more trees than randomly available (Bristow and Ockenfels 2004). Species occurs in a variety of open woodlands but depends on an understory of grasses and forbs (Corman and Wise-Gervais 2005). During ABBA surveys (Corman and Wise-Gervais 2005), 43% of observations were in Madrean evergreen oak woodlands containing alligator juniper and several species of oak (Arizona white, Emory, Mexican blue, and netleaf). The second most observations (13%) were in adjacent semi-arid grassland. Also detected in Madrean pine-oak woodlands (understory of evergreen oaks, juniper, pinyon, and Arizona madrone) and in canyons containing cottonwood, willow, Arizona sycamore, Douglas-fir, maple, and pines. Nests on the ground. Nests found in cool canyons as well as drier grassy and chaparral slopes (Corman and Wise-Gervais 2005). First broods usually seen mid-July (Wallmo 1954) but, in some years, not until August (Stromberg 2000). Brood production varies among years, in part as a function of summer rains (Brown 1979). This species occurs, or potential habitat exists, on 4 of the EMAs on CNF: Peloncillo, Chiricahua, Tumacacori, and Santa Rita (USFS 2009). Projections of suitable climate for vegetation communities forest wide (Chapter 1) predicted declines in suitable climate for all plant community types, with the exception of increases of suitable climate for semi-desert grassland and small increases in Sonoran desert scrub (present in small amounts on the CNF). Given the projected decline in woodland habitats, we predicted that habitat for this species will decrease.	2

Habitat: Montezuma quail (*Cyrtonyx montezumae*)			
Trait/Quality	**Question**	**Background info. & explanation of score**	**Points**
2. Area and distribution: *non-breeding*	Is the area or location of the associated vegetation type used for non-breeding activities by this species expected to change?	Same as breeding habitat (see Habitat, Question 1 above).	2
3. Habitat components: *breeding*	Are specific habitat components required for breeding expected to change?	According to Brown (1979), this species requires perennial bunch grasses for nest construction and concealment. Grasslands are expected to increase over time. However, we considered it unlikely that the species would find open grasslands suitable for nesting without the woodland environment.	-1
4. Habitat components: *non-breeding*	Are specific habitat components required for survival during non-breeding periods expected to change?	Grass cover is also important in the non-breeding season. According to Stromberg (1990), this species roosts at night on the ground in shallow cups; 20-night roosts were located in patches of tall grass (tanglehead [*Heteropogon contortus*]) and typically near rocks where tall grass created a roof.	-1
5. Habitat quality and reproduction	Are features of the habitat associated with better reproductive success expected to change?	No information in Stromberg (2000) on habitat factors associated with differential reproductive success.	0
6. Habitat quality and survival	Are features of the habitat associated with better survival expected to change?	No information in Stromberg (2000) on habitat factors associated with differential survival.	0
7. Ability to colonize new areas	What is this species' capacity and tendency to disperse?	Although little is known about its dispersal, this species appears to undergo fewer movements than many other species of birds. Stromberg (1990) indicated that initial dispersal distance is probably very limited given that covey home ranges after breeding are small (1-2 ha). Pairs are often found in the same small areas (50 m^2) for several years (Bishop 1964 as cited in Stromberg 2000). Also, this species mostly walks and runs as opposed to flying. We scored as "0" because we considered this species "moderately mobile" (expected lower mobility than bird species that migrate long distances or fly more frequently).	0
8. Migratory or transitional habitats	Does this species require additional habitats during migration that are separated from breeding and non-breeding habitats?	No elevational seasonal migrations are documented (Stromberg 2000).	0

Physiology: Montezuma quail (*Cyrtonyx montezumae*)			
Trait/Quality	**Question**	**Background info. & explanation of score**	**Points**
1. Physiological thresholds	Are limiting physiological conditions expected to change?	Occupies arid habitats and Arizona and New Mexico are the northern limits of this species' distribution. It appears that this species does not need to drink free water to survive (Leopold and McCabe 1957 as cited in Stromberg 2000). Not known to bathe in	0

Physiology: Montezuma quail (*Cyrtonyx montezumae*)

Trait/Quality	Question	Background info. & explanation of score	Points
		water even when shallow water is available (Stromberg 2000).	
		No information found on tolerance of extreme heat in Web of Science database, although relatively little is known about this species overall. With the exception of cases of extreme heat rises, presumably could tolerate increases of several degrees C. Shaded habitat (oaks) might reduce effects of solar radiation on rise in body temperature in the short term, but shade from trees expected to decline with time.	
2. Sex ratio	Is sex ratio determined by temperature?	No. Temperature-dependent sex determination is mainly observed in reptiles and fish (Manolakou and others 2006).	0
3. Exposure to extreme weather conditions	Are extreme weather or disturbance events that result in direct mortality or reproductive failure expected to change?	Increased frequency of heat waves is predicted for the southwestern United States. Overall, it is not clear to what extent timing and intensity of heat waves will effect survival and reproduction. We considered it unlikely that heat waves would cause widespread mortality for this species. See also Physiology, Question 1. This species is a year-round resident, so not exposed to potential changes in storms along a migratory route.	0
4. Limitations to active period	Are projected temperature or precipitation regimes that influence activity period of species expected to change?	Individuals forage more in morning and evening; during the middle of the day, they rest, dust, preen, and occasionally dig for food (Stromberg 2000). No information found in Stromberg (2000) indicating limits on activity period relative to high temperatures. With the exception of cases of extreme heat rises, it seems unlikely that seasonal or daily active periods will be directly restricted to the point of significantly reducing survival.	0
5. Metabolic inhibition	Does this species possess an ability to reduce metabolic energy or water requirements?	No information found to indicate that this species uses torpor.	1
6. Survival during resource limitation	Does this species have lower energy requirements or possess the capacity to store energy or water in the long term?	No information found in Stromberg (2000) to indicate that this species stores food.	1
7. Variable life history	Does this species have alternative life history strategies to cope with variable resources or climate conditions?	No variable life history strategies.	0
8. Reproduction in variable environments	Can this species outlive periods where reproduction is limited?	Very little information about longevity in the wild; in captivity, can live as long as 6-7 years (Stromberg 2000) and we assumed that in the wild, mean lifespan is much shorter. Periods of extreme reductions in rainfall may last 5 years. If this condition reduced food resources to the point that birds have insufficient food for breeding, it is expected that most of the population would not survive longer than the period of limited reproduction.	1

Phenology: Montezuma quail (*Cyrtonyx montezumae*)

Trait/Quality	Question	Background info. & explanation of score	Points
1. Cues	Does this species use temperature or moisture cues to initiate activities related to fecundity or survival?	Nesting coincides with summer rains and is reported to be delayed until as late as August if there is little monsoonal rain (Corman and Wise-Gervais 2005). Breeding appears to be triggered by increased humidity and availability of newly emergent vegetation and insects consumed by adults.	1
2. Event timing	Are activities related to species' fecundity or survival tied to discrete events that are expected to change?	See also Phenology, Question 1. Fall covey sizes were positively correlated with summer monsoon rainfall (Stromberg 2000) suggesting a possible association between precipitation and food abundance. It is unclear whether the timing and amount of monsoonal rains will change, but change is considered a potential threat given that reproduction in this species appears to be tied to monsoonal rains.	1
3. Mismatch potential	What is the separation in time or space between cues that initiate activities and discrete events that provide critical resources?	This species is a year-round resident in Arizona. Typically, increases in food abundance (a critical resource) occur in spring, so there is little temporal separation. There is no spatial separation since the species is a year-round resident.	-1
4. Resilience to timing mismatches during breeding	Does this species employ strategies or have traits that increase the likelihood of reproduction co-occurring with important events?	In the wild, no second broods were documented by Leopold and McCabe (1957 as cited in Stromberg 2000).	1

Biotic interactions: Montezuma quail (*Cyrtonyx montezumae*)

Trait/Quality	Question	Background info. & explanation of score	Points
1. Food resources	Are important food resources for this species expected to change?	This species feeds on the ground by digging with its feet (Stromberg 2000). During winter, roots of wood sorrel [*Oxalis* spp.] and underground tubers of sedges (*Cyperus* spp.) are a large proportion of the diet (Stromberg 2000). Adds acorns to the diet in spring and summer; in some areas, may eat acorns year-round. In fall and winter, also eats seeds of a variety of species (e.g., panic grass [*Panicum* spp.], morning glory [*Ipomoea* spp.], nightshade [*Solanum* spp.], brodiaea [*Brodiaea* spp.], yucca, and lupine [*Lupinus* spp.]). Acorns, *Oxalis* spp., and *Cyperus* spp. constitute nearly 80% of year-round diet based on crop analysis (Stromberg 2000). Insects are important in summer, particularly grasshoppers, ants, and beetles (Coleoptera); (references in Stromberg 2000). Stromberg (2000) summarized diet information and indicated that diet differences between individuals in the Huachuca Mountains and in the Santa Rita Mountains reflect differences in plant species composition. Individuals dig for food most commonly in duff and leaves under bushes or trees (Bishop 1964). Overall, unclear whether *Oxalis* spp. and *Cyperus* spp. would decrease in the future. This score reflects the potential reduction in	1

Biotic interactions: Montezuma quail (*Cyrtonyx montezumae*)			
Trait/Quality	Question	Background info. & explanation of score	Points
		acorn crops; reduced acorn crops are expected in the short term as a result of reduced precipitation (Zlotin and Parmenter 2008), and fewer acorns are expected in the long term as a result of reduced tree cover.	
2. Predators	Are important predator populations expected to change?	A variety of predators are known and/or expected. Documented predation by Cooper's hawks, northern goshawks, and coyotes (egg predation) and probable egg predation by various skunk species (Stromberg 2000).	0
3. Symbionts	Are populations of symbiotic species expected to change?	No indication of symbiotic relationships found in Stromberg (2000).	0
4. Disease	Is prevalence of diseases known to cause widespread mortality or reproductive failure in this species expected to change?	No information on diseases and parasites for wild birds; captive birds show ability to contract diseases seen in captive quail (Stromberg 2000).	0
5. Competitors	Are populations of important competing species expected to change?	Stromberg (2000) found no information on inter-specific competition.	0

Literature Cited

Bristow, K.D., and R.A. Ockenfels. 2004. Pairing season habitat selection by Montezuma quail in southeastern Arizona. Journal of Range Management 57:532-538.

Brown, D.E. 1979. Factors influencing reproductive success and population densities in Montezuma quail. Journal of Wildlife Management 43:522-526.

Corman, T.E., and C. Wise-Gervais, eds. 2005. Arizona Breeding Bird Atlas. Albuquerque, NM: University of New Mexico Press.

Stromberg, M.R. 2000. Montezuma Quail (*Cyrtonyx montezumae*). In: Poole, A., ed. The birds of North America online. Ithaca, NY: Cornell Lab of Ornithology. Available: http://bna.birds.cornell.edu/bna/species/524 doi:10.2173/bna.524.

Stromberg, M.R. 1990. Habitat, movements and roost characteristics of Montezuma Quail in southeastern Arizona. Condor 92:229-236.

U.S. Forest Service [USFS]. 2009. Draft Coronado National Forest ecological sustainability report. Tucson, AZ: U.S. Department of Agriculture, Forest Service. Available: http://www fs.fed.us/r3/coronado/plan-revision/documents/final/cnf-ecological-sustainability-report-final-022009.pdf.

Wallmo, O.C. 1954. Nesting of Mearns quail in southeastern Arizona. Condor 56:125-128.

Zlotin, R.I., and Parmenter, R.R. 2008. Patterns of mast production in pinyon and juniper woodlands along a precipitation gradient in central New Mexico (Sevilleta National Wildlife Refuge). Journal of Arid Environments 72:1562-1572.

Habitat: Western yellow-billed cuckoo (*Coccyzus americanus occidentalis*)			
Trait/Quality	**Question**	**Background info. & explanation of score**	**Points**
1. Area and distribution: *breeding*	Is the area or location of the associated vegetation type used for breeding activities by this species expected to change?	**Taxonomic note:** There has been some disagreement over whether there are valid eastern and western sub-species. The U.S. Fish and Wildlife Service (2001) cited the results of Franzreb and Laymon (1993) and recognized a western sub-species (*C. a. occidentalis*) whose listing under the Endangered Species Act was "warranted but precluded by higher priority listing actions." Birds in the north and extreme western portions of Texas to the Pacific Coast were assigned as *C. a. occidentalis*, and other cuckoos in North America as *C. a. americanus* by Ridgeway (1887 as cited in USFWS 2001). Yellow-billed cuckoos prefer "open woodland with clearings and low, dense shrubby vegetation" (Hughes 1999). In Arizona (and elsewhere in the Southwest), they prefer "desert riparian woodlands (Sonoran Zones) comprised of willow, Fremont cottonwood, and dense mesquite" (Hughes 1999) using cottonwoods extensively for foraging and often placing their nests in willows. Nests have also been found in orchards next to river bottoms in Arizona (Hughes 1999). In western United States, nests are also located in Fremont cottonwood, mesquite, hackberry, soapberry, alder, and cultivated fruit trees. For 2-3 weeks before breeding, yellow-billed cuckoos may occupy upland vegetation, including pinyon, oak, juniper, and manzanita (Hamilton and Hamilton 1965; Hughes 1999). In arid regions, individuals are restricted to breeding in "river bottoms, ponds, swampy areas, and damp thickets with relatively high humidity" (Hughes 1999). This species occurs, or potential habitat exists, on two of the EMAs on CNF: Santa Rita and Huachuca (USFS 2009). Projections of suitable climate for vegetation communities forest-wide (Chapter 1) predicted declines in suitable climate for all plant community types, with the exception of increases of suitable climate for semi-desert grassland and small increases in Sonoran desert scrub (present in small amounts on the CNF). Riparian habitats are predicted to decline due to decreased stream flows on average (increased aridity and decreased snowpack), increased fire frequency, and possible changes to the flood regime (earlier peak flows).	2
2. Area and distribution: *non-breeding*	Is the area or location of the associated vegetation type used for non-breeding activities by this species expected to change?	Yellow-billed cuckoos winter primarily in South America. The wintering range of individuals nesting in the western United States is not as well known as that of eastern sub-species, but it is likely that they travel to northwestern South America (Hughes 1999). For the species overall, wintering birds occupy a wide variety of forests, woodlands, and scrubby areas, preferring "woody vegetation bordering fresh water" (Rappole and others 1983 and Stotz and others 1996 as cited in Hughes 1999). Winter habitat for the species is reported as mangroves and riparian habitats in Surinam and Guyana (references in Hughes 1999). In Venezuela, observed in "open woodland, second growth, xerophytic areas, thickets, and páramo" (Meyer de Schauensee and Phelps 1978 as cited in Hughes 1999). Assuming that this sub-species winters in northwestern South America, this would be some of the expected areas occupied. Also found in sub-humid and scrub forest, xerophytic and mesophytic forest edges in other South American locations (Hayes 1995 as cited in Hughes 1999). Overall, future trends in temperature and precipitation in many areas in South America are not clear. Magrin and others (2007) noted some of the observed and possible changes: (1) temperature increases are occurring in many areas (glacier retreat in Columbia, Peru, and Ecuador); (2) climate projected to become more suitable	2

Habitat: Western yellow-billed cuckoo (*Coccyzus americanus occidentalis*)			
Trait/Quality	Question	Background info. & explanation of score	Points
		for tropical vegetation toward the south, and the northern portions of South America drier; (3) tropical forests will be replaced by savannahs and a experience an increased risk of fire; (4) mangroves are threatened by sea level rise; and (4) extreme weather events have been reported, including intense rainfall events in Venezuela (1999 and 2005), flooding in the Argentinean Pampas (2000, 2002), and drought in the Amazon (2005), among others.	
		Overall, preferred wintering habitat for yellow-billed cuckoos (woody vegetation near water) in northern South America is likely to decline due to drying conditions and expected decrease of mangroves.	
3. Habitat components: *breeding*	Are specific habitat components required for breeding expected to change?	Water appears to be important, directly or indirectly. In California, this sub-species was reported to not breed where water is not within 100 m (Gaines 1974 as cited in Hughes 1999). For nesting, suitably sized trees with horizontal branches are required (Laymon 1980 as cited in Hughes 1999). The majority of nests found by ABBA observers (Corman and Wise-Gervais 2005) were along perennial drainages. Hamilton and Hamilton (1965) indicated that "permanent water or some environmental factor closely correlated with it is a basic requirement."	1
		Decrease in average annual stream flows (from reduced precipitation) likely to increase distance to water and reduce suitably sized trees.	
4. Habitat components: *non-breeding*	Are specific habitat components required for survival during non-breeding periods expected to change?	None reported in Hughes (1999).	0
5. Habitat quality and reproduction	Are features of the habitat associated with better reproductive success expected to change?	No information in Hughes (1999).	0
6. Habitat quality and survival	Are features of the habitat associated with better survival expected to change?	No information in Hughes (1999).	0
7. Ability to colonize new areas	What is this species' capacity and tendency to disperse?	Both sexes are highly mobile (populations that breed in Arizona are migratory). We considered birds to be very mobile due to their capacity for flight and, thus, overall able to colonize new areas.	-1
8. Migratory or transitional habitats	Does this species require additional habitats during migration that are separated from breeding and non-breeding habitats?	Yellow-billed cuckoos are long-distance migrants (winter in South America). Migratory routes of western birds are not as well known as for eastern populations. Yellow-billed cuckoos are fairly common spring and fall migrants in Oaxaca, Mexico (Hughes 1999).	1

Physiology: Western yellow-billed cuckoo (*Coccyzus americanus occidentalis*)			
Trait/Quality	**Question**	**Background info. & explanation of score**	**Points**
1. Physiological thresholds	Are limiting physiological conditions expected to change?	In terms of latitude, southern Arizona is in the southeastern portion of the sub-species' range in the United States, and is roughly the southern one-third of the species' breeding range. Yellow-billed cuckoos formerly bred throughout most of North American from southern Canada to northern Mexico (USFWS 2001).	0
		In Arizona, Hamilton and Hamilton (1965) observed an adult shading nestlings in the nest at midday. An incubating adult has been observed panting on hot days (Hughes 1999). Hughes (1999) found no information on water drinking for this species.	
		With the exception of cases of extreme heat rises, presumably could tolerate increases of several degrees C. Shaded habitat might reduce effects of solar radiation on rise in body temperature, although shade from trees expected to decline with time.	
2. Sex ratio	Is sex ratio determined by temperature?	No. Temperature-dependent sex determination is mainly observed in reptiles and fish (Manolakou and others 2006).	0
3. Exposure to extreme weather conditions	Are extreme weather or disturbance events that result in direct mortality or reproductive failure expected to change?	Hughes (1999) reported that migrants may be affected by adverse weather. Veit and Petersen (1993 as cited in Hughes 1999) reported that in 1954, many weakened and starving yellow-billed cuckoos were observed in northeastern states following 3 hurricanes. Hurricane intensity is expected to increase, but frequency predictions are inconsistent (Emanuel 2005); frequency increase would likely be more detrimental overall for migrating birds since hurricane-level winds already are a concern for migrants.	0
		See also Physiology, Question 1.	
4. Limitations to active period	Are projected temperature or precipitation regimes that influence activity period of species expected to change?	See Physiology, Question 1. With the exception of cases of extreme heat rises, seems unlikely for seasonal or daily active periods to be restricted to the point of significantly reducing survival.	0
5. Metabolic inhibition	Does this species possess an ability to reduce metabolic energy or water requirements?	No reports of torpor in Hughes (1999), which reported that metabolism and temperature regulation were poorly known. No citations of torpor in Web of Science database. We assumed that yellow-billed cuckoos do not use torpor.	1
6. Survival during resource limitation	Does this species have lower energy requirements or possess the capacity to store energy or water in the long term?	Feeds most often on insects (Hughes 1999). Hughes (1999) reported no food storage.	1
7. Variable life history	Does this species have alternative life history strategies to cope with variable resources or climate conditions?	No variable life history strategies.	0
8. Reproduction in variable environments	Can this species outlive periods where reproduction is limited?	Little information on longevity; rate of recapture of banded individuals is very low (Hughes 1999). Records from Canadian Wildlife Service indicated a few banded birds at least 4 years old (Hughes 1999).	1

USDA Forest Service RMRS-GTR-273. 2012.

Phenology: Western yellow-billed cuckoo (*Coccyzus americanus occidentalis*)

Trait/Quality	Question	Background info. & explanation of score	Points
1. Cues	Does this species use temperature or moisture cues to initiate activities related to fecundity or survival?	Western yellow-billed cuckoos are predictable breeders, meaning the breeding season occurs at the same time each year (i.e., spring). In predictable breeders, photoperiod is the predominant proximate factor leading to gonadal changes required for reproduction (Dawson and others 2001). Birds, in general, use local predictive information, such as temperature, availability of food, and rainfall, to make short-term adjustments to reproductive timing (Wingfield 2008), although this short-term adjustment is not addressed by this question (see Bagne and others 2011). No information in Hughes (1999) on direct influence of temperature and moisture on cues for this species.	0
2. Event timing	Are activities related to species' fecundity or survival tied to discrete events that are expected to change?	Food abundance in spring is an important factor driving fecundity in bird species breeding in temperate regions (review by Martin 1987). Typically, increases in insect abundance (a critical resource) occur in spring; changes in the timing of precipitation and increases in temperature have the potential to alter the timing of insect availability and abundance and, hence, fecundity. In Indiana, more yellow-billed cuckoo nests were found and the peak of egg-laying was earlier in years when eastern tent caterpillars and cicadas (either periodical or annual species) were abundant (Nolan and Thompson 1975). Unclear whether a similar pattern exists in Arizona.	1
3. Mismatch potential	What is the separation in time or space between cues that initiate activities and discrete events that provide critical resources?	The yellow-billed cuckoo is a migrant that occurs in the CNF in the breeding season. Critical resources for breeding occur far from where individuals over-winter; thus, individuals have no direct information about resource abundance on the breeding grounds when they initiate migration from their wintering grounds. Anders and Post (2006) suggested that warmer winters may lead to earlier spring peaks in the abundance of Lepidoptera species that the yellow-billed cuckoos feed on which could lead to it missing the peak in food abundance since individuals arrive fairly late to the breeding grounds.	1
4. Resilience to timing mismatches during breeding	Does this species employ strategies or have traits that increase the likelihood of reproduction co-occurring with important events?	Populations in the western United States are believed to raise only one brood per season; breeding season in the west is 1-3 months shorter than in the east (Hughes 1999).	1

Biotic interactions: Western yellow-billed cuckoo (*Coccyzus americanus occidentalis*)

Trait/Quality	Question	Background info. & explanation of score	Points
1. Food resources	Are important food resources for this species expected to change?	Yellow-billed cuckoos feed primarily on large insects such as caterpillars, grasshoppers, crickets, katydids, and cicadas; also feed on small lizards, frogs, eggs, and nestlings (Hughes 1999). On wintering grounds, they also feed on fruits and seeds, as well as insects (Hughes 1999). In Arizona, Hamilton and Hamilton (1965) observed consumption of what appeared to be large moth larvae and katydids; the authors stated "the caterpillar of the *Condalia* bush...is the main item taken to the young." Local influxes of yellow-billed cuckoos have been observed in the eastern United States when insect abundance has been high (Veit	0

Biotic interactions: Western yellow-billed cuckoo (*Coccyzus americanus occidentalis*)

Trait/Quality	Question	Background info. & explanation of score	Points
		and Peterson 1993 as cited in Hughes 1999). Peak numbers of yellow-billed cuckoos have been observed following forest tent caterpillar irruptions and gypsy moth outbreaks in Michigan and cicadas in Indiana and Kansas (various citations in Hughes 1999). In eastern populations, Veit and Petersen (1993 in Hughes 1999) considered it likely that more young are raised successfully during years of high caterpillar abundance. However, Hamilton and Hamilton (1965) made no reference to such phenomena related to peaks in insect abundance in Arizona and provided little information on tent caterpillar outbreaks. Yellow-billed cuckoo populations in the eastern United States were found to be lower after warmer years, but the relationship with food is unclear (Anders and Post 2006).	
2. Predators	Are important predator populations expected to change?	Overall, there is a suite of predators. Raptors may be an important predator during migration and upon arrival on wintering grounds (Hector 1985 as cited in Hughes 1999). Snakes, mammals, and avian predators are considered to be egg and nestling predators (Hughes 1999).	0
3. Symbionts	Are populations of symbiotic species expected to change?	Hughes (1999) did not identify important symbiotic relationships.	0
4. Disease	Is prevalence of diseases known to cause widespread mortality or reproductive failure in this species expected to change?	Numerous diseases and parasites have been documented (see Hughes 1999), but we found no information that indicates significant negative effects on populations.	0
5. Competitors	Are populations of important competing species expected to change?	Nests are occasionally parasitized by brown-headed cowbird (*Molothrus ater*) and, in south Texas, rarely by bronzed cowbirds (*Molothrus aeneus*; citations in Hughes 1999). Hughes (1999) indicated it is unlikely that a cowbird chick would fledge successfully and that cowbirds usually select hosts with a longer nestling period than its own nestlings and cuckoos have a shorter nestling period (7-9 days). Overall, cowbird parasitism is probably not a significant issue for this species. Note: The yellow-billed cuckoo is an intraspecific brood parasite, occasionally laying eggs in nests of conspecifics (Hughes 1999).	0

Literature Cited

Anders, A.D., and E. Post. 2006. Distribution-wide effects of climate on population densities of a declining migratory bird. Journal of Animal Ecology 75:221-227.

Bagne, K. E., M.M. Friggens, and D.M. Finch. 2011. A system for assessing vulnerability of species (SAVS) to climate change. Gen. Tech. Rep. RMRS-GTR-257. Fort Collins, CO: U.S. Department of Agriculture, Forest Service, Rocky Mountain Research Station. 28 p.

Corman, T.E., and C. Wise-Gervais, eds. 2005. The Arizona Breeding Bird Atlas. Albuquerque, NM: University of New Mexico Press.

Dawson, A., V.M. King, G.E. Bentley, and G.F. Ball. 2001. Photoperiodic control of seasonality in birds. Journal of Biological Rhythms 16:365-380.

Emanuel, K. 2005. Increasing destructiveness of tropical cyclones over the past 30 years. Nature 436:686-688.

Franzreb, K.E., and S.A. Laymon. 1993. A reassessment of the taxonomic status of the yellow-billed cuckoo. Western Birds 24:17-28.

Hamilton III, W. J. and M. E. Hamilton. 1965. Breeding characteristics of yellow-billed cuckoos in Arizona. Proceedings of the California Academy of Sciences 32:405-432.

Hughes, J.M. 1999. Yellow-billed Cuckoo (*Coccyzus americanus*). In: Poole, A., ed. The birds of North America online. Ithaca, NY: Cornell Lab of Ornithology. Available: http://bna.birds.cornell.edu/bna/species/418.

Magrin, G., C. Gay García, D. Cruz Choque, J.C. Giménez, A.R. Moreno, G.J. Nagy, C. Nobre, and A. Villamizar. 2007: Latin America. In: Parry, M.L., O.F. Canziani, J.P. Palutikof, P.J. van der Linden, and C.E. Hanson, Eds. Climate Change 2007: Impacts, Adaptation and Vulnerability. Contribution of Working Group II to the Fourth Assessment Report of the Intergovernmental Panel on Climate Change. Cambridge, United Kingdom: Cambridge University Press: 581-615.

Martin, T.E. 1987. Food as a limit on breeding birds: a life-history perspective. Annual Review of Ecology and Systematics 18:453-487.

Nolan, V., and C.F. Thompson. 1975. The occurrence and significance of anomalous reproductive activities in two North American non-parasitic cuckoos *Coccyzus sp.* Ibis 117:496-503.

U.S. Fish and Wildlife Service [USFWS]. 2001. 12-month finding for a petition to list the yellow-billed cuckoo (*Coccyzus americanus*) in the western continental United States. Federal Register 66:38611-38626.

U.S. Forest Service [USFS]. 2009. Draft Coronado National Forest ecological sustainability report. Tucson, AZ: U.S. Department of Agriculture, Forest Service. Available: http://www fs fed.us/r3/coronado/plan-revision/documents/final/cnf-ecological-sustainability-report-final-022009.pdf.

Wingfield, J.C. 2008. Comparative endocrinology, environment, and global change. General and Comparative Endocrinology 157:207-216.

Habitat: Elegant trogon (*Trogon elegans*)			
Trait/Quality	Question	Background info. & explanation of score	Points
1. Area and distribution: *breeding*	Is the area or location of the associated vegetation type used for breeding activities by this species expected to change?	U.S. breeding distribution is limited to small areas in southern Arizona and New Mexico (observations in Texas thought to be non-breeding or post-breeding birds; Kunzmann and others 1998). Most or all of the U.S. population is migratory (Kunzmann and others 1998). In Arizona, reported to breed regularly in Atascosa, Chiricahua, Huachuca, and Santa Rita Mountain ranges (Taylor 1994 as cited in Kunzmann and others 1998). In United States, breeding habitat includes high-elevation pine and pine-oak forests and Arizona sycamore riparian woodland (Hall 1996 as cited in Kunzmann and others 1998). At the home range level, "trogons acted as a pine-oak woodland upland species, and used riparian areas with sycamore" while nesting primarily in large sycamores and, to a lesser extent, in oak trees (Kunzmann and others 1998). In Arizona, abundance is greatest in canyons with the greatest cover of "sycamore riparian and edge vegetation, pinyon pine riparian and edge vegetation, juniper riparian, pine riparian, and juniper upland vegetation" (Hall 1996 as cited in Kunzmann and others 1998). Canyons occupied by trogons in Arizona have water flow substantial enough to support sycamore trees; prior work by Taylor (multiple references in Kunzmann and others 1998) suggested that canyons with perennial water are used preferentially, although Hall (1996) found no relationship between abundance and type of water flow (perennial, intermittent, and ephemeral). In southwestern Arizona mountains, most nests are within 300 m of perennial water (multiple references in Kunzmann and others 1998). This species occurs, or potential habitat exists, on 5 of the EMAs on CNF: Peloncillo, Chiricahua, Tumacacori, Santa Rita, and Huachuca	2

Habitat: Elegant trogon (*Trogon elegans*)			
Trait/Quality	**Question**	**Background info. & explanation of score**	**Points**
		(USFS 2009). Projections of suitable climate for vegetation communities forest-wide (Chapter 1) predicted declines in suitable climate for all plant community types, with the exception of increases of suitable climate for semi-desert grassland and small increases in Sonoran desert scrub (present in small amounts on the CNF). Riparian habitats predicted to decline due to decreased stream flows, on average, and increased aridity. Increased risk of fire is also predicted, which is expected to reduce riparian habitats.	
2. Area and distribution: *non-breeding*	Is the area or location of the associated vegetation type used for non-breeding activities by this species expected to change?	Some winter observations of this species in Arizona (Kunzmann and others 1998), but generally, winter range (of migrants and year-round residents) is in Mexico and Central America (including Guatemala, Honduras, and El Salvador), where year-round residents occupy the same kinds of habitats in winter as for breeding. Therefore, we assumed that wintering habitats for migrants that breed in the United States are the same as winter habitats for year-round residents. In Mexico, this habitat ranges from lowlands, foothills, and mountains; more specifically, this includes arid to semi-arid woodland and thorn forest to high-elevation pine and pine-oak forests (Howell and Webb 1995 as cited in Kunzmann and others 1998). Specific projections for change in vegetation in Mexico and Central America were not found. Increases in temperature have been projected for Central America (Magrin and others 2007: Fig. 13.1, Table 13.4). Observed trends in rainfall for Central America vary from increases in some areas to decreases in other areas (Magrin and others 2007: Fig. 13.1) Given the broad geographic scale over which this species potentially occurs in winter (Mexico and Central America) and the absence of specific vegetation projections for those areas, it is difficult to predict how habitat will respond. We took the conservative approach by assuming that increases in temperature will lead to conversion of semi-arid regions to arid, and that reduced high-elevation pine and pine-oak forests will reduce wintering habitat for this species.	2
3. Habitat components: *breeding*	Are specific habitat components required for breeding expected to change?	Commonly nests in abandoned woodpecker (e.g., northern flicker) cavities (Kunzmann and others 1998). Does not excavate its own cavities so it depends on those created by other species. Old reports of this species nesting in banks but Kunzmann and others (1998) found no reliable evidence to support this. Elegant trogon pairs try out different cavities at start of season (Kunzmann and others 1998), indicating that pairs are discriminating (criteria for discrimination unreported). In Arizona, nests may be found in silverleaf oak, Arizona white oak, Apache pine, Chihuahuan pine, and sycamore. Hakes (1983 as cited in Kunzmann and others 1998) showed that this species did not use any of 30 nest boxes placed in the Huachuca Mountains over 4 years. Riparian trees suitable for cavities are expected to decline (see Habitat, Question 1 above) due to projected increase in wildfires.	1
4. Habitat components: *non-breeding*	Are specific habitat components required for survival during non-breeding periods expected to change?	No habitat components for non-breeding season identified in Kunzmann and others (1998).	0
5. Habitat quality and	Are features of the habitat associated	Higher nest success was observed in larger-diameter trees and in trees with taller vegetation south of the nest tree (Hall 1996 as cited	1

Habitat: Elegant trogon (*Trogon elegans*)

Trait/Quality	Question	Background info. & explanation of score	Points
reproduction	with better reproductive success expected to change?	in Kunzmann and others 1998); no relationship was found between nest success and plant species surrounding the nest, nor the average distance to campgrounds, buildings, trails, and water, nor the density of trogons in the area. Large trees are expected to be less abundant in the future due to reduced precipitation and increased fires.	
6. Habitat quality and survival	Are features of the habitat associated with better survival expected to change?	No information in Kunzmann and others (1998).	0
7. Ability to colonize new areas	What is this species' capacity and tendency to disperse?	Kunzmann and others (1998) found no data on initial dispersal from natal site. Both sexes are highly mobile given that populations in Arizona are migratory. We considered birds to be very mobile due to their capacity for flight and, thus, overall able to colonize new areas.	-1
8. Migratory or transitional habitats	Does this species require additional habitats during migration that are separated from breeding and non-breeding habitats?	This species migrates long distances. Individuals breeding in Arizona winter in Mexico and Central America.	1

Physiology: Elegant trogon (*Trogon elegans*)

Trait/Quality	Question	Background info. & explanation of score	Points
1. Physiological thresholds	Are physiological thresholds related to temperature or moisture expected to change?	Unknown whether this species needs drinking water; has been observed drinking, but paucity of observations suggests that water is not a requirement (Kunzmann and others 1998). Need for bathing unknown. Arizona is the northern limit of this species' range. The Trogonidae family is not tolerant of cold temperatures (Kunzmann and others 1998). When migrant individuals arrive in Arizona to breed, mountain ranges used by this species are nearly free of snow (Kunzmann and others 1998). The elegant trogon's northern distribution may be limited due to its sensitivity to cold temperatures (Marshall 1957 as cited in Kunzmann and others 1998). Low resting metabolic rate of a related species (*Trogon rufus*; black-throated trogon) relative to other bird families may reflect low ability to generate heat (Bennett and Harvey 1987 as cited in Kunzmann and others 1998); elegant trogon may have similar physiology. With the exception of cases of extreme heat rises, presumably could tolerate increases of several degrees C. Shaded habitat might reduce effects of solar radiation on rise in body temperature, although shade from trees expected to decline with time.	0
2. Sex ratio	Is sex ratio determined by temperature?	No. Temperature-dependent sex determination is mainly observed in reptiles and fish (Manolakou and others 2006).	0
3. Exposure to extreme weather conditions	Are extreme weather or disturbance events that result in direct mortality or	Increase in frequency of heat waves is predicted for southwestern United States. Overall, not clear to what extent timing and intensity of heat waves will effect survival and reproduction. We considered it unlikely that heat waves would cause widespread mortality for this	0

Physiology: Elegant trogon (*Trogon elegans*)

Trait/Quality	Question	Background info. & explanation of score	Points
	reproductive failure expected to change?	species. Hurricane intensity is expected to increase under global climate change, but frequency predictions are inconsistent (Emanuel 2005); frequency increase likely more detrimental overall to migrating populations than intensity since hurricane-level winds already detrimental to migrants. See also Physiology, Question 1. No information in Kunzmann and others (1998) on significant mortality or failed reproduction due to weather.	
4. Limitations to active period	Are projected temperature or precipitation regimes that influence activity period of species expected to change?	See Physiology, Question 1. With the exception of cases of extreme heat rises, seems unlikely for seasonal or daily active periods to be restricted to the point of significantly reducing survival.	0
5. Metabolic inhibition	Does this species possess an ability to reduce metabolic energy or water requirements?	No reports of torpor in Kunzmann and others (1998). No citations of torpor for elegant trogon in Web of Science database. We assumed that this species does not use torpor.	1
6. Survival during resource limitation	Does this species have lower energy requirements or possess the capacity to store energy or water in the long term?	Food storage not known to occur (Kunzmann and others (1998).	1
7. Variable life history	Does this species have alternative life history strategies to cope with variable resources or climate conditions?	No variable life history strategies.	0
8. Reproduction in variable environments	Can this species outlive periods where reproduction is limited?	Kunzmann and others (1998) found no data on longevity. Based on data for other bird species of this size, not expected to be longer than a few years. Periods of extreme reductions in rainfall may last 5 years. If these conditions reduce food resources to the point that birds have insufficient food for breeding, most of the population would not survive longer than the period(s) of limited reproduction.	1

Phenology: Elegant trogon (*Trogon elegans*)

Trait/Quality	Question	Background info. & explanation of score	Points
1. Cues	Does this species use temperature or moisture cues to initiate activities related to fecundity or survival?	This species is a predictable breeder, meaning its breeding season occurs at the same time each year (i.e., spring). In predictable breeders, photoperiod is the predominant proximate factor leading to gonadal changes required for reproduction (Dawson and others 2001). On the other hand, nesting in individuals of this species in Alamos, Mexico, reported to be timed with summer rainy season (Short 1974 as cited in Kunzmann and others 1998), so it is possible that this species uses moisture as a cue.	1
2. Event timing	Are activities related to species' fecundity or survival tied to	Food abundance in spring is an important factor driving fecundity in bird species breeding in temperate regions (review by Martin 1987). Typically, increases in insect abundance (a critical resource) occur in	1

Phenology: Elegant trogon (*Trogon elegans*)

Trait/Quality	Question	Background info. & explanation of score	Points
	discrete events that are expected to change?	spring; changes in the timing of precipitation and increases in temperature have the potential to alter the timing of insect availability and abundance and, hence, fecundity. In Arizona, breeding initiation dates reported variable among pairs in a 2-year study, with nests begun in May, June, and July (Kunzmann and others 1998).	
3. Mismatch potential	What is the separation in time or space between cues that initiate activities and discrete events that provide critical resources?	Migrant species that occurs in the CNF in the breeding season. Critical resources for breeding occur far from where individuals over-winter; thus, individuals have no direct information about resource abundance on the breeding grounds when they initiate migration from their wintering grounds.	1
4. Resilience to timing mismatches during breeding	Does this species employ strategies or have traits that increase the likelihood of reproduction co-occurring with important events?	In Arizona, most pairs rear one brood per season (Kunzmann and others 1998).	1

Biotic interactions: Elegant trogon (*Trogon elegans*)

Trait/Quality	Question	Background info. & explanation of score	Points
1. Food resources	Are important food resources for this species expected to change?	Main foods are fruit, grasshoppers, and other insects (Kunzmann and others 1998). Fruits include cherries (in orchards), canyon grapes, tropical figs, southwestern chokecherry, and birchleaf buckthorn. Insects include caterpillars, adult and larval butterflies and moths, and species of various other adult and larval insect families (Kunzmann and others 1998). In Arizona, this species mainly forages in oak trees and fruit-bearing plants, when available (Taylor 1994 as cited in Kunzmann and others 1998).	0
2. Predators	Are important predator populations expected to change?	Few data are available on predation (Kunzmann and others 1998). The following observations of predation on elegant trogons were reported by Taylor (1994 as cited in Kunzmann and others 1998): Cooper's Hawk attack on breeding adults, Mexican jay attack on fledglings, and sulphur-bellied flycatchers attack on nestlings. Adult trogons have been observed mobbing great horned owls, and a Sonoran gopher snake moving toward a nest. Breeding adults attacked Mexican fox squirrels and Arizona gray squirrels in Arizona (Taylor 1994 as cited in Kunzmann and others 1998), which may suggest these species are predators (as well as nest cavity predators).	0
3. Symbionts	Are populations of symbiotic species expected to change?	Elegant trogons are obligate secondary cavity nesters, meaning that they do not excavate cavities in trees. We considered this species vulnerable to climate change due to the potential for reduced availability of nest cavities. This species is large enough that natural cavities with large openings must be located or it must use cavities created by woodpeckers (which are expected to be vulnerable to climate change).	1
4. Disease	Is prevalence of diseases known to cause widespread	Kunzmann and others (1998) found no data on diseases, although the authors cited reports on the species carrying a biting lice parasite (*Trogonirmus elegans*; Malcomson 1960). Unidentified nestling	0

Trait/Quality	Question	Background info. & explanation of score	Points
	mortality or reproductive failure in this species expected to change?	parasites were reported by Taylor (1994 as cited in Kunzmamm and others 1998).	
5. Competitors	Are populations of important competing species expected to change?	Intra-specific competition observed in apparent competition for nest cavities (Kunzmann and others 1998). Both males and females defend nest cavities against other species of primary and secondary cavity nesters (e.g., sulphur-bellied flycatcher, northern flicker, eared quetzal, screech-owls). Northern flickers typically win control of contested trogon cavities, and whiskered screech-owls win about 10% of trogon cavities (Taylor 1994 as cited in Kunzmann and others 1998). Breeding adults attacked Mexican fox squirrels and Arizona gray squirrels in Arizona. At least some of these competitor species are expected to be vulnerable to climate change.	-1
		Note: Contrast with Biotic Interactions, Question 3 above, however, where reduction in symbionts results in vulnerability.	
		Brood parasitism not documented (Kunzmann and others 1998).	

Literature Cited

Dawson, A., V.M. King, G.E. Bentley, G.F. Ball. 2001. Photoperiodic control of seasonality in birds. Journal of Biological Rhythms 16:365-380.

Emanuel, K. 2005. Increasing destructiveness of tropical cyclones over the past 30 years. Nature 436:686-688.

Kunzmann, M.R., L.S. Hall, and R.R. Johnson. 1998. Elegant Trogon (Trogon elegans). In: Poole, A., and F. Gill, Eds. The Birds of North America, No. 357. Philadelphia, PA: The Birds of North America, Inc.

Magrin, G., C. Gay García, D. Cruz Choque, J.C. Giménez, A.R. Moreno, G.J. Nagy, C. Nobre, and A. Villamizar. 2007. Latin America. In: Parry, M.L., O.F. Canziani, J.P. Palutikof, P.J. van der Linden, and C.E. Hanson, Eds. Climate Change 2007: Impacts, Adaptation and Vulnerability. Contribution of Working Group II to the Fourth Assessment Report of the Intergovernmental Panel on Climate Change, Cambridge, United Kingdom: Cambridge University Press: 581-615.

Martin, T.E. 1987. Food as a limit on breeding birds: a life-history perspective. Annual Review of Ecology and Systematics 18:453-487.

U.S. Forest Service [USFS]. 2009. Draft Coronado National Forest ecological sustainability report. Tucson, AZ: U.S. Department of Agriculture, Forest Service. Available: http://www.fs.fed.us/r3/coronado/plan-revision/documents/final/cnf-ecological-sustainability-report-final-022009.pdf.

Habitat: Northern buff-breasted flycatcher (*Empidonax fulvifrons pygmaeus*)			
Trait/Quality	**Question**	**Background info. & explanation of score**	**Points**
1. Area and distribution: *breeding*	Is the area or location of the associated vegetation type used for breeding activities by this species expected to change?	Distribution in the United States is southeast Arizona during the breeding season. Outside of the United States, occurs in Mexico and Central America. Very rare in the United States; only 20-40 individuals known annually in the 1980s (Bowers and Dunning 1994). A range-wide survey in 2000 in Arizona estimated the population at 74 individuals (Conway and Kirkpatrick 2007). Two possible records from 1970s in New Mexico (Witzeman and others 1976 as cited in Bowers and Dunning 1994). This is the only sub-species of buff-breasted flycatcher reported to occur in the United States (Bowers and Dunning 1994). Throughout its range, prefers open pine-oak woodlands and montane riparian forests (Bowers and Dunning 1994). Occurs in wide mountain canyons with open growth of pines and/or oaks usually with understory of grasses and small trees. Also uses burned forest with clusters of live pines. Often occurs near riparian areas (Bowers and Dunning 1994). Elevations of breeding sites in Arizona range 1950-2850 m (Bent 1942 as cited in Bowers and Dunning 1994). In Arizona, usually nests in conifer (Bowers and Dunning 1994). Bowers and Dunning (1994) reported the range in the United States as "higher elevations of Huachuca, Chiricahua, Santa Rita, and Santa Catalina Mountains...in past, also known from Rincon, Patagonia, and Pajarito Mountains." During ABBA surveys, found to nest commonly only in specific drainages of the Chiricahua and Huachuca Mountains; some observations were also made in Santa Rita, Rincon, and Santa Catalina Mountains where northern buff-breasted flycatchers may breed on occasion (Corman and Wise-Gervais 2005). Kirkpatrick and others (2007) observed northern buff-breasted flycatchers in the Rincon Mountains in 2000, which was the first documented record there since 1911. Northern buff-breasted flycatchers, or its potential habitat, occur on the following 5 EMAs: Peloncillo, Chiricahua, Santa Rita, Huachuca, Santa Catalina (USFS 2009). Projections of suitable climate for vegetation communities (Chapter 1) predicted declines in suitable conditions for Madrean forest and woodland and Madrean conifer forest and increases in suitable conditions for semi-desert grassland and, to a lesser extent, Sonoran desert scrub. Bowers and Dunning (1994) reported that fire may open new habitat by clearing dense undergrowth that inhibits foraging. They cited a case of a fire in 1976 in the Huachuca Mountains (Carr Canyon) that cleared several hundred acres but left intact small pockets of live trees. Prior to the burn, 1-2 pairs of northern buff-breasted flycatcher were known in this area; by 1980, at least 5 adults were recorded and 9 adults by 1983. Martin and Morrison (1999) indicated that prescribed burning may improve habitat suitability by reducing oak understory, but also indicated that changes in vegetation from fire suppression and grazing may not be completely responsible for the rarity of this species in Arizona, as some apparently suitable habitat remains unoccupied. Conway and Kirkpatrick (2007) found presence of individuals was especially associated with areas containing evidence of high-severity surface fire. At the same time, the authors noted the absence of detections in 5 canyons that had recently burned. Fires that are not stand-replacing but that reduce shrubs may increase habitat for this species. However, fires in the future are likely to be larger and of greater intensity. There was an increase in the area over which stand-replacing fires occurred between 1984 and 2006 in	2

Trait/Quality	Question	Background info. & explanation of score	Points
		portions of California and Nevada, as well as an increase in mean and maximum fire size and the area burned annually (Miller et. al. 2009). The authors indicated that the patterns appeared to be related to hotter air temperatures and reduced precipitation and were not limited by forest fuels. Overall, we expected that projected reductions in forested habitats (e.g., increased aridity, drought, and high intensity fires) will reduce breeding habitat.	
2. Area and distribution: *non-breeding*	Is the area or location of the associated vegetation type used for non-breeding activities by this species expected to change?	Little is known about the wintering ecology (Bowers and Dunning 1994). Reported to occur at elevations lower than breeding habitat in winter; some individuals in Sonora move from pine-oak woodland to low-elevation canyons in thorn scrub near riparian areas (Bowers and Dunning 1994). During migration, has been reported in lowland communities, especially sycamore, cottonwood, and willow riparian forests (see references in Bowers and Dunning 1994). Specific projections for change in vegetation in Mexico and Central America were not found. Increases in temperature have been projected for Central America (Magrin and others 2007: Fig. 13.1, Table 13.4). In southern Mexico from 1960-2004, average and maximum temperatures increased and were generally unrelated to ENSO or PDO (Peralta-Hernandez and others 2009). In this same study, a slight non-statistically significant decrease in precipitation was observed. Observed trends in rainfall for Central America vary from increases in some areas to decreases in other areas (Magrin and others 2007: Fig. 13.1) Given the broad geographic scale over which northern buff-breasted flycatchers potentially occurs in winter (Mexico and Central America) and the absence of specific vegetation projections for those areas, it is difficult to predict how habitat will respond. We assumed that projected increases in temperature and possible reductions in precipitation would lead to conversion of semi-arid regions to arid and that reduced riparian areas would lead to reduced wintering habitat.	2
3. Habitat components: *breeding*	Are specific habitat components required for breeding expected to change?	In Arizona, observed nesting in Chihuahuan pine, ponderosa pine, Arizona sycamore, Arizona white oak, and Douglas-fir; a few nests found in Arizona walnut, big-toothed maple, and alligator juniper (Bowers and Dunning 1994). Percent cover of Chihuahuan pine and Apache pine >10 m tall was the most important variable distinguishing occupied areas from unoccupied areas (Martin and Morrison 1999). Trees expected to decline in abundance.	1
4. Habitat components: *non-breeding*	Are specific habitat components required for survival during non-breeding periods expected to change?	No information about possible habitat components on wintering range.	0
5. Habitat quality and reproduction	Are features of the habitat associated with better reproductive success expected to change?	No information in Bowers and Dunning (1994). Martin and Morrison (1999) indicate that differences in habitat variables between successful and unsuccessful nests were not significant biologically.	0
6. Habitat quality and survival	Are features of the habitat associated with better survival expected to change?	No information in Bowers and Dunning (1994).	0

Habitat: Northern buff-breasted flycatcher (*Empidonax fulvifrons pygmaeus*)

Trait/Quality	Question	Background info. & explanation of score	Points
7. Ability to colonize new areas	What is this species' capacity and tendency to disperse?	Both sexes are highly mobile given that populations in Arizona are migratory. We consider birds to be very mobile due to their capacity for flight and, thus, overall able to colonize new areas.	-1
8. Migratory or transitional habitats	Does this species require additional habitats during migration that are separated from breeding and non-breeding habitats?	Breeds in Arizona but winters in Mexico; little is known about wintering ecology (Bowers and Dunning 1994). Arrives in breeding areas in Arizona between late March and early April (Bowers and Dunning 1994). Individuals that breed in Arizona and northern Sonora, Mexico, move south at least as far as central or southern Sonora in winter (Bowers and Dunning 1994).	1

Physiology: Northern buff-breasted flycatcher (*Empidonax fulvifrons pygmaeus*)

Trait/Quality	Question	Background info. & explanation of score	Points
1. Physiological thresholds	Are limiting physiological conditions expected to change?	No observations of drinking reported (Bowers and Dunning 1994). Metabolism and temperature regulation have not been examined (Bowers and Dunning 1994). Arizona is the northern range limit; considered to be more common in Mexico (Bowers and Dunning 1994). This may suggest that individuals are more tolerant of warm temperatures compared to species whose southern range limit is Arizona. With the exception of cases of extreme heat rises, presumably could tolerate increases of a few degrees C. Shaded habitat would allow escape of direct effects of solar radiation on rise in body temperature, although shade from trees expected to decline with time.	0
2. Sex ratio	Is sex ratio determined by temperature?	No. Temperature-dependent sex determination is mainly observed in reptiles and fish (Manolakou and others 2006).	0
3. Exposure to extreme weather conditions	Are extreme weather or disturbance events that result in direct mortality or reproductive failure expected to change?	Increase in frequency of heat waves is predicted for southwestern United States. Overall, not clear to what extent timing and intensity of heat waves will effect survival and reproduction. We considered it unlikely that heat waves would cause widespread mortality. Hurricane intensity is expected to increase under global climate change, but hurricane frequency predictions are inconsistent (Emanuel 2005); frequency increase likely more detrimental overall to migrating populations than intensity since hurricane-level winds already detrimental to migrants. See also Physiology, Question 1. No information in Bowers and Dunning (1994) on significant mortality or failed reproduction due to weather, although authors indicated little information on causes of mortality.	0
4. Limitations to active period	Are projected temperature or precipitation regimes that influence activity period of species expected to change?	See Physiology, Question 1. With the exception of cases of extreme heat rises, seems unlikely for seasonal or daily active periods to be restricted to the point of significantly reduced survival.	0
5. Metabolic inhibition	Does this species possess an ability to reduce metabolic energy or water requirements?	Little information on temperature regulation or metabolism (Bowers and Dunning 1994). No information to suggest that torpor is used (no citations in Web of Science database).	1

Physiology: Northern buff-breasted flycatcher (*Empidonax fulvifrons pygmaeus*)			
Trait/Quality	Question	Background info. & explanation of score	Points
6. Survival during resource limitation	Does this species have lower energy requirements or possess the capacity to store energy or water in the long term?	Not known to store food (Bowers and Dunning 1994).	1
7. Variable life history	Does this species have alternative life history strategies to cope with variable resources or climate conditions?	No variable life history strategies.	0
8. Reproduction in variable environments	Can this species outlive periods where reproduction is limited?	No information on lifespan or survivorship; only 25 birds banded according to U.S. Bird Banding Laboratory (Bowers and Dunning 1994). In Arizona, 5 individuals re-sighted after banding, making them a minimum of 2 years old; none re-sighted in subsequent years (Bowers and Dunning 1994). Another flycatcher species, the willow flycatcher (*Empidonax trailii*), has an average life span of 1 year (Sedgwick 2000). Longevity record (i.e., longest-lived bird recorded) for the western flycatcher (*E. difficilis*) is 6 years based on 30 recoveries from birds banded through 1981 (Clapp and others 1983 as cited in Lowther 2000). Periods of extreme reductions in rainfall may last 5 years. If these conditions reduce food resources to the point that birds have insufficient food for breeding, most of the population would not survive longer than the periods of limited reproduction.	1

Phenology: Northern buff-breasted flycatcher (*Empidonax fulvifrons pygmaeus*)			
Trait/Quality	Question	Background info. & explanation of score	Points
1. Cues	Does this species use temperature or moisture cues to initiate activities related to fecundity or survival?	Northern buff-breasted flycatchers are predictable breeders, meaning the breeding season occurs at the same time each year (i.e., spring). In predictable breeders, photoperiod is the predominant proximate factor leading to gonadal changes required for reproduction (Dawson and others 2001). It should be noted that, in general, birds also use local predictive information, such as temperature, availability of food, and rainfall, to make short-term adjustments to reproductive timing (Wingfield 2008), although this short-term adjustment is not addressed by this question (see Bagne and others 2011).	0
2. Event timing	Are activities related to species' fecundity or survival tied to discrete events that are expected to change?	Food abundance in spring is an important factor driving fecundity in bird species breeding in temperate regions (review by Martin 1987). Typically, increases in insect abundance (a critical resource) occur in spring; changes in the timing of precipitation and increases in temperature have the potential to alter the timing of insect availability and abundance and, hence, fecundity. In Arizona, most females lay eggs between early May and early August, but in some years, females have laid as early as late April (Corman and Wise-Gervais 2005).	1
3. Mismatch potential	What is the separation in time or space between cues that initiate activities and discrete events that provide critical resources?	Northern buff-breasted flycatchers are migrants that occur in the CNF in the breeding season. Critical resources for breeding occur far from where individuals over-winter; thus, individuals have no direct information about resource abundance on the breeding grounds when they initiate migration from their wintering grounds.	1

USDA Forest Service RMRS-GTR-273. 2012.

Phenology: Northern buff-breasted flycatcher (*Empidonax fulvifrons pygmaeus*)			
Trait/Quality	Question	Background info. & explanation of score	Points
4. Resilience to timing mismatches during breeding	Does this species employ strategies or have traits that increase the likelihood of reproduction co-occurring with important events?	Buff-breasted flycatchers typically rears a single brood (although will re-nest after nest failure; Bowers and Dunning 1994). Martin and Morrison (1999) observed 3 cases of second nesting attempts after pairs successfully reared a brood, although unclear if this is typical.	1

Biotic interactions: Northern buff-breasted flycatcher (*Empidonax fulvifrons pygmaeus*)			
Trait/Quality	Question	Background info. & explanation of score	Points
1. Food resources	Are important food resources for this species expected to change?	Consumes insects, mostly by sallying from a perch; also flies to ground to consume ants and other prey (Bowers and Dunning 1994).Contents of stomach of one individual from Arizona contained ants, wasps, true bugs (Hemiptera), beetles (Coleoptera), and grasshoppers (Cottam and Knappen 1939 as cited in Bowers and Dunning 1994). Large prey identified in bills of breeding Arizona adults: moth, damselfly, spider, cranefly, grasshopper, other insects (Bowers and Dunning 1994). Overall, consumes a variety of insect prey.	0
2. Predators	Are important predator populations expected to change?	Martin and Morrison (1999) found likely predation by jays (Steller's jay and/or Mexican jay) at 20 of 36 failed nests; authors indicated that 100% nest failure (15 nests) in Carr Canyon in 1995 might have been related to high numbers of jays from supplemental feeding at two nearby campgrounds. A variety of other predators is likely.	0
3. Symbionts	Are populations of symbiotic species expected to change?	No information found to suggest that important symbiotic relationships exist.	0
4. Disease	Is prevalence of diseases known to cause widespread mortality or reproductive failure in this species expected to change?	No information (Bowers and Dunning 1994).	0
5. Competitors	Are populations of important competing species expected to change?	Bowers and Dunning (1994) indicated one report of nest parasitism by a brown-headed cowbird followed by the buff-breasted flycatcher abandoning the nest (Bowers and Dunning 1984). Bowers and Dunning (1994) found no reports of this species feeding nestling or fledged cowbirds. Martin and Morrison (1999) found no cowbird eggs or nestlings in the 10 nests that they examined, nor did they find cowbird fledglings among 21 other broods, despite the two species of cowbirds being common in the study areas. Appears that the buff-breasted flycatcher may be an infrequent cowbird host.	0

Literature Cited

Bagne, K.E., M.M. Friggens, and D.M. Finch. 2011. A system for assessing vulnerability of species (SAVS) to climate change. Gen. Tech. Rep. RMRS-GTR-257. Fort Collins, CO: U.S. Department of Agriculture, Forest Service, Rocky Mountain Research Station. 28 p.

Bowers, R.K., Jr., and J.B. Dunning, Jr. 1994. Buff-breasted Flycatcher (*Empidonax fulvifrons*). In: Poole, A., ed. The birds of North America online. Ithaca, NY: Cornell Lab of Ornithology. Available: http://bna.birds.cornell.edu/bna/species/125.

Bowers, R.K., Jr., and J.B. Dunning, Jr. 1984. Nest parasitism by cowbirds on buff-breasted flycatchers, with comments on nest-site selection. Wilson Bulletin 96:718-719.

Conway, C.J., and C. Kirkpatrick. 2007. Effects of forest fire suppression on buff-breasted flycatchers. Journal of Wildlife Management 71:445-457.

Corman, T.E., and C. Wise-Gervais, ed. 2005. The Arizona Breeding Bird Atlas. Albuquerque, NM: University of New Mexico Press.

Dawson, A., V.M. King, G.E. Bentley, G.F. Ball. 2001. Photoperiodic control of seasonality in birds. Journal of Biological Rhythms 16:365-380.

Emanuel, K. 2005. Increasing destructiveness of tropical cyclones over the past 30 years. Nature 436:686-688.

Kirkpatrick, C., C.J. Conway, and D. LaRoche. 2007. Range expansion of the buff-breasted flycatcher (*Empidonax fulvifrons*) into the Rincon Mountains, Arizona. Southwestern Naturalist 52:149-152. Lowther, P.E. 2000. Pacific-slope Flycatcher (*Empidonax difficilis*). In: Poole, A., ed. The birds of North America online. Ithaca, NY: Cornell Lab of Ornithology. Available: http://bna.birds.cornell.edu/bna/species/556a.

Magrin, G., C. Gay García, D. Cruz Choque, J.C. Giménez, A.R. Moreno, G.J. Nagy, C. Nobre and A. Villamizar. 2007. Latin America. In: Parry, M.L., O.F. Canziani, J.P. Palutikof, P.J. van der Linden, and C.E. Hanson, eds. Climate Change 2007: Impacts, Adaptation and Vulnerability. Contribution of Working Group II to the Fourth Assessment Report of the Intergovernmental Panel on Climate Change. Cambridge, United Kingdom: Cambridge University Press: 581-615.

Martin, T.E. 1987. Food as a limit on breeding birds: A life-history perspective. Annual Review of Ecology and Systematics 18:453-487.

Martin, J.A., and M.L. Morrison. 1999. Distribution, abundance, and habitat characteristics of the buff-breasted flycatcher in Arizona. Condor 101:272-281.

Miller, J.D., H.D. Safford, M. Crimmins, and A.E. Thode. 2009. Quantitative evidence for increasing forest fire severity in the Sierra Nevada and southern Cascade Mountains, California and Nevada, USA. Ecosystems 12:16-32.

Peralta-Hernandez, A., R.C. Balling, Jr., and L.R. Barba-Martinez. 2009. Analysis of near-surface diurnal temperature variations and trends in southern Mexico. International Journal of Climatology 29:205-209.

Sedgwick, J.A. 2000. Willow Flycatcher (*Empidonax trailii*). In: Poole, A., and F. Gill, eds. The birds of North America, No. 533. Philadelphia, PA: The Birds of North America, Inc.

U.S. Forest Service [USFS]. 2009. Draft Coronado National Forest ecological sustainability report. Tucson, AZ: U.S. Department of Agriculture, Forest Service. Available: http://www fs fed.us/r3/coronado/plan-revision/documents/final/cnf-ecological-sustainability-report-final-022009.pdf.

Wingfield, J.C. 2008. Comparative endocrinology, environment, and global change. General and Comparative Endocrinology 157:207-216.

Habitat: Mexican long-tongued bat (*Choeronycteris mexicana*)			
Trait/Quality	Question	Background info. & explanation of score	Points
1. Area and distribution: *breeding*	Is the area or location of the associated vegetation type used for breeding activities by this species expected to change?	Distribution of this species is from the southern portion of the Southwest (southern California, southern Arizona, and southwestern New Mexico) through Mexico (northern and central, including Baja) to Honduras and Guatemala (Jones and Carter 1976 as cited in Nowak 1994; Hall 1991 as cited in Arroyo-Cabrales and others 1987). Roosting and habitat needs of this species are poorly understood; fewer than 1500 individuals have been documented (Cryan and Bogan 2003). Observed mostly in arid habitats at 600-2400 m in elevation (Nowak 1994). Hoffmeister (1986) indicated that the species is found "in appropriate shelters in the foothills and above, on mountains that have trees in southeastern Arizona... from the lower edge of the oak zone through the pine-oak woodland to the pine-fir belt." Cryan and Bogan (2003) found this species in New Mexico and Arizona in Madrean	2

Habitat: Mexican long-tongued bat (*Choeronycteris mexicana*)			
Trait/Quality	**Question**	**Background info. & explanation of score**	**Points**
		evergreen woodlands and semi-desert grasslands where species of *Agave* were present; occupied sites were within 1 km of streams.	
		Roosts in caves, mine tunnels, and buildings (Nowak 1994; Arroyo-Cabrales 1987). Hoffmeister (1986) reported that they are found in mine tunnels, caves, rock fissures, and, rarely, in buildings. Females and males roost together, although when young are born, the two sexes may separate (Hoffmeister 1986).	
		This species occurs, or potential habitat exists, on 8 of the 12 EMAs on CNF: Peloncillo, Chiricahua, Dragoon, Tumacacori, Santa Rita, Huachuca, Whetstone, and Santa Catalina (USFS 2009). Projections of suitable climate for vegetation communities forest wide (Chapter 1) predicted declines in suitable climate for all plant community types, with the exception of increases of suitable climate for semi-desert grassland and small increases in Sonoran desert scrub (present in small amounts on the CNF).	
		Projected reductions in woodlands and forested habitats are expected to reduce breeding habitat for this species.	
2. Area and distribution: *non-breeding*	Is the area or location of the associated vegetation type used for non-breeding activities by this species expected to change?	Colonies in southern Arizona thought to migrate to Mexico in winter based on indirect evidence (Nowak 1994). In Mexico, has been collected in a variety of habits, including arid thorn scrub, tropical deciduous forest, and mixed oak-conifer forest (see references in Arroyo-Cabrales and others 1987). We assumed that projected reductions in woodlands and forested habitats for the Southwest likely hold true for Mexico as well, which would mean reduced wintering habitat for this species.	2
3. Habitat components: *breeding*	Are specific habitat components required for breeding expected to change?	Given where this species roosts (Hoffmeister 1986), it does not face the loss of roost sites from vegetation mortality that threatens other bat species. Nectarivorous and frugivorous bats (as is this species) obtain much of their water from food (Hayes and Loeb 2007), so unclear if this species depends on drinking water.	0
4. Habitat components: *non-breeding*	Are specific habitat components required for survival during non-breeding periods expected to change?	See Habitat Question 3.	0
5. Habitat quality and reproduction	Are features of the habitat associated with better reproductive success expected to change?	No information found.	0
6. Habitat quality and survival	Are features of the habitat associated with better survival expected to change?	No information found.	0
7. Ability to colonize new areas	What is this species' capacity and tendency to disperse?	We considered bats to be very mobile due to their capacity for flight and, thus, overall able to colonize new areas. Furthermore, individuals that breed in Arizona are believed to migrate.	-1

Habitat: Mexican long-tongued bat (*Choeronycteris mexicana*)

Trait/Quality	Question	Background info. & explanation of score	Points
8. Migratory or transitional habitats	Does this species require additional habitats during migration that are separated from breeding and non-breeding habitats?	Colonies in southern Arizona are thought to migrate to Mexico in winter based on indirect evidence (Nowak 1994).	1

Physiology: Mexican long-tongued bat (*Choeronycteris mexicana*)

Trait/Quality	Question	Background info. & explanation of score	Points
1. Physiological thresholds	Are limiting physiological conditions expected to change?	Nocturnal forager, so not active during hottest part of day. In a review of the upper critical temperatures for 50 species of bats, the maximum was 41.0 °C and mean was 36.26 °C (Speakman and Thomas 2003); upper critical temperature is the ambient temperature above which an animal's body temperature will increase unless it pants or sweats. In the case of three species of bats roosting in a California barn in summer (*Myotis yumanensis*, *Antrozous pallidus*, and *Tadarida brasiliensis*), when ambient temperature approached 40 °C (104 °F), spacing between individuals tended to increase and most individuals moved to cooler parts of the loft though some did not (Licht and Leitner 1967). Overall, we assumed that temperature would not exceed thresholds. Standing water is expected to become less available, but this is covered in Habitat section.	0
2. Sex ratio	Is sex ratio determined by temperature?	No. Temperature-dependent sex determination is mainly observed in reptiles and fish (Manolakou et al. 2006).	0
3. Exposure to extreme weather conditions	Are extreme weather or disturbance events that result in direct mortality or reproductive failure expected to change?	Increase in frequency of heat waves is predicted for southwestern United States. Overall, not clear to what extent timing and intensity of heat waves will effect survival and reproduction. We considered it unlikely that heat waves would cause widespread mortality for this species. Hurricane intensity is expected to increase under global climate change, but hurricane frequency predictions are inconsistent (Emanuel 2005); frequency increase likely more detrimental overall to migrating populations than intensity (since hurricane-level winds are already detrimental to migrants). See also Physiology, Question 1.	0
4. Limitations to active period	Are projected temperature or precipitation regimes that influence activity period of species expected to change?	Nighttime forager, so avoids being active in hottest part of day; increase in temperatures not likely to reduce foraging time significantly.	0
5. Metabolic inhibition	Does this species possess an ability to reduce metabolic energy or water requirements?	Little information on this species. According to Fleming (1988), no plant-visiting bat is known to hibernate. Another phyllostomid bat (*Carollia perspicillata*) studied in Costa Rica was observed to exhibit daily depression of body temperature (Audet and Thomas 1997); the authors concluded that "hypothermia is a thermoregulatory strategy that allows phyllostomid bats to adjust metabolic rate to feeding success and the level of fat stores". There is some thought that frugivorous bats	-1

USDA Forest Service RMRS-GTR-273. 2012.

Physiology: Mexican long-tongued bat (*Choeronycteris mexicana*)			
Trait/Quality	**Question**	**Background info. & explanation of score**	**Points**
		would not normally use torpor due to the relatively constant food supply in the tropics (McNab 1969 as cited in Audet and Thomas 1997), but depressed body temperature has been observed in some species (Studier and Wilson 1970 as cited in Audet and Thomas 1997).	
6. Survival during resource limitation	Does this species have lower energy requirements or possess the capacity to store energy or water in the long term?	See Physiology, Question 5. We assumed that this species can utilize torpor (daily).	1
7. Variable life history	Does this species have alternative life history strategies to cope with variable resources or climate conditions?	No alternative strategies.	0
8. Reproduction in variable environments	Can this species outlive periods where reproduction is limited?	Bats have been recognized as having an unusual life history; although they are small, they are considered to live long lives (Barclay and Harder 2003). Mean lifespan for species of Family Phyllostomatidae (to which this species belongs) was calculated as 10.9 years (range 7-18), but little information indicating what species were included in this calculation (Barclay and Harder 2003). Litter size is one (Barbour and Davis 1969 as cited in Nowak 1994). Periods of extreme reductions in rainfall may last 5 years. If these conditions reduce resources to the point that bats have insufficient resources for breeding, but conditions recover after the 5 years, we considered it likely that sufficient numbers of individuals would survive long enough to breed once conditions improve.	-1

Phenology: Mexican long-tongued bat (*Choeronycteris mexicana*)			
Trait/Quality	**Question**	**Background info. & explanation of score**	**Points**
1. Cues	Does this species use temperature or moisture cues to initiate activities related to fecundity or survival?	Females are said to become pregnant in Mexico in early spring, and individuals who migrate give birth in June or July (Adams 2003). Temperature and moisture influence flowering, which is important to this species due to its use of nectar and fruit; but since the relationship to parturition would be indirect, this question was scored as "0."	0
2. Event timing	Are activities related to species' fecundity or survival tied to discrete events that are expected to change?	Pregnant females have been collected in the Southwest and Mexico in February, March, June, and September (Wilson 1979 as cited in Nowak 1994). Temperature and moisture influence flowering, which is important to this species due to its use of nectar and fruit. Other species of migratory glossophagine bats (e.g., *Leptonycteris*) are said to require a "nectar trail" (a continual supply of blooming plants), and local changes in environmental factors that affect flowering process could disrupt this process (Arita and Santos-del-Prado 1999).	1
3. Mismatch potential	What is the separation in time or space between cues that initiate activities and	Individuals giving birth in southern Arizona are thought to migrate to Mexico in winter based on indirect evidence (Nowak 1994). Food resources in Arizona where parturition occurs are thus located at a distant location from where the species initiates migration.	1

Phenology: Mexican long-tongued bat (*Choeronycteris mexicana*)

Trait/Quality	Question	Background info. & explanation of score	Points
	discrete events that provide critical resources?		
4. Resilience to timing mismatches during breeding	Does this species employ strategies or have traits that increase the likelihood of reproduction co-occurring with important events?	It appears that this species typically rears only one young per season in a single breeding cycle. Watkins and others (1971 as cited in Arroyo-Cabrales and others 1987) indicated the possibility of a second period of birth (based on a pregnant female being observed in Jalisco in September, but no other information in Arroyo-Cabrales and others (1987) to support this being a common occurrence. Hoffmeister (1986) indicated that young are born in the second half of June or early July. Females are said to become pregnant in Mexico in early spring (Adams 2003).	1

Biotic interactions: Mexican long-tongued bat (*Choeronycteris mexicana*)

Trait/Quality	Question	Background info. & explanation of score	Points
1. Food resources	Are important food resources for this species expected to change?	Some authors have regarded this species as an obligate pollen feeder (Alvarez and Gonzalez 1970 as cited in Arroyo-Cabrales and others 1987), but other evidence suggests this is not the case. Consumes fruit, pollen, nectar, and probably insects; thought to pollinate some plants (Gardner 1977a as cited in Arroyo-Cabrales and others 1987). Hoffmeister (1986) indicated that the food habits of this species are not well known and speculated that individuals may feed primarily on nectar and pollen in Arizona—primarily from *Agave* and *Fouquieria* spp. and other succulents. In central Mexico, forages on cactus (*Stenocereus stellatus*; Arias-Coyotl and others 2006). Less precipitation and increases in higher temperatures (and/or heat waves) may shorten the length of flowering season, which could negatively affect this species due to its apparent strong dependence on what appears to be relatively few species of plants.	1
2. Predators	Are important predator populations expected to change?	Little information. Known to be preyed upon by owls (Mones 1968 as cited in Arroyo-Cabrales and others 1987).	0
3. Symbionts	Are populations of symbiotic species expected to change?	Mutualistic relationships likely exist between this species and its food plants, but little is known about its role as a pollinator or seed disperser (Cryan and Bogan 2003). This species is reported to be one of three bats species that pollinates agaves (although other pollinators may exist; Arizaga and others 2000). The role of the food resources for this species is covered in Biotic Interactions, Question 1.	0
4. Disease	Is prevalence of diseases known to cause widespread mortality or reproductive failure in this species expected to change?	A host to mites (Webb and Loomis 1977 as cited in Arroyo-Cabrales and others 1987) and ticks (Mumford and Zimmerman 1962 as cited in Arroyo-Cabrales and others 1987). No information indicating significant mortality from disease.	0
5. Competitors	Are populations of important competing species expected to change?	Some species of bats roost with other species but this species generally does not (Goodwin 1946 as cited in Arroyo-Cabrales and others 1987). Little information available regarding competitors of this species or of competitive interactions affecting bats in general. An aggressive interaction was observed with a *Leptonycteris* species while foraging on cactus (*Stenocereus stellatus*; Arias-Coyotl and others 2006).	0

USDA Forest Service RMRS-GTR-273. 2012.

Literature Cited

Adams, R.A. 2003. Bats of the Rocky Mountain West. Boulder, CO: University of Colorado Press. 289 p.

Arita, H.T., and K. Santos-del-Prado. 1999. Conservation biology of nectar-feeding bats in Mexico. Journal of Mammalogy 80:31-41.

Arias-Coyotl, E., K.E. Stoner, and A. Casas. 2006. Effectiveness of bats as pollinators of *Stenocereus stellatus* (Cactaceae) in wild, managed in situ, and cultivated populations in La Mixteca Baja, central Mexico. American Journal of Botany 93:1675-1683.

Arizaga, S., E. Excurra, E. Peters, F. Ramirez de Arrellano, and E. Vega. 2000. Pollination ecology of *Agave macroacantha* (Agavaceae) in a Mexican tropical desert. II. The role of pollinators. American Journal of Botany 87:1011-1017.

Arroyo-Cabrales, J., R.R. Hollander, and J.K. Jones, Jr. 1987. *Choeronycteris mexicana*. Mammalian Species 291:1-5. American Society of Mammalogists.

Audet, D., and D.W. Thomas. 1997. Facultative hypothermia as a thermoregulatory strategy in the phyllostomid bats, *Carollia perspicillata* and *Sturnira lilium*. Journal of Comparative Physiology B 167:146-152.

Barclay, M.R., and L.D. Harder. 2003. Life histories of bats: Life in the slow lane. In: Kunz, T.H., and M.B. Fenton, eds. Bat Ecology. Chicago: University of Chicago Press: 209-253.

Cryan, P.M., and M.A. Bogan. 2003. Recurrence of Mexican long-tongued bats (*Choeronycteris mexicana*) at historical sites in Arizona and New Mexico. Western North American Naturalist 63:314-319.

Emanuel, K. 2005. Increasing destructiveness of tropical cyclones over the past 30 years. Nature 436:686-688.

Fleming, T.H. 1988. The Short-tailed Fruit Bat: A Study in Plant-Animal Interactions. Chicago: The University of Chicago Press.

Hayes, J.P., and S.C. Loeb. 2007. The influences of forest management on bats in North America. In: Lacki, M.J., J.P. Hayes, and A. Kurta., eds. Bats in Forests: Conservation and Management. Baltimore, MD: Johns Hopkins University Press: 207-235.

Hoffmeister, D.F. 1986. Mammals of Arizona. University of Arizona Press, and Arizona Game and Fish Department. 602 p.

Licht, P., and P. Leitner. 1967. Behavioral responses to high temperatures in three species of California bats. Journal of Mammalogy 48:52-61.

Manolakou, P., G. Lavranos, and R. Angelopoulou. 2006. Molecular patterns of sex determination in the animal kingdom: A comparative study of the biology of reproduction. Reproductive Biology and Endocrinology 4:59.

Nowak, R.M. 1994. Walker's Bats of the World. Baltimore, MD: The John Hopkins University Press. 287 p.

Speakman, J.R., and D.W. Thomas. 2003. Physiol

ogical ecology and energetic of bats. In: Kunz, T.H., and M.B. Fenton, eds. Bat Ecology. Chicago: University of Chicago Press: 430-490.

U.S. Forest Service [USFS]. 2009. Draft Coronado National Forest ecological sustainability report. Tucson, AZ: U.S. Department of Agriculture. Forest Service. Available: http://www.fs.fed.us/r3/coronado/plan-revision/documents/final/cnf-ecological-sustainability-report-final-022009.pdf.

Habitat: Western yellow bat (*Lasiurus xanthinus*)			
Trait/Quality	**Question**	**Background info. & explanation of score**	**Points**
1. Area and distribution: *breeding*	Is the area or location of the associated vegetation type used for breeding activities by this species expected to change?	**Taxonomic note:** The genus *Lasiurus* comprises the hairy-tailed bats. Until changes began to be considered in the late 1980s, *L. xanthinus* was considered a sub-species of *Lasiurus ega* (specifically, *L. ega xanthinus*), the southern yellow bat. Baker and others (1988) recommended consideration of *L. xanthinus* as a distinct species from *L. ega*. Jones and others (1992) recognized two distinct species—the southern yellow bat (*L. ega*) and the western yellow bat (*L. xanthinus*). Morales and Bickham (1995) also supported recognition of *L. xanthinus*. Some of the information cited here is for *L. ega* since little published information exists for *L. xanthinus* (three references in Web of Science database). Nowak (1994) reported *L. xanthinus* occurring in the southwestern United States, central and western Mexico, and Baja California. In contrast, *L. ega* was indicated as occurring in southern Texas, eastern Mexico to northeastern Argentina (Nowak 1994). In Arizona, Hoffmeister (1986) reported the range as southern Arizona, as far north as Phoenix. *L. xanthinus* has been reported in Nevada, where several hundred captures were made over 2 years; both sexes were captured in all seasons (O'Farrell and others 2004). Recorded in western Texas (Higginbotham and others 2000). NatureServe (2010) indicated that *L. xanthinus* occurs in southern California, southern Arizona, extreme southwestern New Mexico, and Mexico, and is a year-round resident. Species of *Lasiurus* generally occur in wooded areas and roost in foliage and occasionally in tree holes or buildings (Nowak 1994). *L. ega* is reported to live in a variety of habitats (Kurta and Lehr 1995). Use of "palm skirts" in palm trees for roosting in the Southwest appears to be related to recent range extensions of *L. xanthinus* (Constantine 1998). One adult bat in Texas observed to roost in a giant dagger (*Yucca carnerosana*; Higginbotham and others 2000). In southern Nevada (northern-most documented records for the species), occupied extensive California fan palm groves for roosting and foraging and spend more time in riparian woodland than in other vegetation types (O'Farrell and others 2004). Little information on other species of trees used for roosting by this species. Also reported to roost in hackberry and sycamore (Adams 2003). *Lasiurus xanthinus* is reported to occur on all 12 of the EMAs on CNF. Projections of suitable climate for vegetation communities forest wide (Chapter 1) predicted declines in suitable climate for all plant community types, with the exception of increases of suitable climate for semi-desert grassland and small increases in Sonoran desert scrub (present in small amounts on the CNF). Habitat for this species is expected to decline due to increased aridity and increased wildfires (even if limited to naturally occurring palm trees).	2
2. Area and distribution: *non-breeding*	Is the area or location of the associated vegetation type used for non-breeding activities by this species expected to change?	Little information on wintering in this species (as is true for many foliage-roosting bats). Hoffmeister (1986) indicated this species "probably present year-round" in Arizona; live specimens have been collected in southern Arizona in January, February, April, May, September, and October. Score for this question reflects consideration of potential changes to non-breeding habitat in Arizona with the assumption that the same types of areas are used in winter as in summer.	2

USDA Forest Service RMRS-GTR-273. 2012.

Trait/Quality	Question	Background info. & explanation of score	Points
Habitat: Western yellow bat (*Lasiurus xanthinus*)			
3. Habitat components: *breeding*	Are specific habitat components required for breeding expected to change?	*L. xanthinus* is one of many species of bats referred to as "tree bats" as it is believed to rely on trees for roosting throughout the year (Cryan and Veilleux 2007). Lasiurine bats typically do not roost in caves (Kurta and Lehr 1995). In general, lasiurines roost alone or in small family groups (Cryan and Veilleux 2007). Standing water is assumed to be important to this species. In arid environments, water can be a resource that limits the presence of bats (Hayes and Loeb 2007). Insectivorous bats must obtain much of their water intake from free-standing water unlike frugivorous and nectarivorous bats, which obtain much of their water from food (Neuweiler 2000 as cited in Hayes and Loeb 2007). Water availability is expected to be important to successful reproduction since bats lose a large of water to evaporation across their wing membranes (Adams 2003) and because they lactate. Lactating female fringed myotis were found to make significantly more drinking passes over a water source than non-lactating females (Adams and Hayes 2008).	1
4. Habitat components: *non-breeding*	Are specific habitat components required for survival during non-breeding periods expected to change?	See Habitat, Question 3.	1
5. Habitat quality and reproduction	Are features of the habitat associated with better reproductive success expected to change?	No information found.	0
6. Habitat quality and survival	Are features of the habitat associated with better survival expected to change?	No information found.	0
7. Ability to colonize new areas	What is this species' capacity and tendency to disperse?	We considered bats to be very mobile due to their capacity for flight and, thus, overall able to colonize new areas. Bats are capable of moving to more favorable areas (more than 100 km) when seasonal conditions are harsh (Cryan 2003).	-1
8. Migratory or transitional habitats	Does this species require additional habitats during migration that are separated from breeding and non-breeding habitats?	See Habitat, Question 2. O'Farrell et. al. (2004) considered it likely that part of the population in southern Nevada migrates southward in winter. Cryan (2003) concluded that movements in several species of tree bats, including this one, appear to be restricted to movements within the North American continent. Overall, in scoring this question, we assumed that individuals breeding in Arizona do not make long-distance migrations southward.	0

Physiology: Western yellow bat (*Lasiurus xanthinus*)

Trait/Quality	Question	Background info. & explanation of score	Points
1. Physiological thresholds	Are limiting physiological conditions expected to change?	Little information available for *L. xanthinus*. Nocturnal forager, so not active during hottest part of day. In a review of the upper critical temperatures for 50 species of bats, the maximum was 41.0 °C and mean was 36.26 °C (Speakman and Thomas 2003); upper critical temperature is the ambient temperature above which an animal's body temperature will increase unless it pants or sweats. In the case of three species of bats roosting in a California barn in summer (*Myotis yumanensis*, *Antrozous pallidus*, and *Tadarida brasiliensis*), when ambient temperature approached 40 °C (104 °F), spacing between individuals tended to increase and most individuals moved to cooler parts of the loft though some did not (Licht and Leitner 1967). The following applies to red bats: One study found that red bats (*Lasiurus* spp.) in Arizona and New Mexico became active when temperatures reached about 20 °C (Jones 1965 as cited in Shump and Shump 1982); other studies have recorded them flying at temperatures of 13 °C and 19 °C (see references in Shump and Shump 1982). Shump and Shump (1982) indicated that the species seems capable of tolerating drastic temperature fluctuations and observed adaptations to low temperatures, including more insulation than two genera of cave-roosting bats (*Myotis* and *Eptesicus*). Overall, temperature not expected to exceed thresholds. Standing water is expected to become less available, but this is covered in Habitat section.	0
2. Sex ratio	Is sex ratio determined by temperature?	No. Temperature-dependent sex determination is mainly observed in reptiles and fish (Manolakou et al. 2006).	0
3. Exposure to extreme weather conditions	Are extreme weather or disturbance events that result in direct mortality or reproductive failure expected to change?	Increase in frequency of heat waves is predicted for southwestern United States. Overall, not clear to what extent timing and intensity of heat waves will effect survival and reproduction. We considered it unlikely that heat waves would cause widespread mortality for this species. See also Physiology, Question 1.	0
4. Limitations to active period	Are projected temperature or precipitation regimes that influence activity period of species expected to change?	Active in early evening and at night for foraging, so increase in temperatures not likely to reduce foraging time significantly. Warmer winter temperatures may reduce time spent undertaking torpor, but not clear that this will significantly increase active periods.	0
5. Metabolic inhibition	Does this species possess an ability to reduce metabolic energy or water requirements?	According to Cryan and Veilleux (2007), tree bats use torpor to limit energy expenditure during unfavorable conditions, and they cite 4 species of tree bats in which torpor has been documented (silver-haired bat [*Lasionycteris noctivagans*], eastern red bat [*L. borealis*], hoary bat [*L. cinereus*], and evening bat [*Nycticeius humeralis*]). The authors observed no demonstration that torpor can be used for long periods (e.g., >1 week) and indicated that tree bats may use hibernation (a form of torpor in which daily arousal process is inhibited) in some situations but such behavior has not yet been discovered. Cryan and Veilleux (2007) also state that there is "little doubt that lasiurines are capable of withstanding subfreezing temperatures for short periods (<1 month). O'Farrell and others (2004) speculated that reduced period of activity by this species in winter in southern Nevada suggested period of torpor.	−1

USDA Forest Service RMRS-GTR-273. 2012.

Physiology: Western yellow bat (*Lasiurus xanthinus*)

Trait/Quality	Question	Background info. & explanation of score	Points
6. Survival during resource limitation	Does this species have lower energy requirements or possess the capacity to store energy or water in the long term?	See Physiology, Question 5.	1
7. Variable life history	Does this species have alternative life history strategies to cope with variable resources or climate conditions?	No alternative strategies.	0
8. Reproduction in variable environments	Can this species outlive periods where reproduction is limited?	Little species-level information. Bats have been recognized as having an unusual life history; although they are small, they are considered to live long lives (Barclay and Harder 2003). Mean lifespan for species of Family Vespertilionidae (to which *Lasiurus xanthinus* belongs) was calculated as 14.9 years (range 5-34), but little information indicating what species were included in this calculation (Barclay and Harder 2003). Periods of extreme reductions in rainfall may last 5 years. If these conditions reduce resources to the point that bats have insufficient resources for breeding, but conditions recover after the 5 years, we assumed it is likely that sufficient numbers of individuals would survive long enough to breed once conditions improve.	-1

Phenology: Western yellow bat (*Lasiurus xanthinus*)

Trait/Quality	Question	Background info. & explanation of score	Points
1. Cues	Does this species use temperature or moisture cues to initiate activities related to fecundity or survival?	In temperate regions, *Lasiurus* spp. mating takes place in late summer or fall (Nowak 1994); sperm is stored over winter, ovulation and fertilization occurring in the spring, and young are born from late May to July. Bats in the temperate zones give birth in spring, which coincides with insect prey abundance (Arlettaz and others 2001; Frick and others 2010). Since *Lasiurus* spp. are not thought to undergo hibernation (although they appear to use shorter periods of torpor), not clear whether temperature is used as a significant cue for parturition. Temperature and moisture influence insect abundance, but since the relationship to the timing of parturition would be indirect, this question was scored as "0."	0
2. Event timing	Are activities related to species' fecundity or survival tied to discrete events that are expected to change?	Changes in the timing of precipitation and increases in temperature can alter the timing of insect availability and abundance. Warmer temperatures in spring may lead to earlier insect prey availability and possibly earlier parturition (see also Phenology, Question 3).	1
3. Mismatch potential	What is the separation in time or space between cues that initiate activities and discrete events that provide critical resources?	Based on the assumption that females giving birth in Arizona spend the winter there as well, individuals would have local indication of critical resources (e.g., insect prey abundance).	-1

Phenology: Western yellow bat (*Lasiurus xanthinus*)			
Trait/Quality	**Question**	**Background info. & explanation of score**	**Points**
4. Resilience to timing mismatches during breeding	Does this species employ strategies or have traits that increase the likelihood of reproduction co-occurring with important events?	Temperate-breeding bats tend to have only one litter per year (Barclay and Harder 2003). This characteristic increases its vulnerability to a mismatch between resource availability and the breeding period.	1

Biotic interactions: Western yellow bat (*Lasiurus xanthinus*)			
Trait/Quality	**Question**	**Background info. & explanation of score**	**Points**
1. Food resources	Are important food resources for this species expected to change?	Lasiurine bats begin flying in early evening and capture insects in flight ~6-15 m above the ground (one species will land on vegetation) (Nowak (1994). Fecal analysis of individuals of *L. xanthinus* caught in Nevada indicated consumption of the following insect orders: Coleoptera, Diptera, Hemiptera, Homoptera, Lepidoptera, and Orthoptera (O'Farrell and others 2004). Thus, this species appears to consume a variety of prey.	0
2. Predators	Are important predator populations expected to change?	Barn owls are documented predators of *L. ega* (references in Kurta and Lehr 1995). Birds document as predators of other *Lasiurus* species. For example, apparent predation on a western red bat by a scrub jay in northern California orchard (Constantine 1959); observation of a blue jay in Iowa removing a young red bat (*L. borealis*) from breast of its mother and pecking the young bat (presumably predation; Elwell 1962).	0
3. Symbionts	Are populations of symbiotic species expected to change?	No information found to suggest existence of important symbionts.	0
4. Disease	Is prevalence of diseases known to cause widespread mortality or reproductive failure in this species expected to change?	*L. ega* is susceptible to rabies; infection rate is probably less than 1% in wild populations (Constantine and others 1979 as cited in Kurta and Lehr 1995). Other parasites observed, including an intestinal trematode and a cestode (Kurta and Lehr 1995). Others probably exist. However, we found no information indicating significant levels of mortality from disease.	0
5. Competitors	Are populations of important competing species expected to change?	Little information available regarding competitors of this species or of competitive interactions affecting bats in general. Potential competitors are most likely other bat species and/or birds that forage aerially at dusk and dawn (e.g., poorwills, nighthawks; Adams 2003); competition would be for insect prey and/or access to water sources for drinking. Adams (2003) cited work by researchers in Colorado that bat species typically differed in the time of night they visited small water holes. Competition for roosting sites in this species may be mostly intra-specific.	0

Literature Cited

Adams, R.A. 2003. Bats of the Rocky Mountain West. Boulder, Colorado: University of Colorado Press. 289 p.

Adams, R.A., and M.A. Hayes. 2008. Water availability and successful lactation by bats as related to climate change in arid regions of western North America. Journal of Animal Ecology 77:1115:1121.

Arlettaz, R., P. Christe, A. Lugon, N. Perrin, and P. Vogel. 2001. Food availability dictates the timing of parturition in insectivorous mouse-eared bats. Oikos 95:105-111.

Barclay, M.R., and L.D. Harder. 2003. Life histories of bats: Life in the slow lane. In: Kunz, T.H., and M.B. Fenton, eds. Bat Ecology. Chicago: University of Chicago Press: 209-253.

Baker, R.J., J.C Patton, H.H. Genoways, and J.W. Bickham. 1988. Genetic studies of *Lasiurus* (Chiroptera:Vespertilionidae). Occasional Papers of the Museum of Texas Tech University, Number 117.

Constantine, D.G. 1959. Ecological observations on lasiurine bats in the North Bay area of California. Journal of Mammalogy 40:13-15.

Constantine, D.G. 1998. Range extensions of ten species of bats in California. Bulletin of the Southern California Academy of Sciences 97:49-75.

Cryan, P.M. 2003. Seasonal distribution of migratory tree bats (*Lasiurus* and *Lasionycteris*) in North America. Journal of Mammalogy 84:579-593.

Cryan, P.M., and J.P. Veilleux. 2007. Migration and use of autumn, winter, and spring roosts by tree bats. In: Lacki, M.J., J.P. Hayes, and A. Kurta., eds. Bats in Forests: Conservation and Management. Baltimore, MD: Johns Hopkins University Press: 153-175.

Elwell, A.S. 1962. Blue Jay preys on young bats. Journal of Mammalogy 43:434.

Frick, W.F., D.S. Reynolds, and T.H. Kunz. 2010. Influence of climate and reproductive timing on demography of little brown myotis *Myotis lucifigans*. Journal of Animal Ecology 79:128-136.

Hayes, J.P., and S.C. Loeb. 2007. The influences of forest management on bats in North America. In: Lacki, M.J., J.P. Hayes, and A. Kurta., eds. Bats in Forests: Conservation and Management. Baltimore, MD: Johns Hopkins University Press: 207-235.

Higgenbotham, J.L., M.T. Dixon, and L.K. Ammerman. 2000. Yucca provides roost for *Lasiurus xanthinus* (Chiroptera: Vespertilionidae) in Texas. Southwestern Naturalist 45:338-340.

Hoffmeister, D.F. 1986. Mammals of Arizona. University of Arizona Press, and Arizona Game and Fish Department. 602 p.

Jones, J.K., Jr., R.S. Hoffmann, D.W. Rice, C. Jones, R.J. Baker, and M.D. Engstrom. 1992. Revised checklist of North American mammals north of Mexico, 1991. Occasional Papers of the Museum of Texas Tech University, Number 146.

Kurta, A., and G.C. Lehr. 1995. *Lasiurus ega*. American Society of Mammalogists. Mammalian Species No. 515:1-7.

Licht, P., and P. Leitner. 1967. Behavioral responses to high temperatures in three species of California bats. Journal of Mammalogy 48:52-61.

Manolakou, P., G. Lavranos, and R. Angelopoulou. 2006. Molecular patterns of sex determination in the animal kingdom: A comparative study of the biology of reproduction. Reproductive Biology and Endocrinology 4:59.

Morales, J.C., and J.W. Bickham. 1995. Molecular systematic of the genus *Lasiurus* (Chiroptera: Vespertilionidae) based on restriction-site maps of the mitochondrial ribosomal genes. Journal of Mammalogy 76:730-749.

NatureServe. 2010. Comprehensive report for *Lasiurus xanthinus* (Western Yellow Bat). Available: http://www.natureserve.org/explorer/. Accessed March 26, 2010.

Nowak, R.M. 1994. Walker's Bats of the World. Baltimore, MD: The John Hopkins University Press.

O'Farrell, M.J., J.A. Williams, and B. Lund. 2004. Western yellow bat (*Lasiurus xanthinus*) in southern Nevada. Southwestern Naturalist 49:514-518.

Shump, K.A., and A.U. Shump. 1982. *Lasiurus borealis*. American Society of Mammalogists. Mammalian Species No. 183:1-6.

Speakman, J.R., and D.W. Thomas. 2003. Physiological ecology and energetic of bats. In: Kunz, T.H., and M.B. Fenton, eds. Bat Ecology. Chicago: University of Chicago Press.

U.S. Forest Service [USFS]. 2009. Draft Coronado National Forest ecological sustainability report. Tucson, AZ: U.S. Department of Agriculture, Forest Service. Available: http://www fs.fed.us/r3/coronado/plan-revision/documents/final/cnf-ecological-sustainability-report-final-022009.pdf.

Habitat: Western red bat (*Lasiurus blossevillii*)			
Trait/Quality	Question	Background info. & explanation of score	Points
1. Area and distribution: *breeding*	Is the area or location of the associated vegetation type used for breeding activities by this species expected to change?	**Taxonomic note:** This species was formerly considered under two sub-species of *Lasiusus borealis* (*L. borealis teliotus* and *L. borealis frantzii*) but Baker and others (1988) divided *Lasiusus borealis* into several species; Adams (2003) also considered the two to be separate. Fossil evidence suggests that *L. blossevillii* may have been distinct from *L. borealis* since 3.5 million years before present; Czaplewski 1993). In the United States, occurs in the southwest and west (California, Nevada, Utah, Arizona, and parts of New Mexico, with some rare documentation in western Texas). Range extends to Mexico, Central America, and South America; some records from southern British Columbia (Carter and Menzel 2007; NatureServe 2010). Lasiurine bats generally occur in wooded areas and roost in foliage; occasionally in tree holes or buildings (Nowak 1994). They begin flying in early evening and capture insects in flight ~6-15 m above the ground (one species will land on vegetation). *L. borealis* occurs in deciduous and coniferous forest (Shump and Shump 1982). Solitary and roost mostly in trees or shrubs, sometimes near or on the ground (Hall and Kelson 1959 as cited in Shump and Shump 1982). Some individuals of one lasiurine (*L. borealis borealis*) in Iowa observed to change roost sites on different days in summer (Constantine 1966). Red bats commonly roost in habitats adjacent to streams and open fields and in urban areas (references in Shump and Shump 1982). Roosts of *L. borealis* typically have dense shade and cover; no indication to what degree this might be for protection from predators versus exposure to high temperatures. In Arizona, *L. borealis* has been captured over ponds and in riparian areas with cottonwoods, sycamores, and walnut trees in the Huachuca and Graham Mountains (Hoffmeister 1986). Absent from most desert areas (Hoffmeister 1986). Findley and others (1975) noted *L. borealis teliotus* in New Mexico is associated with riparian habitats with deciduous trees and encinal and riparian sycamores and cottonwoods in Hidalgo County. In northern California, reported to roost in fruit trees, including fig, apricot, and orange; apricot trees found to contain this species tended to be 15-20 ft tall and have dark, dense foliage (Constantine 1959). This species occurs, or potential habitat exists, on 9 of the 12 EMAs on CNF (the three exceptions are Winchester, Santa Teresa, and Santa Catalina EMAs; USFS 2009). Projections of suitable climate for vegetation communities forest wide (Chapter 1) predicted declines in suitable climate for all plant community types, with the exception of increases of suitable climate for semi-desert grassland and small increases in Sonoran desert scrub (present in small amounts on the CNF). Projected reductions in riparian habitats would reduce breeding habitat for this species.	2

Trait/Quality	Question	Background info. & explanation of score	Points
Habitat: Western red bat (*Lasiurus blossevillii*)			
2. Area and distribution: *non-breeding*	Is the area or location of the associated vegetation type used for non-breeding activities by this species expected to change?	Little known about migration and winter locations. Seasonal movements may occur in California (Grinnell 1918 as cited in Cryan 2003). Based on a review of museum records, Cryan (2003) indicated that seasonal dispersal of *L. blossevillii* from California is apparently limited. Hoffmeister (1986) stated that *L. borealis* may be present in winter in Arizona.

In California, both males and females occur together at low elevations during winter (Grinnell 1918 and Orr 1950 as cited in Cryan 2003). The patterns of records in Arizona and New Mexico suggest that at least some individuals are moving into the area in spring from elsewhere (Cryan 2003).

Findley and others (1975) reported that individuals that breed in New Mexico probably move south in winter. Shump and Shump (1982) indicated that wintering sites for red bats (*L. borealis*) are not well documented but are "probably in southern states" given that their numbers there increase between December and March. (Note that this citation was written prior to the acceptance of *L. blossevillii* as a separate species, which complicates the understanding of wintering sites.) Considered likely that red bats hibernate in trees in winter (Shump and Shump 1982).

Cryan (2003) concluded, based on patterns in museum records, that there was little evidence for "major movement" between North America and South America by any of the *Lasiurus* species examined (*L. borealis*, *L. blossevillii*, *L. cinereus*, and *L. noctivagans*).

Migration of more than a few hundred kilometers is rare in bats (Fleming and Eby 2003) but is important in those bat species that live in highly seasonal environments. *L. borealis* has been reported to have migrated more than 1000 km between summer and winter roosts (Fleming and Eby 2003), but not clear whether this applies to *L. blossevillii*.

Score for this question reflects consideration of potential changes to non-breeding habitat with the assumption that riparian areas are also important in winter and that this species is likely to decline in Mexico if that is where some breeding individuals over-winter. | 2 |
| 3. Habitat components: *breeding* | Are specific habitat components required for breeding expected to change? | *L. blossevillii* is one of many species of bats referred to as "tree bats." Tree bats are believed to rely on trees for roosting throughout the year (Cryan and Veilleux 2007). The western red bat primarily roosts in foliage (Hayes 2003). Lasiurine bats typically do not roost in caves (Kurta and Lehr 1995). In general, lasiurines roost alone or in small family groups (Cryan and Veilleux 2007).

Standing water is considered an important feature for insectivorous bats in the Southwest (Hayes and Loeb 2007). Jones (2009) found stock tanks and wildlife waterers to be important to bats on the CNF.

Some physiological studies of insectivorous bats during pregnancy and lactation have found that individuals consume water from drinking in addition to that in their insect prey (free-ranging big brown bats [*Eptesicus fuscus*], Kurta and others 1990; and little brown bats [*Myotis lucifugus*], Kurta and others 1989). Female fringed myotis (*Myotis thysanodes*) who were lactating visited an artificial water source in Colorado 13 times more often than non-lactating females (Adams and Hayes 2008). | 1 |
| 4. Habitat components: *non-breeding* | Are specific habitat components required for survival during | See Habitat, Question 3. | 1 |

Trait/Quality	Question	Background info. & explanation of score	Points
	non-breeding periods expected to change?		
5. Habitat quality and reproduction	Are features of the habitat associated with better reproductive success expected to change?	No information found.	0
6. Habitat quality and survival	Are features of the habitat associated with better survival expected to change?	No information found.	0
7. Ability to colonize new areas	What is this species' capacity and tendency to disperse?	We considered bats to be very mobile due to their capacity for flight and, thus, overall able to colonize new areas. Bats are capable of moving more than 100 km to more favorable areas when seasonal conditions are harsh (Cryan 2003).	-1
8. Migratory or transitional habitats	Does this species require additional habitats during migration that are separated from breeding and non-breeding habitats?	Unclear whether Arizona populations of *L. blossevillii* move south. See Habitat, Question 2 for discussion. Scored this question to account for the possibility that this species migrates south for winter. Additional information: Male and female *L. borealis* seem to migrate at different times and have different summer ranges (references in Shump and Shump 1982); in California, males and females winter together, but it is considered possible that they used different areas in summer (Williams and Findley 1979 as cited in Shump and Shump 1982).	1

Habitat: Western red bat (*Lasiurus blossevillii*)

Physiology: Western red bat (*Lasiurus blossevillii*)

Trait/Quality	Question	Background info. & explanation of score	Points
1. Physiological thresholds	Are limiting physiological conditions expected to change?	In a review of the upper critical temperatures for 50 species of bats, the maximum was 41.0 °C and mean was 36.26 °C (Speakman and Thomas 2003); upper critical temperature is the ambient temperature above which an animal's body temperature will increase unless it pants or sweats. In the case of three species of bats roosting in a California barn in summer (*Myotis yumanensis*, *Antrozous pallidus*, and *Tadarida brasiliensis*), when ambient temperature approached 40 °C (104 °F), spacing between individuals tended to increase and most individuals moved to cooler parts of the loft though some did not (Licht and Leitner 1967). One study found that red bats in Arizona and New Mexico became active when temperatures reached about 20 °C (Jones 1965 as cited in Shump and Shump 1982); other studies have found them flying at temperatures of 13 °C and 19 °C (see references in Shump and Shump 1982). Shump and Shump (1982) indicated that the species seems capable of tolerating drastic temperature fluctuations and observed adaptations to low temperatures, including more insulation than two genera of cave-roosting bats (*Myotis* and *Eptesicus*). Nocturnal forager (begins foraging 1-2 hours after sunset; Kunz 1973 as cited in Shump and Shump 1982), so not foraging during hottest part of day. Standing water is expected to become less available, but this is covered in Habitat section.	0

USDA Forest Service RMRS-GTR-273. 2012.

Physiology: Western red bat (*Lasiurus blossevillii*)			
Trait/Quality	**Question**	**Background info. & explanation of score**	**Points**
2. Sex ratio	Is sex ratio determined by temperature?	No. Temperature-dependent sex determination is mainly observed in reptiles and fish (Manolakou et al. 2006).	0
3. Exposure to extreme weather conditions	Are extreme weather or disturbance events that result in direct mortality or reproductive failure expected to change?	Increase in frequency of heat waves is predicted for southwestern United States. Overall, not clear to what extent timing and intensity of heat waves will affect survival and reproduction. We considered it unlikely that heat waves would cause widespread mortality for this species. See also Physiology, Question 1.	0
4. Limitations to active period	Are projected temperature or precipitation regimes that influence activity period of species expected to change?	Active in early evening and at night for foraging, so increase in temperatures not likely to reduce foraging time significantly. Warmer winter temperatures may reduce time spent undertaking torpor, but not clear if this will significantly increase active periods.	0
5. Metabolic inhibition	Does this species possess an ability to reduce metabolic energy or water requirements?	Cryan and Veilleux (2007) indicated that tree bats use torpor to limit energy expenditure during unfavorable conditions, citing 4 species of tree bats in which torpor has been documented (silver-haired bat, eastern red bat, hoary bat, and evening bat). The authors found no indication that torpor can be used for long periods (e.g., >1 week). Cryan and Veilleux (2007) indicated that tree bats may use hibernation (a form of torpor in which daily arousal process is inhibited) in some situations but that such behavior has not yet been discovered.	-1
6. Survival during resource limitation	Does this species have lower energy requirements or possess the capacity to store energy or water in the long term?	See Physiology, Question 5.	1
7. Variable life history	Does this species have alternative life history strategies to cope with variable resources or climate conditions?	No alternative strategies.	0
8. Reproduction in variable environments	Can this species outlive periods where reproduction is limited?	Little species-level information. Bats have been recognized as having an unusual life history; although they are small, they are considered to live long lives (Barclay and Harder 2003). Mean lifespan for species of Family Vespertilionidae (to which *L. xanthinus* belongs) was calculated as 14.9 years (range 5-34), but little information indicating what species were included in this calculation (Barclay and Harder 2003). Periods of extreme reductions in rainfall may last 5 years. If these conditions reduce resources to the point that bats have insufficient resources for breeding, but conditions recover after, we considered it likely that sufficient numbers of individuals would survive long enough to breed once conditions improve.	-1

Phenology: Western red bat (*Lasiurus blossevillii*)			
Trait/Quality	**Question**	**Background info. & explanation of score**	**Points**
1. Cues	Does this species use temperature or moisture cues to initiate activities related to fecundity or survival?	In temperate regions, *Lasiurus* spp. mating takes place in late summer or fall (Nowak 1994); sperm is stored over winter, ovulation and fertilization occur in the spring, and young are born from late May to July. Bats in the temperate zones give birth in spring, which coincides with insect prey abundance (Arlettaz and others 2001; Frick and others 2010). Since *Lasiurus* spp. are not thought to undergo hibernation (although they appear to use shorter periods of torpor), not clear whether temperature is used as a significant cue for parturition.

Temperature and moisture influence insect abundance, but since the relationship to the timing of parturition would be indirect, this question was scored as "0." | 0 |
2. Event timing	Are activities related to species' fecundity or survival tied to discrete events that are expected to change?	Changes in the timing of precipitation and increases in temperature can alter the timing of insect availability and abundance. Warmer temperatures in spring may lead to earlier insect prey availability and possibly earlier parturition (see also Phenology, Question 3).	1
3. Mismatch potential	What is the separation in time or space between cues that initiate activities and discrete events that provide critical resources?	Uncertain to what extent individuals of this species that summer in Arizona also winter in Arizona (see Habitat, Question 8). We scored this question "0" to account for the uncertainty about whether critical resources for parturition are occurring nearby or distant from wintering areas. Potential for this species to be migratory was accounted for in Habitat, Question 8 by us assigning it a "vulnerable" score.	0
4. Resilience to timing mismatches during breeding	Does this species employ strategies or have traits that increase the likelihood of reproduction co-occurring with important events?	Breeds in late summer; fertilization occurs in spring; gestation is 80-90 days (references in Shump and Shump 1982). Temperate-breeding bats tend to have only one litter per year (Barclay and Harder 2003).	1

Biotic interactions: Western red bat (*Lasiurus blossevillii*)			
Trait/Quality	**Question**	**Background info. & explanation of score**	**Points**
1. Food resources	Are important food resources for this species expected to change?	Lasiurine bats begin flying in early evening and capture insects in flight ~6-15 m above the ground (one species will land on vegetation) (Nowak 1994).

Consumes insects. One study in Indiana (Whitaker 1972 as cited in Shump and Shump 1982) found that 26% of stomach contents by volume were moths. Other studies indicated that Homoptera, Coleoptera, Hymenoptera, Diptera, and Lepidoptera have been found in stomachs of red bats (see references in Shump and Shump 1982). Also reported to feed on ground-dwelling crickets, flies, bugs, beetles, cicadas, grain moths, and other insects (references in Shump and Shump 1982).

Thus, this species appears to consume a variety of prey species. | 0 |
| 2. Predators | Are important predator populations expected to change? | Barn owls are documented predators of *Lasiurus ega* (references in Kurta and Lehr 1995). Apparent predation on a western red bat by a scrub jay in northern California orchard (Constantine 1959). Observation of a blue jay in Iowa removing a young red bat (*L.* | 0 |

Biotic interactions: Western red bat (*Lasiurus blossevillii*)			
Trait/Quality	Question	Background info. & explanation of score	Points
		borealis) from breast of its mother and pecking the young bat (presumably predation; Elwell 1962). Mother generally leaves young at the roost site while she forages for food (Shump and Shump 1982), so this can leave young vulnerable to predation, as is the case in other taxa (e.g., birds). Other predators are opossums, house cats, sharp-shinned hawks, American kestrels, merlins, great horned owls, and roadrunners (Shump and Shump 1982).	
3. Symbionts	Are populations of symbiotic species expected to change?	No information found to suggest existence of important symbionts.	0
4. Disease	Is prevalence of diseases known to cause widespread mortality or reproductive failure in this species expected to change?	*L. ega* is susceptible to rabies; infection rate is probably less than 1% in wild populations (Constantine and others 1979 as cited in Kurta and Lehr 1995). Other parasites are an intestinal trematode and a cestode (Kurta and Lehr 1995). Others probably exist. No information indicating significant levels of mortality.	0
5. Competitors	Are populations of important competing species expected to change?	Little information available regarding competitors of this species or of competitive interactions affecting bats in general. Potential competitors are most likely other bat species and/or birds that forage aerially at dusk and dawn (e.g., poorwills and nighthawks; Adams 2003); competition would be for insect prey and/or access to water sources for drinking. Adams (2003) cited work by researchers in Colorado who found that bat species typically differed in the time of night they visited small water holes. Competition for roosting sites in this species may be mostly intra-specific.	0

Literature Cited

Adams, R.A. 2003. Bats of the Rocky Mountain West. Boulder, CO: University of Colorado Press. 289 p.

Adams, R.A., and M.A. Hayes. 2008. Water availability and successful lactation by bats as related to climate change in arid regions of western North America. Journal of Animal Ecology 77:1115-1121.

Arlettaz, R., P. Christe, A. Lugon, N. Perrin, and P. Vogel. 2001. Food availability dictates the timing of parturition in insectivorous mouse-eared bats. Oikos 95:105-111.

Baker, R.J., J.C Patton, H.H. Genoways, and J.W. Bickham. 1988. Genetic studies of *Lasiurus* (Chiroptera:Vespertilionidae). Occasional Papers of the Museum of Texas Tech University, Number 117.

Barclay, M.R., and L.D. Harder. 2003. Life histories of bats: Life in the slow lane. In: Kunz, T.H., and M.B. Fenton, eds. Bat Ecology. Chicago: University of Chicago Press: 209-253.

Carter, T.C., and J.M Menzel. 2007. Behavior and day-roosting ecology of North American foliage-roosting bats. In: Lacki, M.J., J.P. Hayes, and A. Kurta., eds. Bats in Forests: Conservation and Management. Baltimore, MD: Johns Hopkins University Press: 61-81.

Constantine, D.G. 1966. Ecological observations on lasiurine bats in Iowa. Journal of Mammalogy 47:34-41.

Constantine, D.G. 1959. Ecological observations on lasiurine bats in the North Bay area of California. Journal of Mammalogy 40:13-15.

Cryan, P.M. 2003. Seasonal distribution of migratory tree bats (*Lasiurus* and *Lasionycteris*) in North America. Journal of Mammalogy 84:579-593.

Cryan, P.M., and J.P. Veilleux. 2007. Migration and use of autumn, winter, and spring roosts by tree bats. In: Lacki, M.J., J.P. Hayes, and A. Kurta., eds. Bats in Forests: Conservation and Management. Baltimore, MD: Johns Hopkins University Press: 153-175.

Czaplewski, N.J. 1993. Late tertiary bats (Mammalia, Chiroptera) from the southwestern United States. Southwestern Naturalist 38:111-118.

Elwell, A.S. 1962. Blue jay preys on young bats. Journal of Mammalogy 43:434.

Findley, J.S., A.H. Harris, D.E. Wilson, and C. Jones. 1975. Mammals of New Mexico. Albuquerque: University of New Mexico Press.

Fleming, T.H., and P. Eby. 2003. Ecology of bat migration. In: Kunz, T.H., and M.B. Fenton, eds. Bat Ecology. Chicago: University of Chicago Press. 779 p.

Frick, W.F., D.S. Reynolds, and T.H. Kunz. 2010. Influence of climate and reproductive timing on demography of little brown myotis *Myotis lucifigans*. Journal of Animal Ecology 79:128-136.

Hayes, J.P. 2003. Habitat ecology and conservation of bats in western coniferous forests. In: Zabel, C.J., and R.G. Anthony, eds. Mammal Community Dynamics: Management and Conservation in the Coniferous Forests of Western North America. Cambridge, United Kingdom: Cambridge University Press: 81-119.

Hayes, J.P., and S.C. Loeb. 2007. The influences of forest management on bats in North America. In: Lacki, M.J., J.P. Hayes, and A. Kurta., eds. Bats in Forests: Conservation and Management. Baltimore, MD: Johns Hopkins University Press: 207-235.

Hoffmeister, D.F. 1986. Mammals of Arizona. University of Arizona Press and Arizona Game and Fish Department. 602 p.

Jones, L. 2009. Distribution of bats across the Huachuca ecosystem management area: A preliminary assessment for a landscape-level habitat restoration project. 2009 Arizona Bat Conservation Partnership Grant Final Report; December 23, 2009; Submitted to Arizona Game and Fish Department, Phoenix, and U.S. Department of Agriculture, Forest Service, Coronado National Forest, Tucson, AZ. Forest Service Agreement Number 09-CO-11030515-038. Arizona Game and Fish Department Project Number FY-09-06.

Kurta, A., G.P. Bell, K.A. Nagy, T.H. Kunz. 1989. Water balance of free-ranging little brown bats (*Myotis lucifigus*) during pregnancy and lactation. Canadian Journal of Zoology 67:2468-2472.

Kurta, A., T.H. Kunz, K.A. Nagy. 1990. Energetics and water flux of free-ranging big brown bats (*Eptesicus fuscus*) during pregnancy and lactation. Journal of Mammalogy 71:59-65.

Kurta, A., and G.C. Lehr. 1995. *Lasiurus ega*. American Society of Mammalogists. Mammalian Species No. 515:1-7.

Manolakou, P., G. Lavranos, and R. Angelopoulou. 2006. Molecular patterns of sex determination in the animal kingdom: A comparative study of the biology of reproduction. Reproductive Biology and Endocrinology 4:59.

NatureServe. 2010. Comprehensive report for *Lasiurus blossevillii* (Western Red Bat). Available: http://www.natureserve.org/explorer/. Accessed: March 26, 2010.

Nowak, R.M. 1994. Walker's Bats of the World. Baltimore, MD: The Johns Hopkins University Press.

Shump, K.A., and A.U. Shump. 1982. *Lasiurus borealis*. American Society of Mammalogists. Mammalian Species No. 183:1-6.

Speakman, J.R., and D.W. Thomas. 2003. Physiological ecology and energetics of bats. In: Kunz, T.H., and M. Brock Fenton, eds. Bat Ecology. Chicago: University of Chicago Press: 430-490.

U.S. Forest Service [USFS]. 2009. Draft Coronado National Forest ecological sustainability report. Tucson, AZ: U.S. Department of Agriculture, Forest Service. Available: http://www.fs fed.us/r3/coronado/plan-revision/documents/final/cnf-ecological-sustainability-report-final-022009.pdf.

Trait/Quality	Question	Background info. & explanation of score	Points
Habitat: Allen's lappet-browed bat (*Idionycteris phyllotis*)			
1. Area and distribution: *breeding*	Is the area or location of the associated vegetation type used for breeding activities by this species expected to change?	**Taxonomic note:** This species also known under the common name Mexican big-eared bat. Much of the literature refers to this bat as *Plecotus phyllotis* (Czaplewski 1983). It is in the Family Vespertilionidae. Distribution ranges from the southwestern United States (Arizona and portions of California, Nevada, Utah, Colorado, and New Mexico) into Mexico (Czaplewski 1983). In Arizona, reported to occur from the northwest corner of the state to the southeast corner but not reported in the southwestern deserts (Hoffmeister 1986). Most specimens of this species have been collected from altitudes between 1100 m and 2500 m, but specimens range as low as 855 m and as high as 3225 m (Genoways and Jones 1967 as cited in Czaplewski 1983). According to Hoffmeister (1986), this species has been collected most often in ponderosa pine, pinyon juniper, and Mexican woodland; collection locales include elevations as high as white fir and as low as Mohave desert scrub (where *Opuntia* spp., catclaw, yucca, and Joshua trees occur). This species is associated with conifers and often with rocky slopes and nearby cliffs (potential roosting sites) in the eastern portion of Arizona (Hoffmeister 1986). Czaplewski (1983; see references contained therein) indicated that this species primarily occupies forested mountainous regions from pine, fir, and oak forest into riparian woodlands of sycamore, cottonwood, willow, and walnut, with occasional trapping in more arid habitats. Czaplewski (1983) reported that this species occurs from Mojave Desert scrub to fir forest where rocks are near; rocks are assumed to be used as roosting sites. Individuals have often been netted along streams or over ponds (Hoffmeister 1986; Rabe and others 1998) where they may be foraging for insects, drinking water, or both (Hoffmeister 1986). Where this species has been netted in areas below coniferous woodland and coniferous forest, Hoffmeister (1986) indicated that this may be a result of this species seeking drinking water rather than a reflection of preferred habitat. Females separate from males in summer to form maternity colonies (Williams and Findley 1979 as cited in Czaplewski 1983). This species has been observed in nursery (maternity) colonies in caves and collapsed tunnels in Arizona (Hoffmeister 1986). Locations used by individuals for 1-2 years may be abandoned (Hoffmeister 1986). Rabe and others (1998) documented reproductive females of this species using ponderosa pine snags in northern Arizona (Coconino NF) during June and July. This species was not detected during surveys of the Huachuca EMA by Jones (2009). This species occurs, or potential habitat exists, on 3 of the 12 EMAs on CNF: Chiricahua, Pinaleño, and Galiuro (USFS 2009). Projections of suitable climate for vegetation communities (Chapter 1) were for declines in suitable climate for forest, woodland, and Chihuahuan desert scrub and increases in suitable climate for semi-desert grassland and small increases in Sonoran desert scrub (present in small amounts on the CNF). Projected reductions in riparian and forested habitats are expected to reduce breeding habitat for this species.	2

Habitat: Allen's lappet-browed bat (*Idionycteris phyllotis*)			
Trait/Quality	**Question**	**Background info. & explanation of score**	**Points**
2. Area and distribution: *non-breeding*	Is the area or location of the associated vegetation type used for non-breeding activities by this species expected to change?	Tumlison (1993) indicated that migration in this species is not currently known to occur (see also Habitat, Question 8). We assumed that habitat used in winter is similar, or the same as, that used in summer. Little information on winter behavior. Not clear to what extent this species uses torpor in winter. Scored this question on the assumption that the population does not spend a large proportion of winter time hibernating in southern Arizona and that individuals occurring in Arizona in winter would require foraging habitat.	2
3. Habitat components: *breeding*	Are specific habitat components required for breeding expected to change?	This species is reported to roost in mine tunnels and rocks (Czaplewski 1983), but observations of tree use by reproductive females has also been documented. Rabe and others (1998) documented reproductive females of this species using ponderosa pine snags in northern Arizona (Coconino NF) during June and July. Solvesky and Chambers (2009) indicated that this species forms maternity colonies in ponderosa pine snags in Arizona; most were observed in large-diameter snags under sloughing bark, with an average of 11 bats per roost. Bachelor roosts were in vertical sandstone cliff faces in pinyon-juniper woodlands (Solvesky and Chambers 2009). Siders and Jolley (2009) found a maternity roost in Utah in a cliff face. Given that this species can use snags during the breeding season, and snags are expected to decline, we expected that potential maternity roost sites for this species are likely to decline. Standing water appears to be important to this species. Czaplewski (1983) indicated that most specimens were captured over water holes when bats came to drink. In arid environments, water can be a resource limiting the presence of bats (Hayes and Loeb 2007). Insectivorous bats must obtain much of their water intake from free-standing water, unlike frugivorous and nectarivorous bats, which obtain much of their water from food (Neuweiler 2000 as cited in Hayes and Loeb 2007). Water availability is expected to be important to successful reproduction since bats lose a large of water to evaporation across their wing membranes (Adams 2003) and because they lactate. Lactating female fringed myotis were found to make significantly more drinking passes over a water source than non-lactating females (Adams and Hayes 2008).	1
4. Habitat components: *non-breeding*	Are specific habitat components required for survival during non-breeding periods expected to change?	Little information on winter behavior (see also Habitat, Question 2 and Habitat, Question 8). Based on the assumption that this species exhibits some activity in winter, considered likely that it requires standing water during winter. Standing water expected to become less available.	1
5. Habitat quality and reproduction	Are features of the habitat associated with better reproductive success expected to change?	No information found.	0
6. Habitat quality and survival	Are features of the habitat associated with better survival expected to change?	No information found.	0

Habitat: Allen's lappet-browed bat (*Idionycteris phyllotis*)

Trait/Quality	Question	Background info. & explanation of score	Points
7. Ability to colonize new areas	What is this species' capacity and tendency to disperse?	We considered bats to be very mobile due to their capacity for flight and, thus, overall able to colonize new areas. Bats are capable of moving more than 100 km to more favorable areas when seasonal conditions are harsh (Cryan 2003). During June and July, females of this species were captured on average 1.6 km from maternity roosts, and males were captured 12 km from roosts (Solvesky and Chambers 2009), suggesting that these were distances individuals moved in one evening.	-1
8. Migratory or transitional habitats	Does this species require additional habitats during migration that are separated from breeding and non-breeding habitats?	Captured infrequently in surveys during November-March in New Mexico, which suggested that individuals were hibernating there in winter and not regularly active (Geluso 2007). Czaplewski (1983) reported that "seasonal movements and cold-season whereabouts and activities of the species are unknown. All Mexico specimens were collected in summer months...except for the type specimen which was taken on 24 March." Tumlison (1993) indicated that migration in this species is not currently known to occur.	1

Physiology: Allen's lappet-browed bat (*Idionycteris phyllotis*)

Trait/Quality	Question	Background info. & explanation of score	Points
1. Physiological thresholds	Are limiting physiological conditions expected to change?	Little information available for this species. Nocturnal forager, so not active during hottest part of day. In a review of the upper critical temperatures for 50 species of bats, the maximum was 41.00 °C and mean was 36.26 °C (Speakman and Thomas 2003); upper critical temperature is the ambient temperature above which an animal's body temperature will increase unless it pants or sweats. In the case of three species of bats roosting in a California barn in summer (*Myotis yumanensis*, *Antrozous pallidus*, and *Tadarida brasiliensis*), when ambient temperature approached 40 °C (104 °F), spacing between individuals tended to increase and most individuals moved to cooler parts of the loft though some did not (Licht and Leitner 1967). Overall, we assumed that temperature would not exceed thresholds. Standing water is expected to become less available, but this is covered in Habitat section.	0
2. Sex ratio	Is sex ratio determined by temperature?	No. Temperature-dependent sex determination is mainly observed in reptiles and fish (Manolakou et al. 2006).	0
3. Exposure to extreme weather conditions	Are extreme weather or disturbance events that result in direct mortality or reproductive failure expected to change?	Increase in frequency of heat waves is predicted for southwestern United States. Overall, not clear to what extent timing and intensity of heat waves will affect survival and reproduction. We considered it unlikely that heat waves would cause widespread mortality for this species. See also Physiology, Question 1.	0
4. Limitations to active period	Are projected temperature or precipitation regimes that influence activity period of species expected to change?	Active in late evening and at night for foraging, so increase in temperatures not likely to reduce foraging time significantly. Warmer winter temperatures may reduce time spent undertaking torpor (assuming this species uses torpor; see Physiology, Question 5), but not clear if this would significantly increase active periods.	0

Physiology: Allen's lappet-browed bat (*Idionycteris phyllotis*)

Trait/Quality	Question	Background info. & explanation of score	Points
5. Metabolic inhibition	Does this species possess an ability to reduce metabolic energy or water requirements?	Little information on this species. Speakman and Thomas (2003) indicated that "probably all temperate-zones species....are capable of entering regulated torpor on a regular basis." Not clear whether this species is an obligatory hibernator, or whether it would be in this part of its range (Arizona).	-1
6. Survival during resource limitation	Does this species have lower energy requirements or possess the capacity to store energy or water in the long term?	See Physiology, Question 5. We assumed that this species can utilize torpor.	1
7. Variable life history	Does this species have alternative life history strategies to cope with variable resources or climate conditions?	No alternative strategies.	0
8. Reproduction in variable environments	Can this species outlive periods where reproduction is limited?	The longevity record (i.e., longest-lived individuals recorded) for this species is a minimum of 3 years and 2 months (Cockrum 1973 as cited in Czaplewski 1983). Bats have been recognized as having an unusual life history; although they are small, they are considered to live long lives (Barclay and Harder 2003). Mean lifespan for species of Family Vespertilionidae (to which *Idionycteris phyllotis* belongs) was calculated as 14.9 years (range 5-34), but little information indicating what species included in this calculation (Barclay and Harder 2003). Periods of extreme reductions in rainfall may last 5 years. If these conditions reduce resources to the point that bats have insufficient resources for breeding, but conditions recover after, we assumed it is likely that sufficient numbers of individuals would survive long enough to breed once conditions improve.	-1

Phenology: Allen's lappet-browed bat (*Idionycteris phyllotis*)

Trait/Quality	Question	Background info. & explanation of score	Points
1. Cues	Does this species use temperature or moisture cues to initiate activities related to fecundity or survival?	Little information on this species regarding mating and parturition. Pregnant females have been collected in June in New Mexico, Arizona, and Durango, Mexico (references in Czaplewski 1983). Bats in the temperate zones give birth in spring, which coincides with insect prey abundance (Arlettaz and others 2001; Frick and others 2010). Temperature and moisture influence insect abundance, but since the relationship to the timing of parturition would be indirect, this question was scored as "0."	0
2. Event timing	Are activities related to species' fecundity or survival tied to discrete events that are expected to change?	Changes in the timing of precipitation and increases in temperature can alter the timing of insect availability and abundance. Warmer temperatures in spring may lead to earlier insect prey availability and possibly earlier parturition (see also Phenology, Question 3).	1
3. Mismatch potential	What is the separation in time or space between cues that initiate	Based on the assumption that females giving birth in Arizona spend the winter there as well, individuals would have local indication of critical resources (e.g., insect prey abundance).	-1

Phenology: Allen's lappet-browed bat (*Idionycteris phyllotis*)

Trait/Quality	Question	Background info. & explanation of score	Points
	activities and discrete events that provide critical resources?		
4. Resilience to timing mismatches during breeding	Does this species employ strategies or have traits that increase the likelihood of reproduction co-occurring with important events?	Pregnant females collected in June in New Mexico, Arizona, and Durango, Mexico (references in Czaplewski 1983). Temperate-breeding bats tend to have only one litter per year (Barclay and Harder 2003).	1

Biotic interactions: Allen's lappet-browed bat (*Idionycteris phyllotis*)

Trait/Quality	Question	Background info. & explanation of score	Points
1. Food resources	Are important food resources for this species expected to change?	Hoffmeister (1986) indicated that this species of bat flies later in the evening than some other species—most often individuals have been caught in nets after 9 p.m. Appears that insects are gleaned from vegetation or other surfaces or are consumed in flight (Czaplewski 1983). This species is insectivorous and feeds primarily on moths but also on soldier beetles, dung beetles, leaf beetles, roaches, and flying ants (see references in Czaplewski 1983). Flying ants suggested as opportunistic feeding (Ross 1967 as cited in Czaplewski 1983). Overall, appears to feed on a variety of food resources.	0
2. Predators	Are important predator populations expected to change?	According to Czaplewski (1983), no predators of *I. phylottis* are known.	0
3. Symbionts	Are populations of symbiotic species expected to change?	No information found to suggest existence of important symbionts.	0
4. Disease	Is prevalence of diseases known to cause widespread mortality or reproductive failure in this species expected to change?	No blood parasites or other endoparasites have been found in this species (Cain and Studier 1974 as cited in Czaplewski 1983). No ectoparasites were reported according to Czaplewski (1983), although it is likely that some exist. No information indicating significant levels of mortality from diseases or parasites.	0
5. Competitors	Are populations of important competing species expected to change?	This species was observed in the same maternity colony in the Galiuro Mountains in a collapsed cave along with Townsend's big-eared bats, California myotis, and fringed myotis (Hoffmeister 1986). Little information available regarding competitors of this species or of competitive interactions affecting bats in general. Potential competitors are most likely other bat species and/or birds that forage aerially at dusk and dawn (e.g., poorwills and nighthawks; Adams 2003); competition would be for insect prey and/or access to water sources for drinking. Adams (2003) cited work by researchers in Colorado that found that bat species typically differed in the time of night they visited small water holes. Competition for roosting sites in this species may be mostly intra-specific.	0

Literature Cited

Adams, R.A. 2003. Bats of the Rocky Mountain West. Boulder, CO: University of Colorado Press. 289 p.

Adams, R.A., and M.A. Hayes. 2008. Water availability and successful lactation by bats as related to climate change in arid regions of western North America. Journal of Animal Ecology 77:1115:1121.

Arlettaz, R., P. Christe, A. Lugon, N. Perrin, and P. Vogel. 2001. Food availability dictates the timing of parturition in insectivorous mouse-eared bats. Oikos 95:105-111.

Barclay, M.R., and L.D. Harder. 2003. Life histories of bats: Life in the slow lane. In: Kunz, T.H., and M.B. Fenton, eds. Bat Ecology. Chicago: University of Chicago Press: 209-253.

Cryan, P.M. 2003. Seasonal distribution of migratory tree bats (*Lasiurus* and *Lasionycteris*) in North America. Journal of Mammalogy 84:579-593.

Czaplewski, N.J. 1983. *Idionycteris phyllotis*. American Society of Mammalogists. Mammalian Species No. 208:1-4.

Frick, W.F., D.S. Reynolds, and T.H. Kunz. 2010. Influence of climate and reproductive timing on demography of little brown myotis *Myotis lucifigans*. Journal of Animal Ecology 79:128-136.

Geluso, K. 2007. Winter activity of bats over water and along flyways in New Mexico. Southwestern Naturalist 52:482-492.

Hayes, J.P., and S.C. Loeb. 2007. The influences of forest management on bats in North America. In: Lacki, M.J., J.P. Hayes, and A. Kurta., eds. Bats in Forests: Conservation and Management. Baltimore, MD: Johns Hopkins University Press: 207-235.

Hoffmeister, D.F. 1986. Mammals of Arizona. University of Arizona Press and Arizona Game and Fish Department. 602 p.

Jones, L. 2009. Distribution of bats across the Huachuca Ecosystem Management Area: A preliminary assessment for a landscape-level habitat restoration project. 2009 Arizona Bat Conservation Partnership Grant Final Report; December 23, 2009; Submitted to Arizona Game and Fish Department, Phoenix, and USDA Forest Service, Coronado National Forest, Tucson, Arizona. Forest Service Agreement Number 09-CO-11030515-038. Arizona Game and Fish Department Project Number FY-09-06.

Licht, P., and P. Leitner. 1967. Behavioral responses to high temperatures in three species of California bats. Journal of Mammalogy 48:52-61.

Manolakou, P., G. Lavranos, and R. Angelopoulou. 2006. Molecular patterns of sex determination in the animal kingdom: a comparative study of the biology of reproduction. Reproductive Biology and Endocrinology 4:59.

Rabe, M.J., T.E. Morrell, H. Green, J. deVos Jr., and C.R. Miller. 1998. Characteristics of ponderosa pine snag roosts used by reproductive bats in northern Arizona. Journal of Wildlife Management 62:612-621.

Siders, M.S., and W. Jolley. 2009. Roost sites of Allen's lappet-browed bats (*Idionycteris phyllotis*). Southwestern Naturalist 54:201-203.

Solvesky, B.G., and C.L. Chambers. 2009. Roosts of Allen's lappet-browed bat in Northern Arizona. Journal of Wildlife Management 73:677-682.

Speakman, J.R., and D.W. Thomas. 2003. Physiological ecology and energetic of bats. In: Kunz, T.H., and M.B. Fenton, eds. Bat Ecology. Chicago: University of Chicago Press: 430-490.

Tumlison, R. 1993. Geographic variation in the lappet-eared bat, *Idionycteris phyllotis*, with descriptions of subspecies. Journal of Mammalogy 74:412-421.

U.S. Forest Service [USFS]. 2009. Draft Coronado National Forest ecological sustainability report. Tucson, AZ: U.S. Department of Agriculture, Forest Service. Available: http://www.fs fed.us/r3/coronado/plan-revision/documents/final/cnf-ecological-sustainability-report-final-022009.pdf.

Habitat: Townsend's big-eared bat (*Corynorhinus townsendii*)			
Trait/Quality	**Question**	**Background info. & explanation of score**	**Points**
1. Area and distribution: *breeding*	Is the area or location of the associated vegetation type used for breeding activities by this species expected to change?	**Taxonomic note:** Family Vespertilionidae. Formerly designated as *Plecotus townsendii*. Subsequently, sub-genus *Corynorhinus* was given status of genus and *Plecotus townsendii* (along with 2 other *Plecotus* species in North America) were moved into this genus (reviewed in Tumlison and Douglas 1992). Various common names have been used for the species, including western long-nosed bat and western lump-nosed bat, and "pale lump-nosed bat" for this sub-species. Using genetic analysis, Piaggio and Perkins (2005) concluded that *Corynorhinus townsendii townsendii* is the sub-species that occurs in Arizona and *C. townsendii pallescens* occurs in New Mexico and Colorado, which differed from prior work by Handley (1959) who assigned *C. townsendii pallescens* to large areas of the western United States, including Arizona.

This species occurs only infrequently in desert mountains in Arizona (Hoffmeister 1986). In summer, occurs across the state in desert scrub, shelters in desert mountains, oak woodlands, pinyon-juniper, and coniferous forests (Hoffmeister 1986). Handley (1959) reported that this species occurs mainly in Upper Sonoran and Transition life zones, in some places ranging into Lower Sonoran Zone, indicating that it is uncommon in prairie or extreme desert habitats. Occurs in coniferous and deciduous forest throughout much of its range (Kunz and Martin 1982). In California and Washington, reported in coastal areas and hills with mixed vegetation (references in Kunz and Martin 1982). In western coniferous forests, reported in coastal humid forest, pinyon-juniper, montane woodland forest, subalpine forest, forest meadow, and riparian areas (Hayes 2003).

Found during the day mostly in caves or mine tunnels; may use abandoned buildings at night to rest (Hoffmeister 1986). Pregnant females occur in maternity colonies; males generally occur in separate groups from females during the summer (Hoffmeister 1986). Summer colonies in Arizona are generally not large; the largest noted by Hoffmeister (1986) was 100 individuals in the Baboquivari Mountains.

This species occurs, or potential habitat exists, on all 12 of the EMAs on CNF (Jones, personal communication). Surveys by Jones (2009) on Huachuca EMA resulted in no detections of this species. Projections of suitable climate for vegetation communities forest wide (Chapter 1) predicted declines in suitable climate for all plant community types, with the exception of increases of suitable climate for semi-desert grassland and a slight increase in Sonoran desert scrub (present in small amounts on the CNF).

Not clear to what extent this species uses semi-desert grassland on the CNF, which is the plant community that is expected to increase (Chapter 1). Humphrey and Kunz (1976) reported this species in portions of northwestern Oklahoma and south-central Kansas containing mid-grass prairie vegetation invaded by mesquite and sage, as well as riparian vegetation where gypsum hills provide topographic variation that provided roost sites. Fellers and Pierson (2002) found that this species in northern coastal California spent the majority of time near riparian trees and shrubs, occasionally spending time in open habitats (where trees and shrubs occurred), but individuals generally avoided open grassland, both when foraging and traveling between roosting and foraging areas.

Given that this species is rare in prairies (Handley 1959) and the observation that individuals avoided open grassland (Fellers and Pierson 2002), we did not assume that grasslands would substitute for | 2 |

Habitat: Townsend's big-eared bat (*Corynorhinus townsendii*)			
Trait/Quality	**Question**	**Background info. & explanation of score**	**Points**
		predicted losses of oak-woodland, pinyon-juniper, and coniferous forest habitats that Hoffmeister (1986) indicated are used by this species.	
2. Area and distribution: *non-breeding*	Is the area or location of the associated vegetation type used for non-breeding activities by this species expected to change?	Believed to occur in southern Arizona year-round (See Habitat, Question 8). See Habitat, Question 1 for discussion of habitat and scoring. Hoffmeister (1986) found bats both hibernating and active within the same mine in winter (February 1958); he posed the question of whether individuals might need to feed in winter. Three individuals were captured while away from roosts in New Mexico in November and January (Geluso 2007).	2
3. Habitat components: *breeding*	Are specific habitat components required for breeding expected to change?	Females form maternity colonies in the warm parts of caves, mines, and buildings (references in Kunz and Martin 1982). Maternity colonies for this species as large as 1000 females have been reported (Barbour and Davis 1969 as cited in Nowak 1994); in Oklahoma and Kansas, nursery colonies contained 17-40 females (Humphreys and Kunz 1976 as cited in Nowak 1994). Hoffmeister (1986) indicated that summer colonies in Arizona are not large, with the largest being ~100 individuals in the Baboquivari Mountains; in winter, this colony had ~50 individuals, with many hibernacula having fewer. In the Great Basin, Sherwin and others (2003) observed some maternity colonies in mines to move, often multiple times, during the maternity period, some of which was predictable when examined across years, whereas maternity colonies in caves typically used the cave for the entire period as well as among years; however, the authors warned against extrapolating locally derived roosting pattern information to other geographic regions. During the spring, males are reported to typically occupy areas separate from maternity colonies (references in Kunz and Martin 1982), although Sherwin and others (2003) indicated that some roosts sites were observed as both maternity and bachelor colonies (not clear if use for both purposes was simultaneous). Bachelor colonies in the Great Basin were observed to move among a predictable group of mines during each year (Sherwin and others 2003). After an initial bout of feeding at night, individuals use night roosts that are often shared by other species (references in Kunz and Martin 1982). The abundance of caves, mines, and buildings not expected to change as a result of climate change. Standing water is assumed to be important to this species. In arid environments, water can be a resource that limits the presence of bats (Hayes and Loeb 2007). Insectivorous bats must obtain much of their water intake from free-standing water, unlike frugivorous and nectarivorous bats, which obtain much of their water from food (Neuweiler 2000 as cited in Hayes and Loeb 2007). Water availability is expected to be important to successful reproduction since bats lose a large of water to evaporation across their wing membranes (Adams 2003) and because they lactate.	1
4. Habitat components: *non-breeding*	Are specific habitat components required for survival during non-breeding periods expected to change?	Uses hibernacula (caves, mines, or buildings) in winter (Kunz and Martin 1982). This species prefers relatively cold places for hibernation; rarely observed in the warmer parts of winter hibernacula (Humphrey and Kunz 1976; references in Kunz and Martin 1982). Most limestone caves in California are too warm for successful hibernation (Graham 1966 as cited in Kunz and Martin 1982). Sherwin and others (2003) observed that in the Great Basin in winter, colonies often moved among different roosts within a hibernation season.	1

Habitat: Townsend's big-eared bat (*Corynorhinus townsendii*)			
Trait/Quality	**Question**	**Background info. & explanation of score**	**Points**
		The abundance of caves, mines, and buildings not expected to be altered as a result of climate change. See Habitat, Question 3 regarding standing water, which is expected to decrease.	
5. Habitat quality and reproduction	Are features of the habitat associated with better reproductive success expected to change?	No information found.	0
6. Habitat quality and survival	Are features of the habitat associated with better survival expected to change?	No information found.	0
7. Ability to colonize new areas	What is this species' capacity and tendency to disperse?	While females have shown high site fidelity to maternity roosts (Pearson and others 1952; references in Fellers and Pierson 2002), we considered bats capable of colonizing new areas due to their capacity for flight. The longest movement record in California was 32.2 km (Pearson and others 1952), whereas movements of 64 km have been reported in Kentucky and West Virginia (Barbour and Davis 1969 as cited in Kunz and Martin 1982). Three females were observed to move an average of 11.6 km between hibernacula and maternity roosts (Humphrey and Kunz 1976).	-1
8. Migratory or transitional habitats	Does this species require additional habitats during migration that are separated from breeding and non-breeding habitats?	Hoffmeister (1986) indicated that this species occurs in winter south of Mogollon Plateau "but northwest to Ash Fork and Hackberry," which suggests that individuals breeding in northern Arizona may move south in winter. Regardless, it appears that individuals breeding in southeastern Arizona occur there year-round. Kunz and Martin (1982) indicated that the species appears to be relatively sedentary (see references therein) and that no long-distance migrations have been reported.	0

Physiology: Townsend's big-eared bat (*Corynorhinus townsendii*)			
Trait/Quality	**Question**	**Background info. & explanation of score**	**Points**
1. Physiological thresholds	Are limiting physiological conditions expected to change?	Nocturnal forager, so not active during the hottest parts of the day. In Oklahoma and Kansas, individuals in small nursery colonies showed the ability to maintain thermal exchange during pregnancy and lactation, which was facilitated by roosting in dense clusters and was considered to be important to reproductive success (Humphrey and Kunz 1976). Warmer temperatures might reduce physiological demands associated with cold during pregnancy and rearing of young, although there may be no effect if phenology of breeding shifts to earlier in spring. In a review of the upper critical temperatures for 50 species of bats, the maximum was 41.00 °C and mean was 36.26 °C (Speakman and Thomas 2003); upper critical temperature is the ambient temperature above which an animal's body temperature will increase unless it pants or sweats. In the case of three species of bats roosting in a barn in California in summer (*Myotis yumanensis*, *Antrozous pallidus*, and *Tadarida brasiliensis*), when ambient temperature approached 40 °C (104 °F), spacing between individuals tended to increase and most individuals moved to cooler parts of the loft though some did not (Licht and Leitner 1967).	0

Physiology: Townsend's big-eared bat (*Corynorhinus townsendii*)			
Trait/Quality	Question	Background info. & explanation of score	Points
		Overall, we assumed that temperatures are not likely to exceed high temperature thresholds. Standing water is expected to become less available, but this is covered in Habitat section.	
2. Sex ratio	Is sex ratio determined by temperature?	No. Temperature-dependent sex determination is mainly observed in reptiles and fish (Manolakou et al. 2006).	0
3. Exposure to extreme weather conditions	Are extreme weather or disturbance events that result in direct mortality or reproductive failure expected to change?	Increase in frequency of heat waves is predicted for southwestern United States. Overall, not clear to what extent timing and intensity of heat waves will affect survival and reproduction. We assumed it unlikely that heat waves would cause widespread mortality for this species. See also Physiology, Question 1 above.	0
4. Limitations to active period	Are projected temperature or precipitation regimes that influence activity period of species expected to change?	Active at night for foraging; are considered late flyers (Hoffmeister 1986). Given nocturnal foraging activity, increase in temperatures not likely to reduce foraging time significantly. Warmer winter temperatures may reduce time spent in torpor, but not clear whether this will significantly increase activity periods. Furthermore, unclear whether increased activity in winter would have a neutral effect or negative effect on overall energy balance.	0
5. Metabolic inhibition	Does this species possess an ability to reduce metabolic energy or water requirements?	This species is reported to undergo hibernation in winter though some winter activity has been documented. Hibernacula include caves, mines, or buildings (Kunz and Martin 1982). Hoffmeister (1986) found bats both hibernating and active within the same mine in winter (February 1958); Pearson and others (1952) indicated that this species has been observed flying in winter months in northern California. This species appears to arouse from torpor frequently and move its position within the hibernaculum or move to a nearby cave or mine; this behavior contributes to mass loss (Kunz and Martin 1982). Changes in air temperature or humidity can stimulate arousals from torpor. Most roost singly in winter although may form clusters from a few individuals to several dozen (references in Kunz and Martin 1982). Use postures that appear to buffer from environmental extremes but still can lose body mass during hibernation (up to half of the autumn body mass; Humphrey and Kunz 1976). In maternity colonies, females generally are active but may undergo torpor when roost temperatures are low (references in Kunz and Martin 1982). Pearson and others (1952) noted that bats in this genus may undergo periods of torpor in summer in addition to winter. Unclear whether increased winter temperatures would reduce temperatures appropriate for torpor, resulting in inability of individuals to achieve energy savings in winter.	0
6. Survival during resource limitation	Does this species have lower energy requirements or possess the capacity to store energy or water in the long term?	See Physiology, Question 5.	none
7. Variable life history	Does this species have alternative life history strategies to cope with variable resources or climate conditions?	No alternative strategies.	0

USDA Forest Service RMRS-GTR-273. 2012.

Physiology: Townsend's big-eared bat (*Corynorhinus townsendii*)

Trait/Quality	Question	Background info. & explanation of score	Points
8. Reproduction in variable environments	Can this species outlive periods where reproduction is limited?	Pearson and others (1952) estimated for sites in California, median age estimate of 3.1 years and average age of 5.0 years. One lifespan reported by Paradiso and Greenhall (1967) was 16 years 5 months. Periods of extreme reductions in rainfall may last 5 years. If these conditions reduce resources to the point that bats have insufficient resources for breeding, but conditions recover after, it is likely that sufficient numbers of individuals would survive long enough to breed once conditions improve.	-1

Phenology: Townsend's big-eared bat (*Corynorhinus townsendii*)

Trait/Quality	Question	Background info. & explanation of score	Points
1. Cues	Does this species use temperature or moisture cues to initiate activities related to fecundity or survival?	This species reported to undergo hibernation, which is associated with temperature. Rises in spring temperature result in reductions in torpid behavior and are likely one trigger for females with respect to ovulation (copulation occurs in fall and winter, with ovulation occurring in late winter or early spring; Hoffmeister 1986). Pearson and others (1952) reported that in California, gestation in this species lasts from 56-100 days, depending on spring temperatures and the extent of torpor among individuals. On the other hand, the author found that in California, there was no clear support that individuals in colder regions gave birth later than those in warmer regions. Temperature and moisture influence insect abundance (this species is an insectivore). But any relationship to the timing of parturition would be indirect.	1
2. Event timing	Are activities related to species' fecundity or survival tied to discrete events that are expected to change?	Changes in the timing of precipitation and increases in temperature can alter the timing of insect availability and abundance; insect prey assumed to be important to survival of young.	1
3. Mismatch potential	What is the separation in time or space between cues that initiate activities and discrete events that provide critical resources?	Critical resources are assumed to be insect prey. Since this species does not undergo long-distance movements, resources and timing of breeding are closely timed (individuals would have local indication of resource abundance).	-1
4. Resilience to timing mismatches during breeding	Does this species employ strategies or have traits that increase the likelihood of reproduction co-occurring with important events?	Breed in fall and winter; sperm is stored and female ovulates in late winter or early spring (Hoffmeister 1986). Ovulation may occur either before or after females leave hibernacula (Kunz and Martin 1982). A single young is produced.	1

Biotic interactions: Townsend's big-eared bat (*Corynorhinus townsendii*)			
Trait/Quality	**Question**	**Background info. & explanation of score**	**Points**
1. Food resources	Are important food resources for this species expected to change?	Feed mostly on small moths averaging 6 mm long; may take other insects of the Orders Neuroptera, Coleoptera, Diptera, and Hymenoptera (references in Kunz and Martin 1982). Members of this genus capture insects in flight as well as pick insects from foliage while hovering (Nowak 1994). Eastern sub-species said to be Lepidopteran specialists. Given that this species is said to feed primarily on microlepidopterans, we scored this question "1" because there may be limited alternative prey opportunities if microlepidopterans are negatively impacted by climate change.	1
2. Predators	Are important predator populations expected to change?	Pearson and others (1952) considered it unlikely that predation was very high; considered the overall number of suitable winter roosting sites and the number of summer roosting sites surrounded by suitable feeding areas to be the main limits on population size for this species. Fellers (2002) presented evidence suggesting that predation by rats was the primary cause of reproductive failure of a large maternity colony in California located in an abandoned house built in the 1880s. No information found to suggest that predation levels would change as a result of climate change.	0
3. Symbionts	Are populations of symbiotic species expected to change?	No information found to suggest existence of important symbiotic relationships.	0
4. Disease	Is prevalence of diseases known to cause widespread mortality or reproductive failure in this species expected to change?	Rabies virus was found in less than 1% of asymptomatic individuals sampled in New Mexico (Constantine 1967 as cited in Kunz and Martin 1982). Endoparasites reported include 2 nematodes and a cestode; ectoparasites include winged bat flies (Streblidae family), wingless bat flies (Nycteribiidae), macronyssid mites, ticks, a species of chigger, and sarcoptid mites (references in Kunz and Martin 1982; Ritzi and others 2001), but no indication that these cause significant mortality for the species. Pearson and others (1952) considered it unlikely that disease had a substantial role in population control given how rare unhealthy individuals were encountered; the author considered the overall number of suitable winter roosting sites and the number of summer roosting sites surrounded by suitable feeding areas as the main limits on population size for this species.	0
5. Competitors	Are populations of important competing species expected to change?	Little information available regarding competitors of this species or of competitive interactions affecting bats in general. Potential competitors are most likely other bat species and/or birds that forage aerially at dusk and dawn (e.g., poorwills and nighthawks; Adams 2003); competition would be for insect prey and/or access to water sources for drinking. Adams (2003) cited work by researchers in Colorado that found that bat species typically differed in the time of night they visited small water holes.	0

Literature Cited

Adams, R.A. 2003. Bats of the Rocky Mountain West. Boulder, CO: University of Colorado Press. 289 p.

Fellers, G.M. 2002. Predation on *Corynorhinus townsendii* by *Rattus rattus*. Southwestern Naturalist 45:524-527.

Fellers, G.M., and E.D. Pierson. 2002. Habitat use and foraging behavior or Townsend's big-eared bat (*Corynorhinus townsendii*) in coastal California. Journal of Mammalogy 83:167-177.

Geluso, K. 2007. Winter activity of bats over water and along flyways in New Mexico. Southwestern Naturalist 52:482-492.

Handley, C.O., Jr. 1959. A revision of American bats of the Genera Euderma and Plecotus. Proceedings of the United States National Museum 110:95-246.

Hayes, J.P. 2003. Habitat ecology and conservation of bats in western coniferous forests. In: Zabel, C.J., and R.G. Anthony, eds. Mammal Community Dynamics: Management and Conservation in the Coniferous Forests of Western North America. Cambridge, United Kingdom: Cambridge University Press: 81-119.

Hayes, J.P., and S.C. Loeb. 2007. The influences of forest management on bats in North America. In: Lacki, M.J., J.P. Hayes, and A. Kurta., eds. Bats in Forests: Conservation and Management. Baltimore, MD: Johns Hopkins University Press: 207-235.

Hoffmeister, D.F. 1986. Mammals of Arizona. University of Arizona Press and Arizona Game and Fish Department. 602 p.

Humphrey, S.R., and T.H. Kunz. 1976. Ecology of a Pleistocene relict, the Western big-eared bat (*Plecotus townsendii*), in the southern Great Plains. Journal of Mammalogy 57:470-494.

Jones, L. 2009. Distribution of bats across the Huachuca Ecosystem Management Area: A preliminary assessment for a landscape-level habitat restoration project. 2009 Arizona Bat Conservation Partnership Grant Final Report; December 23, 2009; Submitted to Arizona Game and Fish Department, Phoenix, and USDA Forest Service, Coronado National Forest, Tucson, Arizona. Forest Service Agreement Number 09-CO-11030515-038. Arizona Game and Fish Department Project Number FY-09-06.

Jones, Larry. 2010. [Personal communication]. February 17, 2010. Tucson, AZ: U.S. Department of Agriculture, Forest Service, Coronado National Forest, Assistant Program Manager for Wildlife, Fish, and Rare Plants.

Kunz, T.H., and R.A. Martin. 1982. *Plecotus townsendii*. American Society of Mammalogists. Mammalian Species No. 175: 1-6.

Licht, P., and P. Leitner. 1967. Behavioral responses to high temperatures in three species of California bats. Journal of Mammalogy 48:52-61.

Manolakou, P., G. Lavranos, and R. Angelopoulou. 2006. Molecular patterns of sex determination in the animal kingdom: A comparative study of the biology of reproduction. Reproductive Biology and Endocrinology 4:59.

Nowak, R.M. 1994. Walker's Bats of the World. Baltimore, MD: Johns Hopkins University Press.

Paradiso, J.L., and A.M. Greenhall. 1967. Longevity records for American bats. American Midland Naturalist 78:251-252.

Pearson, O.P., M.R Koford, and A.K. Pearson. 1952. Reproduction of the lump-nosed bat (*Corynorhinus rafinesquei*) in California. Journal of Mammalogy 33:272-320.

Piaggio, A.J., and S.L. Perkins. 2005. Molecular phylogeny of North American long-eared bats (Vespertilionidae: Corynorhinus); inter- and intraspecific relationships inferred from mitochondrial and nuclear DNA sequences. Molecular Phylogenetics and Evolution 37:762-775.

Ritzi, C.M., L.K. Ammerman, M.T. Dixon, and J.V. Richerson. 2001. Bat ectoparasites from the Trans-Pecos region of Texas, including notes from Big Bend National Park. Journal of Medical Entomology 38:400-404.

Sherwin, R.E., W.L. Gannon, and J.S. Altenbach. 2003. Managing complex systems simply: understanding inherent variation in the use of roosts by Townsend's big-eared bat. Wildlife Society Bulletin 31:62-72.

Speakman, J.R., and D.W. Thomas. 2003. Physiological ecology and energetic of bats. In: Kunz, T.H., and M.B. Fenton, eds. Bat Ecology. Chicago: University of Chicago Press: 430-490.

Tumlison, R., and M.E. Douglas. 1992. Parsimony analysis and phylogeny of the plecotine bats (Chiroptera: Vespertilionidae). Journal of Mammalogy 73:276-285.

U.S. Forest Service [USFS]. 2009. Draft Coronado National Forest ecological sustainability report. Tucson, AZ: U.S. Department of Agriculture, Forest Service. Available: http://www.fs.fed.us/r3/coronado/plan-revision/documents/final/cnf-ecological-sustainability-report-final-022009.pdf.

Habitat: Abert's squirrel (*Sciurus aberti*)			
Trait/Quality	**Question**	**Background info. & explanation of score**	**Points**
1. Area and distribution: *breeding*	Is the area or location of the associated vegetation type used for breeding activities by this species expected to change?	Range in the Unites States is Wyoming, Colorado, Utah, New Mexico, and Arizona; also occurs in portions of Mexico (from northern Sonora to southern Durango; Nash and Seaman 1977). While typically considered dependent on ponderosa pine for food, cover, and nest sites, this species has been reported in pinyon pine, Douglas-fir, and spruce fir (see review in Hutton and others 2003). On Mount Graham, Hutton and others (2003) documented this species in mixed conifer and spruce-fir between 1989 and 2003. This species is considered invasive on the CNF although native populations occur in northern Arizona. It was introduced into the Pinaleño and Santa Catalina EMAs (Jones, personal communication). Introduction to Mount Graham in the Pinaleño Mountains occurred in the 1940s (Hutton and others 2003). Projections of suitable climate for vegetation communities (Chapter 1) predicted declines in suitable conditions for Madrean forest and woodland, Madrean conifer forest and increases of suitable conditions for semi-desert grassland, and, to a lesser extent, Sonoran desert scrub. Expect that habitat for this species will decrease as a result of climate change.	2
2. Area and distribution: *non-breeding*	Is the area or location of the associated vegetation type used for non-breeding activities by this species expected to change?	Same as breeding habitat (See Habitat, Question 1).	2
3. Habitat components: *breeding*	Are specific habitat components required for breeding expected to change?	Tree squirrels (*Sciurus* and *Tamiasciurus*) use nests for rearing young, rest, predator avoidance, and cover during inclement weather (Steel and Koprowski 2001). Abert's squirrels use tree dreys (spherical twig nests they build) and, to a lesser extent, tree cavities (Edelman and Koprowski 2007). Dreys were more often in trees that were larger and taller than random trees in a study in the Pinaleño Mountains; some individuals used cavities for nests (Edelman and Koprowski 2005a). Cavity nests accounted for ~10% of the nests, and aspen was the most common tree species used for cavity nests (Edelman and Koprowski 2006). Trees, overall, are expected to decline in abundance.	1
4. Habitat components: *non-breeding*	Are specific habitat components required for survival during non-breeding periods expected to change?	Uses nests and cavities in winter (see Habitat, Question 3).	1
5. Habitat quality and reproduction	Are features of the habitat associated with better reproductive success expected to change?	"Survivorship and reproduction of tree squirrels often are positively correlated with tree seed production. This dependence on mature, seed-producing forests is likely one reason that several species of tree squirrels are considered to be threatened or endangered in all or part of their ranges..." (Koprowski and Corse 2001). Recruitment in Abert's Squirrels in north-central Arizona was positively related to the number of interlocking canopy trees (Dodd and others 2003). Mature trees with high mast yields are expected to decline due to fire and increased aridity.	1

Habitat: Abert's squirrel (*Sciurus aberti*)

Trait/Quality	Question	Background info. & explanation of score	Points
6. Habitat quality and survival	Are features of the habitat associated with better survival expected to change?	See Habitat, Question 5. Density of this species was positively related to fecal fungal diversity; winter survival was negatively related to snow cover duration and positively related to dietary fungal diversity (Dodd and others 2003); fecal fungal content in August was, in turn, positively related to basal area for all tree species. Logging has been associated with loss of high-quality foods, which has led to increased mortality (references in Keith 2003), indicating the importance of trees for food.	1
7. Ability to colonize new areas	What is this species' capacity and tendency to disperse?	Tree squirrels are reported to "routinely move distances of 1 km" (references in Koprowski 2005). Little other information found on dispersal. We assumed that both sexes are mobile.	-1
8. Migratory or transitional habitats	Does this species require additional habitats during migration that are separated from breeding and non-breeding habitats?	This species is a year-round resident.	0

Physiology: Abert's squirrel (*Sciurus aberti*)

Trait/Quality	Question	Background info. & explanation of score	Points
1. Physiological thresholds	Are limiting physiological conditions expected to change?	Abert's squirrels are strictly diurnally active (Nash and Seaman 1977). Activity usually begins in the morning with the first light and continues until dusk, with rest periods during the day (Brown 1984). Generally spends the afternoon in a nest or on a foliage-shaded limb (or when cold, may bask in the sun on a limb) (Brown 1984). Squirrels may become inactive outside of the nest when temperatures are high (Gurnell 1987). Rainfall does not typically reduce activity unless it is heavy (references in Gurnell 1987). Squirrels spend most time foraging in trees in summer. Tree squirrels are reported to use evaporative cooling following periods of activity when temperatures are high (may lose heat from sweat glands in feet; Gurnell 1987). We assumed that temperatures will remain below physiological thresholds most of the time.	0
2. Sex ratio	Is sex ratio determined by temperature?	No. Temperature-dependent sex determination is mainly observed in reptiles and fish (Manolakou et al. 2006).	0
3. Exposure to extreme weather conditions	Are extreme weather or disturbance events that result in direct mortality or reproductive failure expected to change?	Increase in frequency of heat waves is predicted for southwestern United States. Overall, not clear to what extent timing and intensity of heat waves will affect survival and reproduction. We assumed it is not likely that heat waves would cause widespread mortality for this species. See also Physiology, Question 1.	0
4. Limitations to active period	Are projected temperature or precipitation regimes that influence activity period of species expected to change?	This species is diurnally active. During summer, squirrels tend to have 2 periods of activity—morning and later afternoon (Gurnell 1987). We assumed that rise in temperatures would not significantly impact morning and evening activity periods. See also Physiology, Question 1.	0

Physiology: Abert's squirrel (*Sciurus aberti*)			
Trait/Quality	Question	Background info. & explanation of score	Points
5. Metabolic inhibition	Does this species possess an ability to reduce metabolic energy or water requirements?	Active year-round, even during inclement winter weather (Golightly and Ohmart 1978). Abert's squirrels will co-occupy nests in winter; the proportion of individuals that nest communally in winter increased with decreasing temperature in a population studied in the Pinaleño Mountains (Edelman and Koprowski 2007). Golightly and Ohmart (1978) studied heterothermy in Abert's squirrels in the wild and in the lab. Body temperature rose in association with periods of intense activity in both winter and summer; this species often sought shade after these periods. In the laboratory, body temperature decreased as ambient temperatures decreased; metabolic expenditures also declined. Although there is not strong evidence that this species uses torpor on a daily basis when temperatures are cold, the fact that squirrels are known to lower body temperature at night and when at rest suggests some ability to reduce energy requirements. This led to the choice of "-1" for this question.	-1
6. Survival during resource limitation	Does this species have lower energy requirements or possess the capacity to store energy or water in the long term?	Brown (1984) indicated that Abert's squirrels generally do not seem to cache many cones. Keith (2003) indicated that this species does not cache food. Appears that squirrels do not deposit large amounts of subcutaneous fat for insulation, although they may increase fat reserves in other parts of the body (Gurnell 1987). This species molts twice a year, with thicker coat in winter.	1
7. Variable life history	Does this species have alternative life history strategies to cope with variable resources or climate conditions?	None reported.	0
8. Reproduction in variable environments	Can this species outlive periods where reproduction is limited?	Barkalow and Soots (1975) cited references that indicate that gray squirrels rarely live longer than 6 years in the wild. In their own study, of 10 wild eastern gray squirrels (*Sciurus carolinensis*), the shortest survival was 6 years and the longest was 12.5 years (Barkalow and Soots 1975). A study of red squirrels (*Tamiasciurus hudsonicus*) in Montana found that 67% of individuals died before 12 months, with a plateau in survivorship occurring at about 36 months and very few individuals surviving past 7 years (Halvorson and Engeman 1983). Periods of extreme reductions in rainfall may last 5 years. If these conditions reduce food resources to the point that squirrels have insufficient food for breeding, most of the population would not survive longer than the periods of limited reproduction.	1

Phenology: Abert's squirrel (*Sciurus aberti*)			
Trait/Quality	Question	Background info. & explanation of score	Points
1. Cues	Does this species use temperature or moisture cues to initiate activities related to fecundity or survival?	The onset of breeding season in this species is reported to coincide with the production of male flowers of the ponderosa pine, reportedly leading to individuals coming into breeding condition (see references in Brown 1984: 26). Keith (2003) questioned this because staminate flower opening is controlled by temperature that generally does not occur until late May or early June (various authors have reported range of mating dates as early as mid-February through June).	0

USDA Forest Service RMRS-GTR-273. 2012.

Phenology: Abert's squirrel (*Sciurus aberti*)

Trait/Quality	Question	Background info. & explanation of score	Points
		It is likely that food availability of some kind is important and that temperature and moisture influence the availability, but since the relationship to squirrel breeding is indirect, this question was scored as "0." Also note that ponderosa pine is not the only tree species consumed by this species (see Biotic Interactions, Question 1), so likely that flowers of other tree species could be important.	
2. Event timing	Are activities related to species' fecundity or survival tied to discrete events that are expected to change?	According to Brown (1984), a female is receptive to breeding for only about 18 hours once each year and that not all females come into estrus each year. Males are in reproductive condition from approximately the end of April to the end of June (although among-individual and among-year variation exists; Brown 1984). If the onset of breeding activity is correlated with flower emergence and consumption of flower parts (Brown 1984; see Phenology, Question 1), warmer temperatures may lead to earlier flowering or to alterations to the availability of other types of food.	1
3. Mismatch potential	What is the separation in time or space between cues that initiate activities and discrete events that provide critical resources?	We considered food a critical resource and assumed a relatively short period of time between food availability and breeding. See Phenology, Question 2.	-1
4. Resilience to timing mismatches during breeding	Does this species employ strategies or have traits that increase the likelihood of reproduction co-occurring with important events?	According to Brown (1984), a female is receptive to breeding for only about 18 hours once each year and not all females come into estrus each year. This characteristic increases its vulnerability to a mismatch between resource availability and the breeding period.	1

Biotic interactions: Abert's squirrel (*Sciurus aberti*)

Trait/Quality	Question	Background info. & explanation of score	Points
1. Food resources	Are important food resources for this species expected to change?	This species does not cache food regularly (references in Keith 2003). Overall, the diet of this species varies by location and season (Keith 2003), presumably based on availability of various foods. Some records indicate that this species is dependent on ponderosa pine for food (including seeds, apical buds, staminate cones, inner bark, and hypogeous [subterranean] fungi associated with ponderosa pine; see references in Edelman and Koprowski 2005b). However, other reports (Edelman and Koprowski 2005b) observed consumption of other species of tree. In the Pinaleño Mountains, seeds of Southwestern white pine and Douglas-fir were most commonly consumed; ponderosa pine seeds were consumed in lesser amounts; and corkbark fir and Englemann spruce seeds were never eaten. Other parts (e.g., apical buds, inner bark, and staminate flowers) of these tree species were consumed, with the preference varying by tree species. In one study, the availability of food (truffles, acorns, cones, and mushrooms) varied annually over a 5-year period (States and others 1988 as cited in Keith 2003)	1

Trait/Quality	Question	Background info. & explanation of score	Points
		In central Arizona, pine seeds were estimated to comprise more than 50% of the diet between June and October, and inner bark was estimated to comprise 50% of the diet between December and May (Keith 1965). Gurnell (1987) indicated that the species in southern United States consumes mostly fungi in summer and autumn and a large proportion of bark in winter; other consumed components are staminate flowers (winter and spring), seeds (all seasons), and buds (spring). Brown (1984) indicated that truffles of the genera *Gautierea*, *Rhizopogon*, and *Morchella* are "probably the most consistent important dietary items." Hoffmeister (1986) indicated that in the Flagstaff, Arizona, area, nearly all cone-producing ponderosa pines are at least 60 years old. On the other hand, over-mature trees are said to produce low-quality cones and the inner bark is reduced in nutritive value. This species appears to be able to vary its diet species, but depends heavily on trees for food, including seeds, and trees are expected to decline.	
2. Predators	Are important predator populations expected to change?	Goshawks have been documented as preying on Abert's squirrels (Reynolds 1963). Gurnell (1987) indicated that red-tailed hawks, red-shouldered hawks, goshawks, and martens hunt squirrels more frequently than other predatory species; however, no species of *Martes* occurs in Arizona. Gurnell (1987) indicated "there is little evidence that predators have any impact on squirrel populations."	0
3. Symbionts	Are populations of symbiotic species expected to change?	Relationship between squirrels and seed crop considered under Biotic Interactions, Question 1. Given that this species not considered to cache large numbers of acorns/seeds, not clear to what extent it acts as a seed disperser for tree species.	0
4. Disease	Is prevalence of diseases known to cause widespread mortality or reproductive failure in this species expected to change?	Squirrels are host to a variety of parasites and diseases (Gurnell 1987). Diseases include distemper, diphtheria, scab disease, myxomatosis (myxoma viral infection), and parapoxvirus infection. Gray squirrels in the Midwest have acquired California encephalitis. Little is known about pathogenicity of most parasite and disease organisms in squirrels. Coccidiosis (infection by protozoan, coccidian in intestinal wall) can cause serious infections that weaken squirrels. Ectoparasites, including fleas, are common in squirrels (Gurnell 1987). Mortality from plague appears to be uncommon in tree squirrels. A search on Web of Science for "plague" and "*Sciurus*" yielded no results. A search of "plague" and "tree squirrels" yielded only Hudson and others (1971), which mentioned a case of eastern fox squirrels (*Sciurus niger*) dying in urban Denver in 1968, some of which were positive for antigens to plague and/or had fleas that were host to *Yersinia pestis* (bacterium that causes plague). A Web of Science search on "Tamiasciurus" and "plague" returned Smith and others (2010), who reported that seroprevalence for *Yersinia pestis* was high in Allen's and long-eared chipmunks (*Tamias senex* and *T. quadrimaculatus*) and in the pine squirrel (*Tamiasciurus douglasii*) in northern California over 28 years of monitoring, but that all 3 were moderately resistant to plague and survived infection. Bot flies (*Cterebra* spp.) lay eggs in nests of several types of squirrels including gray squirrels; the larvae then burrow into the skin of squirrels, eventually re-emerging and dropping off to pupate. West Nile Virus (WNV) was first reported in eastern fox squirrels (*Sciurus niger*) in 2003 (Kiupul and others 2003). Most mammalian	0

Biotic interactions: Abert's squirrel (*Sciurus aberti*)			
Trait/Quality	Question	Background info. & explanation of score	Points
		WNV infections cause no or low morbidity or mortality, although tree squirrels are susceptible to a neurologic disease associated with infection (Padgett and others 2008).	
		Gurnell (1987) indicated that squirrels that are weakened by food shortage may develop a parasite or disease load heavy enough to cause mortality. Large squirrel mortality events were reported in Europe in the early 1900s; coccidiosis was reported to have killed one million Eurasian red squirrels in Finland from 1943-1944 (Lampio 1967 as cited in Gurnell 1987).	
5. Competitors	Are populations of important competing species expected to change?	Mount Graham red squirrel is likely impacted by Abert's squirrel. It has been suggested that red squirrels declined in abundance following the introduction of Abert's squirrel (Hoffmeister 1956 as cited in Hutton and others 2003). Abert's squirrels observed in red squirrel middens on Mount Graham, including being chased from middens by red squirrels (Hutton and others 2003). Possible that the two species may compete for food on Mount Graham (Hutton and others 2003). Mount Graham red squirrel expected to be vulnerable to climate change.	-1

Literature Cited

Barkalow, F.S., Jr., and R.F. Soots, Jr. 1975. Life span and reproductive longevity of the gray squirrel, *Sciurus c. carolinensis* Gmelin. Journal of Mammalogy 56:522-524.

Brown, D.E. 1984. Arizona's Tree Squirrels. Phoenix: Arizona Game and Fish Department. 114 p.

Dodd, N.L., J.S. States, and S.S. Rosenstock. 2003. Tassel-eared squirrel population, habitat condition, and dietary relationships in north-central Arizona. Journal of Wildlife Management 67:622-633.

Edelman, A.J., and J.L. Koprowski. 2007. Communal nesting in asocial Abert's squirrels: The role of social thermoregulation and breeding strategy. Ethology 113:147-154.

Edelman, A.J., and J.L. Koprowski. 2006. Characteristics of Abert's squirrel (*Sciurus aberti*) cavity nests. Southwestern Naturalist 51:64-70.

Edelman, A.J., and J.L. Koprowski. 2005a. Selection of drey sites by Abert's squirrels in an introduced population. Journal of Mammalogy 86: 1220-1226.

Edelman, A.J., and J.L. Koprowski. 2005b. Diet and tree use of Abert's squirrels (*Sciurus aberti*) in a mixed-conifer forest. Southwestern Naturalist 50:461-465.

Edelman, A.J., and J.L. Koprowski. 2001. North American Tree Squirrels. Washington, DC: Smithsonian Institution Press.

Golightly, R.T., Jr., and R.D. Ohmart. 1978. Heterothermy in free-ranging Abert's squirrels (*Sciurus aberti*). Ecology 59:897-909.

Gurnell, J. 1987. The Natural History of Squirrels. New York: Facts on File Publications. 201 p.

Halvorson, C.H., and R.M. Engeman. 1983. Survival analysis for a Red squirrel population. Journal of Mammalogy 64:332-336.

Hoffmeister, D.F. 1986. Mammals of Arizona. University of Arizona Press and Arizona Game and Fish Department. 602 p.

Hudson, B.W., M.I. Goldenberg, J.D. McCluskie, H.E. Larson, C.D. McGuire, A.M. Barnes, and J.D. Poland. 1971. Serological and bacteriological investigations of an outbreak of plague in an urban tree squirrel population. American Journal of Tropical Medicine and Hygiene 20:255-263.

Hutton, K.A., J.L. Koprowski, V.L. Greer, M.I. Alanen, C.A. Schauffert, and P. J. Young. 2003. Use of mixed-conifer and spruce-fir forests by an introduced population of Abert's squirrels (*Sciurus aberti*). Southwestern Naturalist 48:257-260.

Jones, Larry. 2010. [Personal communication]. February 18, 2010. Tucson, AZ: U.S. Department of Agriculture, Forest Service, Coronado National Forest, Assistant Program Manager for Wildlife, Fish, and Rare Plants.

Keith, J.O. 2003. Abert's Squirrel (*Sciurus aberti*): A technical assessment. Online. U.S. Department of Agriculture, Forest Service, Rocky Mountain Region. Available: http://www.fs fed.us/r2/projects/scp/assessments/abertsquirrel.pdf. Accessed: March 26, 2010.

Keith, J.O. 1965. The Abert Squirrel and its dependence on ponderosa pine. Ecology 46:150-163.

Koprowski, J.L., and M.C. Corse. 2001. Food habits of the Chiricahua fox squirrel (*Sciurus nayaritensis chiricahuae*). Southwestern Naturalist 46:62-65.

Koprowski, J.L. 2005. Management and conservation of Tree Squirrels: The importance of endemism, species richness, and forest condition. In: Gottfried, G.J., S. Brooke, L.G. Eskew, C.B. Carleton, comps. Connecting mountain islands and desert seas: Biodiversity and management of the Madrean Archipelago II. 2004 May 11-15; Tucson, AZ. Proc. RMRS-P-36. Fort Collins, CO: U.S. Department of Agriculture, Forest Service, Rocky Mountain Research Station: 245-250.

Manolakou, P., G. Lavranos, and R. Angelopoulou. 2006. Molecular patterns of sex determination in the animal kingdom: A comparative study of the biology of reproduction. Reproductive Biology and Endocrinology 4:59.

Nash, D.J., and R.N. Seaman.1977. *Sciurus aberti*. American Society of Mammalogists. Mammalian Species No. 80.

Padgett, K.A., W.K. Riesen, N. Kahl-Purcell, Y. Fang, B. Cahoon-Young, R. Carney, N. Anderson, L. Zucca, L. Woods, S. Husted, and V.L. Kramer. 2008. West Nile Virus infection in tree squirrels (Rodentia: Sciuridae) in California, 2004-2005. Journal of Wildlife Rehabilitation 29:35-39.

Reynolds, H.G. 1963. Western goshawk takes Abert squirrel in Arizona. Journal of Forestry 61:839.

Smith, C.R., J.R. Tucker, B.A. Wilson, and J.R. Clover. 2010. Plague studies in California: A review of long-term disease activity, flea-host relationships and plague ecology in the coniferous forests of the southern Cascades and northern Sierra Nevada Mountains. Journal of Vector Ecology 35:1-12.

Steele, M.A., and J.L. Koprowski. 2001. North American Tree Squirrels. Washington, DC: Smithsonian Institution Press. 225 p.

U.S. Forest Service [USFS]. 2009. Draft Coronado National Forest ecological sustainability report. Tucson, AZ: U.S. Department of Agriculture, Forest Service. Available: http://www fs.fed.us/r3/coronado/plan-revision/documents/final/cnf-ecological-sustainability-report-final-022009.pdf.

Habitat: Arizona gray squirrel (*Sciurus arizonensis*)			
Trait/Quality	Question	Background info. & explanation of score	Points
1. Area and distribution: *breeding*	Is the area or location of the associated vegetation type used for breeding activities by this species expected to change?	Summarized from Best and Reidel (1995): This species occurs at elevations of 1100 m to greater than 2700 m in Arizona, New Mexico, and Sonora, Mexico. In Arizona, it occurs on the Mogollon Plateau and in many isolated mountain ranges. In Arizona, occurs in "dense, mixed broadleaf communities of riparian-deciduous forest," although in southern parts of the state, it may occur away from deciduous trees where there are tall oaks in uplands. Many populations occur along streams that extend to elevations as low as semi-desert grassland and chaparral but only where the "riparian forest has high species diversity and tall, interlocking canopies." Reported not to occupy more open woodlands that are flood-prone or cottonwood-willow communities at lower elevations (Brown 1984), although in New Mexico, has been reported in floodplains (Frey and others 2008). Occurs in mature forest with tall trees and prefers groves of old sycamore and other large deciduous trees (cottonwood, box elder, Arizona elder, big-tooth maple, ash, willows, and Gambel oak) where cavities are apt to develop. Large evergreen oaks appear to be present throughout their range, even if not readily visible. Arizona walnut, Arizona oak, and Gambel oak are important sources	2

Habitat: Arizona gray squirrel (*Sciurus arizonensis*)			
Trait/Quality	**Question**	**Background info. & explanation of score**	**Points**
		of mast, cavities, and nest platforms. No records of this species in coniferous riparian forests such as blue spruce alliance (Muldavin and others 2000 as cited in Frey and others 2008).	
		In Arizona, uses hollows in deciduous trees. Builds conspicuous leaf nests; uses nest even during winter. An individual may have multiple leaf nests. Platform nests are used in summer for resting; a larger, covered nest is used for a nursery and living, apparently when dens are not available.	
		This species occurs, or potential habitat exists, on the following EMAs: Tumacacori, Santa Rita, Huachuca, and Santa Catalina (USFS 2009). Projections of suitable climate for vegetation communities (Chapter 1) predicted declines in suitable conditions for Madrean forest and woodland and Madrean conifer forest, and increases in suitable conditions for semi-desert grassland and, to a lesser extent, Sonoran desert scrub.	
		We expected that habitat for this species will decrease as a result of climate change.	
2. Area and distribution: *non-breeding*	Is the area or location of the associated vegetation type used for non-breeding activities by this species expected to change?	Same as breeding habitat.	2
3. Habitat components: *breeding*	Are specific habitat components required for breeding expected to change?	Requires tall trees for breeding in dens (hollows in trees) or in leaf nests constructed on branches. Nest trees are greater than 12 m tall and nests are frequently located 11-18 m above the ground (Best and Reidel 1995). Occupies hollows in deciduous trees, including ash, sycamore, and cottonwood (references in Best and Reidel 1995). Nests are most commonly built in different species of oaks, but this species also uses sycamores, walnut trees, alders, maples, cottonwoods, ash trees, and Apache pines (Best and Reidel 1995). Also reported to use flat platform nests in summer for resting.	1
		Trees, overall, are expected to decline in abundance.	
4. Habitat components: *non-breeding*	Are specific habitat components required for survival during non-breeding periods expected to change?	Appears to use hollows and leaf nests in winter as well as in summer; see above Habitat, Question 3.	1
5. Habitat quality and reproduction	Are features of the habitat associated with better reproductive success expected to change?	"Survivorship and reproduction of tree squirrels often are positively correlated with tree seed production. This dependence on mature, seed-producing forests is likely one reason that several species of tree squirrels are considered to be threatened or endangered in all or part of their range (Koprowski and Corse 2001)."	1
		Mature trees with high mast yields are expected to decline.	
6. Habitat quality and survival	Are features of the habitat associated with better survival expected to change?	See Habitat, Question 5.	1

Habitat: Arizona gray squirrel (*Sciurus arizonensis*)

Trait/Quality	Question	Background info. & explanation of score	Points
7. Ability to colonize new areas	What is this species' capacity and tendency to disperse?	Although *Sciurus* and *Tamiasciurus* spp. generally remain in the same area once they are established residents (unless there is a food shortage) (Gurnell 1987), squirrels, in general, are very mobile. Gurnell (1987) cited several studies on movement of gray squirrel in Minnesota, including juveniles moving more than 1 km from their natal area (Gull 1977 as cited in Gurnell 1987).	-1
8. Migratory or transitional habitats	Does this species require additional habitats during migration that are separated from breeding and non-breeding habitats?	An old record indicated that this species may move from high elevations into areas with oaks at lower elevations in summer (Dice and Blossom 1937 as cited in Best and Reidel 1995). However, not clear that this behavior is exhibited regularly or by many populations or that it is a requirement.	0

Physiology: Arizona gray squirrel (*Sciurus arizonensis*)

Trait/Quality	Question	Background info. & explanation of score	Points
1. Physiological thresholds	Are limiting physiological conditions expected to change?	This species is diurnally active. Squirrels may become inactive outside of the nest when temperatures are high (Gurnell 1987). Rainfall does not typically reduce activity unless it is heavy (references in Gurnell 1987). Squirrels spend most time foraging in trees in summer. Tree squirrels are reported to use evaporative cooling following periods of activity when temperatures are high (may lose heat from sweat glands in feet; Gurnell 1987). We assumed temperatures will remain below physiological thresholds most of the time.	0
2. Sex ratio	Is sex ratio determined by temperature?	No. Temperature-dependent sex determination is mainly observed in reptiles and fish (Manolakou et al. 2006).	0
3. Exposure to extreme weather conditions	Are extreme weather or disturbance events that result in direct mortality or reproductive failure expected to change?	Increase in frequency of heat waves is predicted for southwestern United States. Overall, not clear to what extent timing and intensity of heat waves will affect survival and reproduction. We considered it unlikely that heat waves would cause widespread mortality for this species. See also Physiology, Question 1.	0
4. Limitations to active period	Are projected temperature or precipitation regimes that influence activity period of species expected to change?	This species is diurnally active. During summer, squirrels tend to have two periods of activity—morning and later afternoon; Gurnell 1987). We assumed that rise in temperatures will not significantly impact morning and evening activity periods. See also Physiology, Question 1.	0
5. Metabolic inhibition	Does this species possess an ability to reduce metabolic energy or water requirements?	Squirrels are active year-round, and in winter tend to have one main active period each day; in northern areas, activity period may occur closer to the middle of the day than in southern regions (Gurnell 1987). Spend time in nests in winter to conserve body heat. In severe weather conditions, squirrels may remain in nests for several days (references in Gurnell 1987: 55). When at rest, this species' body temperature declines a few degrees, particularly at night when in the nest; this phenomenon has sometimes been referred to as heterothermy (Gurnell 1987). Some evidence to suggest that squirrels are able to employ a form of adaptive hypothermia (see Gurnell 1987: 66).	-1

Physiology: Arizona gray squirrel (*Sciurus arizonensis*)			
Trait/Quality	**Question**	**Background info. & explanation of score**	**Points**
		Although there is not strong evidence that this species uses torpor on a daily basis when temperatures are cold, the fact that squirrels are known to lower body temperature at night and when at rest suggests some ability to reduce energy requirements. This led to the score of "-1" for this question.	
6. Survival during resource limitation	Does this species have lower energy requirements or possess the capacity to store energy or water in the long term?	Best and Reidel (1995) reported that this species does not cache food and usually does not bury nuts but may bury acorns in leaf litter. Brown (1984) also indicated this species is a forager and does not cache food nor regularly bury nuts, although there are some observations of individuals hiding nuts under leaf litter. No information on whether retrieval of buried acorns is a common behavior. Note: Brown (1984) noted that eastern species that are closely related do cache; further support for this from Steele and others (2008) for eastern gray squirrel(*Sciurus carolinensis*). Appears that squirrels do not deposit large amounts of subcutaneous fat for insulation, although they may increase fat reserves in other parts of the body (Gurnell 1987). This species molts twice a year, with thicker coat in winter.	1
7. Variable life history	Does this species have alternative life history strategies to cope with variable resources or climate conditions?	None reported.	0
8. Reproduction in variable environments	Can this species outlive periods where reproduction is limited?	Gurnell (1987) indicated that gray squirrels may survive in the wild as long as 8-10 years (the longevity record for western gray squirrels in captivity is 11 years) but that perhaps only 1% of individuals survive that long. Of 10 wild eastern gray squirrels (*Sciurus carolinensis*), the shortest survival was 6 years and the longest was 12.5 years (Barkalow and Soots 1975); the authors cited references indicating that this species rarely lives longer than 6 years. A study of red squirrels (*Tamiasciurus hudsonicus*) in Montana found that 67% of individuals die before 12 months, with a plateau in survivorship occurring at about 36 months and very few individuals surviving past 7 years (Halvorson and Engeman 1983). Periods of extreme reductions in rainfall may last 5 years. If these conditions reduce food resources to the point that squirrels have insufficient food for breeding, most of the population would not survive longer than the periods of limited reproduction.	1

Phenology: Arizona gray squirrel (*Sciurus arizonensis*)			
Trait/Quality	**Question**	**Background info. & explanation of score**	**Points**
1. Cues	Does this species use temperature or moisture cues to initiate activities related to fecundity or survival?	Onset of breeding activity is correlated with flower emergence and consumption of flower parts (Best and Reidel 1995). Temperature and moisture influence flowering, but since the relationship to squirrel breeding is indirect, this question was scored as "0."	0
2. Event timing	Are activities related to species' fecundity or survival tied to	Estrus for most individuals appears to be in April and early May, but breeding can occur as early as January or February (Brown 1984). It appears that not all females breed each year (Brown 1984).	1

Trait/Quality	Question	Background info. & explanation of score	Points
	discrete events that are expected to change?	The onset of breeding activity is correlated with flower emergence and consumption of flower parts (Best and Reidel 1995); warmer temperatures may lead to earlier flowering (see also Phenology, Question 3).	
3. Mismatch potential	What is the separation in time or space between cues that initiate activities and discrete events that provide critical resources?	Onset of breeding activity is correlated with flower emergence and consumption of flower parts (Best and Reidel 1995). However, given the range of months over which potential species are flowering (i.e., some begin flower as early as January) and the fact that estrus for most individuals appears to be in April and early May (breeding can occur as early as January or February; Brown 1984), unclear how squirrels are timing breeding with respect to consumption of flower parts.	-1
4. Resilience to timing mismatches during breeding	Does this species employ strategies or have traits that increase the likelihood of reproduction co-occurring with important events?	No information that females rear more than one litter per year (Best and Reidel 1995). No evidence that this species has a litter in fall as is the case with fox squirrels and gray squirrels in the eastern United States (Brown 1984). Not all females breed in each year based on the absence of placental scars (Brown 1984). Hoffmeister (1986) cited that Theobald and Brown (1982) also found no evidence of a second litter.	1

Trait/Quality	Question	Background info. & explanation of score	Points
1. Food resources	Are important food resources for this species expected to change?	Squirrels eat tree buds in spring as an important food source when seeds are scarce or in autumn if a seed crop fails (Gurnell 1987). The Arizona gray squirrel consumes mostly tree seeds and fruits, but also fungi, buds, and miscellaneous items; the proportions in the diet vary by season (Gurnell 1987). Consumption of flower parts in breeding season may be related to vitamin content and potential to stimulate breeding (Brown 1984).	1
		This species is a forager and does not cache food or regularly bury nuts; mast said to be 67% of the annual diet, including walnuts, acorns, juniper berries, hackberries, and pine seeds (Brown 1984). When all riparian trees and other flowing species are considered in total, there is a relatively long flowering period (Brown 1984). Occasionally, squirrels eat bird eggs and nestlings and invertebrates (Brown 1984). Hoffmeister (1986) indicated that this species feeds extensively on walnuts.	
		The score reflects the potential for reduction in nut/seed/acorn crops. Reduced crops expected as a result of reduced precipitation in the short term (Zlotin and Parmenter 2008); in the long term, fewer seeds expected as a result of reduced tree abundance.	
2. Predators	Are important predator populations expected to change?	Predators include goshawks (Hobbs 1980 as cited in Brown 1984), red-tailed hawks, and bobcats (Brown 1984). Gurnell (1987) indicated that red-tailed hawks, red-shouldered hawks, goshawks, and martens hunt squirrels more frequently than other predatory species; however, no species of *Martes* occurs in Arizona and red-shouldered hawks are rare in southeast Arizona. Overall, we considered this species to have a "suite of predators." Gurnell (1987) indicated "there is little evidence that predators have any significant impact on squirrel populations."	0

Biotic interactions: Arizona gray squirrel (*Sciurus arizonensis*)			
Trait/Quality	Question	Background info. & explanation of score	Points
3. Symbionts	Are populations of symbiotic species expected to change?	Relationship between squirrels and seed crop considered under Biotic Interactions, Question 1. Given that this species is not considered to cache large numbers of acorns/seeds, not clear to what extent it acts as a seed disperser for tree species.	0
4. Disease	Is prevalence of diseases known to cause widespread mortality or reproductive failure in this species expected to change?	Squirrels are host to a variety of parasites and diseases (Gurnell 1987). Diseases include distemper, diphtheria, scab disease, myxomatosis (myxoma viral infection), and parapoxvirus infection. Gray squirrels in the Midwest have acquired California encephalitis. Little known about pathogenicity of most parasite and disease organisms in squirrels. Coccidiosis (infection by protozoan coccidian in intestinal wall) can cause serious infections that weaken squirrels. Ectoparasites, including fleas, are common in squirrels (Gurnell 1987). Mortality from plague appears to be uncommon in tree squirrels. A Web of Science search for "plague" and "*Sciurus*" yielded no results. A search of "plague" and "tree squirrels" yielded only Hudson and others (1971) who mention a case of eastern fox squirrels (*Sciurus niger*) dying in urban Denver in 1968, some of which were positive for antigens to plague and/or had fleas that were host to *Yersinia pestis* (bacterium that causes plague). A search on "Tamiasciurus" and "plague" returned Smith and others (2010), who reported that seroprevalence for *Yersinia pestis* was high in Allen's and long-eared chipmunks (*Tamias senex* and *T. quadrimaculatus*) and in pine squirrels (*Tamiasciurus douglasii*) in northern California over 28 years of monitoring, but that all 3 were moderately resistant to plague and survived infection.	0
		Bot flies (*Cterebra* spp.) lay eggs in nests of several types of squirrels including Gray Squirrels; the larvae then burrow into skin of squirrel, eventually re-emerging and dropping off to pupate.	
		WNV was first reported in eastern fox squirrels (*Sciurus niger*) in 2003 (Kiupul and others 2003). Most mammalian WNV infections cause no or low morbidity or mortality, although tree squirrels are susceptible to a neurologic disease associated with infection (Padgett and others 2008).	
		Gurnell (1987) indicated that squirrels that are weakened by food shortage may develop a parasite or disease load heavy enough to cause mortality. Large squirrel mortality events were reported in Europe in the early 1900s; coccidiosis was reported to have killed one million Eurasian red squirrels in Finland from 1943-1944 (Lampio 1967 as cited in Gurnell 1987).	
5. Competitors	Are populations of important competing species expected to change?	It has been suggested that the introduction of Abert's squirrels was the cause of the decline of the Arizona gray squirrel in the Santa Catalina Mountains (Lange 1960) where the two species co-occur. The two do not co-occur in other parts of the CNF (Jones, personal communication). Abert's squirrel expected to be vulnerable to climate change, although this would only affect Arizona gray squirrel where the two co-occur (Santa Catalina Mountains).	-1
		A closely related species to Arizona gray squirrel (and thus a potential competitor) is the Chiricahua fox squirrel (*S. nayaritensis chiricahuae*), but it is restricted to the Chiricahua Mountains; Arizona gray squirrel not reported to occur in Chiricahua Mountains (USFS 2009).	

Literature Cited

Barkalow, F.S., Jr., and R.F. Soots, Jr. 1975. Life span and reproductive longevity of the gray squirrel, *Sciurus c. carolinensis* Gmelin. Journal of Mammalogy 56:522-524.

Best, T.L., and S. Riedel. 1995. *Sciurus arizonensis*. American Society of Mammalogists. Mammalian Species No. 496.

Brown, D.E. 1984. Arizona's Tree Squirrels. Phoenix: Arizona Game and Fish Department. 114 p.

Frey, J.K., M.T. Hill, B.L. Christman, J.C. Truett, and S.O. MacDonald. 2008. Distribution and habitat of the Arizona Gray Squirrel (*Sciurus arizonensis*) in New Mexico. Southwestern Naturalist 53:248-255.

Gurnell, J. 1987. The Natural History of Squirrels. New York: Facts on File Publications. 201 p.

Halvorson, C.H., and R.M. Engeman. 1983. Survival analysis for a red squirrel population. Journal of Mammalogy 64:332-336.

Hoffmeister, D.F. 1986. Mammals of Arizona. University of Arizona Press and Arizona Game and Fish . 602 p.

Hudson, B.W., M.I. Goldenberg, J.D.McCluskie, H.E. Larson, C.D. McGuire, A.M. Barnes, and J.D. Poland. 1971. Serological and bacteriological investigations of an outbreak of plague in an urban tree squirrel population. American Journal of Tropical Medicine and Hygiene 20:255-263.

Jones, Larry. 2010. [Personal communication]. February 17, 2010. Tucson, AZ: U.S. Department of Agriculture, Forest Service, Coronado National Forest, Assistant Program Manager for Wildlife, Fish, and Rare Plants.

Kiupul, M., H.A. Simmons, S.D. Fitzgerald, A. Wise, J.G. Sikarskie, T.M. Cooley, S.R. Hollamby, and R. Maes. 2003. West Nile Virus infection in eastern fox squirrels (*Sciurus niger*). Veterinary Pathology 40:703-707.

Koprowski, J.L., and M.C. Corse. 2001. Food habits of the Chiricahua fox squirrel (*Sciurus nayaritensis chiricahuae*). Southwestern Naturalist 46:62-65.

Lange, K.I. 1960. Mammals of the Santa Catalina Mountains, Arizona. American Midland Naturalist 64:436-458.

Manolakou, P., G. Lavranos, and R. Angelopoulou. 2006. Molecular patterns of sex determination in the animal kingdom: A comparative study of the biology of reproduction. Reproductive Biology and Endocrinology 4:59.

Padgett, K.A., W.K. Riesen, N. Kahl-Purcell, Y. Fang, B. Cahoon-Young, R. Carney, N. Anderson, L. Zucca, L. Woods, S. Husted, and V.L. Kramer. 2008. West Nile Virus infection in tree squirrels (Rodentia: Sciuridae) in California, 2004-2005. Journal of Wildlife Rehabilitation 29:35-39.

Smith, C.R., J.R. Tucker, B.A. Wilson, and J.R. Clover. 2010. Plague studies in California: A review of long-term disease activity, flea-host relationships and plague ecology in the coniferous forests of the southern Cascades and northern Sierra Nevada mountains. Journal of Vector Ecology 35:1-12.

Steele, M.A., S.L. Halkin, P.D. Smallwood, T.J. McKenna, K. Mitsopoulos, and M. Beam. 2008. Cache protection strategies of a scatter-hoarding rodent: Do tree squirrels engage in behavioural deception? Animal Behavior 75:705-714.

U.S. Forest Service [USFS]. 2009. Draft Coronado National Forest ecological sustainability report. Tucson, AZ: U.S. Department of Agriculture, Forest Service. Available: http://www.fs fed.us/r3/coronado/plan-revision/documents/final/cnf-ecological-sustainability-report-final-022009.pdf.

Zlotin, R.I., and Parmenter, R.R. 2008. Patterns of mast production in pinyon and juniper woodlands along a precipitation gradient in central New Mexico (Sevilleta National Wildlife Refuge). Journal of Arid Environments 72:1562-1572.

Habitat: Chiricahua fox squirrel (*Sciurus nayaritensis chiricahuae*)			
Trait/Quality	**Question**	**Background info. & explanation of score**	**Points**
1. Area and distribution: *breeding*	Is the area or location of the associated vegetation type used for breeding activities by this species expected to change?	**Taxonomic note:** The Chiricahua fox squirrel is a sub-species of the Mexican fox squirrel (*Sciurus nayaritensis*) and was considered a separate species for a few years (Hoffmeister 1986). This sub-species occurs only in the Chiricahua Mountains where it generally occurs at elevations of ~5500-6500 ft (Hoffmeister 1986). Mexican fox squirrels (*Sciurus nayaritensis*) occur in mixed pine-oak forests of the Upper Sonoran and Transition life zones and occupy Apache pine-oak forest that is somewhat open (not found in areas where trees are very dense); their range includes the Sierra Madre Occidental, Mexico, and south as far as southern Jalisco (Best 1995). They occur in riparian areas with sycamores, ashes, and walnuts, and large evergreen oaks and appear to avoid oak-covered slopes, except possibly where acorns are numerous (Best 1995). High intensity forest fires have been identified as a threat because the fires destroy leaf nests and kill young (Kirkpatrick and Mosby 1981 as cited in Pasch and Koprowski 2005). Projections of suitable climate for vegetation communities forest wide (Chapter 1) predicted declines in suitable climate for all plant community types, with the exception of increases of suitable climate for semi-desert grassland and small increases in Sonoran desert scrub (present in small amounts on the CNF). We expected that habitat for the Chiricahua fox squirrel will decrease as a result of climate change.	2
2. Area and distribution: *non-breeding*	Is the area or location of the associated vegetation type used for non-breeding activities by this species expected to change?	Same as breeding habitat.	2
3. Habitat components: *breeding*	Are specific habitat components required for breeding expected to change?	Tree squirrels (*Sciurus* and *Tamiasciurus*) use nests for rearing young, rest, predator avoidance, and cover during inclement weather (Steele and Koprowski 2001). Hoffmeister (1986) indicated that "nests are said to be much like those of Arizona gray squirrels" and mentioned that nests in Pinery Canyon were in oaks and pines, either in leaf nests on branches or in holes in trees. Pasch and Koprowski (2005) indicated that >95% of Chiricahua fox squirrels use dreys (leaf nests) as nest sites and on average used 4.32 ± 3.33 SD dreys (n=20). The authors also mentioned that lactating females use tree cavities to rear young, then return to dreys following juvenile dispersal. Kneeland and others (2005) report nests in Coronado National Monument in Emory oaks. Pasch and Koprowski (2005) stated that maintaining mature trees in canyon bottoms (at Coronado National Monument, where the study was conducted) is important to prevent low squirrel densities from declining, given that the low numbers of young produced per year limits the ability to recover quickly from environmental disturbances. Trees, overall, are expected to decline in abundance.	1
4. Habitat components: *non-breeding*	Are specific habitat components required for survival during non-breeding periods expected to change?	Individuals use nests in trees in winter (Koprowski and Corse 2005). See Habitat, Question 3.	1

Habitat: Chiricahua fox squirrel (*Sciurus nayaritensis chiricahuae*)			
Trait/Quality	**Question**	**Background info. & explanation of score**	**Points**
5. Habitat quality and reproduction	Are features of the habitat associated with better reproductive success expected to change?	"Survivorship and reproduction of tree squirrels often are positively correlated with tree seed production. This dependence on mature, seed-producing forests is likely one reason that several species of tree squirrels are considered to be threatened or endangered in all or part of their ranges…" (Koprowski and Corse 2001). Pasch and Koprowski (2006b) observed a large increase in home-range size in 2003, the same year of record-low precipitation and attributed this correlation to low food availability in the dry year. Mature trees with high mast yields are expected to decline.	1
6. Habitat quality and survival	Are features of the habitat associated with better survival expected to change?	See Habitat, Question 5.	1
7. Ability to colonize new areas	What is this species' capacity and tendency to disperse?	Although *Sciurus* and *Tamiasciurus* spp. generally remain in the same area once they are established residents unless there is a food shortage (Gurnell 1987), squirrels, in general, are very mobile. Pasch and Koprowski (2006b) observed a female Chiricahua fox squirrel that regularly traveled >1 km to feed on Arizona walnuts.	-1
8. Migratory or transitional habitats	Does this species require additional habitats during migration that are separated from breeding and non-breeding habitats?	Pasch and Koprowski (2006b) indicated that male and female home-range and core-area size varied little from the non-mating season to the mating season. However, males move longer distances during the mating season, presumably due to searching for receptive females.	0

Physiology: Chiricahua fox squirrel (*Sciurus nayaritensis chiricahuae*)			
Trait/Quality	**Question**	**Background info. & explanation of score**	**Points**
1. Physiological thresholds	Are limiting physiological conditions expected to change?	Chiricahua fox squirrels are diurnally active. Squirrels may become inactive outside of the nest when temperatures are high (Gurnell 1987). Rainfall does not typically reduce activity unless it is heavy (references in Gurnell 1987). Squirrels spend most time foraging in trees in summer. Koprowski and Corse (2005) confirmed bimodal daily activity periods in summer in Mexican fox squirrels (becoming active at sunrise with activity peaking during early morning, followed by a lull for 2-3 hours, then another activity peak in late afternoon). In winter, high levels of activity occur throughout the day. Tree squirrels are reported to use evaporative cooling following periods of activity when temperatures are high (may lose heat from sweat glands in feet; Gurnell 1987). Mexican fox squirrel observed in summer resting on a shaded branch with its tail raised, which is assumed to be a method of heat dissipation (Koprowski and Corse 2005). We assumed that temperatures will remain below physiological thresholds most of the time.	0
2. Sex ratio	Is sex ratio determined by temperature?	No. Temperature-dependent sex determination is mainly observed in reptiles and fish (Manolakou et al. 2006).	0

Physiology: Chiricahua fox squirrel (*Sciurus nayaritensis chiricahuae*)			
Trait/Quality	Question	Background info. & explanation of score	Points
3. Exposure to extreme weather conditions	Are extreme weather or disturbance events that result in direct mortality or reproductive failure expected to change?	Increase in frequency of heat waves is predicted for southwestern United States. Overall, not clear to what extent timing and intensity of heat waves will affect survival and reproduction. We considered it unlikely that heat waves would cause widespread mortality. See also Physiology, Question 1.	0
4. Limitations to active period	Are projected temperature or precipitation regimes that influence activity period of species expected to change?	Diurnally active. During summer, tend to have 2 periods of activity—morning and later afternoon; Gurnell 1987; see confirmation of this pattern for this sub-species by Koprowski and Corse [2005] in Physiology, Question 1). We assumed that rise in temperatures will not significantly impact morning and evening activity periods.	0
5. Metabolic inhibition	Does this species possess an ability to reduce metabolic energy or water requirements?	Squirrels are active year-round; tend to have one main active period each day in winter; in northern areas, activity period may be closer to the middle of the day than in southern regions (Gurnell 1987). Spend time in nests in winter to conserve body heat. In severe weather conditions, squirrels may remain in nests for several days (references in Gurnell 1987: 55). When at rest, body temperature declines a few degrees, particularly at night when in the nest; this phenomenon has sometimes been referred to as heterothermy (Gurnell 1987). Some evidence to suggest that squirrels are able to employ a form of adaptive hypothermia (see reference in Gurnell 1987: 66). Chiricahua fox squirrels, like other Holarctic tree squirrels, show higher body mass in winter than in summer (Pasch and Koprowski 2006a). Although there is not strong evidence that this Chiricahua fox squirrels use torpor on a daily basis when temperatures are cold, the fact that diurnal squirrels are known to lower body temperature at night and when at rest suggests some ability to reduce energy requirements. This led to the score of "-1" for this question.	-1
6. Survival during resource limitation	Does this species have lower energy requirements or possess the capacity to store energy or water in the long term?	Brown (1984) indicated that the Chiricahua fox squirrel is a forager and does not cache food or regularly bury nuts. Note: Brown (1984) noted that eastern species that are closely related do cache; further support for this from Steele and others (2008) for eastern gray squirrel (*Sciurus carolinensis*). Appears that squirrels do not deposit large amounts of subcutaneous fat for insulation, although they may increase fat reserves in other parts of the body (Gurnell 1987). Individuals molt twice a year, with thicker coat in winter.	1
7. Variable life history	Does this species have alternative life history strategies to cope with variable resources or climate conditions?	None reported.	0
8. Reproduction in variable environments	Can this species outlive periods where reproduction is limited?	Gurnell (1987) indicated that gray squirrels may survive in the wild as long as 8-10 years (the longevity record for western gray squirrels in captivity is 11 years), but that perhaps only 1% of individuals survive that long. Of 10 wild eastern gray squirrels (*Sciurus carolinensis*), the shortest survival was 6 years and the longest was 12.5 years (Barkalow and Soots 1975); the authors cited references indicating	1

Physiology: Chiricahua fox squirrel (*Sciurus nayaritensis chiricahuae*)			
Trait/Quality	Question	Background info. & explanation of score	Points
		that this species rarely lives longer than 6 years. A study of red squirrels (*Tamiasciurus hudsonicus*) in Montana found that 67% of individuals die before 12 months, with a plateau in survivorship occurring at about 36 months and very few individuals surviving past 7 years (Halvorson and Engeman 1983).	
		Periods of extreme reductions in rainfall may last 5 years. If these conditions reduce food resources to the point that squirrels have insufficient food for breeding, most of the population would not survive longer than the periods of limited reproduction.	

Phenology: Chiricahua fox squirrel (*Sciurus nayaritensis chiricahuae*)			
Trait/Quality	Question	Background info. & explanation of score	Points
1. Cues	Does this species use temperature or moisture cues to initiate activities related to fecundity or survival?	No information found on cues used by Chiricahua fox squirrels. In a similar species, the Arizona gray squirrel, (*Sciurus arizonensis*), onset of breeding activity is correlated with flower emergence and consumption of flower parts (Best and Reidel 1995). Not clear whether Chiricahua fox squirrels follow the same pattern. It is likely that food availability of some kind is important and that temperature and moisture influence the availability, but since the relationship to squirrel breeding is indirect, this question was scored as "0."	0
2. Event timing	Are activities related to species' fecundity or survival tied to discrete events that are expected to change?	In this sub-species, males typically became reproductively active in January and remained scrotal until May (Pasch and Koprowski 2006a). Females come into estrus for only 1 day (Pasch and Koprowski 2006b). Cahalane (1939) indicated that it is likely that parturition occurs in April. Both pregnant and lactating females have been observed in different parts of the range of the Mexican fox squirrel in July (Best 1995). As mentioned above (Phenology, Question 1), not clear what cues are used for breeding. However, we assumed that changes to the timing of precipitation and increases in temperature have the potential to alter the timing of food availability, which, in turn, could alter the timing of breeding and parturition.	1
3. Mismatch potential	What is the separation in time or space between cues that initiate activities and discrete events that provide critical resources?	We considered food a critical resource and assumed that there is a relatively short period of time between food availability and breeding. See Phenology, Questions 1 and 2.	-1
4. Resilience to timing mismatches during breeding	Does this species employ strategies or have traits that increase the likelihood of reproduction co-occurring with important events?	A study by Pasch and Koprowski (2005) from 1994-2003 found that young emerged from nests during May-August, "indicating that a second reproductive bout did not occur during the late summer or early winter season". Females average 1.62 ± 0.51 SD (range 1-2, n=13) offspring per litter. Females come into estrus for only 1 day (Pasch and Koprowski 2006b).	1

Biotic interactions: Chiricahua fox squirrel (*Sciurus nayaritensis chiricahuae*)			
Trait/Quality	**Question**	**Background info. & explanation of score**	**Points**
1. Food resources	Are important food resources for this species expected to change?	Feeds heavily on tree seeds, mistletoe berries, and hypogeous fungi and appears to be dependent on mature trees for food (Koprowski and Corse 2001). Chiricahua fox squirrels spent 56% and 72% of its time foraging on Arizona cypress nuts in summer and winter, respectively, in a study in Chiricahua National Monument (Koprowski and Corse 2001). Hoffmeister (1986) indicated Mexican fox squirrels are thought to feed on seeds of pines, Douglas-fir, acorns, and walnuts. Reported to consume roots, bulbs, and buds when oak mast or other tree seeds are not available (Cahalane 1939).	1
		On the one hand, individuals appear to be able to vary their diets; Koprowski and Corse (2001) indicated that the diverse diet is "likely a response to spatial and temporal variation in seed crops of trees, especially in the drought-prone mountains" in which this species occurs. Pasch and Koprowski (2006b) observed a female that regularly traveled >1 km to feed on Arizona walnuts. On the other hand, individuals depend heavily on trees for food, including seeds, and trees are expected to decline.	
		The score here reflects potential reduction in nut/seed/acorn crops. Reduced crops expected as a result of reduced precipitation in the short term (Zlotin and Parmenter 2008); in the long term, fewer seeds expected as a result of reduced tree abundance.	
2. Predators	Are important predator populations expected to change?	According to Pasch and Koprowski (2005), although Chiricahua fox squirrels are considered sensitive by the USFS, this status does not prohibit hunting of the species. Thus, human hunting can be considered a form of predation, although climate change is not expected to cause direct increases in human populations.	0
		In Coronado National Monument, Kneeland and others (1995) observed interactions between predators and Chiricahua fox squirrels: two instances of a gray fox chasing a squirrel, a gray hawk (*Buteo nitidus*) stooping on a squirrel, and 3 Mexican jays (*Aphelocoma ultramarina*) investigating two different squirrel leaf nests in Emory oaks (an adult squirrel chased the jays). The authors concluded that predation appears to be infrequent. Overall, has a suite of predators.	
3. Symbionts	Are populations of symbiotic species expected to change?	Relationship between squirrels and seed crop considered under Biotic Interactions, Question 1. Given that Chiricahua fox squirrels are not considered to cache large numbers of acorns/seeds, not clear to what extent they act as seed dispersers for tree species.	0
4. Disease	Is prevalence of diseases known to cause widespread mortality or reproductive failure in this species expected to change?	Squirrels are host to a variety of parasites and diseases (Gurnell 1987). Diseases include distemper, diphtheria, scab disease, myxomatosis (myxoma viral infection), and parapoxvirus infection. Gray squirrels in the Midwest have acquired California encephalitis. Little known about pathogenicity of most parasite and disease organisms in squirrels. Coccidiosis (infection by protozoan coccidian in intestinal wall) can cause serious infections that weaken squirrels. Ectoparasites, including fleas, are common in squirrels (Gurnell 1987).	0
		Bot flies (*Cterebra* spp.) lay eggs in nests of several types of squirrels, including Gray Squirrels; larvae then burrow into skin of squirrel, eventually re-emerging and dropping off to pupate.	
		Several species of lice and one species of flea identified for the Chiricahua fox squirrel (Traum and others 1983 as cited in Best 1995). Mortality from plague appears to be uncommon in Tree Squirrels. A search on Web of Science for "plague" and "*Sciurus*" yielded no results. A search of "plague" and "tree squirrels" yielded only Hudson and others (1971), who mentioned a case of eastern fox	

Biotic interactions: Chiricahua fox squirrel (*Sciurus nayaritensis chiricahuae*)			
Trait/Quality	Question	Background info. & explanation of score	Points
		squirrels (*Sciurus niger*) dying in urban Denver in 1968, some of which tested positive for antigens to plague and/or had fleas that were host to *Yersinia pestis* (bacterium that causes plague). A search on "Tamiasciurus" and "plague" returned Smith and others (2010), who reported that seroprevalence for *Yersinia pestis* was high in Allen's and long-eared chipmunks (*Tamias senex* and *T. quadrimaculatus*) and in pine squirrels (*Tamiasciurus douglasii*) in northern California over 28 years of monitoring, but that all 3 were moderately resistant to plague and survived infection.	
		WNV was first reported in eastern fox squirrels (*Sciurus niger*) in 2003 (Kiupul and others 2003). Most mammalian WNV infections cause no or low morbidity or mortality, although tree squirrels are susceptible to a neurologic disease associated with infection (Padgett and others 2008).	
		Squirrels that are weakened by food shortage may develop a parasite or disease load heavy enough to cause mortality (Gurnell 1987). Large squirrel mortality events were reported in Europe in the early 1900s; coccidiosis was reported to have killed one million Eurasian red squirrels in Finland in 1943-1944 (Lampio 1967 as cited in Gurnell 1987).	
		Overall, not clear whether there would be significant increase in disease mortality in association with climate change.	
5. Competitors	Are populations of important competing species expected to change?	Neither the Arizona gray squirrel nor the Abert's squirrel (potential competitors) occurs in the Chiricahua Mountains (USFS 2009). No information found regarding important competitors.	0

Literature Cited

Barkalow, F.S., Jr., and R.F. Soots, Jr. 1975. Life span and reproductive longevity of the gray squirrel, *Sciurus c. carolinensis* Gmelin. Journal of Mammalogy 56:522-524.

Best, T.L. 1995. *Sciurus nayaritensis*. American Society of Mammalogists. Mammalian Species No. 492: 1-5.

Best, T.L., and S. Riedel. 1995. Sciurus arizonensis. American Society of Mammalogists. Mammalian Species No. 496.

Brown, D.E. 1984. Arizona's Tree Squirrels. Phoenix: Arizona Game and Fish Department. 114 p.

Cahalane, V.H. 1939. Mammals of the Chiricahua Mountains, Cochise County, Arizona. Journal of Mammalogy 20:418-440.

Gurnell, J. 1987. The Natural History of Squirrels. New York: Facts on File Publications. 201 p.

Halvorson, C.H., and R.M. Engeman. 1983. Survival analysis for a red squirrel population. Journal of Mammalogy 64:332-336.

Hoffmeister, D.F. 1986. Mammals of Arizona. University of Arizona Press and Arizona Game and Fish Department. 602 p.

Hudson, B.W., M.I. Goldenberg, J.D.McCluskie, H.E. Larson, C.D. McGuire, A.M. Barnes, and J.D. Poland. 1971. Serological and bacteriological investigations of an outbreak of plague in an urban tree squirrel population. American Journal of Tropical Medicine and Hygiene 20:255-263.

Kiupul, M., H.A. Simmons, S.D. Fitzgerald, A. Wise, J.G. Sikarskie, T.M. Cooley, S.R. Hollamby, and R. Maes. 2003. West Nile Virus infection in eastern fox squirrels (*Sciurus niger*). Veterinary Pathology 40:703-707.

Kneeland, M.C., J.L. Koprowski, and M.C. Corse. 1995. Potential predators of Chiricahua fox squirrels (*Sciurus nayaritensis chiricahuae*). Southwestern Naturalist 40:340-342.

Koprowski, J.L. 2005. Management and conservation of tree squirrels: The importance of endemism, species richness, and forest condition. In: Gottfried, G.J., S. Brooke, L.G. Eskew, C.B. Carleton, comps. Connecting mountain islands and desert seas: Biodiversity and management of the Madrean Archipelago II. 2004 May 11-15; Tucson, AZ. Proc. RMRS-P-36. Fort Collins, CO: U.S. Department of Agriculture, Forest Service, Rocky Mountain Research Station: 245-250.

Koprowski, J.L., and M.C. Corse. 2001. Food habits of the Chiricahua fox squirrel (*Sciurus nayaritensis chiricahuae*). Southwestern Naturalist 46:62-65.

Koprowski, J.L., and M.C. Corse. 2005. Time budgets, activity periods, and behavior of Mexican fox squirrels. Journal of Mammalogy 86:947-952.

Manolakou, P., G. Lavranos, and R. Angelopoulou. 2006. Molecular patterns of sex determination in the animal kingdom: A comparative study of the biology of reproduction. Reproductive Biology and Endocrinology 4:59.

Padgett, K.A., W.K. Riesen, N. Kahl-Purcell, Y. Fang, B. Cahoon-Young, R. Carney, N. Anderson, L. Zucca, L. Woods, S. Husted, and V.L. Kramer. 2008. West Nile Virus infection in tree squirrels (Rodentia: Sciuridae) in California, 2004-2005. Journal of Wildlife Rehabilitation 29:35-39.

Pasch, B.S., and J.L. Koprowski. 2005. Correlates of vulnerability in Chiricahua fox squirrels. In: Gottfried, G.J., B.S. Brooke, L.G. Eskew, C.B. Edminster, comps. Connecting mountain islands and desert seas: Biodiversity and management of the Madrean Archipelago II. 2004 May 11-15; Tucson, AZ. Proc. RMRS-P-36. Fort Collins, CO: U.S. Department of Agriculture, Forest Service, Rocky Mountain Research Station: 426-428.

Pasch, B.S., and J.L. Koprowski. 2006a. Annual cycles of body mass and reproduction of Chiricahua fox squirrels (*Sciurus nayaritensis chiricahuae*). Southwestern Naturalist 51:531-535.

Pasch, B.S., and J.L. Koprowski. 2006b. Sex differences in space use of Chiricahua fox squirrels. Journal of Mammalogy 87:380-386.

Smith, C.R., J.R. Tucker, B.A. Wilson, and J.R. Clover. 2010. Plague studies in California: A review of long-term disease activity, flea-host relationships and plague ecology in the coniferous forests of the southern Cascades and northern Sierra Nevada mountains. Journal of Vector Ecology 35:1-12.

Steele, M.A., S.L. Halkin, P.D. Smallwood, T.J. McKenna, K. Mitsopoulos, and M. Beam. 2008. Cache protection strategies of a scatter-hoarding rodent: Do tree squirrels engage in behavioural deception? Animal Behavior 75:705-714.

Steele, M.A., and J.L. Koprowski. 2001. North American Tree Squirrels. Washington, DC: Smithsonian Institution Press. 225 p.

U.S. Forest Service [USFS]. 2009. Draft Coronado National Forest ecological sustainability report. Tucson, AZ: U.S. Department of Agriculture, Forest Service. Available: http://www.fs fed.us/r3/coronado/plan-revision/documents/final/cnf-ecological-sustainability-report-final-022009.pdf.

Zlotin, R.I., and Parmenter, R.R. 2008. Patterns of mast production in pinyon and juniper woodlands along a precipitation gradient in central New Mexico (Sevilleta National Wildlife Refuge). Journal of Arid Environments 72:1562-1572.

Habitat: Mount Graham red squirrel (*Tamiasciurus hudsonicus grahamensis*)			
Trait/Quality	Question	Background info. & explanation of score	Points
1. Area and distribution: *breeding*	Is the area or location of the associated vegetation type used for breeding activities by this species expected to change?	This sub-species occurs only in the Pinaleño Mountains; another sub-species (*Tamiasciurus hudsonicus mogollonensis*) occurs elsewhere in Arizona (Hoffmeister 1986). Mount Graham red squirrels occur only in the highest peaks of the Pinaleño Mountains, generally above 9500 ft (Brown 1984). One estimate of potential habitat is 9083 ha (based on forested area above 2425 m; references in Merrick and others 2007). Estimate of population size is <300 (Koprowski and others 2005). *Tamiasciurus* is a genus of cold climates; thus, in the Southwest, it occurs at high elevations (Brown 1984). Red squirrels in Arizona occur in the larger mountain ranges that contain subalpine conifer forests of spruce and fir; they are rarely found very far below 7500 ft and more	2

Habitat: Mount Graham red squirrel (*Tamiasciurus hudsonicus grahamensis*)			
Trait/Quality	**Question**	**Background info. & explanation of score**	**Points**
		often are above 2530 m (8300 ft; Brown 1984). Hoffmeister (1986) indicated that red squirrels occur where spruce or mixture of spruce and Douglas-fir exist and are rarely found in ponderosa pine or Douglas-fir forests. In the Pinaleño Mountains, Mount Graham red squirrels formerly lived in the fir zone; no large stands of spruce exist in this mountain range (Hoffmeister 1986). Brown (1984) noted that red squirrels in Arizona range from sub-alpine forest to as low as mixed-conifer forest (occasionally in ponderosa pine forest) and that they require cold, moist, shaded conditions. Areas that are most often used are subalpine forests of Englemann spruce and subalpine fir, as well as Douglas-fir and other species (e.g., white fir, southwestern white pine, and ponderosa pine). Stands of blue spruce and southwestern white pine are also frequented by red squirrels.	
		Corkbark fir is an important component of nesting habitat in the mixed conifer transition zone on Mount Graham (Merrick and others 2007).	
		Koprowski and others (2005) documented a significant decline in this sub-species over 1994-2002 in spruce fir forest, with less of a decline in mixed-conifer forest. Over the same time period, significant outbreaks of several conifer pests resulted in significant damage to trees, more so in spruce-fir than in mixed conifer. Pests included a geometrid moth (*Nepytia janetae*; consumes spruce and corkbark fir), a spruce beetle (*Dendroctonus rufipennis* Kirby; attacks spruce), western balsam bark beetle (*Dryocoetes confusus* Swaine; consumes corkbark fir), and a spruce aphid (*Elatobium abietinum* Walker; attacks Englemann spruce).	
		Forest fires (e.g., Clark Peak Fire and Nuttall Complex Fire) and vegetation mortality from bark beetles and spruce aphids have resulted in habitat area reductions (references in Merrick and others 2007). Koprowski and others (2006) documented that survival of radio-collared individuals was lower in areas that burned in the Nuttall Complex Fire (in 2004) relative to unburned areas.	
		Projections of suitable climate for vegetation communities forest wide (Chapter 1) predicted declines in suitable climate for all plant community types, with the exception of increases of suitable climate for semi-desert grassland and small increases in Sonoran desert scrub (present in small amounts on the CNF).	
		We expected that habitat will decrease as a result of climate change.	
2. Area and distribution: *non-breeding*	Is the area or location of the associated vegetation type used for non-breeding activities by this species expected to change?	Same as breeding habitat.	2
3. Habitat components: *breeding*	Are specific habitat components required for breeding expected to change?	Tree squirrels (*Sciurus* and *Tamiasciurus* spp.) use nests for rearing young, rest, predator avoidance, and cover during inclement weather (Steel and Koprowski 2001). Red squirrel nests are made by both sexes in tree cavities, or bolus nests are constructed from conifer twigs, grass, leaves, and moss (Brown 1984). Most squirrels have more than one nest (Vahle 1978 as cited in Brown 1984).	1
		Brown (1984) indicated that red squirrels (like all tree squirrels) prefer areas with large, old trees that offer squirrels the best cone crops and easy movement through the connected canopy. Even-aged and open forests with widely spaced trees are low-quality habitat.	

Habitat: Mount Graham red squirrel (*Tamiasciurus hudsonicus grahamensis*)

Trait/Quality	Question	Background info. & explanation of score	Points
		Merrick and others (2007) found that 3 types of nests were used in the ~100-ha study area: cavity nests, dreys, and occasionally log or ground nests. Nest sites were strongly influenced by stand composition; in particular, important components were: density of corkbark fir, large trees, and decaying logs. Cavity-containing trees and large snags were also important. Cavities were used twice as much as dreys in this study area. Dreys were primarily in Englemann spruce and corkbark fir; cavity nests were primarily in aspen and corkbark fir. Mount Graham red squirrels chose nest sites that had a higher canopy cover and more corkbark fir, decayed logs, and living trees compared to random sites. Cavity trees were on average 1.6 times larger than drey trees or random focal trees. Drey nest trees had almost twice the area of living crown relative to cavity nest trees.	
		A cool microclimate at middens, typically provided by forest structure, is required for cone preservation (Leonard and Koprowski 2009).	
		Trees, overall, are expected to decline in abundance.	
4. Habitat components: *non-breeding*	Are specific habitat components required for survival during non-breeding periods expected to change?	Uses nests in trees winter (Brown 1984). See Habitat, Question 3.	1
5. Habitat quality and reproduction	Are features of the habitat associated with better reproductive success expected to change?	"Survivorship and reproduction of tree squirrels often are positively correlated with tree seed production. This dependence on mature, seed-producing forests is likely one reason that several species of tree squirrels are considered to be threatened or endangered in all or part of their ranges...." (Koprowski and Corse 2001). In various habitat types, mature forest stands are considered to have the highest densities of red squirrels and are thus considered the highest-quality habitat (Layne 1954 as cited in Kemp and Kemp 1970). Even-aged and open forests with widely-spaced trees are low-quality habitat (Brown 1984). Mature trees with high mast yields are expected to decline.	1
6. Habitat quality and survival	Are features of the habitat associated with better survival expected to change?	See Habitat, Question 6.	1
7. Ability to colonize new areas	What is this species' capacity and tendency to disperse?	Although *Sciurus* and *Tamiasciurus* spp. generally remain in the same area, once they are established residents (unless there is a food shortage) (Gurnell 1987), their dependence on middens makes them site faithful. However, squirrels in general are very mobile. Juvenile red squirrels in Canada dispersed up to ~1.6 km from the natal area (Kemp and Keith 1970), although some offspring may establish territories closer to their natal area (Brown 1984). Therefore, we considered the Mount Graham red squirrel as capable of colonizing new areas where appropriate habitat exists.	-1
8. Migratory or transitional habitats	Does this species require additional habitats during migration that are separated from breeding and non-breeding habitats?	Red squirrels defend territories year-around (Brown 1984). Movement out of year-round areas appears to be rare. For example, on the North Kaibab Plateau in 1971, red squirrel populations at high elevations moved into an area where there was a large cone crop of ponderosa pine seeds; squirrels from higher elevations descended to the bumper crop area, established territories, and collected and stored seeds. They moved back upslope after being forced to use other food sources.	0

Physiology: Mount Graham red squirrel (*Tamiasciurus hudsonicus grahamensis*)			
Trait/Quality	**Question**	**Background info. & explanation of score**	**Points**
1. Physiological thresholds	Are limiting physiological conditions expected to change?	Red squirrels are diurnally active (Gurnell 1987), although occasionally they may be active at night (Layne 1954 as cited in Steele 1998). In spring and summer, activity peaks occur in morning and afternoon; in fall, active throughout the day; and in winter, usually one activity peak in the middle of the day (references in Steele 1998). Red squirrels may become less active during periods of heavy rains, snow, and high winds (references in Steele 1998). Squirrels may become inactive outside of the nest when temperatures are high (Gurnell 1987). Clarkson and Ferguson (1969) reported a negative relationship between activity and temperature between 10-35 °C in laboratory conditions. Tree squirrels are reported to use evaporative cooling following periods of activity when temperatures are high (may lose heat from sweat glands in feet; Gurnell 1987). We assumed that temperatures will remain below physiological thresholds most of the time.	0
2. Sex ratio	Is sex ratio determined by temperature?	No. Temperature-dependent sex determination is mainly observed in reptiles and fish (Manolakou and others 2006).	0
3. Exposure to extreme weather conditions	Are extreme weather or disturbance events that result in direct mortality or reproductive failure expected to change?	Increase in frequency of heat waves is predicted for southwestern United States. Overall, not clear to what extent timing and intensity of heat waves will effect survival and reproduction. We considered it unlikely that heat waves would cause widespread mortality. See also Physiology, Question 1.	0
4. Limitations to active period	Are projected temperature or precipitation regimes that influence activity period of species expected to change?	Individuals are diurnally active. In spring and summer, activity peaks occur in morning and afternoon; in fall, active throughout the day; and in winter, usually one activity peak in the middle of the day (references in Steele 1998). We assumed that rise in temperatures will not significantly impact morning and evening activity periods, when temperatures tend to be cooler than mid-day. See also Physiology, Question 1.	0
5. Metabolic inhibition	Does this species possess an ability to reduce metabolic energy or water requirements?	Squirrels are active year-round. When at rest, the body temperature of squirrels declines a few degrees, particularly at night when in the nest; this phenomenon has sometimes been referred to as heterothermy (Gurnell 1987). Some evidence to suggest that squirrels are able to employ a form of adaptive hypothermia (see reference in Gurnell 1987: 66). In fact, Pauls (1979) measured body temperature of two red squirrels in the laboratory and found that they lowered body temperature while in the nest, as well as when active underground, which was considered to potentially result in a significant energy savings. The fact that red squirrels tend to lower body temperature at night and when at rest suggests some ability to reduce energy requirements. This led to the score of "-1" for this question.	-1
6. Survival during resource limitation	Does this species have lower energy requirements or possess the capacity to store energy or water in the long term?	*Tamiasciurus* is the only genus of North America tree squirrels that stores food in any important amount (Brown 1984). Caches are comprised of mounds of unopened cones buried in cone scale debris below a feeding perch; the scale debris is called a midden. They are often near one or more large cone-bearing trees and at the base of a tree of large-diameter or a downed log (Brown 1984). Hollow trees, against stumps, and underground dens and crevices are also used for	-1

Physiology: Mount Graham red squirrel (*Tamiasciurus hudsonicus grahamensis*)

Trait/Quality	Question	Background info. & explanation of score	Points
		cone storage. The primary cache is strongly defended. Moisture in the cache keeps the cones from opening, so locations must be in shaded areas, depressions, or north-facing locations that stay moist. In Arizona, middens are often placed under ponderosa pine (Hoffmeister 1986). Mount Graham red squirrel female body mass did not increase in winter (Koprowski 2005).	
7. Variable life history	Does this species have alternative life history strategies to cope with variable resources or climate conditions?	None reported.	0
8. Reproduction in variable environments	Can this species outlive periods where reproduction is limited?	Not all female red squirrels breed each year (Brown 1984). In a related species, it was observed that in years of low food, most chickarees (*Tamiasciurus douglasii*) did not breed in spring and none bred in fall (Smith 1968 as cited in Brown 1984). In Montana, Halvorson and Engeman (1983) found that most mortality (67%) occurred before 12 months of age, with few red squirrel individuals surviving more than 7 years. The median longevity for males was 3 months and 6 months for females. Periods of extreme reductions in rainfall may last 5 years. If these conditions reduce food resources to the point that squirrels have insufficient food for breeding, most of the population would not survive longer than the periods of limited reproduction.	1

Phenology: Mount Graham red squirrel (*Tamiasciurus hudsonicus grahamensis*)

Trait/Quality	Question	Background info. & explanation of score	Points
1. Cues	Does this species use temperature or moisture cues to initiate activities related to fecundity or survival?	Little information on cues that trigger breeding. Steele (1998) noted that compared to ground squirrels, red squirrel females are asynchronous in the timing of estrus (can vary up to 1-2 months). Individuals are often consistent in estrus timing among years, however. Becker (1993) concluded that timing of estrus in red squirrels (*T. hudsonicus*) appears to result from an interaction between an endogenous circannual reproductive cycle (such as day length) and net energy gain (e.g., food availability). The consumption of certain high-quality food may be involved (Steele 1998). Kemp and Keith (1970) indicated that red squirrels may come into breeding condition in response to feeding on spruce flower buds. It is likely that food availability of some kind is important, and that temperature and moisture influence the availability of food, but since the relationship to squirrel breeding would be indirect, this question was scored as "0."	0
2. Event timing	Are activities related to species' fecundity or survival tied to discrete events that are expected to change?	As previously mentioned (Phenology, Question 1), to what extent environmental factors trigger breeding is unclear, but it appears likely that food availability plays some key role. The timing of precipitation and increases in temperature can alter the timing of food availability.	1

Phenology: Mount Graham red squirrel (*Tamiasciurus hudsonicus grahamensis*)

Trait/Quality	Question	Background info. & explanation of score	Points
3. Mismatch potential	What is the separation in time or space between cues that initiate activities and discrete events that provide critical resources?	Consider food a critical resource and assumed relatively short period of time between food availability and breeding. See Phenology, Questions 1 and 2.	-1
4. Resilience to timing mismatches during breeding	Does this species employ strategies or have traits that increase the likelihood of reproduction co-occurring with important events?	Brown (1984) reported that red squirrels typically have only one litter per year but Layne (1954) reported two litters in one year in New York. Smith (1968) also cited that females come into estrus for only one day per year (usually in late March or early April [Brown 1984]) (although females are not synchronous), gestation is 35 days, and young remain in the nest for 45 days or more. After leaving the nest, they remain with the adult female for another 2-3 weeks. Litter size is generally 2-4. Hoffmeister (1986) indicated that red squirrels in Arizona (including in the Pinaleño Mountains) may produce two litters (one in spring and a second in summer). However, Koprowski (2005) cited references indicating that red squirrels typically have a single reproductive season in late spring or early summer. Steele (1998) cited references indicating that, particularly in the western and northwestern portion of their range, red squirrels typically produce only 1 litter per year.	1

Biotic interactions: Mount Graham red squirrel (*Tamiasciurus hudsonicus grahamensis*)

Trait/Quality	Question	Background info. & explanation of score	Points
1. Food resources	Are important food resources for this species expected to change?	From Brown (1984): Conifer seeds are an important component of the diet of red squirrels; important species in Arizona include white fir, subalpine fir, blue spruce, Engelmann spruce, white pine, ponderosa pine, and Douglas-fir. In late winter, terminal buds of conifers are eaten in addition to seeds from stored cones. Terminal buds can be an important component of the diet in a severe winter or if cone stores are insufficient. Inner bark and cambium are also consumed. Male cones, available in the early spring, are not stored nor defended. In summer, branches containing female cones are chewed off; the seeds are either eaten or the cones are stored. Other food includes false truffles and other fungi (sometimes stored), nestling birds, insects, and carrion. Cones are dug out of caches for harvesting of seeds. In winter, squirrels keep a path open to the cache via paths under the snow. See Physiology, Question 6 for more information on caches. Epigeous and hypogeous mycorrhizal fungi can be important to red squirrels in summer and other periods of food shortage (references in Steele 1998). Although it would appear that Mount Graham red squirrels vary their diet, it depends heavily on trees for food, including seeds. Trees, in general, are expected to decline. The score here reflects potential for reduction in seed crops.	1
2. Predators	Are important predator populations expected to change?	Goshawks are considered a predator of red squirrels; pine martens do not occur in Arizona (Brown 1984). Schauffert and others (2002) observed five predation attempts in ~41,000 hours of field time over 7 years; predators included Mexican spotted owl, bobcat, and northern goshawk. Other potential predators included Cooper's	0

Biotic interactions: Mount Graham red squirrel (*Tamiasciurus hudsonicus grahamensis*)			
Trait/Quality	**Question**	**Background info. & explanation of score**	**Points**
		hawks, sharp-shinned hawks, greathorned owls, and gray foxes, all of which are reported as known predators by Steele (1998). Overall, it appears that Mount Graham red squirrels have a suite of predators. Furthermore, Schauffert and others (2002) indicated that their low number of observations suggest that successful predation attempts appear to be low.	
3. Symbionts	Are populations of symbiotic species expected to change?	Relationship between squirrels and seed crop considered under Biotic Interactions, Question 1.	0
4. Disease	Is prevalence of diseases known to cause widespread mortality or reproductive failure in this species expected to change?	From Yahner (2003): A variety of endoparasites, ectoparasite, and diseases have been reported for red squirrels, including, sucking lice, nematodes, tapeworms, fleas, ticks, chiggers, and mites, and they are known to be susceptible to sarcocysts, botfly, tularemia, and various other infections, some viral. It appears that mortality from plague is uncommon in tree squirrels. Smith and others (2010) reported that seroprevalence for *Yersinia pestis* (bacterium that causes plague) was high in Allen's and long-eared chipmunks (*Tamias senex* and *T. quadrimaculatus*) and in the pine squirrel (*Tamiasciurus douglasii*) in northern California over 28 years of monitoring, but that all 3 were moderately resistant to plague and survived infection. A search on Web of Science for "plague" and "*Tamiasciurus*" yielded only this citation (Smith and others 2010), and a search on Web of Science for "plague" and "*Sciurus*" yielded no results. A search of "plague" and "tree squirrels" yielded only Hudson and others (1971) who mentioned a case of eastern fox squirrels dying in urban Denver in 1968, some of which tested positive for antigens to plague and/or had fleas that were host to *Yersinia pestis*. Overall, not clear whether there would be a significant increase in disease mortality in association with climate change.	0
5. Competitors	Are populations of important competing species expected to change?	Steele (1998) indicated that red squirrels experience little, if any, competition with tree and ground squirrels and chipmunks due to differences in habitats and food resources from other species. However, discussion exists regarding the impact on Abert's squirrel on this sub-species of red squirrel. Abert's squirrels, which were introduced into the Pinaleño Mountains, may have contributed to the decline of the Mount Graham red squirrel (Hoffmeister 1986). Brown (1984) cited Layne (1954) that red squirrels in New York were not able to prevent pilfering of their caches by eastern gray squirrels, leading to exclusion by the gray squirrels. Abert's squirrels are considered to have the potential to reduce population viability of the Mount Graham red squirrel by reducing food resources (see references in Rushton and others 2006); in some areas, Abert's squirrels have been reported to reduce cone crops by as much as 74%. Using remote cameras at 9 occupied Mount Graham red squirrel middens, 7 unoccupied middens, and 7 random sites, Edelman and others (2005) found that Abert's squirrels were recorded only at unoccupied middens. The authors concluded that kleptoparasitism of red squirrel middens by Abert's squirrel appeared to be uncommon, possibly due to territorial defense. Edelman and others (2009) concluded, based on work in mixed conifer habitat, that competition for nest sites appeared unlikely given that Abert's squirrels used dreys mostly, whereas red squirrels used mostly cavity nests. Abert's squirrel nests were in areas that were more open and contained greater species diversity, whereas red squirrel nest sites were in more densely	-1

Biotic interactions: Mount Graham red squirrel (*Tamiasciurus hudsonicus grahamensis*)			
Trait/Quality	Question	Background info. & explanation of score	Points
		forested areas dominated by corkbark fir.	
		Overall, unclear to what extent Abert's squirrel directly impacts numbers of Mount Graham red squirrel, but the potential appears to exist.	
		Abert's squirrels were identified as being vulnerable to climate change as part of this assessment.	

Literature Cited

Becker, C.D. 1993. Environmental cues of estrus in the North American red squirrel (*Tamiasciurus hudsonicus* Bangs). Canadian Journal of Zoology 71:1326-1333.

Brown, D.E. 1984. Arizona's Tree Squirrels. Phoenix: Arizona Game and Fish Department. 114 p.

Clarkson, D.P., and J.H. Ferguson. 1969. Effect of temperature upon activity in the red squirrel. American Zoologist 9:1110.

Edelman, A.J., J.L. Koprowski, and S.R. Bertelsen. 2009. Potential for nest site competition between native and exotic tree squirrels. Journal of Mammalogy 90:167-174.

Edelman, A.J., J.L Koprowski, and J.L Edelman. 2005. Kleptoparasitic behavior and species richness at Mt. Graham red squirrel middens. In: Gottfried, G.J., S. Brooke, L.G. Eskew, C.B. Carleton, comps. Connecting mountain islands and desert seas: Biodiversity and management of the Madrean Archipelago II. 2004 May 11-15; Tucson, AZ. Proc. RMRS-P-36. Fort Collins, CO: U.S. Department of Agriculture, Forest Service, Rocky Mountain Research Station: 395-398.

Gurnell, J. 1987. The Natural History of Squirrels. New York: Facts on File Publications. 201 p.

Halvorson, C.H., and R.M. Engeman. 1983. Survival analysis for a red squirrel population. Journal of Mammalogy 64:332-336.

Hoffmeister, D.F. 1986. Mammals of Arizona. University of Arizona Press and Arizona Game and Fish Department. 602 p.

Kemp, G.A., and L.B. Keith. 1970. Dynamics and regulation of red squirrel (*Tamiasciurus hudsonicus*) populations. Ecology 51:763-779.

Koprowski, J.L., K.M. Leonard, C.A. Zugmeyer, and J.L. Jolley. 2006. Direct effects of fire on endangered Mount Graham red squirrels. Southwestern Naturalist 51:59-63.

Koprowski, J.L. 2005. Management and conservation of tree squirrels: The importance of endemism, species richness, and forest condition. In: Gottfried, G.J., S. Brooke, L.G. Eskew, C.B. Carleton, comps. Connecting mountain islands and desert seas: Biodiversity and management of the Madrean Archipelago II. 2004 May 11-15; Tucson, AZ. Proc. RMRS-P-36. Fort Collins, CO: U.S. Department of Agriculture, Forest Service, Rocky Mountain Research Station: 245-250.

Koprowski, J.L., M.I. Alanen, and A.M. Lynch. 2005. Nowhere to run and nowhere to hide: Response of endemic Mt. Graham red squirrels to catastrophic forest damage. Biological Conservation 126:491-498.

Koprowski, J.L., and M.C. Corse. 2001. Food habits of the Chiricahua fox squirrel (*Sciurus nayaritensis chiricahuae*). Southwestern Naturalist 46:62-65.

Gurnell, J. 1987. The Natural History of Squirrels. New York: Facts on File Publications. 201 p.

Hudson, B.W., M.I. Goldenberg, J.D. McCluskie, H.E. Larson, C.D. McGuire, A.M. Barnes, and J.D. Poland. 1971. Serological and bacteriological investigations of an outbreak of plague in an urban tree squirrel population. American Journal of Tropical Medicine and Hygiene 20:255-263.

Leonard, K.M., and J.L. Koprowski. 2009. A comparison of habitat use and demography of red squirrels at the southern edge of their range. American Midland Naturalist 162:125-138.

Manolakou, P., G. Lavranos, and R. Angelopoulou. 2006. Molecular patterns of sex determination in the animal kingdom: A comparative study of the biology of reproduction. Reproductive Biology and Endocrinology 4:59.

Merrick, M.J., S.R. Bertelsen, and J.L. Koprowski. 2007. Characteristics of Mount Graham red squirrel nest sites in a mixed conifer forest. Journal of Wildlife Management 71:1958-1963.

Pauls, R.W. 1979. Body temperature dynamics of the red squirrel (*Tamiasciurus hudsonicus*): Adaptations for energy conservation. Canadian Journal of Zoology 57:1349-1354.

Schauffert, C.A., J.L Koprowski, V.L. Greer, M.I. Alanen, K.A. Hutton, and P.J. Young. 2002. Interactions between predators and Mt. Graham red squirrels (*Tamiasciurus hudsonicus grahamensis*). Southwestern Naturalist 47:498-501.

Smith, C.R., J.R. Tucker, B.A. Wilson, and J.R. Clover. 2010. Plague studies in California: A review of long-term disease activity, flea-host relationships and plague ecology in the coniferous forests of the southern Cascades and northern Sierra Nevada mountains. Journal of Vector Ecology 35:1-12.

Steele, M.A. 1998. *Tamiasciurus hudsonicus*. American Society of Mammalogists. Mammalian Species No. 586: 1-9.

Steele, M.A., and J.L. Koprowski. 2001. North American Tree Squirrels. Washington, DC: Smithsonian Institution Press. 225 p.

U.S. Forest Service [USFS]. 2009. Draft Coronado National Forest ecological sustainability report. Tucson, AZ: U.S. Department of Agriculture, Forest Service. Available: http://www fs fed.us/r3/coronado/plan-revision/documents/final/cnf-ecological-sustainability-report-final-022009.pdf.

Yahner, R.H. 2003. Pine Squirrels. In: Feldhamer, G.C., B.C. Thompson, and J.A. Chapman, eds. Wild mammals of North America: Biology, management, and conservation. Baltimore, MD: Johns Hopkins University Press:268-275.

Habitat: Mesquite mouse (*Peromyscus merriami*)			
Trait/Quality	Question	Background info. & explanation of score	Points
1. Area and distribution: *breeding*	Is the area or location of the associated vegetation type used for breeding activities by this species expected to change?	**Taxonomic note:** This species is closely related to, and formerly included in, *Peromyscus eremicus*. The two can be very difficult to distinguish morphologically (Hoffmeister and Lee 1963), although not genetically, and some museum specimens may have been incorrectly identified (Kingsley 2006). In Arizona, this species occurs in the southern-middle portion of the state; range extends into Mexico (Hoffmeister 1986). The majority of known records for this species in Arizona are in Pima County along the Santa Cruz River and its tributaries (Kingsley 2006). Is almost entirely restricted to mesquite forests (bosques: Hoffmeister 1986). Hoffmeister (1986) indicated that it occurs in heavy, forest-like stands of mesquite (such stands were more abundant in the past). Kingsley (2006) found in Pima County, individuals occur not just in large velvet mesquite (*Prosopis vetulina*) bosques, but "in a wider variety of mesquite-dominated communities on floodplain soils." This species was not found in isolated patches of mesquite surrounded by urban development, narrow rocky washes with few mesquites, mesquite-invaded grassland, or upland vegetation. This species occurs, or potential habitat exists, on the following EMAs: Tumacacori, Santa Rita, Huachuca, and Santa Catalina (Jones, personal communication). Projections of suitable climate for vegetation communities (Chapter 1) predicted declines in suitable climate for plains grassland, Madrean forest and woodland, and Madrean conifer forest, and increases of suitable climate for semi-desert grassland. Sonoran desert scrub is also predicted to increase, to a small degree, on the Santa Catalina EMA. Velvet mesquite is a facultative riparian species native to the Sonoran biotic region (Stromberg and others 1993). The wettest habitats in which this species occurs are riverine floodplains with perennially available groundwater. Riparian communities are expected to decrease in area.	2

Trait/Quality	Question	Background info. & explanation of score	Points
Habitat: Mesquite mouse (*Peromyscus merriami*)			
2. Area and distribution: *non-breeding*	Is the area or location of the associated vegetation type used for non-breeding activities by this species expected to change?	See Habitat, Question 1.	2
3. Habitat components: *breeding*	Are specific habitat components required for breeding expected to change?	No information found on this topic. A similar species, *P. eremicus*, often lives in abandoned burrows of other mammals or in part of a wood rat house (Hoffmeister 1986).	0
4. Habitat components: *non-breeding*	Are specific habitat components required for survival during non-breeding periods expected to change?	No information found on this topic.	0
5. Habitat quality and reproduction	Are features of the habitat associated with better reproductive success expected to change?	No information found on this topic.	0
6. Habitat quality and survival	Are features of the habitat associated with better survival expected to change?	No information found on this topic.	0
7. Ability to colonize new areas	What is this species' capacity and tendency to disperse?	Home ranges of a similar species, *P. eremicus,* averaged 0.3 ha (Ogston 1974 as cited in Veal and Caire 1979). Reports of distances travelled by other species in the genus vary. *Peromyscus maniculatus* has been observed to move 50-1320 m, which is considered "long distance" (Rehmeier and others 2004) and >3 km (Murie and Murie 1931 as cited in Maier 2002). *Peromyscus leucopus* has been reported to have moved >14 km (Maier 2002). Overall, we considered *Peromyscus* spp. to be relatively poor dispersers.	1
8. Migratory or transitional habitats	Does this species require additional habitats during migration that are separated from breeding and non-breeding habitats?	No information to suggest that this species undertakes migratory movements.	0

USDA Forest Service RMRS-GTR-273. 2012.

Physiology: Mesquite mouse (*Peromyscus merriami*)			
Trait/Quality	**Question**	**Background info. & explanation of score**	**Points**
1. Physiological thresholds	Are limiting physiological conditions expected to change?	*Peromyscus* spp. are nocturnally active (Burt and Grossenheider 1976), so they avoid activity during the hottest part of the day. We assumed that this species estivates, as does *P. eremicus* (see Physiology, Question 5), so assumed it can respond to higher temperatures and lower moisture availability. We assumed that temperatures will remain below physiological thresholds most of the time.	0
2. Sex ratio	Is sex ratio determined by temperature?	No. Temperature-dependent sex determination is mainly observed in reptiles and fish (Manolakou and others 2006).	0
3. Exposure to extreme weather conditions	Are extreme weather or disturbance events that result in direct mortality or reproductive failure expected to change?	Increase in frequency of heat waves is predicted for southwestern United States. Overall, not clear to what extent timing and intensity of heat waves will affect survival and reproduction. We considered it unlikely that heat waves would cause widespread mortality for this species. See also Physiology, Question 1.	0
4. Limitations to active period	Are projected temperature or precipitation regimes that influence activity period of species expected to change?	*Peromyscus* spp. are nocturnally active (Burt and Grossenheider 1976). The closely related *P. eremicus* was found to be most active on moonlit nights, in comparison to *P. californicus*, which was most active on moonless nights (Owings and Lockard 1971 as cited in Veal and Caire 1979).	0
5. Metabolic inhibition	Does this species possess an ability to reduce metabolic energy or water requirements?	In the closely related *P. eremicus,* torpor mostly occurs on a daily basis (active at night, torpid during the day) and can be used any time energy supplies are limited (references in Veal and Caire 1979). Torpor occurred at any ambient temperature below 30 °C (Macmillen 1965). Winter torpor appears to result only from food restriction, as compared to summer torpor (estivation), which results from food limitation or a negative water balance; estivation can last several weeks (Macmillen 1965). We assumed that the above biology applies to *P. merriami* as well.	-1
6. Survival during resource limitation	Does this species have lower energy requirements or possess the capacity to store energy or water in the long term?	The closely-related *P. eremicus* was found to exhibit the highest level of food hoarding among five *Peromyscus* taxa; the amount of hoarding was not apparently related to ambient temperature or photoperiod (Barry 1976 as cited in Veal and Caire 1979). We assumed that hoarding behavior also occurs in *P. merriami*.	-1
7. Variable life history	Does this species have alternative life history strategies to cope with variable resources or climate conditions?	None reported.	0
8. Reproduction in variable environments	Can this species outlive periods where reproduction is limited?	In the closely related *P. eremicus*, the average age at first conception is 10 months with, on average, 50 days between litters (Davis and Davis 1979 as cited in Veal and Caire 1979). "Suspect that mesquite mice are born in nearly every month, much as with *P. eremicus*" (Hoffmeister 1986). Such a high reproductive rate suggests that this species is relatively short-lived. *P. leucopus* is said to have a complete population turn-over each year from mortality (Snyder 1956 in	1

Physiology: Mesquite mouse (*Peromyscus merriami*)			
Trait/Quality	Question	Background info. & explanation of score	Points
		Lackey and others 1985), so we assumed a similar situation for *P. merriami*.	
		Periods of extreme reductions in rainfall may last 5 years. If these conditions eliminate breeding (e.g., insufficient food), most of the population would not survive longer than the periods of limited reproduction.	

Phenology: Mesquite mouse (*Peromyscus merriami*)			
Trait/Quality	Question	Background info. & explanation of score	Points
1. Cues	Does this species use temperature or moisture cues to initiate activities related to fecundity or survival?	"Suspect that mesquite mice are born in nearly every month, much as with *P. eremicus*..." (Hoffmeister 1986). If this is the case, it appears that reproduction is not related to specific cues.	0
2. Event timing	Are activities related to species' fecundity or survival tied to discrete events that are expected to change?	No apparent connection to discrete events (see Phenology, Question 1).	0
3. Mismatch potential	What is the separation in time or space between cues that initiate activities and discrete events that provide critical resources?	Reproduction occurs year-round (see Phenology, Question 1). Resources do not appear to be particularly limited in general.	-1
4. Resilience to timing mismatches during breeding	Does this species employ strategies or have traits that increase the likelihood of reproduction co-occurring with important events?	"Suspect that mesquite mice are born in nearly every month, much as with *P. eremicus*..." Hoffmeister (1986). The closely related *P. eremicus* appears to curtail reproduction in hot dry periods in summer (Moor 1968 as cited in Veal and Caire 1979).	-1

Biotic interactions: Mesquite mouse (*Peromyscus merriami*)			
Trait/Quality	Question	Background info. & explanation of score	Points
1. Food resources	Are important food resources for this species expected to change?	Little information on this species. In the closely related *P. eremicus* in the California coastal sage scrub community, the diet consisted primarily of fruit and flowers of shrubs (Meserve 1976 as cited in Veal and Caire 1979). Also reported to consume seeds, insects, and green vegetation based on seasonal availability (references in Veal and Caire 1979). Other studies of *P. eremicus* reported that diet consists of seeds and desert annuals, in addition to mesquite beans, hackberry, nutlets, insects, and green vegetation; some studies reported insects as being an important part of the diet (references in Veal and Caire 1979).	0

Biotic interactions: Mesquite mouse (*Peromyscus merriami*)			
Trait/Quality	**Question**	**Background info. & explanation of score**	**Points**
		Assuming that *P. merriami* has a similar diet breadth to *P. eremicus*, species consumes a variety of prey.	
2. Predators	Are important predator populations expected to change?	We assumed that this species is preyed upon by a variety of predators. In the closely related *P. eremicus*, documented predation by barn owls in Sonora, Mexico, screech owl, and king snake (references in Veal and Caire 1979).	0
3. Symbionts	Are populations of symbiotic species expected to change?	No information to suggest important symbiotic relationships exist.	0
4. Disease	Is prevalence of diseases known to cause widespread mortality or reproductive failure in this species expected to change?	*P. eremicus* is host to a variety of parasites, including the nematode *Gongylonema peromysci*, and several species of mites, chiggers, ticks, fleas, and biting lice; in Mexico, documented to have bot fly larvae (*Cuterebra* spp.) under the skin (references in Veal and Caire 1979). Bot fly infestation has not been observed to have detectable effects on several measured host characteristics, including body mass, length and mass of testes, fecundity, and tolerance to cold stress (see references in Nichols 1994). Antibodies to Sin Nombre Virus, a type of hantavirus, were identified in *Peromyscus eremicus* in southeastern Arizona (Kuenzi and others 1999), but no indication that there has been widespread mortality due to this.	0
5. Competitors	Are populations of important competing species expected to change?	Little information. An experiment where three species of *Dipodomys* were excluded resulted in the authors concluding that *Peromyscus eremicus* and the 3 other species of small mammals were in direct competition (Heske and others 1994). This relationship may hold for *P. merriami*. The range of *Dipodomys ordii* and *D. merriami* overlap with that of *Peromyscus merriami*, and at least some of their habitat affinities seem similar. Possible that other species compete with *P. merriami* as well, so likely to have a variety of competitive relationships.	0

Literature Cited

Burt, W.H., and R.P. Grossenheider. 1976. A Field Guide to the Mammals of North America North of Mexico (3rd ed.). Boston: Houghton Mifflin Company.

Heske, E.J., J.H. Brown, and S. Mistry. 1994. Long-term experimental study of a Chihuahuan Desert rodent community: 13 years of competition. Ecology 75:438-445.

Hoffmeister, D.F. 1986. Mammals of Arizona. University of Arizona Press and Arizona Game and Fish Department. 602 p.

Hoffmeister, D.F., and M. R. Lee. 1963. The status of the sibling species *Peromyscus merriami* and *Peromyscus eremicus*. Journal of Mammalogy 44:201-213.

Jones, Larry. 2010. [Personal communication]. February 17, 2010. Tucson, AZ: U.S. Department of Agriculture, Forest Service, Coronado National Forest, Assistant Program Manager for Wildlife, Fish, and Rare Plants.

Jones, Larry. 2011. [Personal communication]. May 18, 2011. Tucson, AZ: U.S. Department of Agriculture, Forest Service, Coronado National Forest, Assistant Program Manager for Wildlife, Fish, and Rare Plants.

Kingsley, K.J. 2006. Evaluation of mesquite mouse (*Persomyscus merriami*) status in Pima County, Arizona. Prepared for: Pima County Regional Flood Control Distict, Water Resources Division, Public Works Center, Tucson, AZ. Arizona Game and Fish Department, Heritage Grant Program #I05001. Available: http://www.pima.gov/cmo/sdcp/reports/d30/EvaluationMesquite%20MouseStatus.pdf.

Kuenzi, A.J., M.L. Morrison, D.E. Swann, P.C. Hardy, and G.T. Downard. 1999. A longitudinal sutdy of Sin Nombre Virus prevalence in rodents, southwestern Arizona. Emerging Infectious Diseases 5:113-117.

Lackey, J.A., D.G. Huckaby, and B. G. Ormiston. 1985. *Peromyscus leucopus*. American Society of Mammalogists. Mammalian Species No. 247.

Macmillen, R.E. 1965. Aestivation in the cactus mouse, *Peromyscus eremicus*. Comparative Biochemistry and Physiology 16:247-248.

Manolakou, P., G. Lavranos, and R. Angelopoulou. 2006. Molecular patterns of sex determination in the animal kingdom: A comparative study of the biology of reproduction. Reproductive Biology and Endocrinology 4:59.

Maier, T.J. 2002. Long-distance movements by female white-footed mice, *Peromyscus leucopus*, in extensive mixed-wood forest. Canadian Field-Naturalist 116:108-111.

Nichols, L.B. 1994. The effect of bot fly (*Cuterebra*) infestation on cold-night trap mortality in cactus mice (*Peromyscus eremicus*). Southwestern Naturalist 39:383-385.

Rehmeier, R.L., G.A. Kaufman, and D.W. Kaufman. 2004. Long-distance movements of the deer mouse in tallgrass prairie. Journal of Mammalogy 85:562-568.

Stromberg, J.C., S.D. Wilkins, and J.A. Tress. 1993. Vegetation-hydrology models: Implications for management of *Prosopis velutina* (velvet mesquite) riparian ecosystems. Ecological Applications 3:307-314.

U.S. Forest Service [USFS]. 2009. Draft Coronado National Forest ecological sustainability report. Tucson, AZ: U.S. Department of Agriculture, Forest Service. Available: http://www fs fed.us/r3/coronado/plan-revision/documents/final/cnf-ecological-sustainability-report-final-022009.pdf.

Veal, R., and W. Caire. 1979. *Peromyscus eremicus*. American Society of Mammalogists. Mammalian Species No. 118.

Habitat: White-bellied long-tailed vole (*Microtus longicaudus leucophaeus*)			
Trait/Quality	**Question**	**Background info. & explanation of score**	**Points**
1. Area and distribution: *breeding*	Is the area or location of the associated vegetation type used for breeding activities by this species expected to change?	This sub-species occurs in the Pinaleño Mountains (Hoffmeister 1986). Note that the long-tailed vole has a large range throughout most of the western United States and Canada to eastern Alaska, with 14 sub-species, as identified by Hall 1981 (as cited in Smolen and Keller 1987). Hoffmeister (1986) identified 4 sub-species as occurring in Arizona. Across its range, *M. longicaudus* occurs in a variety of habitats ranging from forests, forest-meadow ecotones, and riparian areas, to grassy or sagebrush areas (see references in Smolen and Keller 1987). In Arizona, long-tailed voles occur in meadows, grassy valleys, grassy clearings in forests, sagebrush flats, and rocky slopes near or in coniferous forest (Hoffmeister 1986). In the Pinaleño Mountains, it was reported that this sub-species could be found "in any of the meadows or flats…above 8000 feet, where the grass is tall and thick and becomes heavily saturated with dew…. Frequently, there was standing water among the grass where they lived." (Hoffmeister 1956 as cited in Hoffmeister 1986). Hoffmeister (1986) also indicated that in Arizona, where long-tailed voles occur in the absence of *Microtus montanus*, they may occupy more mesic areas than elsewhere in the Southwest. Spicer (1985) indicated that the sub-species occurs in the Pinaleño Mountains from 1829-3269 m and in a variety of grassy habitats ranging from wet to dry. This includes areas containing "meadows, cienegas, and creeks; narrows strips along creeks, openings in coniferous forest and along roadsides; occasionally steep slopes with	2

Habitat: White-bellied long-tailed vole (*Microtus longicaudus leucophaeus*)			
Trait/Quality	**Question**	**Background info. & explanation of score**	**Points**
		openings of bunchgrasses…although such habitats are found in heavily forested areas above 2930 m…most occur between 2650 m and 2930 m on the relatively gently rolling semi-plateau of the crest of the range." The author indicated it is most abundant in areas with the thickest grass and grass-like vegetation in meadows and near water.	
		Van Horne (1982) reported that long-tailed voles are atypical voles in that they tend to occupy shrubby or forest edge areas rather than primarily in grasslands, except in high elevations where they may occupy meadows. The highest populations observed consistently in coastal coniferous forest in Alaska were on 7-10 year-old clear cut areas; densities were lower in mature timber stands than in successional stands (Van Horne 1982). Pugh and others (2003) indicated that for voles "…optimal habitat contains stable amounts of moisture and moisture-laden plant food, influenced by permanent water sources including the water table or by elevation and microclimate effects of geomorphology."	
		For the Pinaleño EMA, projections of suitable climate for vegetation communities (Chapter 1) predicted declines in suitable climate for Chihuahua desert scrub, Madrean forest and woodland, and Rocky Mountain conifer forest, with increases of suitable climate for semi-desert grassland, and little change by year 2090 for Madrean conifer forest and Sonoran desert scrub.	
		Reports for Arizona suggest this sub-species occurs more abundantly in association with more mesic areas (which may or may not include forests and riparian areas).	
		We considered it likely that habitat will decline due to reduced moisture (increased aridity). Not clear whether habitat might increase at higher elevations where temperatures are colder.	
2. Area and distribution: *non-breeding*	Is the area or location of the associated vegetation type used for non-breeding activities by this species expected to change?	Non-breeding habitat the same as breeding habitat; see Habitat, Question 1.	2
3. Habitat components: *breeding*	Are specific habitat components required for breeding expected to change?	Not clear if long-tailed voles require standing water. The presence of standing water was not considered a requirement by some authors (Borell and Ellis 1934 as cited in Smolen and Keller 1987). In Nevada, long-tailed voles have been found as far as 0.81 km from water (Hall 1946 as cited in Smolen and Keller 1987). Findley and others (1975) indicated that in the laboratory, *Microtus longicaudus* appeared to have greater drinking water needs than *M. mexicanus* or *M. montanus*, and that short-term water deprivation was often fatal. Not clear how this translates to field conditions.	0
		Voles build nests for rearing young, resting, and protection from extreme environmental conditions (Pugh and others 2003). Nests are formed from dried grass and plant fibers, and can either be above- or belowground and placed under rocks or logs, near boards or fenceposts, or in brush piles.	
		Overall, not clear if there are identifiable habitat components that will be altered by climate change.	
4. Habitat components:	Are specific habitat components required	No clear information on relationships.	0

Habitat: White-bellied long-tailed vole (*Microtus longicaudus leucophaeus*)

Trait/Quality	Question	Background info. & explanation of score	Points
non-breeding	for survival during non-breeding periods expected to change?	In Alaska, herbs were considered critical for over-winter survival (Van Horne 1982); covered under Biotic Interactions, Question 1.	
5. Habitat quality and reproduction	Are features of the habitat associated with better reproductive success expected to change?	In Alaskan coastal coniferous forest, long-tailed voles occurred in the greatest density (which was related to high productivity) where herb and shrub cover was high (Van Horne 1982). Not clear whether this translates to current occupied areas for this sub-species.	0
6. Habitat quality and survival	Are features of the habitat associated with better survival expected to change?	Recruitment and over-winter survival decreased as forb cover decreased through forest succession and shading increased (Van Horne 1982). Not clear whether this was related to food or something else; also unclear whether this applies to current occupied areas for this sub-species. See Habitat, Question 5.	0
7. Ability to colonize new areas	What is this species' capacity and tendency to disperse?	Individuals appear to move only small distances. The average distance moved of *Microtus* spp. among multiple capture sites in California was 59 m for males and 49 m for females, with 3 males moving >1000 m (Jenkins 1948 as cited in Smolen and Keller 1987). Van Horne (1982) documented 4 long-tailed voles moving 0.5 km, and one adult male that moved 1.1 km.	1
8. Migratory or transitional habitats	Does this species require additional habitats during migration that are separated from breeding and non-breeding habitats?	No information found to indicate that additional habitats are used.	0

Physiology: White-bellied long-tailed vole (*Microtus longicaudus leucophaeus*)

Trait/Quality	Question	Background info. & explanation of score	Points
1. Physiological thresholds	Are limiting physiological conditions expected to change?	In captivity, above 35 °C, long-tailed voles spent 90% of their time lying flat on their stomachs (Beck and Anthony 1971). In captivity, they appear to have no behavioral mechanisms for temperature regulation when ambient temperatures are above 30 °C. Temperatures above 35 °C are lethal to *M. montanus* within 2 hours (Packard 1968 as cited in Beck and Anthony 1971). Voles are not known to have specific physiological traits for conserving body water and are not considered "arid adapted" (Pugh and others 2003). Voles build nests for rearing young, resting, and protection from extreme environmental conditions, and nests can either be above- or belowground, and under rocks or logs (Pugh and others 2003). We assumed that temperatures will remain below physiological thresholds most of the time. See also Physiology, Questions 3 and 4.	0
2. Sex ratio	Is sex ratio determined by temperature?	No. Temperature-dependent sex determination is mainly observed in reptiles and fish (Manolakou and others 2006).	0
3. Exposure to extreme weather	Are extreme weather or disturbance events that result in	Increase in frequency of heat waves is predicted for southwestern United States. Overall, not clear to what extent timing and intensity of heat waves will affect survival and reproduction. We assumed it	0

Physiology: White-bellied long-tailed vole (*Microtus longicaudus leucophaeus*)			
Trait/Quality	**Question**	**Background info. & explanation of score**	**Points**
conditions	direct mortality or reproductive failure expected to change?	unlikely that heat waves would cause widespread mortality. See also Physiology, Questions 1 and 4.	
4. Limitations to active period	Are projected temperature or precipitation regimes that influence activity period of species expected to change?	Spicer (1985) indicated that voles are active diurnally and nocturnally and that this sub-species was trapped at night and during the day. In Alaska, long-tailed voles were observed to be active mostly at night (Van Horne 1982). Voles must eat frequently, so activity tends to be intermittent (Pugh and others 2003). Not clear that activity periods overall will be reduced. See also Physiology, Questions 1 and 3.	0
5. Metabolic inhibition	Does this species possess an ability to reduce metabolic energy or water requirements?	Voles are homeotherms; they have not been documented to use seasonal hibernation, daily torpor, or prolonged fasting (Wunder 1985 as cited in Pugh and others 2003). Pugh and others (2003) described physiological, morphological, and behavioral traits for dealing with cold temperatures.	1
6. Survival during resource limitation	Does this species have lower energy requirements or possess the capacity to store energy or water in the long term?	Voles may clip grass for winter storage (Wunder 1978 in Pugh and others 2003). *Microtus xanthognathus* has been reported to store rhizomes (Wolff and Lidicker 1980 as cited in Pugh and others 2003). Little documentation of vole food storage (Wunder 1985 as cited in Pugh and others 2003). Mattson (2004) documented bears consuming vole caches (*Microtus* spp.) in Yellowstone National Park. We assumed that, at high elevations where snow cover exists in winter, food storage would be primary method of survival since voles are not known to use torpor (see Physiology, Question 5).	-1
7. Variable life history	Does this species have alternative life history strategies to cope with variable resources or climate conditions?	None reported.	0
8. Reproduction in variable environments	Can this species outlive periods where reproduction is limited?	Long-tailed voles rarely live more than 1 year (Jenkins 1948 as cited in Smolen and Keller 1987). Females may ovulate as early as 3 weeks of age and gestation is 20-23 days; this effectively allows the population to increase during favorable environmental conditions (Pugh and others 2003). This ability to increase population size rapidly would not appear to offer specific resistance against unfavorable conditions, however. While, Van Horne (1982) indicated that long-tailed voles are thought to exhibit annual fluctuations in density (though not multi-annual fluctuations as in some other vole species), Spicer (1985) indicated that this sub-species is not known to have population irruptions. Periods of extreme reductions in rainfall may last 5 years. If these conditions reduce food resources to the point that voles have insufficient food for breeding, most of the population would not survive longer than the periods of limited reproduction.	1

Phenology: White-bellied long-tailed vole (*Microtus longicaudus leucophaeus*)			
Trait/Quality	**Question**	**Background info. & explanation of score**	**Points**
1. Cues	Does this species use temperature or moisture cues to initiate activities related to fecundity or survival?	In Nevada, the breeding season is from May-October with June and July showing the most reproductive activity (Hall 1946 as cited in Smolen and Keller 1987). Ovulation appears to be induced by copulation or hormonal stimulation (Seabloom 1985 as cited in Pugh and others 2003). Jannett (1982) indicated that estrus is male-induced and is not an estrus cycle. Odor is the predominant cue used to evaluate reproductive status and receptivity. Little information on this topic, although Van Horne (1982) suggested that in Alaskan coniferous forest, reproduction may be cued to day length and temperature proximately, but ultimately to a berry crop.	0
2. Event timing	Are activities related to species' fecundity or survival tied to discrete events that are expected to change?	Little information available. Changes in precipitation and increases in temperature can alter timing of food availability, which could alter timing of breeding.	1
3. Mismatch potential	What is the separation in time or space between cues that initiate activities and discrete events that provide critical resources?	Critical resources for breeding probably involve food but relationship is unclear.	0
4. Resilience to timing mismatches during breeding	Does this species employ strategies or have traits that increase the likelihood of reproduction co-occurring with important events?	Long-tailed vole young are born at least from late April-September; believed that females have more than 1 litter during the year (Hoffmeister 1986). Van Horne (1982) observed that at least half of the females produced 2 litters in a season (in Alaska); number of litters may differ according to latitude. Females reported to produce no more than 2 litters in their lifetime (Smolen and Keller 1987); this observed by Van Horne (1982) in Alaska. The mean number of embryos was 4.51 (range 2-7; n=39 females that had embryos).	-1

Biotic interactions: White-bellied long-tailed vole (*Microtus longicaudus leucophaeus*)			
Trait/Quality	**Question**	**Background info. & explanation of score**	**Points**
1. Food resources	Are important food resources for this species expected to change?	Voles are herbivores. Pugh and others (2003) indicated that most species of *Microtus* consume a wide variety of food items (mostly green succulent vegetation), and that items may change in relative proportions and species from one season to the next and from one year to the next. *Microtus* spp. may consume roots, bark, and fungi; rarely do they consume insects or meat. In Alaska, herbs were considered critical for over-winter survival (Van Horne 1982). Long-tailed voles consume fruits and seeds mostly, but also dicots and some monocots (Van Horne 1982). In Wyoming, diets consisted of 38% green plant material by volume, 1% seed fragments, and 61% unidentified matter (n=14; Clark 1973 as cited in Smolen and Keller 1987). Other items recorded include fungus and sagebrush bark and leaves in Nevada in winter (see references in Smolen and Keller 1987).

Growth rates of the first and second cohorts of *Microtus montanus* offspring in Wyoming were significantly lower in a year of low summer rainfall (1988) than in a summer of heavy rainfall (1987), and production from a third cohort was lower. Grasses and sedges were | 1 |

Biotic interactions: White-bellied long-tailed vole (*Microtus longicaudus leucophaeus*)			
Trait/Quality	**Question**	**Background info. & explanation of score**	**Points**
		shorter in 1988 than in 1987.	
		Although long-tailed voles eat a variety of foods, their dependence on green vegetation will potentially be reduced by increased aridity.	
2. Predators	Are important predator populations expected to change?	Predators include barn owls, great horned owls, long-eared owls, short-eared owls, prairie falcon, ermines, long-tailed weasels, and pine martens (see references in Smolen and Keller 1987). Most species of raptors feed on voles; during vole irruptions, other species may prey on them (e.g., shrikes, magpies, crows, white-tailed kites, great blue herons, and bitterns; references in Pugh and others 2003). Other mammalian predators of voles include short-tailed shrews, badgers, coyotes, skunks, weasels, and bobcats; reptile predators include a variety of snakes (references in Pugh and others 2003). Long-tailed Voles have a suite of predators.	0
3. Symbionts	Are populations of symbiotic species expected to change?	No information found to suggest existence of important symbionts.	0
4. Disease	Is prevalence of diseases known to cause widespread mortality or reproductive failure in this species expected to change?	Long-tailed voles have been reported to have a variety of parasites. Reported endoparasites include *Giardia* spp. and three species of nematodes (see references in Smolen and Keller 1987). Reported ectoparasites include mites, fleas, lice, and ticks. Also cestodes (Pugh and others 2003). Dead voles have been found harboring the bacterium that causes tularemia (*Francisella tularensis*), but not clear what role this disease had in mortality observed during vole irruptions (Pugh and others 2003). Plague bacillus (*Yersinia pestis*) has been found in *Microtus californicus*. Pugh and others (2003) reported no clear relationships of widespread mortality to disease.	0
5. Competitors	Are populations of important competing species expected to change?	Hoffmeister (1986) indicated that in Arizona, *M. montanus* occurs only in the White Mountains (Apache and Greenlee Counties); *M. mexicanus* indicated as occurring in areas north of CNF.	0

Literature Cited

Beck, L.R., and R.G. Anthony. 1971. Metabolic and behavioral thermoregulation in the long-tailed vole, *Microtus longicaudus*. Journal of Mammalogy 52:404-412.

Hoffmeister, D.F. 1986. Mammals of Arizona. University of Arizona Press and Arizona Game and Fish Department. 602 p.

Jannett, F.J., Jr. 1982. Male-induced estrus in the long-tail vole (*Microtus longicaudus*) and the sagebrush vole (*Lagurus curtatus*). American Zoologist 22:932.

Manolakou, P., G. Lavranos, and R. Angelopoulou. 2006. Molecular patterns of sex determination in the animal kingdom: A comparative study of the biology of reproduction. Reproductive Biology and Endocrinology 4:59.

Mattson, D.J. 2004. Consumption of voles and vole food caches by Yellowstone grizzly bears: Exploratory analyses. Ursus 15:218-226.

Pugh, S.R., S. Johnson, and R.H. Tamarin. 2003. Voles. In: Feldhamer, G.C., B.C. Thompson, and J.A. Chapman, eds. Wild mammals of North America: Biology, management, and conservation. Baltimore, MD: Johns Hopkins University Press. 1216 p.

Smolen, M.J., and B.L. Keller. 1987. *Microtus longicaudus*. American Society of Mammalogists. Mammalian Species No. 271: 1-7.

Spicer, R.B. 1985. Status of the white-bellied vole, *Microtus longicaudus leucophaeus* Allen, of southeastern Arizona. Prepared for: Office of Endangered Species, U.S. Fish and Wildlife Service,

Albuquerque, NM. Prepared by: Arizona Game and Fish Department, Phoenix. Contract # 14-16-0002-82-216.

U.S. Forest Service. 2009. Draft Coronado National Forest ecological sustainability report. Tucson, AZ: U.S. Department of Agriculture, Forest Service. Available: http://www fs.fed.us/r3/coronado/plan-revision/documents/final/cnf-ecological-sustainability-report-final-022009.pdf.

Van Horne, B. 1982. Demography of the longtail vole *Microtus longicaudus* in seral stages of coastal coniferous forest, southeast Alaska. Canadian Journal of Zoology 60:1690-1709.

Habitat: Coues' white-tailed deer (*Odocoileus virginianus couesi*)			
Trait/Quality	Question	Background info. & explanation of score	Points
1. Area and distribution: *breeding*	Is the area or location of the associated vegetation type used for breeding activities by this species expected to change?	The white-tailed deer has a large range, from southern Canada throughout most of the coterminous United States, to northern South America (although not present in Utah and rare in Nevada and California; Smith 1991). The sub-species that occurs in Arizona is *Odocoileus virginianus couesi* (in eastern New Mexico and Texas, *O. v. texanus* occurs; Hoffmeister 1986). White-tailed deer inhabit a wide range of habitats in North America (from north-temperate to subtropical and semi-arid environments) and is most abundant east of the Mississippi River (McCabe and McCabe 1984 as cited in Smith 1991). Within arid regions, this species occurs in the more mesic areas; most of its range within the Southwest received >25 cm of rain each years; areas with ~40 cm per year have the highest numbers of individuals (Smith 1991). In Mexico, they are most abundant in pine-oak forests, and in Central America, most abundant in second-growth forests, thickets, and forest-savannah ecotones. In Arizona, they occur in mountain ranges in southeastern Arizona, as well as on the Mogollon Plateau and other areas; also observed in desert ranges (Ajos, Growlers, and Saucedas; Hoffmeister 1986). In Arizona, found mostly in woodlands (evergreen oaks or oak-juniper-pinyon) but also in ponderosa pine forest, desert scrub, and deciduous forest, and occasionally in spruce-fir in the Graham Mountains (Hoffmeister 1986). Hoffmeister (1986) indicated that probably more than three-quarters of individuals in Arizona occur in the oaks, junipers, pinyon, Apache, and Chihuahuan pines. Overall, habitat for white-tailed deer has increased in some areas through increases in second-growth forest, openings, and farmlands as a result of logging, clearing, and agriculture; forest openings and early-successional habitats have benefitted the species (Smith 1991). Expansion into west Texas and other arid regions has been encouraged by irrigation. Tree removal improved forage in previously unoccupied portions of northern boreal forests (Smith 1991). Seasonal drought is thought to exclude white-tailed deer from western Arizona; the disappearance of isolated populations from western-most portions of the range in Arizona were thought to be correlated with an increased propensity for spring drought since 1950 (Brown and Henry 1981). Coues' white-tailed deer occur, or potential habitat exists, on all 12 of the EMAs on CNF (USFS 2009). Projections of suitable climate for vegetation communities forest wide (Chapter 1) predicted declines in suitable climate for all plant community types, with the exception of increases of suitable climate for semi-desert grassland and small increases in Sonoran desert scrub (present in small amounts on the CNF).	2

Habitat: Coues' white-tailed deer (*Odocoileus virginianus couesi*)			
Trait/Quality	Question	Background info. & explanation of score	Points
		Although white-tailed deer have been observed to prefer early successional forests, in the Southwest, woodlands and pine forests may already be fairly open compared to northern-latitude forests. Thus, we expected that wildfire and increased aridity have the potential to reduce habitat rather than increase it.	
2. Area and distribution: *non-breeding*	Is the area or location of the associated vegetation type used for non-breeding activities by this species expected to change?	Although high-elevation individuals may move to lower elevations in winter, we assumed that they still utilize woodlands in winter. See Habitat, Question 1.	2
3. Habitat components: *breeding*	Are specific habitat components required for breeding expected to change?	Abundance of white-tailed deer in the Great Plains is limited by the quality and amount of vegetative cover (references in Smith 1991). In areas not heavily forested, the density and distribution is lower in areas with less riparian and other woody cover (references in Smith 1991). Free-standing water appears to be utilized by desert mule deer (*O. hemionus crooki*) in the region, and we assumed these trends apply to *O. virginianus*. Several tagged desert mule deer in Arizona (Picacho Mountains) observed at 6 catchments, 1 spring, and ephemeral rain pools, visited water sources generally once per day, consuming 1.5-6.0 L per visit (Hazam and Krausman 1988). Large males were not observed at catchments in summer. Females in summer consumed the largest amounts of water (possibly related to lactation). There is debate over whether mule deer require free-standing water (see references in Kie and others 2003). It appears that the absence of standing water represents marginal conditions (Severson and Medina 1983 as cited in Kie and others 2003). A study of 9 female desert mule deer in Arizona (Belmont and Bighorn Mountains) found that the mean distance to water during fawning was not different from the non-fawning season (2.7 km and 2.5 km, respectively; Fox and Krausman 1994). In this same study, home ranges of females usually contained or were near one water source at a minimum; such proximity has been attributed to an increased need for water during hot weather. During summer (when temperatures are high and water availability is decreased), diurnal bed sites are considered important in enabling this sub-species to maintain body temperature and water balance (Knipe 1977 as cited in Ockenfels and Brooks 1994). Tree density, tree species richness, and tree canopy cover were greater in bed sites than at random sites in the Santa Rita Mountain foothills. Overall, reductions in natural water sources and reductions in trees are expected to reduce habitat components.	1
4. Habitat components: *non-breeding*	Are specific habitat components required for survival during non-breeding periods expected to change?	Reductions in free-standing water potentially will negatively impact Coues' white-tailed deer during the non-breeding season. A study of 9 female desert mule deer in Arizona (Belmont and Bighorn Mountains) found that the mean distance to water during fawning was not different from the non-fawning season (2.7 km and 2.5 km, respectively; Fox and Krausman 1994).	1
5. Habitat quality and reproduction	Are features of the habitat associated with better	A study of 9 female desert mule deer in Arizona (Belmont and Bighorn Mountains) showed that thermal and hiding cover were important components of habitat for fawns (as would be expected);	1

Habitat: Coues' white-tailed deer (*Odocoileus virginianus couesi*)

Trait/Quality	Question	Background info. & explanation of score	Points
	reproductive success expected to change?	fawns were bedded near vegetation that provided shade (Fox and Krausman 1994). It has been suggested that the condition and type of cover available for fawning influences the survival rate of fawns (see discussion in Fox and Krausman 1994).	
6. Habitat quality and survival	Are features of the habitat associated with better survival expected to change?	Cover for hiding and concealment may be critical to ungulate population, but not clear that this is distinct from habitat needs covered in Habitat, Question 1 (Kie and others 2003).	0
7. Ability to colonize new areas	What is this species' capacity and tendency to disperse?	While white-tailed deer tend to occupy well-defined home ranges for multiple years (Staines 1974 as cited in Smith 1991), they have the ability to disperse long distances. Movements are correlated with age, sex, density, social interactions, latitude, season, and habitat characteristics (Smith 1991). Males move farther than females; young deer move farther than adults. Average seasonal migrations between 15-23 km are common in northern and montane populations (Marchinton and Hirth 1984 as cited in Smith 1991).	-1
8. Migratory or transitional habitats	Does this species require additional habitats during migration that are separated from breeding and non-breeding habitats?	Individuals at high elevations often migrate to lower elevations. Those at highest elevations on the CNF expected to migrate to lower elevations for winter.	1

Physiology: Coues' white-tailed deer (*Odocoileus virginianus couesi*)

Trait/Quality	Question	Background info. & explanation of score	Points
1. Physiological thresholds	Are limiting physiological conditions expected to change?	Mule deer (*O. hemionus*) tolerate a wide range of temperatures, from below -15 °C in winter to >30 °C in summer in southern regions; Wallmo 1981 as cited in Kie and others 2003). We assumed that white-tailed deer have similar tolerances. This sub-species in Oklahoma was least active >30 °C; at high temperatures, deer use areas with shade trees (Ockenfels and Brooks 1994). We assumed that temperatures will remain below physiological thresholds for the most part.	0
2. Sex ratio	Is sex ratio determined by temperature?	No. Temperature-dependent sex determination is mainly observed in reptiles and fish (Manolakou and others 2006).	0
3. Exposure to extreme weather conditions	Are extreme weather or disturbance events that result in direct mortality or reproductive failure expected to change?	Extensive snow cover reduces movement and the availability of forage, which can lead to increase winter mortality (references in Smith 1991); this appears to be more of a problem in northern portions of North America. Snow depths of 25-30 cm may interfere with movements of mule deer in Colorado, with depths >50 cm having the potential to completely prevent access (Loveless 1967 as cited in Kie and others 2003). Again, we assumed that populations at high elevations would move down slope to areas with lower snow cover in the event of extreme snowfall events. Likely that snow cover will be reduced as a result of higher temperatures, causing more precipitation to fall as rain than as snow. Increase in frequency of heat waves is predicted for southwestern United States. Overall, not clear to what extent timing and intensity of heat waves will affect survival and reproduction. We considered it	0

Physiology: Coues' white-tailed deer (*Odocoileus virginianus couesi*)			
Trait/Quality	**Question**	**Background info. & explanation of score**	**Points**
		unlikely that heat waves would cause widespread mortality. See also Physiology Question 1 above.	
4. Limitations to active period	Are projected temperature or precipitation regimes that influence activity period of species expected to change?	Foraging is most extensive for 1-2 hours around sunrise and sunset (Hoffmeister 1986). In hot environments, feeding at night reduces thermal stress but possibly takes advantage of daily cycles of water content in forage species (Taylor 1969 as cited in Kie and others 2003). We assumed that rise in temperatures will not significantly impact morning and evening activity periods.	0
5. Metabolic inhibition	Does this species possess an ability to reduce metabolic energy or water requirements?	No.	1
6. Survival during resource limitation	Does this species have lower energy requirements or possess the capacity to store energy or water in the long term?	No long-term food, fat, or water storage ability.	1
7. Variable life history	Does this species have alternative life history strategies to cope with variable resources or climate conditions?	No alternative life history strategies.	0
8. Reproduction in variable environments	Can this species outlive periods where reproduction is limited?	Females do not breed before they are 18 months old; many do not produce young in their first breeding effort (Hoffmeister 1986). Females usually produce 1 young in first birth, twins in later breeding seasons. As many as 65% of the fawns born in most years do not survive to be counted in winter surveys (Knipe 1977 as cited in Hoffmeister 1986). Few individuals live more than 10 years (Halls 1978 as cited in Smith 1991). Life expectancy is 2.5 years in Illinois (Calhoun and Loomis 1974 as cited in Smith 1991); in Pennsylvania, life expectancy is 2 years for males and 3 years for females (Forbes and others 1971 as cited in Smith 1991). Note that seasonal drought is thought to exclude white-tailed deer from western Arizona; the disappearance of isolated populations from western-most portions of its range in Arizona was thought to be correlated with an increased propensity for spring drought since 1950 (Brown and Henry 1981). If these conditions reduce resources to the point that individuals have insufficient resources for breeding for several years, but conditions recover, we considered it likely that sufficient numbers of individuals would survive long enough to breed once conditions improve.	–1

Phenology: Coues' white-tailed deer (*Odocoileus virginianus couesi*)			
Trait/Quality	**Question**	**Background info. & explanation of score**	**Points**
1. Cues	Does this species use temperature or moisture cues to initiate activities related to fecundity or survival?	Breeding activity of females is influenced by the presence of a mature rutting male, physical condition, and genetics (Smith 1991). "The ultimate determinant of breeding season is availability of adequate nutrition which is cued by photoperiodism (Verme and Ullrey 1984 as cited in Smith 1991). Females generally come into estrus in autumn (Sauer 1984 as cited in Smith 1991).

In Arizona, the fawning season for mule deer coincides with the summer monsoon (Fox and Krausman 1994); however, not clear that this is a cue or an ultimate evolutionary factor.

Temperature and moisture influence food abundance, but since the relationship to the timing of parturition would be indirect, this question was scored as "0." | 0 |
2. Event timing	Are activities related to species' fecundity or survival tied to discrete events that are expected to change?	Changes in the timing of precipitation and increases in temperature in spring can alter the timing of new growth in plants (see diet description in Biotic Interactions, Question 1), but not clear how white-tailed deer time breeding relative to consumption of new growth and whether new growth (versus other plant parts) is critical.	0
3. Mismatch potential	What is the separation in time or space between cues that initiate activities and discrete events that provide critical resources?	See Phenology, Question 2.	0
4. Resilience to timing mismatches during breeding	Does this species employ strategies or have traits that increase the likelihood of reproduction co-occurring with important events?	Single breeding event per year. Females typically don't breed until 1.5 years of age (Halls 1978 as cited in Smith 1991) and usually produce 1 young in first birth, twins in later breeding seasons (Hoffmeister 1986).	1

Biotic interactions: Coues' white-tailed deer (*Odocoileus virginianus couesi*)			
Trait/Quality	**Question**	**Background info. & explanation of score**	**Points**
1. Food resources	Are important food resources for this species expected to change?	From Hoffmeister (1986): Diet changes throughout the year although much of what they consume is from shrubs. white-tailed deer eat leaves from many broad-leafed trees, including fallen leaves (both green and dry). A diet analysis in the Mazatzal Mountains (north of Phoenix) across several seasons found: (1) in midsummer, ate fruits of turbinella oak, skunk bush, mesquite, Emory oak, yellow-leaf silktassel, and catclaw acacia, as well as sagebrush; (2) in November-December, ate more shrubs (e.g., blackbrush, sagebrush, spurges, calliandra, and spiderwort); (3) in January, ate old leaves of shrubs (e.g., buckthorn, buckbrush, buckwheats, and sagebrush); (4) in late winter, ate new grass growth, filaree, and bromes; (5) and in the spring, ate new growth of sugar sumac, buckbrush, buckhorn, scrub oak, calliandra, and ratany (McCulloch 1973 as cited in Hoffmeister 1986).

Anthony (1976) observed that during a year-long drought (~half the annual average precipitation) in southeastern Arizona, both white- | 0 |

Trait/Quality	Question	Background info. & explanation of score	Points
		tailed and mule deer fed more on evergreen and drought-resistant species and less on deciduous shrubs. Overall, white-tailed deer consume a variety of forage species and appear capable of switching forage species in periods of low rainfall.	
2. Predators	Are important predator populations expected to change?	Predation is listed as one of several proximate causes of death; other causes include disease, fence entanglement, automobile collisions, predation, hunter crippling, old age, and poaching (Halls 1984 as cited in Smith 1991). Predators include coyotes, bobcats, mountain lions, feral dogs, golden eagles; gray fox, owls, and hawks are considered predators on fawns (Hoffmeister 1986). Overall, white-tailed deer have a suite of predators.	0
3. Symbionts	Are populations of symbiotic species expected to change?	No information found to suggest existence of important symbionts.	0
4. Disease	Is prevalence of diseases known to cause widespread mortality or reproductive failure in this species expected to change?	Disease is listed as one of several proximate causes of death (others include fence entanglement, automobile collisions, predation, hunter crippling, old age, and poaching (Halls 1984 as cited in Smith 1991). White-tailed deer are host to more than 100 species of internal and external parasites (Samuel 1994 as cited in Miller and others 2003). High levels of mortality in southeastern U.S. populations have occurred due to epizootic hemorrhagic disease, and while mortality from this disease has occurred in Arizona, it has not been recognized as a significant problem in cervids in Arizona (Noon and others 2002). Chronic wasting disease, a neurological disease caused by an infectious prion, affects captive and free-ranging deer in North America; appears that it has not been observed in Arizona (Williams and others 2002). Not clear whether climate change would affect spread or susceptibility to this disease. Overall, did not find cases of significant mortality from disease in Arizona.	0
5. Competitors	Are populations of important competing species expected to change?	Mule deer also occurs in Arizona (Hoffmeister 1986). Where the two species occur together, white-tailed deer generally occur at higher elevations. Mule deer are considered better adapted to arid conditions than white-tailed deer based on distributional differences (Brown and Henry 1981). Brown and Henry (1981) indicated that the desert mule deer may have replaced or displaced white-tailed deer in lower elevations; not clear whether this is due to direct competition or whether changes in habitat over time reduced suitability for white-tailed deer. Anthony and Smith (1977) studied the two species in the San Cayetano and Dos Cabeza Mountains in southeastern Arizona; in the former, there was a "buffer zone" between the two species, but the two were sympatric in the latter area, and mule deer were dominant over white-tails in behavioral interactions. The authors concluded that the zone of non-overlap suggested exclusion of white-tails by mule deer. Overall, even if changes in conditions favor mule deer over white-tailed deer, not clear that the former will be positively affected by climate change.	0

Literature Cited

Anthony, R.G. 1976. Influence of drought on diets and numbers of desert deer. Journal of Wildlife Management 40:140-144.

Anthony, R.G., and N. S. Smith. 1977. Ecological relationships between mule deer and white-tailed deer in southeastern Arizona. Ecological Monographs 47:255-277.

Brown, D.E., and R.S. Henry. 1981. On relict occurrences of white-tailed deer within the Sonoran Desert in Arizona. Southwestern Naturalist 26:147-152.

Fox, K.B., and P.R. Krausman. 1994. Fawning habitat of desert mule deer. Southwestern Naturalist 39:269-275.

Hazam, J.E., and P.R Krausman. 1988. Measuring water consumption of desert mule deer. Journal of Wildlife Management 52:529-534.

Hoffmeister, D.F. 1986. Mammals of Arizona. University of Arizona Press and Arizona Game and Fish Department. 602 p.

Kie, J.G., T. Bowyer, and K.M. Stewart.2003. Ungulates in western coniferous forests: Habitat relationships, population dynamics, and ecosystem processes. In: Zabel, C.J., and R.G. Anthony, eds. Mammal community dynamics: Management and conservation in the coniferous forests of Western North America. Cambridge, United Kingdom: Cambridge University Press: 296-340.

Manolakou, P., G. Lavranos, and R. Angelopoulou. 2006. Molecular patterns of sex determination in the animal kingdom: A comparative study of the biology of reproduction. Reproductive Biology and Endocrinology 4:59.

Miller, K.V., L.I. Muller, and S. Demaris. 2003. White-tailed Deer. In: Feldhamer, G.C., B.C. Thompson, and J.A. Chapman. Wild mammals of North America: Biology, management, and conservation. Baltimore, MD: Johns Hopkins University Press: 906-930.

Noon, T.H., S.L. Wesche, J. Heffelfinger, A. Fuller, G.A. Bradley, and C. Regglardo. 2002. Hemorrhagic disease in deer in Arizona. Journal of Wildlife Diseases 38:177-181.

Ockenfels, R.A., and D.E. Brooks. 1994. Summer diurnal bed sites of Coues white-tailed deer. Journal of Wildlife Management 58:70-75.

Smith, W.P. 1991. *Odocoileus virginianus*. American Society of Mammalogists. Mammalian Species No. 388.

U.S. Forest Service [USFS]. 2009. Draft Coronado National Forest ecological sustainability report. Tucson, AZ: U.S. Department of Agriculture, Forest Service. Available: http://www fs fed.us/r3/coronado/plan-revision/documents/final/cnf-ecological-sustainability-report-final-022009.pdf.

Williams, E.S., M.W. Miller, T.J. Kreeger, R.H. Kahn, and E.T. Thorne. 2002. Chronic wasting disease of deer and elk: A review with recommendations for management. Journal of Wildlife Management 66:551-563.

Habitat: Desert bighorn sheep (*Ovis canadensis mexicana*)			
Trait/Quality	Question	Background info. & explanation of score	Points
1. Area and distribution: *breeding*	Is the area or location of the associated vegetation type used for breeding activities by this species expected to change?	*Ovis canadensis mexicana* is one of 6 extant sub-species of *Ovis canadensis*; it occurs in Arizona, southwestern New Mexico, western Texas, and portions of northern New Mexico (Shackleton 1985). Desert bighorn sheep range from 78 m below sea-level (Death Valley, California) to >4200 m (Shackleton 1985). Its habitat tends to include vegetation associations that are adapted to dry, rocky, or sandy soils containing arid-adapted plants (Krausman and Bowyer 2003). In Arizona, prefers precipitous, rocky desert ranges; vegetation is rarely thick or tall, and individuals often use the highest ridges as lookouts (Hoffmeister 1986). Buechner (1960) suggested that the most productive habitat in Arizona is between 3000-4000 ft in jojoba (*Simmondsia* spp.) communities as well as riparian communities. Hoffmeister (1986) mentioned that suitable habitat includes creek beds or near natural tanks; several plant species may be more abundant there (ocotillo, saguaro, cacti, and brittlebrush). Cliff and rock areas are required for escape habitat. Alderman and others (1989) observed common use of desert washes in Arizona.	0

Habitat: Desert bighorn sheep (*Ovis canadensis mexicana*)			
Trait/Quality	**Question**	**Background info. & explanation of score**	**Points**
		Cain and others (2005) considered Sonoran desert scrub, Madrean oak woodland, and semi-desert grassland as potential habitat in the Santa Catalina Mountains.	
		Visibility is an important habitat feature for bighorn sheep to avoid predators; some areas that had once been occupied no longer support sheep because vegetation increased following fire suppression (see references in Krausman and Bowyer 2003). Maturing chaparral resulted in reduced visibility, which lowered its suitability for bighorn (DeForge 1980 as cited in Krausman and Bowyer 2003). Wilson and others (1980) indicated that areas of dense vegetation over 30 inches tall are generally used less than areas with shorter vegetation, or are avoided. Low-severity fires may not significantly reduce vegetation that impedes visibility for desert bighorn sheep (Cain and others 2005).	
		Surveys by the Arizona Game and Fish Department documented bighorn sheep within the last 5 years in the Galiuro and Peloncillo Mountains (Brochu, personal communication). Sheep in the Galiuro Mountains were observed on CNF lands. Hoffmeister (1986) indicated that in 1974, 14 individuals were reported in the Santa Catalina's and 60 in the early 1980s. Desert bighorn sheep may no longer regularly occupy the Santa Catalina range (Heffelfinger, personal communication).	
		Desert bighorn sheep occur, or potential habitat exists, on the Galiuro, Peloncillo and Santa Catalina EMAs on CNF (USFS 2009). Projections of suitable climate for vegetation communities on these three EMAs (Chapter 1) predicted declines in suitable climate for Madrean forest and woodland and Madrean coniferous forest, an increase in semi-desert grassland, and a small increase in Sonoran desert scrub.	
		Assuming that desert bighorn sheep can utilize semi-desert grassland that is expected to increase, we expected that habitat will be type-converted.	
2. Area and distribution: *non-breeding*	Is the area or location of the associated vegetation type used for non-breeding activities by this species expected to change?	We assumed that non-breeding habitat is similar to breeding habitat on the CNF. See Habitat, Question 1.	0
3. Habitat components: *breeding*	Are specific habitat components required for breeding expected to change?	The importance/requirement of sources of free-standing water is debated. Water is obtained through food (e.g., saguaro, cholla, prickly pear and other cacti, and agave; Hoffmeister 1986). Bradley (1963) suggested that bighorn sheep probably need to drink at least every few weeks. Krausman and Bowyer (2003) did not indicate that bighorn sheep require free-standing water. Desert bighorn sheep occupy the Little Harquahala Mountains in Arizona where free-standing water is not known to occur (Alderman and others 1989).	0
		We did not consider free-standing water a habitat component required for breeding.	
		Females seek steep, rugged terrain to be secluded while giving birth (Krausman and Bowyer 2003; Bangs and others 2005a). Parturition sites are used for only a few days (Bangs and others 2005a). This availability not expected to change as a direct result of climate change.	

Habitat: Desert bighorn sheep (*Ovis canadensis mexicana*)

Trait/Quality	Question	Background info. & explanation of score	Points
4. Habitat components: *non-breeding*	Are specific habitat components required for survival during non-breeding periods expected to change?	See Habitat, Question 3 for discussion of water. Bighorn sheep need cliffs and other precipitous terrain for escaping predators; rarely far from such cover (references in Krausman and Bowyer 2003). In New Mexico, locations were nearer to topography with 60% slope than were random locations (Bangs and others 2005b). Availability of steep terrain not expected to change as a direct result of climate change.	0
5. Habitat quality and reproduction	Are features of the habitat associated with better reproductive success expected to change?	The distribution of water holes in Nevada influenced patterns of home-range use in *O. c. nelsoni* (references in Shackleton 1985). Some researchers have suggested that water is the most limiting factor for desert bighorn sheep (references in Broyles and Cutler 1999). Other research (generally, more recent studies) indicated that the presence of perennial water sources (which provides water during the hottest parts of year) may not limit populations (references in Broyles and Cutler 1999). Broyles and Cutler (1999) detected no difference in relative abundance or in various measures of reproductive output in 4 ranges with perennial surface water compared to 3 ranges without (Cabeza Prieta National Wildlife Refuge in Arizona). Cain and others (2008) removed water catchments in Cabeza Prieta NWR and compared pre- and post-removal indices in a "treatment" mountain range and a control range. The authors did not detect changes in home-range area, movement rates, or distance that sheep were from water during hotter months. Krausman and Bowyer (2003; see references therein) indicated that the value of water sources has been questioned because there is a lack of empirical evidence that artificial water sources benefit populations. Hoffmeister (1986) indicated that rainfall in Arizona's desert ranges is infrequent enough that natural catchments dry up during much of the year. See also Habitat, Question 3.	0
6. Habitat quality and survival	Are features of the habitat associated with better survival expected to change?	See Habitat, Question 5.	0
7. Ability to colonize new areas	What is this species' capacity and tendency to disperse?	Considered very mobile. Some populations/sub-species of bighorn sheep move between summer and winter ranges as many as ~48 km (see Shackleton 1985). See also Habitat, Question 8.	-1
8. Migratory or transitional habitats	Does this species require additional habitats during migration that are separated from breeding and non-breeding habitats?	Some populations/sub-species of bighorn move between seasonal home ranges, moving to lower elevations for winter; populations occupying low desert ranges do not (Geist 1971 as cited in Shackleton 1985). Krausman and Bowyer (2003) indicated that most desert bighorn populations "are restricted to small areas during hot summer months due to suboptimal distribution of resources." While most populations remain in isolated areas, others move among mountain ranges, move in elevation, or move to/from water sources (McQuivey 1978 as cited in Krausman and Bowyer 2003). Does not appear that desert bighorn individuals move down-slope in winter (Gerhart, personal communication; Heffelfinger, personal communication). Flesch and others (2010) studied desert bighorn sheep in the Cabeza Prieta Mountains and Pinta Mountains on Cabeza Prieta NWR. They did not observe movements between the two mountain ranges (separated by an 11-km wide valley), but within mountain ranges,	1

USDA Forest Service RMRS-GTR-273. 2012.

Habitat: Desert bighorn sheep (*Ovis canadensis mexicana*)

Trait/Quality	Question	Background info. & explanation of score	Points
		average distance moved was 1.6 km, and more movements were documented in late summer and fall than in winter. Overall, seasonal movements appear to be undertaken by at least some individuals.	

Physiology: Desert bighorn sheep (*Ovis canadensis mexicana*)

Trait/Quality	Question	Background info. & explanation of score	Points
1. Physiological thresholds	Are limiting physiological conditions expected to change?	Desert bighorn sheep can tolerate extremes in air temperature from 20 °F to 120 °F (Wilson and others 1980). Bighorns are diurnal but may be active on moonlit nights (Shackleton 1985). Desert bighorn sheep use both vegetation and caves as sources of thermal cover during the hottest parts of the day (Cain and others 2008). To dissipate heat, sheep pant and sweat (references in Simmons 1969). At Cabeza Prieta NWR (elevational range 740-3300 ft), on hot days in summer, where bighorn sheep were observed to bed up to 7 hours per day; "much of the feeding was done at night (Simmons 1969)." See Habitat, Questions 3 and 5 for discussion of drinking water. We assumed temperatures will remain below physiological thresholds for the most part, but see Physiology, Question 4 regarding activity periods.	0
2. Sex ratio	Is sex ratio determined by temperature?	No. Temperature-dependent sex determination is mainly observed in reptiles and fish (Manolakou and others 2006).	0
3. Exposure to extreme weather conditions	Are extreme weather or disturbance events that result in direct mortality or reproductive failure expected to change?	Increase in frequency of heat waves is predicted for southwestern United States. Overall, not clear to what extent timing and intensity of heat waves will affect survival and reproduction. We considered it unlikely that heat waves would cause widespread mortality. See Physiology, Question 4 for discussion of activity periods.	0
4. Limitations to active period	Are projected temperature or precipitation regimes that influence activity period of species expected to change?	Bighorns are diurnal but may be active on moonlit nights (Shackleton 1985). Daily patterns are comprised of alternating feeding bouts and rest-rumination bouts. Feeding bouts usually occur near dawn or dusk. Total daily feeding time remained relatively constant throughout the year, except when daylight decreased in winter, although the mean number of feeding bouts may change from one season to the next (Eccles 1981 as cited in Krausman and Bowyer 2003). Activity of desert bighorn is affected by temperature (Chilelli and Krausman 1981 as cited in Krausman and Bowyer 2003). In Arizona (Cabeza Prieta NWR), when wet-bulb temperatures were >19 °C, sheep bedded in the shade on average 7 hours each day (Simmons 1969; wet bulb temperatures are lower than dry-bulb temperatures when air is not 100% saturated). Average dry-bulb temperature when sheep bedded was 32 °C (90 °F; Simmons 1969). Heat stress in summer is an important issue; bedding during the hottest parts of the day and feeding and watering on shaded slopes helps to minimize negative affects (Krausman and Bowyer 2003). During spring and summer, desert bighorn rested 60% of the day in Arizona (Alderman and others 1989). The hourly amount of time that females spent foraging was negatively correlated with mean temperature in all seasons. Sheep were active 39% of the night during summer, fall, and winter, and 26% of the night during spring.	1

Physiology: Desert bighorn sheep (*Ovis canadensis mexicana*)

Trait/Quality	Question	Background info. & explanation of score	Points
		Nocturnal activity was not influenced by temperature; the same degree of activity occurred in winter. Although this sub-species occurs in arid regions, it is identified as being sensitive to temperature. We considered it possible that increases in temperature would result in reduced activity.	
5. Metabolic inhibition	Does this species possess an ability to reduce metabolic energy or water requirements?	No information to suggest use of torpor.	1
6. Survival during resource limitation	Does this species have lower energy requirements or possess the capacity to store energy or water in the long term?	Active year-round.	1
7. Variable life history	Does this species have alternative life history strategies to cope with variable resources or climate conditions?	No alternative strategies.	0
8. Reproduction in variable environments	Can this species outlive periods where reproduction is limited?	Although mortality for the first year of life can be as high as 90% (references in Krausman and Bowyer 2003), male *O. c. canadensis* frequently lives 15 or 16 years (Geist 1971 as cited in Shackleton 1985). Appears that females have a higher mortality rate than males, although this may be in part due to problems with properly aging females older than 5 years (references in Shackleton 1985). Bender and Weisenberger (2005) found that population size and trend for populations in New Mexico were best described by a model that included only precipitation as a covariate, and that the ratio of lambs females was positively related to the current year's precipitation total (period from late gestation through weaning), most likely because precipitation influenced forage quality and quantity. Periods of extreme reductions in rainfall may last 5 years. If these conditions reduce resources to the point that bighorn sheep have insufficient resources for breeding, but conditions recover after, likely that sufficient numbers of individuals would survive long enough to breed once conditions improve.	–1

Phenology: Desert bighorn sheep (*Ovis canadensis mexicana*)

Trait/Quality	Question	Background info. & explanation of score	Points
1. Cues	Does this species use temperature or moisture cues to initiate activities related to fecundity or survival?	Cues for mating and parturition not clearly related to temperature or moisture. Considering the range of bighorn sheep, differences in mating period characteristics (onset, extent of synchrony, and mating period duration) and timing of lambing are related to local environmental conditions, which appear to be related to the timing of plant growth; for example, the lambing period begins earlier and ends later in southern populations (references in Thompson and Turner 1982; Shackleton 1985). The mating season (rut) begins with males joining	0

Phenology: Desert bighorn sheep (*Ovis canadensis mexicana*)			
Trait/Quality	**Question**	**Background info. & explanation of score**	**Points**
		maternal groups; courtship begins when an estrous female is detected by a male using olfaction (Shackleton 1985).	
		Bighorn sheep have an extended mating period (references in Krausman and Bowyer 2003); births are documented in the Sonoran Desert in all months except October. Poor correlation between start and length of growing season and lambing period thought to be due to unpredictable precipitation patterns. This may be an adaptive strategy to varying and unpredictable forage production.	
2. Event timing	Are activities related to species' fecundity or survival tied to discrete events that are expected to change?	Bighorn sheep have an extended mating period (references in Krausman and Bowyer 2003); births are documented in the Sonoran Desert in all months except October. Poor correlation between start and length of growing season and lambing period thought to be due to unpredictable precipitation patterns. This may be an adaptive strategy to varying and unpredictable forage production.	-1
3. Mismatch potential	What is the separation in time or space between cues that initiate activities and discrete events that provide critical resources?	See Phenology, Question 1.	0
4. Resilience to timing mismatches during breeding	Does this species employ strategies or have traits that increase the likelihood of reproduction co-occurring with important events?	Females generally do not breed until they are 2.5 years old (Hoffmeister 1986). Only one breeding event per year; breeding occurs between July and September (peak in August) and young are born usually in February in Arizona (Russo 1956 as cited in Hoffmeister 1986).	1

Biotic interactions: Desert bighorn sheep (*Ovis canadensis mexicana*)			
Trait/Quality	**Question**	**Background info. & explanation of score**	**Points**
1. Food resources	Are important food resources for this species expected to change?	Bighorn sheep are considered relatively opportunistic in their diet with relative proportions of browse, forbs, and grass varying by sub-species, population, sex, and age (references in Krausman and Bowyer 2003). Desert bighorn tend to consume more browse than grasses and forbs. Preferred foods are fruits and leaves of mesquite, ironwood, palo verde, catclaw, coffeeberry, bush muhly, jojoba, brittlebrush, and calliandra; also feed on dry leaves of three-awn, fillaree, galleta, and fluff grass, as well as scrape the ground to access roots (Hoffmeister 1986). Near Yuma at the Kofa NWR (Sonoran zone), plants that are considered important include Mormon tea, grama, agave, ratany, desert mallow, prickly pear, bursage, desertthorn, and plantain (Halloran and Crandall 1953). Diet breadth can vary from one day to the next; numerous species of plants may be consumed in one day, but the next day, only one or a few species may be consumed (Hoffmeister 1986).	0
		Sheep in Chihuahua, Mexico, "like all other sheep of the southern deserts including Texas and Arizona" ate little grass but ate a large variety of desert vegetation, including cactus and its fruit (Sheldon 1925 as cited in Halloran and Crandall 1953). In Texas, sheep were "especially fond of the browse of mountain mahogany, syringa,	

Biotic interactions: Desert bighorn sheep (*Ovis canadensis mexicana*)			
Trait/Quality	**Question**	**Background info. & explanation of score**	**Points**
		Ceanothus, and other common shrubs and feed to a great extent on the smaller plants" and may feed to a small extent on grasses (Bailey 1928 as cited in Halloran and Crandall 1953). Hoffmeister (1986) indicated that "water is considered as important as food;" some of the plants that consume provide water (e.g., saguaro, cholla, prickly pear, other cacti, and agave). Saguaro fruits are especially sought for food (Hoffmeister 1986). Overall, a variety of forage species are consumed.	
2. Predators	Are important predator populations expected to change?	Young sheep may be preyed upon by eagles, coyotes, and bobcats (Hoffmeister 1986). Coyote predation is mostly on young sheep; cougars are also documented predators (references in Shackleton 1985). Mountain lion predation was documented for desert bighorn sheep (mostly adults) in the Sierra Ladron Mountains in New Mexico (Rominger 2004) following the introduction of bighorn sheep to this area, which was not known to support them historically. Overall, bighorn sheep have a suite of predators.	0
3. Symbionts	Are populations of symbiotic species expected to change?	No information found to suggest existence of important symbionts.	0
4. Disease	Is prevalence of diseases known to cause widespread mortality or reproductive failure in this species expected to change?	Disease can be a significant cause of mortality for bighorn sheep with sudden mortality of notable numbers of individuals reported as common (see references in Krausman and Bowyer 2003). Hoffmeister (1986) indicated that they "readily and frequently have bacterial infections, some of which are lethal. They also have tapeworms and lung infections." Bighorns are susceptible to bluetongue (caused by bluetongue virus), contagious ecthyma, parainfluenza, encephalitis, and various bacterial infections (Shackleton 1985). A significant source of mortality can result from chronic sinusitis in this sub-species (Bunch 1980 as cited in Shackleton 1985). Introduced mites of domestic sheep cause scabies in bighorn sheep, which can result in significant mortality (references in Shackleton 1985). Lungworm-pneumonia complex can result in association with infections by lungworms (*Protostrongylus stilesi* and *P. rushi*; Buechner 1960). Hemorrhagic septicemia, which can lead to pneumonia, was attributed to a large die-off in Colorado in the 1920s (the majority of a herd of 350 sheep); this condition is caused by a bacterium *Pasteurella oviseptica* (Buechner 1960). However, there was some debate as to whether this was the actual cause of mortality. The virus causing epizootic hemorrhagic disease was found in tissues of a desert bighorn sheep in Arizona that also possessed lesions typical of the disease (Noon and others 2002) and was thought to be the first record of this disease in Arizona bighorn. Not clear that above diseases will increase in prevalence as a result of projected changes in climate.	0
5. Competitors	Are populations of important competing species expected to change?	Overgrazing by cattle and desert bighorn is said to limit the density of sheep through competition for space and forage (Krausman and Bowyer 2003). Competition from domestic sheep and goats historically has been the most serious type of competition for desert bighorn. Diet and habitat overlap with other ungulates (Shackleton 1985). Deer often use the same habitat; cattle are said to have same diet but do not overlap in steep terrain (references in Shackleton 1985). Domestic sheep and Barbary sheep (native to Africa) are considered the biggest competitive threats to bighorn sheep across	0

Biotic interactions: Desert bighorn sheep (*Ovis canadensis mexicana*)			
Trait/Quality	Question	Background info. & explanation of score	Points
		their range. Feral burros consume browse species of plants in many areas, which suggests forage competition with bighorns where the two species co-occur (see references in Krausman and Bowyer 2003). Not expected that above competitors will increase as a result of projected changes in climate.	

Literature Cited

Alderman, J.A., P.R. Krausman, and B. D. Leopold. 1989. Diel activity of female desert bighorn sheep in western Arizona. Journal of Wildlife Management 53:264-271.

Bangs, P.D., P.R. Krausman, K.E. Kunkel, and Z.D. Parsons. 2005a. Habitat use by desert bighorn sheep during lambing. European Journal of Wildlife Research 51:178-184.

Bangs, P.D., P.R. Krausman, K.E. Kunkel, and Z.D. Parsons. 2005b. Habitat use by female desert bighorn sheep in the Fra Cristobal Mountains, New Mexico, USA. European Journal of Wildlife Research 51:77-83.

Bender, L.C., and M.E. Weisenberger. 2005. Precipitation, density, and population dynamics of desert bighorn sheep on San Andres National Wildlife Refuge, New Mexico. Wildlife Society Bulletin 33:956-964.

Bradley, W.G. 1963. Water metabolism in desert mammals. Transactions of the Desert Bighorn Council 7:26-39. Available: http://www.desertbighorncouncil.org/transactions_old.html.

Brochu, Ben. 2011. [Personal communication]. May 25, 2011. Tucson, AZ: Arizona Game and Fish Department, Wildlife Manager.

Broyles, B., and T.L. Cutler. 1999. Effect of surface water on desert bighorn sheep in the Cabeza Prieta National Wildlife Refuge, southwestern Arizona. Wildlife Society Bulletin 27:1082-1088.

Buechner, H.K. 1960. The bighorn sheep in the United States, its past, present, and future. Wildlife Monographs 4:1-174.

Cain, J.W., III, H.E. Johnson, and P.R. Krausman. 2005. Wildfire and desert bighorn Sheep habitat, Santa Catalina Mountains, Arizona. Southwestern Naturalist 50:506-513.

Cain, J.W., III, P.R. Krausman, J.R. Morgart, B.D. Jansen, and M.P. Pepper. 2008. Responses of desert bighorn sheep to removal of water sources. Wildlife Monographs 171:1-30.

Flesch, A.D., C.W. Epps, J.W. Cain, III, M. Clark, P.D. Krausman, and J.R. Morgart. 2010. Potential effects of the United States-Mexico border fence on wildlife. Conservation Biology 24:171-181.

Halloran, A.F., and H.B. Crandell. 1953. Notes on bighorn food in the Sonoran Zone. Journal of Wildlife Management 17:318-320.

Heffelfinger, Jim. 2010. [Personal communication]. May 20, 2010. Tucson, AZ: Arizona Game and Fish Department, Game Specialist.

Hoffmeister, D.F. 1986. Mammals of Arizona. University of Arizona Press and Arizona Game and Fish Department. 602 p.

Krausman, P.R., and R.T. Bowyer. 2003. Mountain sheep. In: Feldhamer, G.C., B.C. Thompson, and J.A. Chapman, eds. Wild mammals of North America: Biology, management, and conservation. Baltimore, MD: Johns Hopkins University Press: 1095-1115.

Manolakou, P., G. Lavranos, and R. Angelopoulou. 2006. Molecular patterns of sex determination in the animal kingdom: A comparative study of the biology of reproduction. Reproductive Biology and Endocrinology 4:59.

Noon, T.H., S.L. Wesche, D. Cagle, D.G. Mead, E.J. Bicknell, G.A. Bradley, S. Riplog-Peterson, D. Edsall, and C. Reggiardo. Hemorrhagic disease in bighorn sheep in Arizona. Journal of Wildlife Diseases 38:172-176.

Rominger, E.M., H.A. Whitlaw, D.L. Weybright, W.C. Dunn, and W.B. Ballard. 2004. The influence of mountain lion predation on bighorn sheep translocations. Journal of Wildlife Management 68:993-999.

Shackleton, D.M. 1985. *Ovis canadensis*. American Society of Mammalogists. Mammalian Species No. 230:1-9.

Simmons, N.M. 1969. Heat stress and bighorn behavior in the Cabeza Prieta Game Range, Arizona. Transactions of the Desert Bighorn Council 13:55-63. Available: http://www.desertbighorncouncil.org/transactions_old html.

Thompson, R.W., and J.C. Turner. 1982. Temporal geographic variation in the lambing season of bighorn sheep. Canadian Journal of Zoology 60:1781-1793.

U.S. Forest Service [USFS]. 2009. Draft Coronado National Forest ecological sustainability report. Tucson, AZ: U.S. Department of Agriculture, Forest Service. Available: http://www fs fed.us/r3/coronado/plan-evision/documents/final/cnf-ecological-sustainability-report-final-022009.pdf.

Wilson, L.O., J. Blaisdell, G. Welsh, [and others]. 1980. Desert Bighorn habitat requirements and management recommendations. Transactions of the Desert Bighorn Council 24:1-7. Available: http://www.desertbighorncouncil.org/transactions_old html.

Habitat: Sonoran desert tortoise (*Gopherus agassizii*, Sonoran population)			
Trait/Quality	Question	Background info. & explanation of score	Points
1. Area and distribution: *breeding*	Is the area or location of the associated vegetation type used for breeding activities by this species expected to change?	*Gopherus agassizii* occurs in southern Utah, southern Nevada, western Arizona, and southeastern California, most of Sonora to northwestern Sinaloa, Mexico (Auggenberg and Franz 1978). Two geographic assemblages of tortoise have been identified among desert tortoises in the United States by genetic analyses; the "Mohave assemblage" generally coincides with the range of the Mohave Desert (north and west of the Colorado River) and the "Sonoran assemblage" (south and east of the Colorado River; Lamb and McLuckie 2002). Recently, a study provided evidence to support recognition of desert tortoise populations south and east of the Colorado River (i.e., the Sonoran population) as a distinct species, *Gopherus morafkai* (Murphy and others 2011). We have retained the use of *G. agassizii* for this report.

In Arizona, the range of the Sonoran desert tortoise occurs in Sonoran desert scrub (Van Devender 2002a). In the Sonoran Desert, tortoises typically occur on rocky slopes and bajadas and deeply incised washes emanating from rocky bajadas, are absent from intermountain valley floors (Riedle and others 2008). Averill-Murray and Averill-Murray (2005) found this species in intermountain valleys in low densities in Ironwood Forest National Monument in Arizona. This species has been reported in ecotonal areas comprised of Sonoran desert scrub with "elements" of Mohave desert scrub, juniper woodland, interior chaparral, and desert grassland (Averill-Murray and others 2002b).

This species occurs, or potential habitat exists for this species, on the following EMAs: Tumacacori, Galiuro, and Santa Catalina (USFS 2009). Projections of suitable climate for vegetation communities (Chapter 1) predicted declines in suitable climate for Madrean forest and woodland, Madrean conifer forest, with increases of suitable climate for semi-desert grassland and small increases on Chiricahua EMA for Sonoran desert scrub.

Overall, expect that projected changes in Sonoran desert scrub would not result in significant reductions in desert scrub for this species, and possibly would increase it. | 0 |

Habitat: Sonoran desert tortoise (*Gopherus agassizii*, Sonoran population)			
Trait/Quality	Question	Background info. & explanation of score	Points
2. Area and distribution: *non-breeding*	Is the area or location of the associated vegetation type used for non-breeding activities by this species expected to change?	Same as breeding habitat; see Habitat, Question 1.	0
3. Habitat components: *breeding*	Are specific habitat components required for breeding expected to change?	Requires burrows, which may be formed by erosion, desert tortoises, or other animals (Averill-Murray and others 2002a). Tortoise nests are typically inside burrows (female buries eggs; Averill-Murray and others 2002b). In the Mohave Desert of southwestern Nevada, desert tortoises spend up to 95% of their life within a shelter (Nagy and Medica 1986 as cited in Riedle and others 2008). Uses burrows for nesting, courtship, escape from temperature extremes, to avoid predators (references in Riedle and others 2008). Desert tortoises show high fidelity to burrows, including returning to same hibernacula or nest sites in successive years (references in Riedle and others 2008). They use multiple shelters during the year (Averill-Murray and others 2002a) and in a fenced population have been observed to use multiple burrows per day (Nagy and Medica 1986). In the Sonoran Desert, use a variety of substrates for shelter, generally under rocks, but also they use woodrat middens, burrows dug by other animals, or caliche caves (references in Riedle and others 2008). In south-central Arizona (Florence Military Reservation), utilized caliche caves as shelter more than other types of shelter (Riedle and others 2008). Shelter availability in the Sonoran Desert depends on the "complexity and geological structure of the terrain (Averill-Murray and others 2002a)." Availability of burrows not expected to change as a result of climate change.	0
4. Habitat components: *non-breeding*	Are specific habitat components required for survival during non-breeding periods expected to change?	Requires burrows for over-wintering; see Habitat, Question 3.	0
5. Habitat quality and reproduction	Are features of the habitat associated with better reproductive success expected to change?	Found no information on variation in reproductive success as related to habitat features for the Sonoran desert tortoise. It appears that there is little or none for desert tortoise in general.	0
6. Habitat quality and survival	Are features of the habitat associated with better survival expected to change?	In the Sonoran Desert, density and abundance of desert tortoise varies widely; differences in the density of shelter sites may partly explain these differences (Averill-Murray and others 2002b). Availability of burrows not expected to change as a result of climate change.	0
7. Ability to colonize new areas	What is this species' capacity and tendency to disperse?	Desert tortoises show high fidelity to burrows, including returning to same hibernacula or nest sites in successive years (references in Riedle and others 2008). Mean home range estimates in the Sonoran Desert averaged over several studies ranged from 9.2-25.8 ha for females and 2.6-23.3 ha for males (Averill-Murray and others 2002a). Dispersal by Sonoran desert tortoises away from rocky ridge habitats is rare, although there are instances of individuals of both sexes moving up to 3 km away from their activity centers over a period of a	1

Habitat: Sonoran desert tortoise (*Gopherus agassizii*, Sonoran population)			
Trait/Quality	**Question**	**Background info. & explanation of score**	**Points**
		few weeks (Averill-Murray and others 2002b). In some locations, individuals may occur at low density in valleys between mountain ranges and such valleys may be important to maintaining population viability (Averill-Murray and Averill-Murray 2005).	
8. Migratory or transitional habitats	Does this species require additional habitats during migration that are separated from breeding and non-breeding habitats?	No information to indicate that additional habitats are required.	0

Physiology: Sonoran desert tortoise (*Gopherus agassizii*, Sonoran population)			
Trait/Quality	**Question**	**Background info. & explanation of score**	**Points**
1. Physiological thresholds	Are limiting physiological conditions expected to change?	Desert tortoises cannot tolerate body temperatures above 39.5-43.0 °C (Brattstrom 1965 as cited in Averill-Murray and others 2002a). Four desert tortoise populations in Arizona were active at temperatures between 20 °C and 45 °C (Woodman and others 1996 as cited in Averill-Murray and others 2002a). Desert tortoises are reported to use burrows as shelter from temperature extremes (references in Riedle and others 2008). Tortoises drink standing water from puddles produced by thunderstorms and have been observed eating damp soil and obtaining water from the ground surface through their nose (Averill-Murray and others 2002a). Sufficient hydration allows tortoises to acquire energy from plants. Also, drinking water allows them to flush excess salts and rehydrate their bladders (see Biotic Interactions, Question 1 for more information on ion balance). Thus, water is particularly important for desert tortoise (Peterson 1996). Expect that this species would seek out burrows to avoid exceeding temperature thresholds as they do currently, but reductions in precipitation have the potential to reduce periods with rainfall which could alter the ability of desert tortoises to find drinking water. Thus, score of "1" was assigned.	1
2. Sex ratio	Is sex ratio determined by temperature?	Temperature-dependent sex determination has been reported for this family (Testudinidae; Vitt and Caldwell 2009). In the northeastern Mojave Desert, nest temperatures exceeding 32 °C produced females, whereas lower temperatures produced males (Spotila and others 1994 as cited in Averill-Murray and others 2002a); the authors indicated that it is likely that this threshold temperature varies across the range of desert tortoise. Baxter and others (2008) found some support that temperature during the early to middle part of incubation (day 15-45 of a ~90-day incubation period) may play a role in sex determination in the Mojave Desert populations of desert tortoise.	1
3. Exposure to extreme weather conditions	Are extreme weather or disturbance events that result in direct mortality or reproductive failure expected to change?	Desert tortoises are reported to use burrows as shelter from temperature extremes (references in Riedle and others 2008). We assumed that desert tortoises could survive short periods of high temperature by utilizing burrows.	0

Physiology: Sonoran desert tortoise (*Gopherus agassizii*, Sonoran population)			
Trait/Quality	**Question**	**Background info. & explanation of score**	**Points**
4. Limitations to active period	Are projected temperature or precipitation regimes that influence activity period of species expected to change?	There is a bimodal activity pattern. Active in late March or April after leaving winter hibernacula (though appear to be less active during this period than in summer). Activity declines in the dry season ("foresummer") in May and June, and then activity increases again following start of monsoon in late July and August (Averill-Murray and others 2002a). Spring activity may be important for acquiring energy resources for egg-laying which occurs near the onset of the rainy season. Also, desert tortoises are generally inactive during midday during the hottest times of year (references in Averill-Murray and others 2002a).

An increase in temperature and changes in precipitation have the potential to alter seasonal activity periods given that currently active periods coincide with periods of food abundance and in summer, water availability. | 1 |
| 5. Metabolic inhibition | Does this species possess an ability to reduce metabolic energy or water requirements? | Cycles of dormancy are common in amphibians and reptiles, and hibernation is most likely primarily a response to cold temperatures and less so to a change in resource availability (Vitt and Caldwell 2009). While hibernating, activity mostly ceases, body temperature depends on temperature of the hibernation site, and physiological processes are reduced. Such inactivity is called brumation in ectotherms, not hibernation.

Desert tortoises hibernate during the cool months of the year (November-February; Averill-Murray and others 2002a). Accumulates fat during summer for winter hibernation (Van Devender 2002a). Hibernating tortoises in a semi-natural setting (fenced population) did not lose significant levels of body mass or body water over winter (Nagy and Medica 1986). Desert tortoises also estivate (Nagy and Medica 1986).

We assumed that wintering sites would be largely buffered from increased temperatures. | 0 |
| 6. Survival during resource limitation | Does this species have lower energy requirements or possess the capacity to store energy or water in the long term? | Ectotherm. | -1 |
| 7. Variable life history | Does this species have alternative life history strategies to cope with variable resources or climate conditions? | No alternative strategies. | 0 |
| 8. Reproduction in variable environments | Can this species outlive periods where reproduction is limited? | Desert tortoises are long-lived species. In natural populations, Sonoran populations thought to reach sexual maturity at about 16 years of age (Germano and others 2002). Sonoran desert tortoises have been observed to live as long as 35 years (Germano 1992 as cited in Averill-Murray and others 2002b). Survivorship of desert tortoises tends to be high (Averill-Murray and others 2002b).

Periods of extreme reductions in rainfall may last 5 years. If these conditions reduce resources to the point that this species has insufficient resources for breeding, but conditions recover after, we considered it likely that sufficient numbers of individuals would survive long enough to breed once conditions improve. | -1 |

Phenology: Sonoran desert tortoise (*Gopherus agassizii*, Sonoran population)			
Trait/Quality	**Question**	**Background info. & explanation of score**	**Points**
1. Cues	Does this species use temperature or moisture cues to initiate activities related to fecundity or survival?	Temperature is an important cue in reptiles (Licht 1972). Tortoises emerge from burrows in spring, but the emergence can be protracted, and females appear to emerge earlier than males (Averill-Murray and others 2002a). Also, "temperature probably plays a more important role than day length in the onset of hibernation at a particular location." Rainfall appears to be a cue for emerging from burrows and feeding in summer. In a fenced population of desert tortoise in southern Nevada, 10 of 11 tortoises emerged from estivating in their burrows before or during a thunderstorm in mid-July, and some constructed shallow basins in which rainwater pooled, after which they fed on dry vegetation (Nagy and Medica 1986). Increased activity, drinking and feeding following summer rain was also observed in California (Minnich 1977 as cited in Nagy and Medica 1986). There is a lag of about 10 days between the start of summer rains and when "perennials have substantial new growth or summer annuals germinate and accumulate much biomass (Averill-Murray and others 2002a)."	1
2. Event timing	Are activities related to species' fecundity or survival tied to discrete events that are expected to change?	In the Sonoran desert tortoise, egg-laying typically occurs between early June and early August near the start of the rainy season, although mean egg-laying date "does not appear to be directly related to recent rainfall (Averill-Murray and others 2002b)."	1
3. Mismatch potential	What is the separation in time or space between cues that initiate activities and discrete events that provide critical resources?	The number of Sonoran desert tortoise females breeding in a given year and clutch size shows a relationship to recent rainfall (Averill-Murray and Klug 2000 as cited in Averill-Murray and others 2002b). Also shown to relate to rainfall from prior winter, presumably via food (i.e., spring annual plant production; Averill-Murray 2002).	-1
4. Resilience to timing mismatches during breeding	Does this species employ strategies or have traits that increase the likelihood of reproduction co-occurring with important events?	Sonoran desert tortoises lay a maximum of one clutch per year, although females may not reproduce in every year (references in Averill-Murray and others 2002b).	1

Biotic interactions: Sonoran desert tortoise (*Gopherus agassizii*, Sonoran population)			
Trait/Quality	**Question**	**Background info. & explanation of score**	**Points**
1. Food resources	Are important food resources for this species expected to change?	Desert tortoises are considered opportunistic herbivores, eating many different types of plants (Van Devender and others 2002b). This includes plant material from trees and shrubs, sub-shrubs and woody vines, spring annual grasses, succulents, herbaceous perennials, and dicot annuals. For relationship to consuming water, see Physiology, Question 1. Potassium intake in food may currently be a problem for desert tortoises, and increasing levels may cause tortoises to reduce feeding, or possibly stop feeding, with increasing aridity (Nagy and Medica 1986). Desert tortoise lack functional extrarenal salt glands, unlike	0

Biotic interactions: Sonoran desert tortoise (*Gopherus agassizii*, Sonoran population)

Trait/Quality	Question	Background info. & explanation of score	Points
		other desert reptiles, like chuckwallas and desert iguanas, which have nasal salt glands through which they can excrete excess potassium. Thus, tortoises have to excrete potassium through urine, which uses body water.	
2. Predators	Are important predator populations expected to change?	Mortalities have been attributed to mountain lions, which are considered to be one of the few natural predators with the ability to break the shell of an adult tortoise (references in Averill-Murray and others 2002b). Other carnivores, such as coyotes, bobcats, foxes, badgers, and common ravens, may prey on hatchlings, juveniles, or eggs. Golden eagles and other raptors, and greater roadrunner may also be predators. Gila monsters are documented predators. Overall, this species has a variety of predators.	0
3. Symbionts	Are populations of symbiotic species expected to change?	No information found regarding important symbiotic relationships.	0
4. Disease	Is prevalence of diseases known to cause widespread mortality or reproductive failure in this species expected to change?	Upper Respiratory Tract Disease in desert tortoises is caused by *Mycoplasma agassizii* (Dickinson and others 2002) and also has been associated with *Pasteurella testudinis*, an irodovirus (Sandmeier and others 2009). Physical signs include discharge from the eyes and nose, conjunctivitis, and eyelid swelling (Jacobsen and others 1991 as cited in Dickinson and others 2002). Arizona Fish and Game conducted health studies of Mojave and Sonoran populations of tortoise. The 5-year study in Arizona took place in the Arizona Upland habitats (study plots near Bagdad and Aguila) beginning in 1990. Sonoran populations had a low incidence of obvious *Mycoplasma agassizii* infection compared to Mohave tortoises (Dickinson and others 2002). Not clear that this disease causes consistent levels of mortality across the Mojave (Dickinson and others 2002). Shell disease (cutaneous dyskeratosis) was associated with a mortality rate of 70% in a population of Mohave tortoises (1982-1988). Dickinson and others (2002) indicated that this disease may not be a serious problem for Sonoran populations, but more studied is recommended for it and Mojave populations. Dickinson and others (2002) indicated that disease does not appear to be a major limiting favor of Sonoran desert tortoise. No clear indication that climate change would increase propensity for mortality from disease.	0
5. Competitors	Are populations of important competing species expected to change?	No information found on competitors.	0

Literature Cited

Auffenberg, W., and R. Franz. 1978. *Gopherus agassizii*. No. 212. Catalogue of American Amphibians and Reptiles. Society for the Study of Amphibians and Reptiles.

Averill-Murray, R.C. 2002. Reproduction of *Gopherus agassizii* in the Sonoran Desert, Arizona. Chelonian Conservation and Biology 4:295-301.

Averill-Murray, R.C., and A. Averill-Murray. 2005. Regional-scale estimation of density and habitat use of the desert tortoise (*Gopherus agassizii*) in Arizona. Journal of Herpetology 39:65-72.

Averill-Murray, R.C., B.E. Martin, S.J. Bailey, and E.B. Wirt. 2002a. Activity and behavior of the Sonoran Desert tortoise in Arizona. In: Van Devender, T.R., ed. The Sonoran Desert Tortoise: Natural history, biology, and conservation. Tucson: The University of Arizona Press: 135-158.

Averill-Murray, R.C., A.P. Woodman, and J.M. Howland. 2002b. Population ecology of the Sonoran Desert tortoise in Arizona. In: Van Devender, T.R., ed. The Sonoran Desert Tortoise: Natural history, biology, and conservation. Tucson: The University of Arizona Press: 109-134.

Baxter, P.C., D.S. Wilson, and D.J. Morafka. 2008. The effects of nest date and placement of eggs in burrows on sex ratios and potential survival of hatchling desert tortoises, *Gopherus agassizii*. Chelonian Conservation and Biology 7:52-59.

Dickinson, V.M., J.L. Jarchow, M.H. Trueblood, and J.C. deVos. 2002. Are free-ranging Sonoran Desert tortoises healthy? In: Van Devender, T.R., ed. The Sonoran Desert tortoise: natural history, biology, and conservation. Tucson: The University of Arizona Press: 242-263.

Germano, D.J., F.H. Pough, D.J. Morafka, E.M. Smith, and M.J. Demlong. 2002. Growth of desert tortoises: Implications for conservation and management. In: Van Devender, T.R., ed. The Sonoran Desert tortoise: Natural history, biology, and conservation. Tucson: The University of Arizona Press: 263-288.

Lamb, T., and A.M. McLuckie. 2002. Genetic differences among geographic races of the desert tortoise. In: Van Devender, T.R., ed. The Sonoran Desert tortoise: Natural history, biology, and conservation. Tucson: The University of Arizona Press: 67-85.

Licht, P. 1972. Environmental physiology of reptilian breeding cycles: Role of temperature. General and Comparative Endocrinology Supplement 3:477-488.

Murphy, R.W, K.H. Berry, T. Edwards, A.E. Leviton, A. Lathrop, and J.D. Riedle. 2011. The dazed and confused identity of Agassiz's

land tortoise, *Gopherus agassizii* (Testudines, Testudinidae) with the description of a new species, and its consequences for conservation. ZooKeys 113: 39-71.

Nagy, K.A., and P.A. Medica. 1986. Physiological ecology of Desert tortoises in southern Nevada. Herpetologica 42:73-92.

Peterson, C.C. 1996. Ecological energetics of the desert tortoise (*Gopherus agassizii*): Effects of rainfall and drought. Ecology 77:1831-1844.

Riedle, J.D., R.C. Averill-Murray, C.L. Lutz, and D.K. Bolen. 2008. Habitat use by desert tortoises (*Gopherus agassizii*) on alluvial fans in the Sonoran Desert, south-central Arizona. Copeia 2008 2:414-420.

Sandmeier, F.C., C.R. Tracy, S. dePré, and K. Hunter. 2009. Upper respiratory tract disease (URTD) as a threat to desert tortoise populations: A reevaluation. Biological Conservation 142:1255-1268.

U.S. Forest Service [USFS]. 2009. Draft Coronado National Forest ecological sustainability report. Tucson, AZ: U.S. Department of Agriculture, Forest Service. Available: http://www fs fed.us/r3/coronado/plan-revision/documents/final/cnf-ecological-sustainability-report-final-022009.pdf.

Van Devender, T.R. 2002a. Natural history of the Sonoran Tortoise in Arizona. In: Van Devender, T.R., ed. The Sonoran Desert tortoise: Natural history, biology, and conservation. Tucson: The University of Arizona Press: 3-28.

Van Devender, T.R. 2002b. Grasses, mallows, desert vine, and more: Diet of the desert tortoise in Arizona and Sonora. In: Van Devender, T.R., ed. The Sonoran Desert tortoise: natural history, biology, and conservation. Tucson: The University of Arizona Press: 159-173.

Vitt, L.J., and J.P. Caldwell. 2009. Herpetology. Oxford, United Kingdom: Elsevier. 697 p.

Habitat: Slevin's bunchgrass lizard (*Sceloporus slevini*)			
Trait/Quality	**Question**	**Background info. & explanation of score**	**Points**
1. Area and distribution: *breeding*	Is the area or location of the associated vegetation type used for breeding activities by this species expected to change?	**Taxonomic note:** This species was formerly considered *Sceloporus scalaris slevini* (Watkins-Colwell and others 2003). From Painter (2009): This species occurs in montane habitats (including woodlands and forests dominated by pines), intermountain valleys, and riparian areas. In Arizona, elevation range is from 1300 m in the Sonoita Plains to ~2600 m in the Chiricahua Mountains (Barfoot Park). Range of this species in the United States is southeastern Arizona and southwestern New Mexico. It is common on east- and south-facing slopes where dense grasses occur. Reported in Santa Rita, Dragoon, Huachuca, and Chiricahua Mountains in Arizona. Bock and others (1990) indicated that this species was abundant in lowland semi-desert grassland (dominated by 5 species of grama grass) in an area that had been protected from livestock grazing for 20 years (Sonoita Plain, Santa Cruz County); authors indicated that "apparent restriction of *Sceloporus scalaris* to montane meadows may be an historic artifact associated with chronic and ubiquitous grazing of lower-elevation perennial grasslands." This species does not survive at lower elevations where cattle graze as a result of loss of bunchgrass cover (Watkins-Colwell and others 2003). This species occurs, or potential habitat exists, for this species, on the following EMAs: Peloncillo, Chiricahua, Dragoon, Santa Rita, Huachuca, and Whetstone (USFS 2009). Projections of suitable climate for vegetation communities (Chapter 1) predicted declines in suitable climate for Madrean forest and woodland, Madrean conifer forest, and Plains grassland, with increases of suitable climate for semi-desert grassland, and small increases on Chiricahua EMA for Sonoran desert scrub. Overall, areas with suitable climate for semi-desert grassland expected to increase, which is expected to increase total amount of habitat for this species.	-1
2. Area and distribution: *non-breeding*	Is the area or location of the associated vegetation type used for non-breeding activities by this species expected to change?	Same as breeding habitat; see Habitat, Question 1.	-1
3. Habitat components: *breeding*	Are specific habitat components required for breeding expected to change?	Clumps of thick grass have been called essential (Painter 2009; Watkins-Colwell and others 2003). In valley grasslands, grasses may include sacatons, grammas, panic grasses, and tobosa; in montane areas, bromes and muhlys are typical (Painter 2009). Grasses serve as cover from predators and sites for thermoregulation. Bock and others (1990) found this species in grazed areas lacking dense grass cover but where other debris occurred (boards and other surface litter) under which lizards were found; not clear what kind of surface litter was involved and whether this typically occurs in sufficient quantities in areas absent bunchgrass. Overall, semi-desert grassland likely to increase, which would involve increase in grass cover.	-1
4. Habitat components: *non-breeding*	Are specific habitat components required for survival during	See Habitat, Question 3; grass cover especially important in winter for thermoregulation in winter months (Painter 2009).	-1

Habitat: Slevin's bunchgrass lizard (*Sceloporus slevini*)

Trait/Quality	Question	Background info. & explanation of score	Points
	non-breeding periods expected to change?		
5. Habitat quality and reproduction	Are features of the habitat associated with better reproductive success expected to change?	No information.	0
6. Habitat quality and survival	Are features of the habitat associated with better survival expected to change?	In the Chiricahua Mountains, higher population densities were observed in areas with ~90% cover of grasses (*Blepharoneuron tricholepsis*, *Muhlenbergia virescens*, and *Bromus frondosus*; Ballinger and Congdon 1981). Ballinger and Congdon (1996) attributed loss of grasses from cattle grazing on the CNF in the Chiricahua Mountains to the severe declines of densities of this lizard species that in the 1970s had been 100-200 individuals per ha. Expect grass cover to increase.	-1
7. Ability to colonize new areas	What is this species' capacity and tendency to disperse?	Most amphibians and reptiles move relatively little across their lifetime except when breeding (Vitt and Caldwell 2009). No information found on this species. However, in another spiny lizard in Texas, *Sceloporus merriami*, home ranges averaged $100m^2$ in females and $150\text{-}250m^2$ in males.	1
8. Migratory or transitional habitats	Does this species require additional habitats during migration that are separated from breeding and non-breeding habitats?	No information found to indicate that additional habitats are required.	0

Physiology: Slevin's bunchgrass lizard (*Sceloporus slevini*)

Trait/Quality	Question	Background info. & explanation of score	Points
1. Physiological thresholds	Are limiting physiological conditions expected to change?	Members of this family (Phrynosomatidae) are diurnally active (Leaché 2009). This species remains active throughout the year (Painter 2009). Individuals actively thermoregulate and maintain body temperature well above that of the surrounding ambient temperature; body temperature in Arizona individuals (n=851) averaged 32.6 °C (Painter 2009). Critical thermal maximum, the temperature at which individuals lose their righting response, was measured in this species by Mathies and Andrews (1995); median values from individuals from high elevation populations and low-elevation populations were 44.8 °C and 44.6 °C, respectively. The genus *Sceloporus* maintains relatively high and stable body temperatures during activity, which is thought to be associated in part with open vegetation that allows for easy thermoregulation (Andrews 1998). Mean body temperatures of this genus in temperate latitudes were 35 °C (96 °F) throughout their elevational range (Andrews 1998). It's likely that lizards would seek refuge in burrows to escape temperature extremes (Huey and others 2010).	0
2. Sex ratio	Is sex ratio determined by temperature?	Vitt and Caldwell (2009) did not provide information on whether temperature-dependent sex determination occurs in Phrynosomatidae, suggesting that it may be unknown. In some members of Iguania (the	0

	Physiology: Slevin's bunchgrass lizard (*Sceloporus slevini*)		
Trait/Quality	Question	Background info. & explanation of score	Points
		infraorder of Squamata that contains this family as well as other groups), sex determination is known to be genetically based, while in others (e.g., Agamidae) temperature-dependent sex determination has been observed.	
3. Exposure to extreme weather conditions	Are extreme weather or disturbance events that result in direct mortality or reproductive failure expected to change?	Increase in frequency of heat waves is predicted for southwestern United States. We assumed that lizards could survive short periods of high temperature by utilizing burrows, even if foraging opportunities were reduced for several days.	0
4. Limitations to active period	Are projected temperature or precipitation regimes that influence activity period of species expected to change?	Members of this family (Phrynosomatidae) are diurnally active (Leaché 2009). This species remains active throughout the year (Painter 2009). Newlin (1974), working in the Chiricahua Mountains at ~2500 m elevation, found no significant differences in mean hourly capture rate or observation rate between 0900-1500, but observed reduced activity from 0800-0900 and 1500-1600 (observations for all months appear to be lumped; study conducted May-August, September, October and February). In summer, activity in summer ended ~2 hours earlier in the afternoon at cooler high-elevation sites (2664 m, 2852 m) than at warmer low-elevation sites (1463 m) (Mathies and Andrews 1995). Warmer temperatures may increase activity periods for populations at high elevations, but not likely to increase activity periods at low elevations. At low elevations, which are warmer overall, activity during summer has the potential to be reduced. Dunham (1993) predicted that a rise of 2 °C would severely reduce the number of hours per day *Sceloporus merriami* in Texas could be active given specific assumptions (i.e., if this species was active only at body temperatures of 32.2 °C); less restrictive assumptions resulted in less reduction in activity. The score of "1" for this question reflects possible effect on low-elevation populations.	1
5. Metabolic inhibition	Does this species possess an ability to reduce metabolic energy or water requirements?	Although cycles of dormancy are common in amphibians and reptiles, this species remains active throughout the year (Ballinger and Congdon 1981; Painter 2009). Able to maintain body temperature above ambient; mean body temperature of 23 lizards was 31 °C when ambient temperature was 12 °C (Ballinger and Congdon 1981). Newlin (1974) observed active in February when temperatures were 10-20 °C and snow existed in portions of the study area.	1
6. Survival during resource limitation	Does this species have lower energy requirements or possess the capacity to store energy or water in the long term?	Ectotherm.	–1
7. Variable life history	Does this species have alternative life history strategies to cope with variable resources or climate conditions?	Females of this species retain eggs in the body longer than other 2 *Sceloporus* species that occur at lower altitudes; this may be an adaptation to reduce the development time of embryos in cold climates (DeMarco 1992). Not clear whether increases in temperature would result in this species reducing the time to oviposition following fertilization, and if so, whether this would have an effect (positive or negative) on fitness.	0
8. Reproduction	Can this species outlive periods	Individuals become reproductively active in their first year after hatching in September (Ballinger and Congdon 1981). In a mark-	1

Physiology: Slevin's bunchgrass lizard (*Sceloporus slevini*)

Trait/Quality	Question	Background info. & explanation of score	Points
in variable environments	where reproduction is limited?	recapture 4-year study in the Chiricahua Mountains, lizards were observed at a minimum of 2, 3, or 4 years of age. Yearling mortality was estimated at 75%; although individuals as old as 5 years have been observed, only ~6% survived to 2 years of age or older.	
		In 1997, Smith and others (1998) observed dramatic reductions in numbers of this species on the Sonoita Plain where previously numbers had been high; they attributed the reduction in density to drought (low rainfall) in the preceding two years.	
		Periods of extreme reductions in rainfall may last 5 years. If these conditions eliminate breeding (e.g., insufficient food), most of the population would not survive longer than the periods of limited reproduction.	

Phenology: Slevin's bunchgrass lizard (*Sceloporus slevini*)

Trait/Quality	Question	Background info. & explanation of score	Points
1. Cues	Does this species use temperature or moisture cues to initiate activities related to fecundity or survival?	Temperature is an important cue in reptiles; it has been called the "most important and widespread of the timing cues for saurian reproduction (Licht 1972)."	1
		This species is oviparous (Watkins-Colwell, and others 2003), which makes it unlike many reptiles in cold environments that bear live young. Newlin (1974) observed that in 1973, egg laying began in late July, with all females having deposited eggs by mid-August. Egg laying in this species coincides with the onset of summer rains (Ballinger and Congdon 1981), although it is not clear whether this is a cue for laying. Newlin (1974) indicated that mating probably occurs between February and May.	
		The typical pattern for temperate-zone lizards is for low-elevation populations to initiate reproduction earlier in spring than at higher, cooler elevations. However, a different trend has been observed in this species. High-elevation females began ovulating 2-3 weeks earlier than low-elevation females and retained their eggs longer (~40 days at "high" versus ~20 days at "low;" Mathies and Andrews 1995).	
2. Event timing	Are activities related to species' fecundity or survival tied to discrete events that are expected to change?	See Phenology, Question 1.	1
		The length of the cold season is an important constraint on how long the reproductive season lasts in reptiles, and soil temperatures are high enough only in summer for embryonic development to occur rapidly enough (Vitt and Caldwell 2009). Increased temperatures may alter the length of the breeding season.	
		Clutch size did not appear to vary significantly with variations in rainfall (Ballinger and Congdon 1981).	
		Changes in the timing of precipitation and increases in temperature can alter the timing of prey availability and abundance.	
3. Mismatch potential	What is the separation in time or space between cues that initiate activities and discrete events that provide critical resources?	Cues and critical resources (e.g., food) expected to be closely related in time and space.	-1

Phenology: Slevin's bunchgrass lizard (*Sceloporus slevini*)

Trait/Quality	Question	Background info. & explanation of score	Points
4. Resilience to timing mismatches during breeding	Does this species employ strategies or have traits that increase the likelihood of reproduction co-occurring with important events?	In southeastern Arizona at higher elevation, mating occurs in April, oviposition in late June through early July, and hatching in September; these events probably occur earlier at lower elevations (Painter 2009). Only one clutch of eggs is produced per year per female (Newlin 1974; Ballinger and Congdon 1981; Painter 2009).	1

Biotic interactions: Slevin's bunchgrass lizard (*Sceloporus slevini*)

Trait/Quality	Question	Background info. & explanation of score	Points
1. Food resources	Are important food resources for this species expected to change?	In a study in the Chiricahua Mountains, the two most important groups of prey based on stomach analyses were Homoptera/Hemiptera (31% by volume), and Hymenoptera (17% by volume); Coleoptera were 10% and larvae were 10% (Newlin 1974). In Durango, Mexico, in a 2-year study, individuals of this species consumed adult beetles (40%), ants (35%), hemipterans (26%) grasshoppers (68%), and beetles (35%), with differences among years in terms of the type of prey most consumed (Degenhardt 1996). Overall, species consumes a variety of prey species.	0
2. Predators	Are important predator populations expected to change?	Specific information lacking on predators of this species. Newlin (1974) noted that Twin-spotted rattlesnakes (*Crotalus pricei*) might be predators. We assumed that this species has a variety of predators, such as birds (e.g., roadrunner) and mammals and other reptiles. In general, lizard predators include birds, mammals, snakes, other lizards, fish, spiders, centipedes, scorpions, and tailless whip scorpions (Pianka and Vitt 2003). Predation tends to be heaviest on lizard eggs and juveniles.	0
3. Symbionts	Are populations of symbiotic species expected to change?	No information found to indicate existence of important symbionts.	0
4. Disease	Is prevalence of diseases known to cause widespread mortality or reproductive failure in this species expected to change?	Little information. Helminths were reported in individuals collected in California; that only immature helminthes (no adults) were found suggested to the authors that this lizard species host a limited parasitic fauna (Goldbert and Bursey 1992).	0
5. Competitors	Are populations of important competing species expected to change?	Newlin (1974) indicated that Yarrow's spiny lizard (*Sceloporus jarrovi*) occurs sympatrically and is considered to a potential competitor, but the author considered it likely that the two species are separated ecologically due to different habitat preferences. Pygmy short-horned lizard (*Phrynosoma douglasi*) was also considered a potential competitor, but not readily observed in Newlin's study. Not clear that strong competition exists between this species and those mentioned above.	0

Literature Cited

Andrews, R.M. 1998. Geographic variation in field body temperature of *Sceloporus* lizards. Journal of Thermal Biology 23:329-334.

Ballinger, R.E., and J.D. Congdon. 1996. Status of the bunch grass lizard, *Sceloporus scalaris*, in the Chiricahua Mountains of southeastern Arizona. Bulletin of the Maryland Herpetological Society 32:67-69.

Ballinger, R.E., and J.D. Congdon. 1981. Population ecology and life history strategy of a montane lizard (*Sceloporus scalaris*) in southeastern Arizona. Journal of Natural History 15:213-222.

Bock, C.E., H.M. Smith, and J.H. Bock. 1990. The effect of livestock grazing upon abundance of the lizard, *Sceloporus scalaris*, in southeastern Arizona. Journal of Herpetology 24:445-446.

Degenhardt, W.G., C.W. Painter, and A.H. Price. 1996. The amphibians and reptiles of New Mexico. Albuquerque: University of New Mexico Press. 433 p.

DeMarco, V. 1992. Embryonic development times and egg retention in four species of sceloporine lizards. Functional Ecology 6:436-444.

Dunham, A.E. 1993. Population responses to environmental change: operative environments, physiologically structured models, and population dynamics. In: Kareiva, P.M., J.G. Kingsolver, and R.B. Huey, eds. Biotic Interactions and Global Change. Sunderland, Massachusetts: Sinauer Associates, Inc.: 95-119.

Goldberg, S.R., and C.R. Bursey. 1992. Helminths of the bunch grass lizard, *Sceloporus scalaris slevini* (Iguanidae). Journal of the Helminthological Society 59:130-131.

Huey, R.B., J.B. Losos, and C. Moritz. 2010. Are lizards toast? Science 328:832-833.

Leaché, A.D. 2009. Family Phrynosomatidae: Phrynosomatid Lizards (Zebra-tailed, Earless, Fringe-toed, Spiny, Tree, Brush, Side-blotched, California Rock, and Horned Lizards). In: Jones, L.L.C., and R.E. Lovich, eds. Lizards of the American Southwest: A Photographic Field Guide. Tucson, AZ: Rio Nuevo Publishers: 139-141.

Licht, P. 1972. Environmental physiology of reptilian breeding cycles: Role of temperature. General and Comparative Endocrinology Supplement 3:477-488.

Mathies, T., and R.M. Andrews. 1995. Thermal and reproductive biology of high and low elevation populations of the lizard *Sceloporus scalaris*: implications for the evolution of viviparity. Oecologia 104:101-111.

Newlin, M.E. 1974. Reproduction, trophic ecology, and other aspects of natural history in the bunch grass lizard, *Sceloporus scalaris*. Thesis. Angelo State University, San Angelo, TX. 111 p.

Painter, C.W. 2009. Slevin's Bunchgrass Lizard. In: Jones, L.L.C., and R.E. Lovich, eds. Lizards of the American Southwest: A Photographic Field Guide. Tucson, AZ: Rio Nuevo Publishers: 250-253.

Pianka, E.R., and L.J. Vitt. 2003. Lizards: Windows to the Evolution of Diversity. Berkeley: University of California Press.

Smith, H.M., D. Chiszar, A. Chiszar, [and others]. 1998. Slevin's bunch grass lizard (*Sceloporus slevini*) decimated on the Sonoita Plain, Arizona. Herpetological Review 29:225-226.

U.S. Forest Service [USFS]. 2009. Draft Coronado National Forest ecological sustainability report. Tucson, AZ: U.S. Department of Agriculture, Forest Service. Available: http://www.fs fed.us/r3/coronado/plan-revision/documents/final/cnf-ecological-sustainability-report-final-022009.pdf.

Vitt, L.J., and J.P. Caldwell. 2009. Herpetology. Oxford, United Kingdom: Elsevier. 697 p.

Watkins-Colwell, G.J., H.M. Smith, and D. Chiszar. 2003. *Sceloporus slevini* Smith. No. 771. Catalogue of American Amphibians and Reptiles. Society for the Study of Amphibians and Reptiles.

Habitat: Giant spotted whiptail (*Aspidoscelis burti strictogrammus*)			
Trait/Quality	**Question**	**Background info. & explanation of score**	**Points**
1. Area and distribution: *breeding*	Is the area or location of the associated vegetation type used for breeding activities by this species expected to change?	**Taxonomic note:** The genus for North American whiptails fairly recently changed from *Cnemidophorus* to *Aspidoscelis* (Persons and Wright 2009). The giant spotted whiptail is the only sub-species of *Aspidoscelis burti* in the United States. It occurs in southeastern Arizona and extreme southwestern New Mexico (Rosen 2009). Canyon spotted whiptail is the common name used for *Aspidoscelis burti* (Degenhardt and others 1996, Rosen 2009). From Rosen (2009): *A. burti* occurs primarily in "thorn scrub environments, in mountain canyons, in semi-desert grassland, the Arizona Upland portion of the Sonoran Desert, and the lower Madrean Oak Woodland. It also occurs along perennial streams, cienegas, and surrounding thorn scrub in arid valleys." The types of plants that occur in preferred thickets in thorn scrub include velvet mesquite, desert hackberry, catclaw acacia, etc. These lizards utilize riparian woodland and nearby thickets, occur mostly between ~822-1219 m, and use rock slopes, embankments in arroyos, and vegetated bottomlands that are densely vegetated. Occur mainly in canyons in the Santa Catalina, Rincon, Santa Rita, Whetstone, Galiuro, Pinaleño, and Santa Teresa Mountains. Rosen (2009) indicated that *A. burti* is found in canyon-bottom thickets especially near perennial water. In New Mexico, *A. burti* occurs in riparian areas dominated by sycamore, cottonwood, and ash and grasses and forbs, including open areas of bunch grass within riparian areas (Degenhardt and others 1996). Drying of valleys streams and frequent damage to riparian vegetation appear to have resulted in reductions in occurrence of this habitat in valleys (Rosen 2009). The giant spotted whiptail occurs, or potential habitat exists, on all EMAs except for three (Chiricahua, Dragoon, and Whetstone; USFS 2009). Projections of suitable climate for vegetation communities on all EMAs combined (Chapter 1) predicted declines in suitable climate for all plant community types, with the exception of increases of suitable climate for semi-desert grassland, and small increases in Sonoran desert scrub (present in small amounts on the CNF). Individuals appear to use more than one habitat, including Madrean oak woodland and desert riparian habitat, both of which are expected to decline.	2
2. Area and distribution: *non-breeding*	Is the area or location of the associated vegetation type used for non-breeding activities by this species expected to change?	Non-breeding habitat is same as breeding habitat. See Habitat, Question 1.	2
3. Habitat components: *breeding*	Are specific habitat components required for breeding expected to change?	No information found to indicate existence of specific habitat components for breeding.	0
4. Habitat components: *non-breeding*	Are specific habitat components required for survival during non-breeding	No information found to indicate existence of specific habitat components for survival during non-breeding periods.	0

Habitat: Giant spotted whiptail (*Aspidoscelis burti strictogrammus*)			
Trait/Quality	Question	Background info. & explanation of score	Points
	periods expected to change?		
5. Habitat quality and reproduction	Are features of the habitat associated with better reproductive success expected to change?	No information found.	0
6. Habitat quality and survival	Are features of the habitat associated with better survival expected to change?	No information found.	0
7. Ability to colonize new areas	What is this species' capacity and tendency to disperse?	Rosen (2009) indicated that individuals tend to actively forage in an area about 150 m in diameter.	1
8. Migratory or transitional habitats	Does this species require additional habitats during migration that are separated from breeding and non-breeding habitats?	No indication that individuals undergo movements that require them to use additional habitats.	0

Physiology: Giant spotted whiptail (*Aspidoscelis burti strictogrammus*)			
Trait/Quality	Question	Background info. & explanation of score	Points
1. Physiological thresholds	Are limiting physiological conditions expected to change?	Most members of the Family Teiidae are active foragers with high preferred body temperatures (Persons and Wright 2009). Whiptails (consist of the genus *Aspidoscelis*) are diurnal and are active during the warmest times of day. Body temperatures are usually in the range of 37-42 °C; individuals can retain heat in their large mass which allows them to forage well into shade (Rosen 2009). They are active through the heat of the day generally, although they may spend more time in shade (Rosen 2009). The high body temperatures of whiptails in part support their high activity levels (Pianka and Vitt 2003). Considered likely that lizards would seek refuge in burrows to escape temperature extremes (Huey and others 2010).	0
2. Sex ratio	Is sex ratio determined by temperature?	In Vitt and Caldwell (2009), genetic sex determination is reported for the Teiidae family; i.e., temperature-dependent sex determination not known occur in this family. Note that females lay eggs (i.e., not viviparous).	0
3. Exposure to extreme weather conditions	Are extreme weather or disturbance events that result in direct mortality or reproductive failure expected to change?	Increase in frequency of heat waves is predicted for southwestern United States. We assumed that lizards could survive short periods of high temperature by utilizing burrows; even if foraging opportunities were reduced for several days (see also Physiology, Question 1).	0

Physiology: Giant spotted whiptail (*Aspidoscelis burti strictogrammus*)			
Trait/Quality	**Question**	**Background info. & explanation of score**	**Points**
4. Limitations to active period	Are projected temperature or precipitation regimes that influence activity period of species expected to change?	Whiptails are diurnal, and are active during the warmest times of day, and therefore have shorter active seasons than other species that may occur in the same areas (Persons and Wright 2009). Individuals become active in late April to mid-May and remain active until mid-September or October (Rosen 2009). In temperate North America, whiptails go underground in fall (Pianka and Vitt 2003). Winne and Keck (2004) tested the hypothesis that high soil temperatures are required for whiptails to initiate and cease daily activity and found that circadian cycles in two bisexual species of *Aspidoscelis* (*A. inornata heptagramma* and *A. gularis septemvittatus*) can play an important role in both the initiation and cessation of daily activity. Thus, not clear the relative contribution of temperature versus circadian cycle to daily activity period. Score of "0" reflects possibility that seasonal activity period may increase if spring months are warmer for longer periods, but may be offset if temperatures during warmest part of day become hotter. See also Physiology, Question 1.	0
5. Metabolic inhibition	Does this species possess an ability to reduce metabolic energy or water requirements?	Cycles of dormancy are common in amphibians and reptiles; hibernation (some refer to hibernation in ectotherms as "brumation") is most likely primarily a response to cold temperatures and less so to a change in resource availability (Vitt and Caldwell 2009). While hibernating, activity mostly ceases, body temperature depends on temperature of the hibernation site, and physiological processes are reduced. Individuals are inactive in winter (see Physiology, Question 4) when they occupy burrows. Most temperate zone lizards become inactive during winter, and move underground to sites that do not freeze. We assumed these areas would be largely buffered from increased temperatures.	0
6. Survival during resource limitation	Does this species have lower energy requirements or possess the capacity to store energy or water in the long term?	Ectotherm.	-1
7. Variable life history	Does this species have alternative life history strategies to cope with variable resources or climate conditions?	Both males and females comprise this sub-species (Rosen 2009), unlike some other whiptails which consist of only females that reproduce by parthenogenesis (Persons and Wright 2009). No known variable life history strategies.	0
8. Reproduction in variable environments	Can this species outlive periods where reproduction is limited?	No information found on longevity but we assumed it to be a few years on average in the wild. Longevity record of individuals in captivity was 3 years for the New Mexico whiptail (*Cnemidophorus neomexicanus*/*Aspidoscelis neomexicana*; Bowler 1975). Periods of extreme reductions in rainfall may last 5 years. If these conditions eliminate breeding (e.g., insufficient food), most of the population would not survive longer than the periods of limited reproduction.	1

Phenology: Giant spotted whiptail (*Aspidoscelis burti strictogrammus*)			
Trait/Quality	**Question**	**Background info. & explanation of score**	**Points**
1. Cues	Does this species use temperature or moisture cues to initiate activities related to fecundity or survival?	Temperature is an important cue in reptiles; it has been called the "most important and widespread of the timing cues for saurian reproduction (Licht 1972)." In temperate zone lizards that become inactive in winter, decreasing day length and cooler temperatures trigger a response of the pituitary gland leading to changes in hormones that lead to the urge to become inactive (Pianka and Vitt 2003). Goldberg (1987b) indicated that individuals emerged in April or early May "depending on yearly climatic conditions."	1
2. Event timing	Are activities related to species' fecundity or survival tied to discrete events that are expected to change?	Most temperate zone lizards become inactive during winter, and move underground to sites that do not freeze; such inactivity is called brumation in ectotherms (not hibernation). Decreasing day length and colder temperatures trigger a hormonal response that leads to inactivity (Pianka and Vitt 2003). Pianka and Vitt (2003) indicated that in temperate North America, whiptails go underground in fall.	1
3. Mismatch potential	What is the separation in time or space between cues that initiate activities and discrete events that provide critical resources?	Cues and critical resources (e.g., food) expected to be closely related in time and space.	-1
4. Resilience to timing mismatches during breeding	Does this species employ strategies or have traits that increase the likelihood of reproduction co-occurring with important events?	Females produce one or more clutches from early June through mid-July (Rosen 2009). Goldberg (1987b) found evidence of a female producing >1 clutch per season.	-1

Biotic interactions: Giant spotted whiptail (*Aspidoscelis burti strictogrammus*)			
Trait/Quality	**Question**	**Background info. & explanation of score**	**Points**
1. Food resources	Are important food resources for this species expected to change?	Rosen (2009) indicated that the diet probably includes arthropods as well as small juvenile lizards. Individuals dig in organic debris and under trees to find arthropods. Pianka and Vitt (2003) indicated that most whiptails eat a variety of insects (particularly termites) and spiders. Overall, appears that giant spotted whiptails consume a variety of prey.	0
2. Predators	Are important predator populations expected to change?	Predators thought to include Sonora whipsnakes and greater roadrunners (Rosen 2009). In general, lizard predators include birds, mammals, snakes, other lizards, fish, spiders, centipedes, scorpions, tailless whip scorpions, with predation tending to be heaviest on lizard eggs and juveniles (Pianka and Vitt 2003).	0
3. Symbionts	Are populations of symbiotic species expected to change?	No information found regarding symbiotic relationships.	0
4. Disease	Is prevalence of diseases known to cause widespread mortality or	Four nematodes and two cestodes known in this sub-species (n=57) (Goldberg 1987a; Goldberg and others 1989). No information found indicating widespread mortality from disease.	0

Biotic interactions: Giant spotted whiptail (*Aspidoscelis burti strictogrammus*)			
Trait/Quality	Question	Background info. & explanation of score	Points
	reproductive failure in this species expected to change?		
5. Competitors	Are populations of important competing species expected to change?	Rosen (2009) indicated that important competitors may be the unisexual parthenogenetic species resulting from hybridization. These unisexuals do well in areas disturbed by humans. Not clear that these unisexuals would be positively impacted by climate change.	0

Literature Cited

Bowler, J.K., 1975. Longevity of reptiles and amphibians in North American collections as of 1 November, 1975. Society for the Study of Amphibians and Reptiles, Miscellaneous Publications, Herpetological Circular 6:1-32.

Degenhardt, W.G., C.W. Painter, and A.H. Price. 1996. The amphibians and reptiles of New Mexico. Albuquerque: University of New Mexico Press.

Goldberg, S.R. 1987a. Larval cestodes (*Mesocestoides* sp.) in the giant spotted whiptail, *Cnemidophorus burti strictogrammus*. Journal of Herpetology 21:337.

Goldberg, S.R. 1987b. Reproductive cycle of the giant spotted whiptail, *Cnemidophorus burti strictogrammus*, in Arizona. Southwestern Naturalist 32:510-511.

Goldberg, S.R., and C.R. Bursey. 1989. Helminths of the giant spotted whiptail, *Cnemidophorus burti strictogrammus* (Sauria: Teiidae). Proceedings of the Helminthological Society 56:86-87.

Licht, P. 1972. Environmental physiology of reptilian breeding cycles: Role of temperature. General and Comparative Endocrinology Supplement 3:477-488.

Pianka, E.R., and L.J. Vitt. 2003. Lizards: Windows to the evolution of diversity. Berkeley: University of California Press.

Persons, T.B., and J.W. Wright. 2009. Family Teiidae: Whiptails and their allies. In: Jones, L.L.C., and R.E. Lovich, eds. Lizards of the American Southwest: a photographic field guide. Tucson, AZ: Rio Nuevo Publishers: 322-325.

Rosen, P.C. 2009. Canyon Spotted Whiptail. In: Jones, L.L.C., and R.E. Lovich, eds. Lizards of the American Southwest: a photographic field guide. Tucson, AZ: Rio Nuevo Publishers: 330-333.

U.S. Forest Service [USFS]. 2009. Draft Coronado National Forest ecological sustainability report. Tucson, AZ: U.S. Department of Agriculture, Forest Service. Available: http://www fs fed.us/r3/coronado/plan-revision/documents/final/cnf-ecological-sustainability-report-final-022009.pdf.

Vitt, L.J., and J.P. Caldwell. 2009. Herpetology. Oxford, United Kingdom: Elsevier. 697 p.

Winne, C.T., and M.B. Keck. 2004. Daily activity patterns of whiptail lizards (Squamata: Teiidae: *Aspidoscelis*): A proximate response to environmental conditions or an endogenous rhythm? Functional Ecology 18:314-321

Habitat: Northern Mexican gartersnake (*Thamnophis eques megalops*)			
Trait/Quality	**Question**	**Background info. & explanation of score**	**Points**
1. Area and distribution: *breeding*	Is the area or location of the associated vegetation type used for breeding activities by this species expected to change?	In the United States, this sub-species has been primarily known from central and southern Arizona, with a limited distribution in New Mexico; also known from Mexico (Rosen and Schwalbe 1988; USFWS 2006). It is the only sub-species that occurs in the United States (Rosen and Schwalbe 1988). Across its range, observed at 40-2590 m (130-8496 ft) in elevation (USFWS 2006). Most localities in which individuals were observed by Rosen and Schwalbe (1988) ranged from 914-1524 m (3000-5000 ft). Considered to be restricted to riparian areas, except when dispersing (USFWS 2006). In Arizona, found to be most abundant in "source-area wetlands" around cienegas, cienega-streams, and stock tanks (Rosen and Schwalbe 1988). In New Mexico, most observations of *Thamnophis eques* have been at a few shallow stock tanks with abundant shoreline vegetation (e.g., often with abundant cattails; Degenhardt and others 1996). Rosen and Schwalbe (1988) also identified large river riparian woodlands and forests and streamside gallery forests (well-developed broadleaf deciduous riparian forests) as habitats. Cienegas are mid-elevation wetlands characterized by permanently saturated, highly organic, reducing soils (Hendrickson and Minckley 1984 as cited in USFWS 2006). The northern Mexican gartersnake occurs, or potential habitat exists, on the following EMAs: Tumacacori, Santa Rita, and Huachuca (USFS 2009). Projections of suitable climate for vegetation communities on all EMAs combined (Chapter 1) predicted declines in suitable climate for all plant community types, with the exception of increases of suitable climate for semi-desert grassland and small increases in Sonoran desert scrub (present in small amounts on the CNF). Riparian habitats predicted to decline due to decreased water flows on average, increased fire frequency, and possibly changes to the flood regime (earlier peak flows).	2
2. Area and distribution: *non-breeding*	Is the area or location of the associated vegetation type used for non-breeding activities by this species expected to change?	Non-breeding habitat is same as breeding habitat. See Habitat, Question 1.	2
3. Habitat components: *breeding*	Are specific habitat components required for breeding expected to change?	Dense bank and aquatic vegetation is considered an essential component of suitable habitat (Rosen and Schwalbe 1988), and is particularly important for neonates (references in USFWS 2006). Individuals use riparian herbaceous vegetation for cover, thermoregulation, and foraging. Removal of vegetation for even one season has to potential to lead to extirpation of a population (Rosen and Schwalbe 1988). Seldom seen more than 15 m from permanent water; *T. eques* is closely tied to permanent water (Rosen and Schwalbe 1988).	1
4. Habitat components: *non-breeding*	Are specific habitat components required for survival during non-breeding periods expected to change?	See Habitat, Question 3.	1

Habitat: Northern Mexican gartersnake (*Thamnophis eques megalops*)

Trait/Quality	Question	Background info. & explanation of score	Points
5. Habitat quality and reproduction	Are features of the habitat associated with better reproductive success expected to change?	No information (see Habitat, Question 3).	0
6. Habitat quality and survival	Are features of the habitat associated with better survival expected to change?	No information (see Habitat, Question 4).	0
7. Ability to colonize new areas	What is this species' capacity and tendency to disperse?	Most amphibians and reptiles move relatively little across their lifetime except when breeding (Vitt and Caldwell 2009). Rosen and Schwalbe (1988) reported that individuals are rarely seen >15 m from permanent water, "although it may occasionally wander overland."	1
8. Migratory or transitional habitats	Does this species require additional habitats during migration that are separated from breeding and non-breeding habitats?	No information found indicating that individuals undergo seasonal movements involving additional habitats.	0

Physiology: Northern Mexican gartersnake (*Thamnophis eques megalops*)

Trait/Quality	Question	Background info. & explanation of score	Points
1. Physiological thresholds	Are limiting physiological conditions expected to change?	Northern Mexican gartersnakes are surface active at ambient temperatures between 22-33 °C (71-91 °F) and forage along banks of water bodies (USFWS 2006). Thermal preferendum for the *Thamnophis* genus appears to be near 30 °C (Rosen 1991). Not clear that physiological threshold would regularly be exceeded. Forages in water and in areas with vegetative cover.	0
2. Sex ratio	Is sex ratio determined by temperature?	In Vitt and Caldwell (2009), genetic sex determination was reported for the Colubridae family; i.e., temperature-dependent sex determination not known occur in this family.	0
3. Exposure to extreme weather conditions	Are extreme weather or disturbance events that result in direct mortality or reproductive failure expected to change?	Individuals occupying streams may be exposed to increased levels of flooding (proportionally greater streamflow in winter and early spring as snow melts earlier) which could increase mortality. Increase in frequency of heat waves is predicted for southwestern United States. We assumed that snakes could survive short periods of high temperature by utilizing vegetative cover and/or standing water, even if foraging opportunities were reduced for several days.	1
4. Limitations to active period	Are projected temperature or precipitation regimes that influence activity period of species expected to change?	*T. eques* is active during the warm months of the year (Degenhardt and others 1996). The body temperature during the active season in Arizona of 18 individuals averaged 27.26 °C (22-33 °C; Rosen 1991). Forages along watercourses; seeks shelter from predators in thick streamside vegetation or in the stream (Degenhardt and others 1996). In Chihuahua, Mexico, this sub-species had peak activity between 1000-1100 hours in summer (Van Devender and Lowe 1977). Swims above and below water while foraging or escaping. After summer rains that begin in late June, individuals were observed frequently on the road at night. Association with water suggests that daily activity period will not be limited as long as water is present.	1

Trait/Quality	Question	Background info. & explanation of score	Points
		However, reduced precipitation could reduce the length of seasonal activity periods by reducing water in pools/tanks, potentially leading to earlier retreats to hibernacula.	
5. Metabolic inhibition	Does this species possess an ability to reduce metabolic energy or water requirements?	Cycles of dormancy are common in amphibians and reptiles; hibernation (some refer to hibernation in ectotherms as "brumation") is most likely primarily a response to cold temperatures and less so to a change in resource availability (Vitt and Caldwell 2009). While hibernating, activity mostly ceases, body temperature depends on temperature of the hibernation site, and physiological processes are reduced. We assumed that burrows would be largely buffered from increased temperatures.	0
6. Survival during resource limitation	Does this species have lower energy requirements or possess the capacity to store energy or water in the long term?	Ectotherm.	–1
7. Variable life history	Does this species have alternative life history strategies to cope with variable resources or climate conditions?	No information found to suggest alternative life history strategies.	0
8. Reproduction in variable environments	Can this species outlive periods where reproduction is limited?	Males thought to mature at 2 years of age, and females at 2-3 years (Rosen and Schwalbe 1988). Only ~50% of the females bear young each year (Rosen and Schwalbe 1988). Follicular enlargement begins in autumn for the next year's litter (Rosen and Schwalbe 1988). No longevity record for *T. eques* in Snider and Bowler (1992). Low survivorship of neonates and possibly yearlings was observed in Arizona (Rosen and Schwalbe 1988). Periods of extreme reductions in rainfall may last 5 years, which could reduce ponds and other water sources on which individuals depend for breeding. If these conditions eliminate breeding, we expected that most of the population would not survive longer than the periods of limited reproduction given: (1) the time to maturity, (2) that only about half of the females breed every year, and (3) individuals are probably not particularly long-lived.	1

Phenology: Northern Mexican gartersnake (*Thamnophis eques megalops*)			
Trait/Quality	Question	Background info. & explanation of score	Points
1. Cues	Does this species use temperature or moisture cues to initiate activities related to fecundity or survival?	Temperature is an important cue in reptiles (Licht 1972). *T. eques* is active during the warm months of the year (Degenhardt and others 1996).	1
2. Event timing	Are activities related to species' fecundity or	Follicular enlargement begins in autumn for the next year's litter (Rosen and Schwalbe 1988). Ovulation begins in late March or early April (Rosen and Schwalbe 1988); the authors indicate that mating probably	1

Phenology: Northern Mexican gartersnake (*Thamnophis eques megalops*)

Trait/Quality	Question	Background info. & explanation of score	Points
	survival tied to discrete events that are expected to change?	occurs in fall and very likely also occurs in early spring. Timing of temperature increases in late winter/early spring and rainfall patterns are likely important to this species.	
3. Mismatch potential	What is the separation in time or space between cues that initiate activities and discrete events that provide critical resources?	Cues and critical resources (e.g., food) expected to be closely related in time and space.	–1
4. Resilience to timing mismatches during breeding	Does this species employ strategies or have traits that increase the likelihood of reproduction co-occurring with important events?	In Arizona, 8 females produced 7-26 neonates (averaged 13.6; Rosen and Schwalbe 1988). Females typically move to warm microenvironments a few meters from water and give birth from early June to early July, with ~50% of the females bearing young each year (Rosen and Schwalbe 1988).	1

Biotic interactions: Northern Mexican gartersnake (*Thamnophis eques megalops*)

Trait/Quality	Question	Background info. & explanation of score	Points
1. Food resources	Are important food resources for this species expected to change?	Frogs, tadpoles, and fish are dominant prey; also lizards and mice and likely earthworms (Rosen and Schwalbe 1988). The most important prey were considered to be leopard frogs, Woodhouse's toads, Gila and roundtail chubs, and very likely other small fish, especially Gila topminnow (Rosen and Schwalbe 1988). Substantial numbers of individuals were only observed where anurans and prey fish were abundant. The authors thought that native prey species appear to play a larger role in the ecology of this sub-species than for other striped gartersnakes in Arizona. Forages using a variety of behaviors including ambush (both in water and on land), active foraging in riffles, vegetation mats and occasionally open water, and it capitalizes on transitory concentrations of prey (Rosen and Schwalbe 1988). Diet consists mostly of amphibians (adult and larval forms) and fishes (adult and juvenile forms); and may also include tree frogs, deer mice, lizards (*Aspidoscelis* and *Sceloporus*, larval tiger salamanders), and leeches (USFWS 2006). In one study in Mexico, differences in diet were found—large snakes fed mainly on fish, frogs, and salamander larvae, and leeches, and small snakes fed mostly on earthworms and leeches (Garcia and Drummond 1988). Overall, it appears that a variety of prey species are consumed. However, the northern Mexican gartersnake appears especially vulnerable to the loss of native prey species, such as leopard frogs (multiple references in USFWS 2006) that are expected to be vulnerable to climate change. USFWS (2006) stated "if an area is solely comprised of nonnative fish, the northern Mexican gartersnake may be faced with nutritional stress or face starvation." Thus a score of "1" was assigned to this question.	1
2. Predators	Are important predator populations	Rosen and Schwalbe (1988) considered that bullfrogs might influence populations of gartersnakes through predation. The authors indicated that during surveys in Arizona, "Mexican garter snakes were rare, and in	–1

Biotic interactions: Northern Mexican gartersnake (*Thamnophis eques megalops*)			
Trait/Quality	**Question**	**Background info. & explanation of score**	**Points**
	expected to change?	some localities possible extirpated, where bullfrogs were abundant." Authors also conjectured that bias toward large adults at the San Bernardino NWR was due to predation of small snakes by bullfrogs. A variety of predators is thought to prey on northern Mexican gartersnakes, including birds of prey, other snakes, wading birds, raccoons, skunks, and coyotes (Rosen and Schwalbe 1988). Bullfrog and crayfish are thought to be the biggest threat to northern Mexican gartersnakes (references in USFWS 2006). Overall, there are a suite of predators. However, USFWS (2006) indicated that the expansion of nonnative predators (bullfrogs, crayfish and green sunfish) is the primary cause of decline in this sub-species in southeastern New Mexico. These aquatic predators of the northern Mexican gartersnake are likely to be vulnerable to climate change as well. Thus, a score of "-1" was assigned.	
3. Symbionts	Are populations of symbiotic species expected to change?	No information found regarding symbiotic relationships.	0
4. Disease	Is prevalence of diseases known to cause widespread mortality or reproductive failure in this species expected to change?	Disease in this sub-species has not been identified as a major threat, but little information about diseases in snakes, in general, exists (USFWS 2006). *Batrachochytrium* (fungus causing chytrid infections) has not been reported on reptilian hosts in the wild (USFWS 2006). Individuals in Mexico documented to be host to various helminth parasites but no discussion of impacts from these parasites (Jimenez-Ruiz and others 2002).	0
5. Competitors	Are populations of important competing species expected to change?	Nonnative species (e.g., bullfrogs, nonnative fish, and crayfish) compete with northern Mexican gartersnake for prey (USFWS 2006). Crayfish alter the abundance and structure of aquatic and semi-aquatic vegetation used by gartersnakes (USFWS 2006). These aquatic species are likely to be vulnerable to climate change as well. Marcy's checkered gartersnake (*T. marcianus marcianus*) is a semi-terrestrial species; it may be out-competing northern Mexican gartersnakes at San Bernardino National Refuge in southern Arizona (Rosen and others 2001 as cited in USFWS 2006). Thus, we assigned a score of "0" because non-native aquatic competitors are likely to decrease but Marcy's checkered gartersnake may increase.	0

Literature Cited

Degenhardt, W.G., C.W. Painter, and A.H. Price. 1996. The amphibians and reptiles of New Mexico. Albuquerque: University of New Mexico Press.

Garcia, C.M., and H. Drummond. 1988. Seasonal and ontogenetic variation in the diet of the Mexican garter snake, *Thamnophis eques*, in Lake Tecosomulco, Hidalgo. Journal of Herpetology 22:129-134.

Jimenez-Ruiz, F.A., L. Garcia-Prieto, and G. Perez-Ponce de Leon. 2002. Helminth infracommunity structure of the sympatric garter snakes *Thamnophis eques* and *Thamnophis megalongaster* from the Mesa Central of Mexico. Journal of Parasitology 88:454-460.

Licht, P. 1972. Environmental physiology of reptilian breeding cycles: Role of temperature. General and Comparative Endocrinology Supplement 3:477-488.

Rosen, P.C. 1991. Comparative field study of thermal preferenda in garter snakes (*Thamnophis*). Journal of Herpetology 25:301-312.

Rosen, P.C., and C.R. Schwalbe. 1988. Status of the Mexican and narrow-headed garter snakes (*Thamnophis eques megalops* and *Thamnophis rufipunctatus*) in Arizona. Unpublished report from

Arizona Game and Fish Department, Phoenix, AZ, to U.S. Fish and Wildlife Service, Albuquerque, NM. 88 p.

Snider, A.T., and J.K. Bowler. 1992. Longevity of reptiles and amphibians in North American collections. Second edition. Herpetological Circular No. 21. Society for the Study of Amphibians and Reptiles. 40 p.

U.S. Fish and Wildlife Service [USFWS]. 2006. 12-Month finding on a petition to list the Northern Mexican Gartersnake (*Thamnophis eques megalops*) as threatened or endangered with critical habitat. Federal Register 71:56227-56256.

U.S. Forest Service [USFS]. 2009. Draft Coronado National Forest ecological sustainability report. Tucson, AZ: U.S. Department of Agriculture, Forest Service. Available: http://www.fs fed.us/r3/coronado/plan-revision/documents/final/cnf-ecological-sustainability-report-final-022009.pdf.

Van Devender, T.R., and C.H. Lowe, Jr. 1977. Amphibians and reptiles of Yepómera, Chihuahua, Mexico. Journal of Herpetology 11:41-50.

Vitt, L.J., and J.P. Caldwell. 2009. Herpetology. Oxford, United Kingdom: Elsevier. 697 p.

Habitat: Arizona ridge-nosed rattlesnake (*Crotalus willardi willardi*)			
Trait/Quality	**Question**	**Background info. & explanation of score**	**Points**
1. Area and distribution: *breeding*	Is the area or location of the associated vegetation type used for breeding activities by this species expected to change?	In the United States, this sub-species occurs in southern Arizona between 4000 and 9000 ft in elevation and has been reported in the Huachuca, Santa Rita, Canelo, Patagonia, and Whetstone Mountains (Degenhardt and others 1996; Brennan 2008). Often occurs in Madrean evergreen woodland, in or near drainages that contain abundant canopy cover and leaf litter. In the Huachuca Mountains, the most frequently occurring perennial plants within 2.5 m of individuals when they were captured were bullgrass (*Muhlenbergia emersleyi*), Mexican pinyon (*Pinus cembroides*), Emory oak (*Quercus emoryi*), and Arizona white oak (*Q. arizonica*; McCrystal and others 1996). In the Patagonia Mountains, they were silverleaf oak (*Q. hypoleucoides*), Mexican pinyon, squaw bush (*Rhus trilobata*), and bullgrass. Rado and Rowlands (1981) found an individual under bark near a decomposing log where dominant vegetation included Arizona sycamore, Mexican pinyon, one seed juniper, Arizona ash, Emory oak, and Mexican blue oak. Degenhardt and others (1996) called *Crotalus willardi obscurus* in New Mexico a "montane generalist…occurring mostly above 1800m." In New Mexico and northern Mexico, most have been collected "in and along steep rocky canyons with intermittent streams or on exposed talus slopes." Authors indicated that dominant vegetation where *C .w. obscurus* occurs includes various species of oaks, Apache and Chihuahuan pine, alligator juniper, Arizona cypress, Arizona madrone, Manzanita, and various grasses. Arizona ridge-nosed rattlesnakes occur, or potential habitat exists for this species, on the following EMAs: Santa Rita, Huachuca, and Whetstone (USFS 2009). Projections of suitable climate for vegetation communities (Chapter 1) predicted declines in suitable climate for Madrean forest and woodland, Madrean conifer forest, and plains grassland, with increases of suitable climate for semi-desert grassland. Overall, we expected that projected reductions in pine-oak woodland habitats (from increased aridity, drought, and high intensity fires) will reduce breeding habitat.	2
2. Area and distribution: *non-breeding*	Is the area or location of the associated vegetation type used for non-	Same as breeding habitat; See Habitat, Question 1.	2

Habitat: Arizona ridge-nosed rattlesnake (*Crotalus willardi willardi*)			
Trait/Quality	**Question**	**Background info. & explanation of score**	**Points**
	breeding activities by this species expected to change?		
3. Habitat components: *breeding*	Are specific habitat components required for breeding expected to change?	No information found to indicate existence of specific habitat components for breeding.	0
4. Habitat components: *non-breeding*	Are specific habitat components required for survival during non-breeding periods expected to change?	Requires over-wintering sites. McCrystal and others (1996) conducted a study in autumn and indicated that Arizona ridge-nosed rattlesnakes are semi-fossorial and are "generalized in the cover they choose when opportunities are varied." The authors indicated that they seemed to prefer burrows or holes in the ground, but that they have been observed to use holes under rocks, holes in rock piles (possibly leading to holes in the ground) and occasionally clumps of bunch grass. Refuge was rarely sought under dead logs. In areas with less rock cover, individuals seemed to use bunchgrass and burrow more frequently. Not clear to authors whether bunchgrass clumps were used in winter; no feces or shed skins were found there as at other refugia. In Mexico, ridge-nosed rattlesnakes have been found over-wintering 40-46 cm deep in talus (Degenhardt and others 1996). Availability of such holes/burrows/rock piles not expected to change as a direct result of climate change.	0
5. Habitat quality and reproduction	Are features of the habitat associated with better reproductive success expected to change?	No information found on habitat quality and reproduction.	0
6. Habitat quality and survival	Are features of the habitat associated with better survival expected to change?	No information found on habitat quality and survival.	0
7. Ability to colonize new areas	What is this species' capacity and tendency to disperse?	Most amphibians and reptiles move relatively little during their lifetime except when breeding (Vitt and Caldwell 2009). Smith and others (2001) found that 3 radio-tagged *C. w. obscurus* had a daily activity area of 5.6-74.4 m^2 during May-July 1997. Six individuals of *C. w. willardi* were found 0-105 m from where originally located across 6-1097 days (McCrystal and others 1996)	1
8. Migratory or transitional habitats	Does this species require additional habitats during migration that are separated from breeding and non-breeding habitats?	No information found to suggest that Arizona ridge-nosed rattlesnakes undergo seasonal movements.	0

USDA Forest Service RMRS-GTR-273. 2012.

Physiology: Arizona ridge-nosed rattlesnake (*Crotalus willardi willardi*)			
Trait/Quality	**Question**	**Background info. & explanation of score**	**Points**
1. Physiological thresholds	Are limiting physiological conditions expected to change?	In Mexico, ridge-nosed rattlesnakes have been found basking both at air temperatures of 6-9 °C (43-48 °F) in the shade and 26 °C (79 °F) in the sun (Degenhardt and others 1996). Body temperatures of *C. w. willardi* in the Huachuca and Patagonia Mountains during fall surveys averaged 24.2 °C (McCrystal and others 1996). Armstrong and Murphy (1979) indicated that this sub-species appears to prefer the "more humid canyon bottoms of pine-oak habitats as opposed to the arid slopes where *C. lepidus* and *C. pricei* are common." The authors indicated that although this preference seemed to exist, an individual was also observed on an east-facing slope in scrub oak. In Sonora, Mexico, individuals were found to be common in rocky stream beds where pools of water stood following summer rains; two species of *Sceloporus* were common here (thought to be important prey). Authors thought this sub-species was more active on warm, humid days when there was intermittent sunlight, particularly before and after rain showers in the afternoons when the temperature was 24-29 °C. McCrystal and others (1996) indicated that this sub-species "does not exhibit regular surface activity when conditions are hot and dry, but will be found active during cool times, providing there is access to the sun for basking. We have found them moving in the rain, and have seen them basking in every month of the year, including basking on dry sunlit rocks less than 3 meters from snow." We chose the score of "1" due to the potential that Arizona ridge-nosed rattlesnakes are sensitive to higher temperatures.	1
2. Sex ratio	Is sex ratio determined by temperature?	In Vitt and Caldwell (2009), genetic sex determination is reported for the Viperidae family; i.e., temperature-dependent sex determination not known occur in this family.	0
3. Exposure to extreme weather conditions	Are extreme weather or disturbance events that result in direct mortality or reproductive failure expected to change?	Increase in frequency of heat waves is predicted for southwestern United States. We assumed that snakes could survive short periods of high temperature by utilizing cover; even if foraging opportunities were reduced for several days (see also Physiology, Question 1). Eight radio-tagged rattlesnakes (*Crotalus* spp.) exposed to low-intensity fire survived, and were in subterranean retreats following the fire (Smith and others 2001), suggesting the ability to escape high intensity temperatures.	0
4. Limitations to active period	Are projected temperature or precipitation regimes that influence activity period of species expected to change?	Ridge-nosed rattlesnakes are primarily diurnally active but occasionally they are crepuscular or occasionally nocturnally active at lower elevations (Brennan 2008). Not active during late fall and winter. Possible that seasonal activity period may increase if non-winter months are warmer for longer periods, but may be offset if temperatures during warmest part of day become hotter. Score of "1" reflects information that activity associated with intermittent sunlight, and before and after rain showers at moderate temperatures (see Physiology, Question 1), suggesting that Arizona ridge-nosed rattlesnakes may be more sensitive to higher temperatures than other reptiles.	1
5. Metabolic inhibition	Does this species possess an ability to reduce metabolic energy or water requirements?	Cycles of dormancy are common in amphibians and reptiles, and hibernation is most likely primarily a response to cold temperatures and less so to a change in resource availability (Vitt and Caldwell 2009). While hibernating, activity mostly ceases, body temperature depends on temperature of the hibernation site, and physiological processes are reduced. Such inactivity is called brumation in ectotherms (not hibernation). Inactive in winter. In Mexico, ridge-nosed rattlesnakes have been found over-wintering 40-46 cm deep in talus (Degenhardt and others 1996).	0

Physiology: Arizona ridge-nosed rattlesnake (*Crotalus willardi willardi*)			
Trait/Quality	**Question**	**Background info. & explanation of score**	**Points**
		We assumed that wintering sites would be largely buffered from increased temperatures.	
6. Survival during resource limitation	Does this species have lower energy requirements or possess the capacity to store energy or water in the long term?	Ectotherm.	–1
7. Variable life history	Does this species have alternative life history strategies to cope with variable resources or climate conditions?	Females appear to reproduce every other year or at greater intervals (Holycross and Goldberg 2001), but not clear that this is a benefit to variable resources or climate conditions.	0
8. Reproduction in variable environments	Can this species outlive periods where reproduction is limited?	Little information on survivorship in the wild. The longevity record for captive *C. w. willardi* is 21 years (Bowler1975); 34 longevity records for *Crotalus* spp. in captivity range 3 years to 3-30 years (Bowler1975), suggesting that this genus may have relatively long lifespans (Bowler1975). Periods of extreme reductions in rainfall may last 5 years. If these conditions reduce resources to the point that Arizona ridge-nosed rattlesnakes have insufficient resources for breeding, but conditions recover after, we assumed it is likely that sufficient numbers of individuals would survive long enough to breed once conditions improve.	–1

Phenology: Arizona ridge-nosed rattlesnake (*Crotalus willardi willardi*)			
Trait/Quality	**Question**	**Background info. & explanation of score**	**Points**
1. Cues	Does this species use temperature or moisture cues to initiate activities related to fecundity or survival?	Temperature is an important cue in reptiles (Licht 1972). Temperature may be an important cue for departing and returning to over-wintering sites.	1
2. Event timing	Are activities related to species' fecundity or survival tied to discrete events that are expected to change?	See Phenology, Question 1. The length of the cold season is an important constraint on how long the reproductive season lasts in reptiles (Vitt and Caldwell 2009). Increased temperatures may alter the length of the breeding season. Young (2-9) are born from late July-August (Holycross and Goldberg 2001). This coincides with the start of summer rains and the appearance of juvenile *Sceloporus*, a prey species; it is possible that parturition is timed to coincide with the increase of prey availability. Ovulation and fertilization probably occur in early spring, with a 4-5-month gestation period after that. Copulation occurs in mid-summer to early fall. However, reproduction appears to biennial or longer.	1
3. Mismatch potential	What is the separation in time or space between cues that initiate activities and discrete events that provide critical resources?	Cues and critical resources (e.g., food) expected to be closely related in time and space.	–1

Phenology: Arizona ridge-nosed rattlesnake (*Crotalus willardi willardi*)			
Trait/Quality	Question	Background info. & explanation of score	Points
4. Resilience to timing mismatches during breeding	Does this species employ strategies or have traits that increase the likelihood of reproduction co-occurring with important events?	Individuals mate in summer or fall, and young are born the following summer (Brennan 2008). Females appear to produce young every other year or at longer intervals (Holycross and Goldberg 2001).	1

Biotic interactions: Arizona ridge-nosed rattlesnake (*Crotalus willardi willardi*)			
Trait/Quality	Question	Background info. & explanation of score	Points
1. Food resources	Are important food resources for this species expected to change?	Brennan (2008) indicated that this sub-species consumes mostly lizards, mice and centipedes, occasionally birds and scorpions. McCrystal and others (1996) concluded that this sub-species appears to be a food generalist. In a study of *C. w. obscurus*, adults fed primarily on small mammals (62.3%), lizards (26.4%) and occasionally passerine birds (9.4%). *Peromyscus* spp. comprised 64.9% of the small mammals consumed and *Sceloporus* spp. for 68.4% of lizards. Juveniles consumed a diet of 57% lizards and 71% of these were identified as *Sceloporus* spp.; centipedes constituted 33% of the diet (Holycross and others 2001a). Multiple prey species are consumed, although not as wide of a variety of prey as some species.	0
2. Predators	Are important predator populations expected to change?	Little information on predators exists (Holycross and others 2001b). One observation of a snake carcass (*C. w. obscurus*) was believed to have been preyed upon by a Mexican spotted owl or a red-tailed hawk (Holycross and others 2001b).	0
3. Symbionts	Are populations of symbiotic species expected to change?	No information found that indicates important symbiotic relationships.	0
4. Disease	Is prevalence of diseases known to cause widespread mortality or reproductive failure in this species expected to change?	Little information. McAllister and others (1996) indicated theirs is the first published report on parasites of *C. willardi obscurus*. The authors found oocysts and sporocysts of *Sarcocystis* spp. (protozoans) in the feces of individuals in Mexico. No information on whether the parasite was causing visible illness in the individuals snakes. Salmonella has been reported in captive populations of *C. willardi* (Grupka and others 2006); not clear whether this might apply to wild individuals.	0
5. Competitors	Are populations of important competing species expected to change?	No information found on competitors.	0

Literature Cited

Armstrong, B.L., and J.B. Murphy. 1979. The natural history of Mexican rattlesnakes. University of Kansas Museum of Natural History Special Publication No. 5. vii + 88 p.

Bowler, J.K., 1975. Longevity of reptiles and amphibians in North American collections as of 1 November, 1975. Society for the Study of Amphibians and Reptiles, Miscellaneous Publications, Herpetological Circular 6:1-32.

Brennan, T.C. 2008. Ridge-nosed Rattlesnake (*Crotalus willardi*). Online field guide to the reptiles and amphibians of Arizona. Available: http://www.reptilesofaz.org/Snakes-Subpages/h-c-willardi.html.

Degenhardt, W.G., C.W. Painter, and A.H. Price. 1996. The amphibians and reptiles of New Mexico. Albuquerque: University of New Mexico Press.

Grupka, L.M., E.C. Ramsay, and D.A. Bemis. 2006. Salmonella surveillance in a collection of rattlesnakes (*Crotalus* spp.). Journal of Zoo and Wildlife Medicine 37:306-312.

Holycross, A.T., and S.R. Goldberg. 2001. Reproduction in northern populations of the ridgenose rattlesnake, *Crotalus willardi* (Serpentes: Viperidae). Copeia 2001: 473-481.

Holycross, A.T., C.W. Painter, D.G. Barker, and M.E. Douglas. 2001a. Foraging ecology of the threatened New Mexico ridge-nosed rattlesnake (*Crotalus willardi obscurus*). In: Schuett, G.W., M. Hoggren, M.E. Douglas, and H.W. Greene, eds. Biology of the Vipers. Eagle Mountain, UT: Eagle Mountain Publishing: 243-251.

Holycross, A.T., L.K. Kamees, and C.W. Painter. 2001b. Observations of predation on *Crotalus willardi obscurus* in the Animas Mountains, New Mexico. Southwestern Naturalist 46:363-364.

Licht, P. 1972. Environmental physiology of reptilian breeding cycles: Role of temperature. General and Comparative Endocrinology Supplement 3:477-488.

McAllister, C.T., S.J. Upton, D.G. Barker, and C.W. Painter. 1996. *Sarcocystis sp.* (Apicomplexa) from the New Mexico ridgenose rattlesnake, *Crotalus willardi obscurus* (Serpentes: Viperidae) from Sonora, Mexico. Journal of the Helminthological Society of Washington 63:128-130.

McCrystal, H.K., C.R. Schwalbe, and D.F. Retes. 1996. Selected aspects of the ecology of the Arizona ridge-nosed rattlesnake (*Crotalus willardi willardi*) and the banded rock rattlesnake (*Crotalus lepidus klauberi*) in Arizona. Final Report. Arizona Game and Fish Department. Heritage Grant IIPAM 192304. Submitted to Heritage Program, Arizona Game and Fish Department, Phoenix, AZ. September 13, 1996.

Rado, T.A., and P.G. Rowlands. 1981. A range extension and low elevation record for the Arizona ridge-nosed rattlesnake (*Crotalus w. willardi*). Herpetological Review 12:15.

Smith, L.J., A. T. Holycross, C.W. Painter, and M.E. Douglas. 2001. Montane rattlesnakes nd prescribed fire. Southwestern Naturalist 46:54-61.

U.S. Forest Service [USFS]. 2009. Draft Coronado National Forest ecological sustainability report. Tucson, AZ: U.S. Department of Agriculture, Forest Service. Available: http://www.fs.fed.us/r3/coronado/plan-revision/documents/final/cnf-ecological-sustainability-report-final-022009.pdf.

Vitt, L.J., and J.P. Caldwell. 2009. Herpetology. Oxford, United Kingdom: Elsevier. 697 p.

Habitat: Sonoran tiger salamander (*Ambystoma tigrinum stebbinsi*)			
Trait/Quality	Question	Background info. & explanation of score	Points
1. Area and distribution: *breeding*	Is the area or location of the associated vegetation type used for breeding activities by this species expected to change?	Tiger salamanders overall have a wide distribution, but this sub-species is historically only known from Santa Cruz and Cochise counties and currently occurs only in the San Rafael Valley (Storfer and others 2004). The San Rafael Valley consists of plains grassland and Madrean evergreen woodland (Collins and others 1988). Across their range, tiger salamanders tend to occur in grasslands, savannahs, and woodland edges (Lannoo and Phillips 2005). Terrestrial adults of this sub-species utilize grassland habitats and adjacent slopes in the San Rafael Valley (Brooks and Rorabaugh 1997). Actual breeding is aquatic (affect of climate change on water sources covered in Habitat, Question 3), but terrestrial adults move from surrounding uplands they use for over-wintering to access breeding areas. Habitat for the Sonoran tiger salamander occurs only on the Huachuca EMA (USFS 2009). Climate change projections for vegetation communities (Chapter 1) on the Huachuca EMA predicted declines in suitable conditions for Madrean forest and woodland, Madrean conifer	0

Habitat: Sonoran tiger salamander (*Ambystoma tigrinum stebbinsi*)

Trait/Quality	Question	Background info. & explanation of score	Points
		forest, and Plains grassland, and increases in suitable conditions for semi-desert grassland. Increased grasslands would lead to an increase in terrestrial habitat, although decline of Madrean oak woodland would constitute a loss, which could result in no net gain in habitat area.	
2. Area and distribution: *non-breeding*	Is the area or location of the associated vegetation type used for non-breeding activities by this species expected to change?	Same as Habitat, Question 1.	0
3. Habitat components: *breeding*	Are specific habitat components required for breeding expected to change?	Breeding in tiger salamanders is aquatic (Lannoo and Phillips 2005), so permanent or semi-permanent water sources are required. Utilizes non-flowing water (Degenhardt and others 1996). Water sources must persist seasonally at least long enough for larvae to metamorphose into terrestrial forms if populations are to persist. Larval stage lasts at least 10 weeks but can be longer; varies with environmental factors (e.g., food, temperature, salamander density, etc.). Some larvae develop into terrestrial adults, a morph that lacks gills; others develop into gilled aquatic adults (referred to by various names including branchiate adults, neotenic adults, and paedomorphs; Lannoo and Phillips 2005). Larvae may not metamorphose in their first year and instead over-winter in permanent water sources (USFWS 2002). All known extant and historical aquatic populations are restricted to the cattle tanks (human-made earthen stock ponds) or impounded cienegas with 31 km of Lochiel, Arizona (Brooks and Rorabaugh 1997). Historically probably bred in springs, natural cienegas or possibly backwater pools (Brooks and Rorabaugh 1997). Some ranchers have maintained water in cattle ponds to support tiger salamanders (Snyder 1988 as cited in USFWS 2002). In the San Rafael Valley, many ponds that contain salamanders do not have aquatic or bank-line vegetation; thus, this appears not to be required for presence of this sub-species (USFWS 2002). Presence of ponds expected to decline with increased aridity. Several stock ponds went dry during droughts in 1994 and 1996 (Brooks and Rorabaugh 1997).	1
4. Habitat components: *non-breeding*	Are specific habitat components required for survival during non-breeding periods expected to change?	Year-round water is required by aquatic morphs (neotenic adults) and larvae that have not yet undergone metamorphosis. Collins and others (1988) noted that only ~17-40% of animals actually metamorphose to terrestrial form each year based on data from Bodie Tank in San Raphael Valley. Neotenic adults may not be able to undergo metamorphosis when threatened by drought (Lannoo and Phillips 2005). Juveniles may stay near wet areas and feed, or may move to upland areas to burrow (Lannoo and Phillips 2005). Note that there is often significant, but naturally occurring, larval mortality in tiger salamanders that breed in semi-permanent water sources when they dry each year, as is often the case with amphibians (Lannoo and Phillips 2005), yet populations persist. No indication that neotenic adults can burrow into mud and aestivate if ponds dry (Lannoo and Phillips 2005); thus, if they cannot metamorphose before their water source dries they are subject to mortality. Sub-adult tiger salamanders have been observed burrowing in mud cracks when a cattle tank dried up (Webb 1969 as cited in Degenhardt 1996 and others). Furthermore, occasional drying of ponds reduces predator	1

Habitat: Sonoran tiger salamander (*Ambystoma tigrinum stebbinsi*)

Trait/Quality	Question	Background info. & explanation of score	Points
		populations (fish, bullfrogs), which could ultimately benefit breeding and non-breeding Sonoran tiger salamanders. Overall, if the percentage of individuals that Collins and others (1988) observed as undergoing metamorphosis at Bodie Tank is indicative of individuals across the population of this sub-species, we assumed that year-round ponds are important to the persistence of the population. Terrestrial adults require deep friable soils for burrowing (they can dig their own burrows, but often are associated with mammal burrows; references in Lannoo and Phillips 2005). However, no expected significant reduction in friable soils under climate change.	
5. Habitat quality and reproduction	Are features of the habitat associated with better reproductive success expected to change?	Little information. In field enclosures during summer months, Holomuzki (1986) found that larval survivorship and growth were generally greater in vegetated shallows than in enclosures in the limnetic zone (well-lit surface waters away from shore); this variation was correlated with lower food levels, lower temperatures, and lower oxygen in deeper limnetic areas. Further, the authors found significant variation in fitness among years despite the fact that food, temperature, and oxygen remained relatively constant, suggesting that other unmeasured factors were important.	0
6. Habitat quality and survival	Are features of the habitat associated with better survival expected to change?	Little information; see Habitat, Question 5.	0
7. Ability to colonize new areas	What is this species' capacity and tendency to disperse?	Terrestrial adults move from over-wintering sites in uplands to wet areas for breeding (Lannoo and Phillips 2005). One tagged male moved 162 m to an upland site (Semlitsch 1983a as cited in Lannoo and Phillips 2005). Brooks and Rorabaugh (1997) noted an account of a single terrestrial salamander being found at a location that was probably 1 km from an aquatic site. In other *Ambystoma* spp., adults usually return to breed in the same ponds where they hatched (USFWS 2002). Considered to have low ability to disperse.	1
8. Migratory or transitional habitats	Does this species require additional habitats during migration that are separated from breeding and non-breeding habitats?	Terrestrial adults move from over-wintering sites in uplands to wet areas for breeding (Lannoo and Phillips 2005). In some populations of tiger salamander, newly metamorphosed individuals stay near aquatic habitat rather than migrating into uplands (Lannoo and Phillips 2005). However, these transitional areas are not expected to be substantially different from wintering areas.	0

Physiology: Sonoran tiger salamander (*Ambystoma tigrinum stebbinsi*)

Trait/Quality	Question	Background info. & explanation of score	Points
1. Physiological thresholds	Are limiting physiological conditions expected to change?	This sub-species is tolerant of a wide temperature range; temporary ponds can range in temperature across the year from <5 °C to 30 °C; temperature in terrestrial environments can range from below 0 °C to >35 °C (USFWS 2002). We assumed that water or air temperature will not exceed thresholds. Standing water expected to become less available, but this is covered in Habitat section. Decrease in precipitation and increased evaporation (due to increased temperatures) may reduce the amount of moisture available for adults to move between breeding ponds and over-wintering areas, and/or survive during over-wintering periods (increases probability of desiccation).	1

Physiology: Sonoran tiger salamander (*Ambystoma tigrinum stebbinsi*)			
Trait/Quality	Question	Background info. & explanation of score	Points
2. Sex ratio	Is sex ratio determined by temperature?	Vitt and Caldwell (2009) indicated that salamanders do not experience temperature-dependent sex determination.	0
3. Exposure to extreme weather conditions	Are extreme weather or disturbance events that result in direct mortality or reproductive failure expected to change?	Increase in frequency of heat waves is predicted for southwestern United States. Overall, not clear that heat waves during summer would reduce survival and reproduction due to high probability that terrestrial forms would be in or near water at this time of year.	0
4. Limitations to active period	Are projected temperature or precipitation regimes that influence activity period of species expected to change?	Reduced precipitation could reduce the length of seasonal activity periods by reducing water in pools/tanks and leading to earlier retreats to hibernacula.	1
5. Metabolic inhibition	Does this species possess an ability to reduce metabolic energy or water requirements?	Cycles of dormancy are common in amphibians and reptiles; hibernation (some refer to hibernation in ectotherms as "brumation") is most likely primarily a response to cold temperatures and less so to a change in resource availability (Vitt and Caldwell 2009). While hibernating, activity mostly ceases, body temperature depends on temperature of the hibernation site, and physiological processes are reduced. Terrestrial adults occupy burrows during winter (Lannoo and Phillips 2005). We assumed that burrows would be largely buffered from increased temperatures.	0
6. Survival during resource limitation	Does this species have lower energy requirements or possess the capacity to store energy or water in the long term?	Ectotherm.	-1
7. Variable life history	Does this species have alternative life history strategies to cope with variable resources or climate conditions?	The presence of both aquatic and terrestrial adult forms is considered a benefit in that populations can survive the non-breeding season on land in burrows, and thus do not depend on ponds during the non-breeding season. Tiger salamanders have a cannibal morph larvae, which may eat conspecifics among other prey and have proportionally large heads and teeth (Lannoo and Phillips 2005). The authors did not indicate this as a sub-species where this morph has been documented in wild populations, but do note that it has been induced in laboratory conditions. Cannibal morphs are not observed in all years in those populations in which they are known to occur; conspecific density appears to trigger their presence (references in Lannoo and Phillips 2005). Five individuals of this morph have been observed out of thousands of individuals in the San Rafael Valley (USFWS 2002).	-1
8. Reproduction in variable environments	Can this species outlive periods where reproduction is limited?	Little information on this sub-species. Branchiate adults of the sub-species *A. t. nebulosum* have survived for up to 8 years in captivity (USFWS 2002). Based on 150 individuals of this same sub-species taken from the wild, none were estimated to be older than 6 years (USFWS 2002). In the eastern tiger salamander, most individuals die before they can breed a second time (Church and others 2007). Periods of extreme reductions in rainfall may last 5 years, which can	1

Physiology: Sonoran tiger salamander (*Ambystoma tigrinum stebbinsi*)			
Trait/Quality	Question	Background info. & explanation of score	Points
		reduce ponds and other water sources on which individuals depend for breeding. If these conditions eliminate breeding, most of the population would not survive longer than the periods of limited reproduction.	

Phenology: Sonoran tiger salamander (*Ambystoma tigrinum stebbinsi*)			
Trait/Quality	Question	Background info. & explanation of score	Points
1. Cues	Does this species use temperature or moisture cues to initiate activities related to fecundity or survival?	Amphibians, in general, respond to temperature and moisture cues in the timing of breeding (Carey and Alexander 2003). This sub-species has been known to breed as early as January and as late as early May; rarely breed after monsoon rains in July and August (USFWS 2002). Migrations to breeding areas from wintering sites are triggered by warm spring rains in northern wetlands (references in Lannoo and Phillips 2005); considered possible that temperature triggers migration in Arizona (given that rains are mostly in winter and summer). Wet or rainy weather may stimulate terrestrial activity (Degenhardt and others 1996).	1
2. Event timing	Are activities related to species' fecundity or survival tied to discrete events that are expected to change?	Known to breed as early as January and as late as early May; rarely breed after monsoon rains in July and August (USFWS 2002). Eggs hatch 2-4 weeks after being laid; eggs develop more quickly in warm water than in cold water (USFWS 2002). Possible that eggs will develop more quickly under climate change, but unclear how much warmer the water in ponds will be.

In as few as 2 months, larvae of this sub-species can develop into the size required to metamorphose (>45 mm snout-vent length) into terrestrial adults; in the San Rafael Valley, however, because many of the sites hold water year-long, larvae often do not metamorphose as quickly as this, or they develop into branchiate adults instead of metamorphosing (USFWS 2002). In some cases, branchiate adults can metamorphose into terrestrial morphs if their pond starts to dry up, but these individuals often do not successfully complete metamorphosis (USFWS 2002).

The timing of metamorphosis in tiger salamanders in high elevations of the Rocky Mountains was related to the temperature of the water (Bizer 1978 as cited in Degenhardt and others1996). | 1 |
| 3. Mismatch potential | What is the separation in time or space between cues that initiate activities and discrete events that provide critical resources? | Individuals are non-migratory. Cues and critical resources (e.g., food) expected to be closely related in time and space. | -1 |
| 4. Resilience to timing mismatches during breeding | Does this species employ strategies or have traits that increase the likelihood of reproduction co-occurring with important events? | This sub-species has been known to breed as early as January and as late as early May; rarely breed after monsoon rains in July and August (USFWS 2002). Breeding season is short in tiger salamanders, and males typically arrive at ponds before females (Degenhardt and others 1996). Allison and others (1994) reported an opportunistic second breeding attempt in *A. t. nebulosum* following the drying and re-filling of a lake in late summer. Not clear that this pattern is typical in either sub-species. | 1 |

Biotic interactions: Sonoran tiger salamander (*Ambystoma tigrinum stebbinsi*)			
Trait/Quality	**Question**	**Background info. & explanation of score**	**Points**
1. Food resources	Are important food resources for this species expected to change?	Tiger salamander larvae are size-selective feeders (being gape-limited) but are generalists, consuming zooplankton, ostracods, aquatic insect larvae and adults, mollusks, oligochaetes, leeches, crayfish, anuran tadpoles, small fish, and in the case of cannibalistic morph, conspecifics (references in Lannoo and Phillips 2005). The diet of neotenic adults typically is similar to that of large larvae (references in Lannoo and Phillips 2005). Terrestrial adults consume a variety of invertebrates associated with soil and soil surfaces, such as annelids and insects (larvae and adults); also reported to consume small vertebrates (e.g., field mice, lizards). Non-breeding terrestrial adults may forage in wetlands lacking fish (Lannoo and Phillips 2005). Overall, tiger salamanders consume a variety of prey.	0
2. Predators	Are important predator populations expected to change?	Tiger salamanders have a variety of predators (predators consume eggs, larvae, and adults, see references in Lannoo and Phillips 2005), including caddis flies, dragonfly naiads, predaceous diving beetles, giant water bugs, newts, salamanders, snakes, a wide range of birds, and a variety of mammals (e.g., bobcats, raccoons, and coyotes). Predation occurs despite terrestrial individuals producing secretions along the dorsal surface of the tail that contain neurotoxins. Neotenic adults tend to require fishless water sources (Lannoo and Phillips 2005). In San Rafael Valley, exotic fish tend to eliminate salamanders (Collins and others 1988). Bullfrogs were introduced into the SRV; bullfrog larvae may eat eggs of tiger salamanders, and adult bullfrogs may prey on larval salamanders (Collins and others 1988). USFWS (2002) indicated that many ponds in San Rafael Valley have not maintained consistently high densities of bullfrogs and their effect on this sub-species is unclear. Overall, there is a suite of predators.	0
3. Symbionts	Are populations of symbiotic species expected to change?	No information found to indicate existence of important symbionts.	0
4. Disease	Is prevalence of diseases known to cause widespread mortality or reproductive failure in this species expected to change?	Disease is considered one of the biggest threats to this sub-species (Brooks and Rorabaugh 1997). Collins and others (1988) reported mortality from an undiagnosed disease whose symptoms were similar to *Aeromonas* spp. infection (red leg disease) that killed all aquatic individuals in at least three sites in the San Rafael Valley in 1985. Epizootics are not uncommon in tiger salamanders, including this sub-species (Jancovich and others 1997). Further study identified a virus as the primary pathogen involved in epizootics, and was named ATV (*Ambystoma tigrinum* virus; Jancovich and others 1997). The virus is highly infectious. Recolonization following die-offs has been observed in the San Rafael Valley. Little information found on triggers for epizootics involving this virus. Chytrid fungal infections known to occur in this sub-species although minimal symptoms were observed in many individuals of this sub-species during a laboratory study (Davidson and others 2003). There is conflicting evidence about whether changes in climate are affecting susceptibility of amphibians to chytrid fungal infections (Lips and others 2008). Recurring mass mortality of tiger salamanders has been observed in an oligotrophic lake in Utah with the proximate cause of death caused by epizoic bacteria (*Acinetobacter* spp.; Worthylake and Hovingh 1989). The authors suggested that high bacteria levels seemed likely due to high levels of nitrogen from atmospheric sources and from sheep. Stress can induce outbreaks of red-leg disease in tiger salamanders;	0

Biotic interactions: Sonoran tiger salamander (*Ambystoma tigrinum stebbinsi*)			
Trait/Quality	Question	Background info. & explanation of score	Points
		e.g., heavy siltation of a pond associated with a nearby construction project leading to zooplankton crash was thought to be related to the only outbreak of this disease noted in a population in the Midwest (Lannoo and Phillips 2006). Parasitic nematodes occur in tiger salamanders (Lannoo and Phillips 2005). Leeches can infect some populations of tiger salamanders; effects of leeches on *Ambyostoma tigrinum nebulosum* were unclear, although they have been reported to cause significant mortality in larvae in other amphibian populations (Holomuzki 1986). Not clear that climate change would directly increase widespread mortality from diseases.	
5. Competitors	Are populations of important competing species expected to change?	Other sub-species that occur in Arizona are the Arizona tiger salamander (*A. t. nebulosum*) and the barred tiger salamander (*A. t. mavortium*). Storfer and others (2004) conducted a genetic study to evaluate whether these two sub-species might have been introduced into the range of *A. t. stebbinsi*. The results suggested that introgression from introduced *A. t. mavortium* may be altering the gene pool of *A. t. stebbinsi*. Not clear that climate change would increase competition of this sub-species with other sub-species.	0

Literature Cited

Allison, L.J., P.E. Brunkow, and J.P. Collins. 1994. Opportunistic breeding after summer rains by Arizona tiger salamanders. Great Basin Naturalist 54:376-379.

Brooks, A., and J. Rorabaugh. 1997. 50 CFR Part 17. Endangered and threatened wildlife and plants: Determination of endangered status for three wetland species found in southern Arizona and northern Sonora, Mexico. Federal Register Volume 62, Number 3: 665-689.

Carey, C., and M.A. Alexander 2003. Climate change and amphibian declines: Is there a link? Diversity and Distributions 9: 111-121.

Church, D. R., L.L. Bailey, H.M. Wilbur, W.L. Kendall, and J. E. Hines. 2007. Iteroparity in the variable environment of the salamander *Ambystoma tigrinum*. Ecology 88: 891-903.

Collins, J.P., T.R. Jones, and H.J. Berna. 1988. Conserving genetically distinctive populations: The case of the Huachuca tiger salamander (*Ambystoma tigrinum stebbinsi* Lowe). In: Szaro, R.C., K.C. Severson, and D.R. Patten, eds. Management of amphibians, reptiles, and small mammals in North America. Fort Collins, CO: USDA Forest Service GTR-RM-166: 43-53.

Davidson, E.W., M. Parris, J.P. Collins, J.E. Longcore, A.P. Pessier, and J. Brunner. 2003. Pathogenicity and transmission of chyrtridiomycosis in tiger salamanders (Ambystoma tigrinum). Copeia 2003:601-607.

Degenhardt, W. G., C. W. Painter, and A.H. Price. 1996. Amphibians and reptiles of New Mexico. Albuquerque: University of New Mexico Press. 431 p.

Holomuzki, J.R. 1986. Effect of microhabitat on fitness components of larva tiger salamanders, *Ambystoma tigrinum nebulosum*. Oecologia 71:142-148.

Jancovich, J. K., E. W. Davidson, J. F. Morado, B. L. Jacobs, and J. P. Collins. 1997. Isolation of a lethal virus from the endangered tiger salamander, Ambystoma tigrinum stebbinsi Lowe. Diseases of Aquatic Organisms 31: 161-167.

Lannoo, M.J., and C.A. Phillips. 2005. Tiger salamander. In: Lannoo, M., ed. Amphibian declines: The conservation status of United States species. Berkeley: University of California Press: 636-639. Species accounts also available: http://amphibiaweb.org/index.html.

Lips, K.R., J. Diffendorfer, J.R. Mendelson, III, and M.W. Sears. 2008. Riding the wave: Reconciling the roles of disease and climate change in amphibian declines. PLoS Biology 6:e72. doi:10.1371/journal.pbio.0060072.

Manolakou, P., G. Lavranos, and R. Angelopoulou. 2006. Molecular patterns of sex determination in the animal kingdom: A comparative study of the biology of reproduction. Reproductive Biology and Endocrinology 4: 59.

Storfer, A., S.G. Mech, M.W. Reudink, R.E. Ziemba, J. Warren, and J.P. Collins. 2004. Evidence for introgression in the endangered Sonora tiger salamander, *Ambystoma tigrinum stebbinsi* (Lowe). Copeia 4: 783-796.

U.S. Fish and Wildlife Service [USFWS]. 2002. Sonora tiger salamander (*Ambystoma tigrinum stebbinsi*) recovery plan. Phoenix, AZ: U.S. Fish and Wildlife Service. iv + 67 p.

U.S. Forest Service [USFS]. 2009. Draft Coronado National Forest ecological sustainability report. Tucson, AZ: U.S. Department of Agriculture, Forest Service. Available: http://www.fs.fed.us/r3/coronado/plan-revision/documents/final/cnf-ecological-sustainability-report-final-022009.pdf.

Vitt, L.J., and J.P. Caldwell. 2009. Herpetology. Oxford, United Kingdom: Elsevier. 697 p.

Worthylake, K.M., and P. Hovingh. 1989. Mass mortality of salamanders (*Ambystoma tigrinum*) by bacteria (*Acinetobacter*) in an oligotrophic seepage mountain lake. Great Basin Naturalist 49:364-372.

Habitat: American bullfrog (*Rana catesbeiana*)			
Trait/Quality	**Question**	**Background info. & explanation of score**	**Points**
1. Area and distribution: *breeding*	Is the area or location of the associated vegetation type used for breeding activities by this species expected to change?	This species is widespread across North America, although introduced in the western part of the continent (Casper and Hendricks 2005). Bullfrogs breed in permanent bodies of water, in shallow areas with vegetation. Adult bullfrogs are mostly aquatic and prefer warm, still-water habitats but also occupy shorelines of lakes and streams. In New Mexico, generally occurs below 2100 m (Degenhardt and others 1996). This species occurs, or potential habitat exists for this species, on all 12 of the EMAs on CNF (Jones, personal communication). Projections of suitable climate for vegetation communities on all EMAs combined (Chapter 1) predict declines in suitable climate for all plant community types, with the exception of increases of suitable climate for semi-desert grassland, and small increases in Sonoran desert scrub (present in small amounts on the CNF). Permanent water sources are expected to decline with projected conditions.	2
2. Area and distribution: *non-breeding*	Is the area or location of the associated vegetation type used for non-breeding activities by this species expected to change?	Same as above (Habitat, Question 1).	2
3. Habitat components: *breeding*	Are specific habitat components required for breeding expected to change?	Breeds in permanent water including ponds, lakes, rivers, and irrigation ponds. Some variation in metamorphosis duration and also some use of temporary ponds (Bury and Whelan 1984 as cited in Casper and Hendricks 2005). Permanent water sources are expected to decline with projected conditions.	1

Habitat: American bullfrog (*Rana catesbeiana*)			
Trait/Quality	**Question**	**Background info. & explanation of score**	**Points**
4. Habitat components: *non-breeding*	Are specific habitat components required for survival during non-breeding periods expected to change?	Winter hibernation usually takes place under water (Treanor and Nichola 1972 as cited in Casper and Hendricks 2005). Record of a bullfrog found in winter under leaf litter in a soil pocket in Michigan (Bohnsack 1952 as cited in Casper and Hendricks 2005). A radiotelemetry study in Ohio in winter of 6 individuals found 5 over-wintering in relatively shallow areas in the corners of ponds and one frog 1-2 m from a pond (Stinner and others 1994). Of the 208 times frogs were located, they were submerged in each case (Stinner and others 1994). Permanent water sources are expected to decline with projected conditions.	1
5. Habitat quality and reproduction	Are features of the habitat associated with better reproductive success expected to change?	Embryo mortality occurs when water temperatures exceed 32° C (Howard 1978b as cited in Casper and Hendricks 2005), but we assumed that water in most ponds rarely, if ever, gets this hot. Tadpoles prefer warm waters (24-30 °C; Brattstrom 1962b as cited in Casper and Hendricks 2005) but move into deep water until just before metamorphosis; avoid predators by seeking cover. Water temperature might increase due to increased air temperatures, which could favor tadpole development.	-1
6. Habitat quality and survival	Are features of the habitat associated with better survival expected to change?	Some sources cited need for deep water for hibernation (Degenhardt and others 1996), but have also been found in shallow water. Some reductions in water depth may be expected, but unknown connection between water depth (and changes to water depth) and winter survival.	0
7. Ability to colonize new areas	What is this species' capacity and tendency to disperse?	Movement over land occurs on warm, rainy nights; this includes adults as well as dispersing of newly metamorphosed individuals (see references in Casper and Hendricks 2005). Can move up to 159 m in one night and has been found at isolated temporary ponds (Degenhardt and others 1996). In New York, a mean movement of 402 m and maximum movement of 1600 m was observed (Ingram and Raney 1943 as cited in Casper and Hendricks 2005). While low rainfall may reduce dispersal to new areas, we assumed it will be sufficient to allow dispersal, at least in some years. Although our sources did not suggest that there is sex-biased dispersal in this species, we considered this species "mobile," though not "very mobile" relative to organisms that fly (e.g., birds and bats) and larger mammals, hence the score of "0."	0
8. Migratory or transitional habitats	Does this species require additional habitats during migration that are separated from breeding and non-breeding habitats?	Seasonal movements are considered limited and transitional habitats not required.	0

Physiology: American bullfrog (*Rana catesbeiana*)			
Trait/Quality	**Question**	**Background info. & explanation of score**	**Points**
1. Physiological thresholds	Are limiting physiological conditions expected to change?	Embryo mortality occurs when water temperatures exceed 32 °C (Howard 1978b as cited in Casper and Hendricks 2005), but we assumed that water in most ponds rarely, if ever, gets this hot. We assumed that water temperature will not exceed thresholds. Standing water expected to become less available, but this is covered in Habitat section.	0

Physiology: American bullfrog (*Rana catesbeiana*)

Trait/Quality	Question	Background info. & explanation of score	Points
2. Sex ratio	Is sex ratio determined by temperature?	No information in Casper and Hendricks (2005) to indicate temperature-dependent sex determination. Vitt and Caldwell (2009) indicated that frogs do not experience temperature-dependent sex determination.	0
3. Exposure to extreme weather conditions	Are extreme weather or disturbance events that result in direct mortality or reproductive failure expected to change?	Individuals occupying edges of streams may be exposed to increased flooding in spring (proportionally greater streamflow in winter and early spring as snow melts earlier), which could increase mortality. No information in Casper and Hendricks (2005) to indicate that direct mortality from flooding has been a problem to date. Since this species is aquatic, not likely to be seriously affected by temperatures associated with heat waves.	1
4. Limitations to active period	Are projected temperature or precipitation regimes that influence activity period of species expected to change?	Association with water suggests that activity period will not be limited as long as water is present. Movements occur on warm nights when rainy; possible that reduced precipitation will affect summer monsoonal rains to the point of limiting movements post-metamorphosis.	1
5. Metabolic inhibition	Does this species possess an ability to reduce metabolic energy or water requirements?	Cycles of dormancy are common in amphibians and reptiles, and hibernation is most likely primarily a response to cold temperatures and less so to a change in resource availability (Vitt and Caldwell 2009). While hibernating, activity mostly ceases, body temperature depends on temperature of the hibernation site, and physiological processes are reduced. Bullfrogs are not tolerant of freezing conditions (Casper and Hendricks 2005). A study in Missouri reported that adults become torpid before frost occurs and juveniles remain active until freezing temperatures occur (Willis and others 1956). In contrast, Stinner and others (1994) suggested that bullfrogs in Ohio in winter remain active in winter and prefer warm, relatively shallow water. See also Habitat, Questions 4 and 6. Not clear whether this species would hibernate in areas where freezing or near-freezing temperatures do not occur regularly (e.g., low elevations in Arizona). Overall, scored as "0" (neutral) to account for this species occurring in waters where it does go torpid in winter.	0
6. Survival during resource limitation	Does this species have lower energy requirements or possess the capacity to store energy or water in the long term?	Ectotherm.	–1
7. Variable life history	Does this species have alternative life history strategies to cope with variable resources or climate conditions?	The time to metamorphosis from tadpole to juvenile is negatively correlated with the average length of the frost-free period (references in Casper and Hendricks 2005). Low water temperatures during development have been associated with increased time to metamorphosis (references in Collins 1979). Based on this, considered possible that bullfrogs at higher elevations currently take longer to metamorphose than bullfrogs at lower elevations. With increased temperatures tadpoles where water temperature is a limiting factor would be expected to metamorphose in a shorter period of time in the future. Yearling males do not maintain territories when male-male competition is intense and instead attempt to intercept females	–1

Physiology: American bullfrog (*Rana catesbeiana*)

Trait/Quality	Question	Background info. & explanation of score	Points
		attracted to larger males (Howard 1984). No known relationship between these strategies and climate.	
8. Reproduction in variable environments	Can this species outlive periods where reproduction is limited?	Longevity estimated as 8-10 years (Casper and Hendricks 2005). Multi-year droughts expected, which have the potential to reduce ponds and other water sources on which this species depends dry up. Blair (1961) reported that bullfrogs declined in the late 1950s and then were extirpated when there was a severe drought and the tank under study dried up. Survival rates of tadpoles in ponds in Kentucky were 11.8-17.6% (Cecil and Just 1979).	1

Phenology: American bullfrog (*Rana catesbeiana*)

Trait/Quality	Question	Background info. & explanation of score	Points
1. Cues	Does this species use temperature or moisture cues to initiate activities related to fecundity or survival?	Amphibians, in general, respond to temperature and moisture cues in the timing of breeding (Carey and Alexander 2003). Ambient temperature strongly influences reproduction in frogs (Gibbs and Breisch 2001). Breeding occurs earlier in southern latitudes (Casper and Hendricks 2005) as for many vertebrates. In Texas, breeds from March through October (Blair 1961). In Kansas, calling begins when air temperatures are above 21 °C (Fitch 1956c as cited in Casper and Hendricks 2005). Calling season of this species in Texas corresponded more to hot summer season than other anurans, and evening calling associated with higher temperatures (Blair 1961) and individuals called after rainfall events. Adults tend to remain inactive until water temperatures reach 15 °C (Harding 1977 as cited in Casper and Hendricks 2005).	1
2. Event timing	Are activities related to species' fecundity or survival tied to discrete events that are expected to change?	Species uses still water for breeding. Changes to timing of peak flow in spring could alter the timing of when still waters are achieved in the spring. On the other hand, breeding may occur earlier due to temperature rises, as breeding activity is associated with temperature and rainfall (see Phenology, Question 1).	1
3. Mismatch potential	What is the separation in time or space between cues that initiate activities and discrete events that provide critical resources?	Cues and critical resources (e.g., food) expected to be closely related in time and space.	-1
4. Resilience to timing mismatches during breeding	Does this species employ strategies or have traits that increase the likelihood of reproduction co-occurring with important events?	Double clutching has been observed in Michigan (Emlen 1977 as cited in Casper and Hendricks 2005) and expected to occur elsewhere, particularly in southern latitudes. Older females may produce two clutches per year (Howard 1978b as cited in Casper and Hendricks 2005). Reproductive period is prolonged as there is large variation in date of sexually receptivity for individual females and males remain reproductively active (Degenhardt and others 1996).	-1

Biotic interactions: American bullfrog (*Rana catesbeiana*)

Trait/Quality	Question	Background info. & explanation of score	Points
1. Food resources	Are important food resources for this species expected to change?	An opportunistic predator; preys on almost any animal it can capture (smaller than it) including conspecifics (Casper and Hendricks 2005). Consumes invertebrates, snakes, rodents, frogs, and salamanders. Often eats beetles and snails in New Mexico (Degenhardt and others 1996).	0
2. Predators	Are important predator populations expected to change?	Various predators. Tadpoles relatively unpalatable to fish (references in Casper and Hendricks 2005). Tadpoles eaten by salamanders, other frogs, turtles, snakes, birds, mammals, as well as adult bullfrogs (Casper and Hendricks 2005).	0
3. Symbionts	Are populations of symbiotic species expected to change?	No known symbionts.	0
4. Disease	Is prevalence of diseases known to cause widespread mortality or reproductive failure in this species expected to change?	Chytridiomycosis is a disease associated with amphibian declines. Laboratory studies suggest that bullfrogs are an efficient carrier of the pathogen (although they appear to be resistant to clinical effects of the disease (Daszak and others 2004). Conflicting evidence about whether changes in climate are affecting susceptibility of amphibians to chytrid fungal infections (Lips and others 2008).	0
5. Competitors	Are populations of important competing species expected to change?	Bullfrog tadpoles have been shown to out-compete native tadpoles such as yellow-legged frog (*Rana boylii*) and Pacific tree frogs (*Hyla regilla*) in California (Kupferberg 1997). No known major competitors.	0

Literature Cited

Blair, W.F. 1961. Calling and spawning seasons in a mixed population of anurans. Ecology 42:99-110.

Carey, C., and M.A. Alexander 2003. Climate change and amphibian declines: Is there a link? Diversity and Distributions 9:111-121.

Casper, G.S. and R. Hendricks. 2005. American Bullfrog. In: Lannoo, M., ed. Amphibian declines: The conservation status of United States species. Berkeley: University of California Press: 540-546. Species accounts also available: http://amphibiaweb.org/index html.

Cecil, S.G., and J.J. Just. 1979. Survival rate, population density and development of a naturally occurring anuran larvae (*Rana catesbeiana*). Copeia 3:447-453.

Collins, J.P. 1979. Intrapopulation variation in the body size at metamorphosis and timing of metamorphosis in the bullfrog, *Rana catesbeiana*. Ecology 60:738-749.

Daszak, P., A. Strieby, A.A. Cunningham, J.E. Longcore, C.C. Brown, and D. Porter. 2004. Experimental evidence that the bullfrog (*Rana catesbeiana*) is a potential carrier of chytridiomycosis, an emerging fungal disease of amphibians. Herpetological Journal 14:201-207.

Degenhardt, W.G., C.W. Painter, and A.H. Price. 1996. Amphibians and reptiles of New Mexico. Albuquerque: University of New Mexico Press. 431 p.

Gibbs, J.P., and A.R. Breisch. 2001. Climate warming and calling phenology of frogs near Ithaca, New York, 1900-1999. Conservation Biology 15:1175-1178.

Howard, R. 1984. Alternative mating behaviors of young male bullfrogs. American Zoologist 24:397-406.

Jones, Larry. 2010. [Personal communication]. February 17, 2010. Tucson, AZ: U.S. Department of Agriculture, Forest Service, Coronado National Forest, Assistant Program Manager for Wildlife, Fish, and Rare Plants.

Kupferberg, S. 1997. Bullfrog (*Rana catesbeiana*) invasion of a California river: The role of larval competition. Ecology 78:1736-1751.

Lips, K.R., J. Diffendorfer, J.R. Mendelson. III, and M.W. Sears. 2008. Riding the wave: Reconciling the roles of disease and climate change in amphibian declines. PLoS Biology 6:e72. doi:10.1371/journal.pbio.0060072.

Manolakou, P., G. Lavranos, and R. Angelopoulou. 2006. Molecular patterns of sex determination in the animal kingdom: A comparative study of the biology of reproduction. Reproductive Biology and Endocrinology 4:59.

Stinner, J., N. Zarlinga, and S. Orcutt. 1994. Overwintering behavior of adult bullfrogs, *Rana catesbeiana*, in northeastern Ohio. Ohio Journal of Science 94:8-13.

U.S. Forest Service [USFS]. 2009. Draft Coronado National Forest ecological sustainability report. Tucson, AZ: U.S. Department of Agriculture, Forest Service. Available: http://www.fs fed.us/r3/coronado/plan-revision/documents/final/cnf-ecological-sustainability-report-final-022009.pdf.

Vitt, L.J., and J.P. Caldwell. 2009. Herpetology. Oxford, United Kingdom: Elsevier. 697 p.

Willis, Y.L., D.L. Moyle, and T.S. Baskett. 1956. Emergence, breeding, hibernation, movements, and transformation of the bullfrog, *Rana catesbeiana*, in Missouri. Copeia 1:30-41.

Habitat: Chiricahua leopard frog (*Rana chiricahuensis*)			
Trait/Quality	Question	Background info. & explanation of score	Points
1. Area and distribution: *breeding*	Is the area or location of the associated vegetation type used for breeding activities by this species expected to change?	Occurs in Arizona, New Mexico, and Mexico (Platz and Mecham 1979). Found chiefly in oak, mixed oak, and pine woodlands and pine forests; ranges into chaparral, grassland, and even desert (Stebbins 1985). Distribution of species is fragmented by aridity (Mecham 1968c as cited in Sredl and Jennings 2005). Elevational range is 1000-2710 m (Platz and Mecham 1979). Breeds in still waters in a range of natural and human-created systems (multiple references in Sredl and Jennings [2005]; see Habitat, Question 3). At thermal springs in New Mexico this species had prolonged annual activity including year-round activity at one site and including winter breeding (Scott and Jennings 1985). This species occurs, or potential habitat exists for this species, on seven of the EMAs on CNF: Peloncillo, Chiricahua, Dragoon, Tumacacori, Santa Rita, Huachuca, and Galiuro (USFS 2009). Projections of suitable climate for vegetation communities on all EMAs combined (Chapter 1) predicted declines in suitable climate for all plant community types, with the exception of increases of suitable climate for semi-desert grassland and small increases in Sonoran desert scrub (present in small amounts on the CNF). Riparian and forested habitats predicted to decline due to decreased stream flows on average, increased aridity, and increased fire risk.	2
2. Area and distribution: *non-breeding*	Is the area or location of the associated vegetation type used for non-breeding activities by this species expected to change?	Individuals likely over-winter near breeding sites, but information about locations of hibernation areas not well known (Sredl and Jennings 2005). Generally considered a habitat generalist (Sredl and Jennings 2005). Juvenile habitat not well studied, but in a closely-related species, *Rana yavapaiensis*, juveniles were more frequently found in small ponds and marshy areas, whereas adults were more often associated with large pools (Sredl 1994 as cited in Sredl and Jennings 2005). Adult habitat ranges from perennial to near-perennial (Sredl and Jennings 2005). Not known how this species survives loss of surface water, but other species of leopard frog in the Southwest have been observed burrowing into cracks in the mud (Howland and others 1997 as cited in Sredl and Jennings 2005).	2

Habitat: Chiricahua leopard frog (*Rana chiricahuensis*)

Trait/Quality	Question	Background info. & explanation of score	Points
		Predicted changes in habitat considered same as for breeding habitat; see Habitat, Question 1.	
3. Habitat components: *breeding*	Are specific habitat components required for breeding expected to change?	Requires water for breeding (Sredl and Jennings 2005). Breeding areas include rivers, permanent streams and pools, intermittent streams, wetlands, and springs. Also observed in earthen tanks and drinkers (for livestock), wells, abandoned swimming pools, backyard ponds, etc. (Sredl and Jennings 2005). Shallow water with emergent and perimeter vegetation provide adult and tadpole basking areas; deeper water, root masses, and undercut banks offer refuge from predators and may offer hibernacula (unpublished data cited in Sredl and Jennings 2005). Important breeding areas include those with few predators (fish, bullfrogs, and crayfish). Some studies have found frogs and eggs masses to be most abundant in areas with warmer water (Jennings 1988, 1990 as cited in Sredl and Jennings 2005). Thermal springs in New Mexico provide winter breeding opportunities (Sredl and Jennings 2005). Unclear how much water temperature in southern Arizona streams would increase. Potential for water during breeding season to be reduced we considered a larger impact than potential increased suitability for breeding by increase in water temperature.	1
4. Habitat components: *non-breeding*	Are specific habitat components required for survival during non-breeding periods expected to change?	See Habitat, Question 3. Reduced precipitation could reduce ability to survive during non-breeding season.	1
5. Habitat quality and reproduction	Are features of the habitat associated with better reproductive success expected to change?	Little information.	0
6. Habitat quality and survival	Are features of the habitat associated with better survival expected to change?	Year-round water supply, areas with undercut banks for escape from predation and potential hibernacula (Sredl and Jennings 2005).	1
7. Ability to colonize new areas	What is this species' capacity and tendency to disperse?	Male home ranges have been estimated at 161 m^2 and 357 m^2 in the dry and wet seasons, respectively (unpublished data in Sredl and Jennings 2005). One male moved 3.5 km in one direction over a 2-month period. Overall, considered to have a low ability to disperse given small home range and given absence of data suggesting this species consistently moves long distances.	1
8. Migratory or transitional habitats	Does this species require additional habitats during migration that are separated from breeding and non-breeding habitats?	Unlike some other amphibians, breeding migrations have not been noted in this species (Sredl and Jennings 2005). Maintaining corridors for dispersal of juveniles and adults may be critical to preserving populations (Jennings and Scott 1991 as cited in Sredl and Jennings 2005), but we considered this beyond the scope of this question.	0

Physiology: Chiricahua leopard frog (*Rana chiricahuensis*)			
Trait/Quality	Question	Background info. & explanation of score	Points
1. Physiological thresholds	Are physiological thresholds related to temperature or moisture expected to change?	Decrease in precipitation and increased evaporation (due to increased temperatures) may reduce the amount of moisture available for this species to survive during over-wintering periods (increases probability of desiccation). We assumed that water temperature will not exceed thresholds. Standing water expected to become less available, but this is covered in Habitat section above.	1
2. Sex ratio	Is sex ratio determined by temperature?	Vitt and Caldwell (2009) indicated that frogs do not experience temperature-dependent sex determination.	0
3. Exposure to extreme weather conditions	Are extreme weather or disturbance events that result in direct mortality or reproductive failure expected to change?	Individuals occupying edges of streams may be exposed to increased flooding (proportionally greater streamflow in winter and early spring as snow melts earlier) which could increase mortality. Since this species is aquatic, not likely to be seriously affected by air temperatures associated with short-term heat waves.	1
4. Limitations to active period	Are projected temperature or precipitation regimes that influence activity period of species expected to change?	Adult habitat ranges from perennial to near-perennial (Sredl and Jennings 2005); not known how this species survives loss of surface water (other species of leopard frog in the Southwest have been observed burrowing into cracks in the mud [Howland and others 1997 as cited in Sredl and Jennings 2005]). Thus, reduced precipitation could reduce activity periods through increased aridity of the environment.	1
5. Metabolic inhibition	Does this species possess an ability to reduce metabolic energy or water requirements?	Cycles of dormancy are common in amphibians and reptiles, and hibernation is most likely primarily a response to cold temperatures more than to a change in resource availability (Vitt and Caldwell 2009). While hibernating, activity mostly ceases, body temperature depends on temperature of the hibernation site, and physiological processes are reduced. Post-metamorphic individuals are generally not active November-February, although few studies have been conducted on wintertime activity (Sredl and Jennings 2005). Individuals likely over-winter near breeding sites but information about locations of hibernation areas not well known (Sredl and Jennings 2005). Considered possible that hibernacula would be exposed to increased temperatures (thus, score of "1").	1
6. Survival during resource limitation	Does this species have lower energy requirements or possess the capacity to store energy or water in the long term?	None. Ectotherm.	-1
7. Variable life history	Does this species have alternative life history strategies to cope with variable resources or climate conditions?	Frogs have tadpole stage, but this is not considered a benefit since water is also required for this stage.	0
8. Reproduction	Can this species outlive periods	Multi-year droughts are projected. Preliminary estimates suggest that individuals can live as long as 6 years (Durkin 1995 as cited in Sredl	1

Physiology: Chiricahua leopard frog (*Rana chiricahuensis*)			
Trait/Quality	Question	Background info. & explanation of score	Points
in variable environments	where reproduction is limited?	and Jennings 2005), although most individuals expected to live shorter periods than this. In 2002/2003 surveys, Jones and Sredl (2005) observed apparent local extirpations that coincided with a drought that began in 1996/1997 at a large numbers of sites.	

Phenology: Chiricahua leopard frog (*Rana chiricahuensis*)			
Trait/Quality	Question	Background info. & explanation of score	Points
1. Cues	Does this species use temperature or moisture cues to initiate activities related to fecundity or survival?	Amphibians in general respond to temperature and moisture cues in the timing of breeding (Carey and Alexander 2003). Ambient temperature strongly influences reproduction in frogs (Gibbs and Breisch 2001). Proximate cues that stimulate mating are not well studied in this species (Sredl and Jennings 2005). One unpublished report on a closely related species, *Rana subaquavocalis* (Platz 1997 as cited in Sredl and Jennings 2005) indicated that oviposition appeared to be correlated with changes in water temperature and not precipitation.	1
2. Event timing	Are activities related to species' fecundity or survival tied to discrete events that are expected to change?	Species requires still water for breeding. Changes to timing in peak flow in spring flow (earlier peak flow) and timing of rise in water temperatures likely to change.	1
3. Mismatch potential	What is the separation in time or space between cues that initiate activities and discrete events that provide critical resources?	Species is non-migratory. Resources are closely timed.	-1
4. Resilience to timing mismatches during breeding	Does this species employ strategies or have traits that increase the likelihood of reproduction co-occurring with important events?	Egg masses have been reported in all months except November, December, and January (references in Sredl and Jennings 2005). Egg-laying in this species in Arizona and New Mexico appears to differ according to elevation of occupied habitat; during 1972-1979, populations below ~1800 m generally deposited eggs from spring to late summer (most before June), whereas those above 1800 m laid in June, July, and August (Frost and Platz 1983).	-1

Biotic interactions: Chiricahua leopard frog (*Rana chiricahuensis*)			
Trait/Quality	Question	Background info. & explanation of score	Points
1. Food resources	Are important food resources for this species expected to change?	No comprehensive study of diet of larval or adult forms has been conducted (Sredl and Jennings 2005). Larvae are herbivorous; adults likely eat a diverse array of insects (Degenhardt and others 1996 as cited in Sredl and Jennings 2005). Analyses of stomach contents showed invertebrates and vertebrates (fish, conspecific and heterospecific frogs, and birds; Stebbins 1951 as cited in Sredl and Jennings 2005).	0

Biotic interactions: Chiricahua leopard frog (*Rana chiricahuensis*)			
Trait/Quality	**Question**	**Background info. & explanation of score**	**Points**
2. Predators	Are important predator populations expected to change?	Detailed studies have not been conducted (Sredl and Jennings 2005). Considered likely that tadpoles are preyed upon by aquatic insects and vertebrates (birds, snakes, and non-native fish). Juvenile and adult frogs likely preyed upon by fish (native and non-native), American bullfrogs, gartersnakes, birds, and a variety of mammals (Sredl and Jennings 2005). Likely predators—giant water bugs (belostomatids) and black-necked gartersnakes (*Thamnophis cyrtopsis*)—were observed during surveys by Jones and Sredl (2005). Presence of American bullfrogs, crayfish, and predatory fish are negatively correlated with presence of this species (references in Sredl and Jennings 2005) although in New Mexico, many populations have declined in the absence of bullfrogs (Jennings and Scott 1991 as cited in Sredl and Jennings 2005). Overall, this species considered to be preyed upon by a suite of predators.	0
3. Symbionts	Are populations of symbiotic species expected to change?	No information on this species in Sredl and Jennings (2005) regarding symbiotic relationships.	0
4. Disease	Is prevalence of diseases known to cause widespread mortality or reproductive failure in this species expected to change?	Six species of trematode and one nematode were found in this species (Goldberg and others 1998b as cited in Sredl and Jennings 2005). In late 1980s, high mortality of this species in earthen cattle tanks in New Mexico was observed, including extirpation of many populations over 3 years; "post-metamorphic death syndrome" was implicated although chytrid fungus may have played a role (Sredl and Jennings 2005). Chytrid fungus is present in Arizona and many species, including this one, have been affected (Sredl and Jennings 2005). Outbreaks of the fungus have occurred during the cool season (Sredl and others 2000 as cited in Sredl and Jennings 2005). The fungus was confirmed present in populations in New Mexico that declined (Sredl and Jennings 2005). Conflicting evidence about whether changes in climate are affecting susceptibility of amphibians to chytrid fungal infections (Lips and others 2008).	0
5. Competitors	Are populations of important competing species expected to change?	Negative association with American bullfrogs (Rosen and others 1995 as cited in Sredl and Jennings 2005) considered to be predatory, not competitive. No clear relationships found regarding important competition with other species.	0

Literature Cited

Carey, C., and M.A. Alexander 2003. Climate change and amphibian declines: Is there a link? Diversity and Distributions 9:111-121.

Frost, J.S., and J.E. Platz. 1983. Comparative assessment of modes of reproductive isolation among four species of leopard frogs (*Rana pipiens* complex). Evolution 37:66-78.

Gibbs, J.P., and A.R. Breisch. 2001. Climate warming and calling phenology of frogs near Ithaca, New York, 1900-1999. Conservation Biology 15:1175-1178.

Jones, L.L.C., and M.J. Sredl. 2005. Chiricahua leopard frog status in the Galiuro Mountains, Arizona, with a monitoring framework for the species' entire range. In: Gottfried, G.J., B.S. Gebow, L.G. Eskew, C.B. Carleton, comps. Connecting mountain islands and desert seas: Biodiversity and management of the Madrean Archipelago II. Proc. RMRS-P-36. Fort Collins, CO: U.S. Department of Agriculture, Forest Service, Rocky Mountain Research Station: 88-91.

Lips, K.R., J. Diffendorfer, J.R. Mendelson, III, and M.W. Sears. 2008. Riding the wave: Reconciling the roles of disease and climate change in amphibian declines. PLoS Biology 6:e72. doi:10.1371/journal.pbio.0060072.

Manolakou, P., G. Lavranos, and R. Angelopoulou. 2006. Molecular patterns of sex determination in the animal kingdom: A comparative study of the biology of reproduction. Reproductive Biology and Endocrinology 4:59.

Platz, J.E., and J.S. Mecham. 1979. *Rana chiricahuensis*, a new species of leopard frog (*Rana pipiens* complex) from Arizona. Copeia 1979:383-390.

Scott, N.J., Jr., and R.D. Jennings. 1985. The tadpoles of five species of New Mexican leopard frogs. Museum of Southwestern Biology, Occasional Papers, Number 3. Albuquerque: University of New Mexico.

Sredl, M.J., and R.D. Jennings. 2005. Chiricahua Leopard Frogs. In: Lannoo, M., ed. Amphibian declines: The conservation status of United States species. Berkeley: University of California Press: 546-549. Species accounts also available: http://amphibiaweb.org/index html.

Stebbins, R.C. 1985. A Field Guide to Western Amphibians and Reptiles (Second edition). New York: Houghton Mifflin.

U.S. Forest Service [USFS]. 2009. Draft Coronado National Forest ecological sustainability report. Tucson, AZ: U.S. Department of Agriculture. Available: http://www fs.fed.us/r3/coronado/plan-revision/documents/final/cnf-ecological-sustainability-report-final-022009.pdf.

Vitt, L.J., and J.P. Caldwell. 2009. Herpetology. Oxford, United Kingdom: Elsevier. 697 p.

Habitat: Tarahumara frog (*Rana tarahumarae*)			
Trait/Quality	**Question**	**Background info. & explanation of score**	**Points**
1. Area and distribution: *breeding*	Is the area or location of the associated vegetation type used for breeding activities by this species expected to change?	From Rorabaugh and Hale (2005): This species is known from 63 locations in montane canyons, from southeastern Arizona, south to Mexico (parts of Sinaloa and Chihuahua). Historically, this species was known from 6 locations in the United States (3 in Santa Rita Mountains and 3 in the Atascosa-Pajarito-Tumacacori Mountains complex), but by 1983, it had been extirpated from Arizona. Declines in some sites in Mexico occurred around the same time (Rorabaugh and others 2005). Individuals were re-established in the Santa Rita Mountains in 2004 (Big Casa Blanca Canyon). Zweifel (1968) provided (historical) locality information in Arizona, all of which was within 20 km of the Mexican border; elevational range 457-1828 m (1500-6000 ft) Rorabaugh and others (2005) and Hale and May (1983) also reviewed historical locations. Breeding habitat is oak and pine-oak woodlands; juveniles appear to use same habitat as adults (references in Rorabaugh and Hale 2005). Zweifel (1955) indicated that cottonwoods and willows frequently shade pools used by this species. Large streams are generally avoided, probably due to the greater variation in flow rates and greater propensity for remaining flooded longer in spring from winter snowmelt (Hale and May 1983). This species occurs, or potential habitat exists for this species, only in the Santa Rita EMA on CNF (USFS 2009). Projections of suitable climate for vegetation communities on this EMAs (Chapter 1) predicted declines in suitable climate for Madrean forest and woodland and Madrean coniferous forest and an increase in semi-desert grassland. Riparian and woodland habitats predicted to decline due to decreased stream flows on average, increased aridity, and increased fire risk.	2
2. Area and distribution: *non-breeding*	Is the area or location of the associated vegetation type used for non-	Non-breeding habitat considered to be same as breeding habitat. See Habitat, Question 1. Hibernacula covered in Habitat, Question 4.	2

Habitat: Tarahumara frog (*Rana tarahumarae*)

Trait/Quality	Question	Background info. & explanation of score	Points
	breeding activities by this species expected to change?		
3. Habitat components: *breeding*	Are specific habitat components required for breeding expected to change?	This species has aquatic reproduction and requires a permanent water source for metamorphosis (Rorabaugh and Hale 2005). Generally breeds April-May, when permanent water is often limited to springs and pools >1 m in depth in bedrock or among boulders. Best breeding habitat are such pools with low mean flows (<0.2 cubic ft/sec and relatively steep gradients; "plunge pools"). Tadpole metamorphosis has been reported to take 2 years (Hale and May 1983); in semi-wild conditions, most took >10 months. Water sources are expected to decline.	1
4. Habitat components: *non-breeding*	Are specific habitat components required for survival during non-breeding periods expected to change?	This species requires a permanent water source for metamorphosis (Rorabaugh and Hale 2005). See also Habitat, Question 3. An important feature is the presence of hibernacula that allow individuals to remain moist and offers protection from predators and freezing temperatures; such hibernacula include moist areas around rocks or boulders along streams and at "plunge pools" (Hale and May 1983). Water sources are expected to decline.	1
5. Habitat quality and reproduction	Are features of the habitat associated with better reproductive success expected to change?	No information found.	0
6. Habitat quality and survival	Are features of the habitat associated with better survival expected to change?	Both boulder plunge pools (formed by boulders creating a barrier across a streambed) and bedrock plunge pools (formed when bedrock is exposed along the streambed) are highly favorable habitat for this species (Hale and May 1983). Climate change would not alter the abundance of boulders or bedrock; water availability covered in Habitat, Questions 3 and 4.	0
7. Ability to colonize new areas	What is this species' capacity and tendency to disperse?	Capacity to disperse appears to be low. In Big Casa Blanca Canyon in Arizona, juveniles and males reported to move <1885 m, and females <651 m and were along stream courses; authors indicated limited overland movements might have occurred (Hale and May 1983). Authors also indicated that some individuals prefer to remain in specific pools or stream reaches. Tadpoles likely are transported downstream. Hale and May (1983) documented upstream movements by most frogs during the summer rainy season; closer to autumn, frogs moved mostly downstream, although some may move upstream to reach hibernacula.	1
8. Migratory or transitional habitats	Does this species require additional habitats during migration that are separated from breeding and non-breeding habitats?	Rorabaugh and Hale (2005) indicated it is unknown if this species undertakes breeding migrations. Seasonal short-distance movements documented in Hale and May (2003). In Big Casa Blanca Canyon in Arizona, juveniles and males reported to move <1885 m, and females <651 m along stream courses (Hale and May 1983). See also Habitat, Question 7 for additional information.	0

Physiology: Tarahumara frog (*Rana tarahumarae*)			
Trait/Quality	**Question**	**Background info. & explanation of score**	**Points**
1. Physiological thresholds	Are limiting physiological conditions expected to change?	Decrease in precipitation and increased evaporation (due to increased temperatures) may reduce the amount of moisture available for this species to survive during over-wintering periods (increases probability of desiccation). We assumed that water temperature will not exceed thresholds. Standing water expected to become less available, but this is covered in Habitat section.	1
2. Sex ratio	Is sex ratio determined by temperature?	No information in Rorabaugh and Hale (2005) to indicate this occurs in *Rana tarahumarae*. Vitt and Caldwell (2009) indicated that frogs do not experience temperature-dependent sex determination.	0
3. Exposure to extreme weather conditions	Are extreme weather or disturbance events that result in direct mortality or reproductive failure expected to change?	Individuals occupying stream edges may be exposed to increased flooding (proportionally greater streamflow in winter and early spring as snow melts earlier) which could increase mortality. Since this species is aquatic, not likely to be seriously affected by air temperatures associated with heat waves.	1
4. Limitations to active period	Are projected temperature or precipitation regimes that influence activity period of species expected to change?	Appears to feed nocturnally and diurnally depending on when prey species are active (Rorabaugh and Hale 2005). Rorabaugh and Hale (2005) indicated that during the dry season before the summer rains, most individuals probably reside in plunge pools to avoid desiccation. But the authors indicated that Hale and May (1983) suggested that this species may aestivate during this period. Reduced precipitation could reduce the length of seasonal activity periods by reducing water depth in plunge pools and leading to earlier retreats to hibernacula.	1
5. Metabolic inhibition	Does this species possess an ability to reduce metabolic energy or water requirements?	Cycles of dormancy are common in amphibians and reptiles, and hibernation is most likely primarily a response to cold temperatures more than to a change in resource availability (Vitt and Caldwell 2009). While hibernating, activity mostly ceases, body temperature depends on temperature of the hibernation site, and physiological processes are reduced. In Big Casa Blanca Canyon, this species was not active in February when water temperatures were ~8 °C; when water temperatures averaged ~15 °C many frogs were active (Hale and May 1983). Authors indicated that they appear to hibernate very near the water line, "perhaps in air pockets behind partially submerged boulders near pools." Boulder plunge pool habitat offers places for frogs to retreat during periods of cold weather (Hale and May 1983). During the dry season, although some frogs may aestivate, most congregate in pools that have not gone dry. Given that many individuals appear to over-winter in areas that do not appear to be largely protected from temperature fluctuations as would underwater burrowing into mud, considered possible that hibernacula would be exposed to increased temperatures (thus, score of "1").	1
6. Survival during resource limitation	Does this species have lower energy requirements or possess the capacity to store energy or water in the long term?	Ectotherm.	-1

Physiology: Tarahumara frog (*Rana tarahumarae*)

Trait/Quality	Question	Background info. & explanation of score	Points
7. Variable life history	Does this species have alternative life history strategies to cope with variable resources or climate conditions?	Frogs have a tadpole stage, but this is not considered a benefit since water is required for this stage.	0
8. Reproduction in variable environments	Can this species outlive periods where reproduction is limited?	Hale and May (1983) estimated that the oldest frogs in Big Casa Blanca Canyon (Arizona) were 6 years post-metamorphosis at the least. Larvae take 2 years to complete metamorphosis (Hale and May 1983). Periods of extreme reductions in rainfall may last 5 years, which can reduce ponds and other water sources on which this species depends. If these conditions eliminate breeding, most of the population would not survive longer than the periods of limited reproduction.	1

Phenology: Tarahumara frog (*Rana tarahumarae*)

Trait/Quality	Question	Background info. & explanation of score	Points
1. Cues	Does this species use temperature or moisture cues to initiate activities related to fecundity or survival?	Amphibians, in general, respond to temperature and moisture cues in the timing of breeding (Carey and Alexander 2003). Ambient temperature strongly influences reproduction in frogs (Gibbs and Breisch 2001). Hale and May (1983) indicated that spring emergence is directly related to water temperatures (which vary by elevation, exposure, flow rates, and water source).	1
2. Event timing	Are activities related to species' fecundity or survival tied to discrete events that are expected to change?	Changes to timing in spring flow (earlier peak flow) and timing of rise in water temperatures likely to change.	1
3. Mismatch potential	What is the separation in time or space between cues that initiate activities and discrete events that provide critical resources?	Species is non-migratory. Cues and critical resources (e.g., food) expected to be closely related in time and space.	-1
4. Resilience to timing mismatches during breeding	Does this species employ strategies or have traits that increase the likelihood of reproduction co-occurring with important events?	Hale and May (1983) reported that amplectic frogs and egg masses were generally found from April to mid-May. Thus, the species does not appear to have a prolonged breeding period.	1

Biotic interactions: Tarahumara frog (*Rana tarahumarae*)			
Trait/Quality	**Question**	**Background info. & explanation of score**	**Points**
1. Food resources	Are important food resources for this species expected to change?	Larvae are likely omnivorous with a tendency to consume algae, as are most ranid tadpoles (Rorabaugh and Hale 2005). Adults consume a variety of prey ranging from juvenile Sonoran mud turtles, Sonora chubs, snakes, beetles, moths, water bugs, scorpions, centipedes, grasshoppers, mantids, wasps, spiders, crickets, caddis flies, and katydids (references in Zweifel 1955; Rorabaugh and Hale 2005). Appears to feed nocturnally and diurnally, depending on time that prey species are known to be active (Rorabaugh and Hale 2005). Overall, species consumes a variety of prey species.	0
2. Predators	Are important predator populations expected to change?	From Rorabaugh and Hale (2005) and references therein: Frog adults, tadpoles, and egg masses are expected to have a variety of predators including gartersnakes and other snake species, birds, frogs, salamanders, fish, invertebrates, and water bugs (*Belostoma* and *Lethocerus* genera). Non-native fish (e.g., green sunfish [*Lepomis cyanellus*], but also largemouth bass [*Micropterus salmoides*]) and American bullfrog predation may have been partly responsible for the elimination of Tarahumara frog from Pena Blanca Canyon in Arizona. Large chub species (*Gila* sp.) may have eliminated this species from one site in Mexico. Overall, preyed upon by a suite of predators.	0
3. Symbionts	Are populations of symbiotic species expected to change?	No information on this species in Rorabaugh and Hale (2005) regarding symbiotic relationships.	0
4. Disease	Is prevalence of diseases known to cause widespread mortality or reproductive failure in this species expected to change?	During a die-off in Sycamore Canyon (Arizona) in 1974, individuals of this species were collected that were infected with chytridiomycosis; the chytrid fungus has also been found in frogs collected in Mexico (Rorabaugh and Hale 2005). The fungus is considered as a possible factor involved in the extirpation of this species in Arizona (Hale and others 2005); these authors consider that cold may play a role in creating stress for frogs that may make them more susceptible to infection. Other factors considered to have potentially contributed to the extirpation of this species in Arizona are: heavy metal poisoning (acid rain from copper smelters may have mobilized naturally-occurring metals in streamside deposits into the water), predation, competition, flooding or severe drought, and winter cold (Rorabaugh and Hale 2005). Conflicting evidence about whether changes in climate are affecting susceptibility of amphibians to chytrid fungal infections (Lips and others 2008). Individuals mildly infected with nematodes and trematodes reported in Sonora, Mexico (Hale and Jarchow 1988).	0
5. Competitors	Are populations of important competing species expected to change?	In southern Arizona, this species was found in association with Chiricahua leopard frogs, and in most locations where this species occurs, canyon tree frogs (*Hyla arenicolor*) have been observed (Rorabaugh and Hale 2005). No information in Rorabaugh and Hale (2005) indicating strong competition between *R. tarahumarae* and these species.	0

Literature Cited

Carey, C., and M.A. Alexander 2003. Climate change and amphibian declines: Is there a link? Diversity and Distributions 9:111-121.

Gibbs, J.P., and A.R. Breisch. 2001. Climate warming and calling phenology of frogs near Ithaca, New York, 1900-1999. Conservation Biology 15:1175-1178.

Hale, S.F., P.C. Rosen, J.L. Jarchow, and G.A. Bradley. 2005. Effects of the chytrid fungus on the Tarahumara frog (*Rana tarahumarae*) in Arizona and Sonora, Mexico. In: Gottfried, G.J., B.S. Gebow, L.G. Eskew, C.B. Edminster, comps. Connecting mountain islands and desert seas: Biodiversity and management of the Madrean Archipelago II. 2004 May 11-15; Tucson, AZ. Proc. RMRS-P-36. Fort Collins, CO: U.S. Department of Agriculture, Forest Service, Rocky Mountain Research Station: 407-411.

Hale, S.F., and J.L. Jarchow. 1988. The status of the Tarahumara frog (*Rana tarahumarae*) in the United States and Mexico: Part II. Prepared for: Arizona Game and Fish Department, and Office of Endangered Species, U.S. Fish and Wildlife Service, Albuquerque, NM.

Hale, S.F., and C.J. May. 1983. Status report for the *Rana tarahumarae* Boulenger. Prepared for: Office of Endangered Species, U.S. Fish and Wildlife Service, Albuquerque, NM. Prepared by Stephen F. Hale, Arizona Natural Heritage Program, Tucson, AZ, and Clayton J. May, Pima Community College, Tucson, AZ.

Lips, K.R., J. Diffendorfer, J.R. Mendelson, III, and M.W. Sears. 2008. Riding the wave: Reconciling the roles of disease and climate change in amphibian declines. PLoS Biology 6:e72. doi:10.1371/journal.pbio.0060072.

Manolakou, P., G. Lavranos, and R. Angelopoulou. 2006. Molecular patterns of sex determination in the animal kingdom: A comparative study of the biology of reproduction. Reproductive Biology and Endocrinology 4:59.

Rorabaugh, J.C., and S.F. Hale. 2005. Tarahumara Frog. In: Lannoo, M., ed. Amphibian declines: The conservation status of United States species. Berkeley: University of California Press: 593-595. Species accounts also available: http://amphibiaweb.org/index html.

Rorabaugh, J.C., S.F. Hale, M.J. Sredl, and C. Ivanyi. 2005. Return of the Tarahumara frog to Arizona. In: Gottfried, G.J., B.S. Gebow, L.G. Eskew, C.B. Edminster, comps. Connecting mountain islands and desert seas: biodiversity and management of the Madrean Archipelago II. 2004 May 11-15; Tucson, AZ. Proc. RMRS-P-36. Fort Collins, CO: U.S. Department of Agriculture, Forest Service, Rocky Mountain Research Station: 345-348.

U.S. Forest Service [USFS]. 2009. Draft Coronado National Forest ecological sustainability report. Tucson, AZ: U.S. Department of Agriculture, Forest Service. Available: http://www fs.fed.us/r3/coronado/plan-revision/documents/final/cnf-ecological-sustainability-report-final-022009.pdf.

Vitt, L.J., and J.P. Caldwell. 2009. Herpetology. Oxford, United Kingdom: Elsevier. 697 p.

Zweifel, R.G. 1955. Ecology, distribution, and systematic of frogs of the *Rana boylei* group. University of California Publications in Zoology: 54:207-292. Berkeley: University of California Press.

Zweifel, R.G. 1968. *Rana tarahumarae* Boulenger. No. 66. Catalogue of American Amphibians and Reptiles. Society for the Study of Amphibians and Reptiles.